Nazi Intelligence Operations
in Non-Occupied Territories

AF008334

Nazi Intelligence Operations in Non-Occupied Territories

Espionage Efforts in the United States, Britain, South America and Southern Africa

CHRISTOPHER VASEY

McFarland & Company, Inc., Publishers
Jefferson, North Carolina

LIBRARY OF CONGRESS CATALOGUING-IN-PUBLICATION DATA

Names: Vasey, Christopher, 1980– author.
Title: Nazi intelligence operations in non-occupied territories : espionage efforts in the United States, Britain, South America and Southern Africa / Christopher Vasey.
Description: Jefferson, North Carolina : McFarland & Company, Inc., Publishers, 2016. | Includes bibliographical references and index.
Identifiers: LCCN 2016025064| ISBN 9781476663531 (softcover : alkaline paper) ∞
Subjects: LCSH: World War, 1939–1945—Military intelligence—Germany. | Espionage, German—United States—History—20th century. | Espionage, German—Great Britain—History—20th century. | Espionage, German—South America—History—20th century. | Espionage, German—Africa, Southern—History—20th century.
Classification: LCC D810.S7 V27 2016 | DDC 940.54/8743—dc23
LC record available at https://lccn.loc.gov/2016025064

BRITISH LIBRARY CATALOGUING DATA ARE AVAILABLE

ISBN (print) 978-0-4766-6353-1
ISBN (ebook) 978-1-4766-2458-7

© 2016 Christopher Vasey. All rights reserved

No part of this book may be reproduced or transmitted in any form or by any means, electronic or mechanical, including photocopying or recording, or by any information storage and retrieval system, without permission in writing from the publisher.

Front cover: Wilhelm Canaris, chief of the German military intelligence agency Abwehr; (background) 1944 world map (U.S. Army Map Service)

Printed in the United States of America

McFarland & Company, Inc., Publishers
 Box 611, Jefferson, North Carolina 28640
 www.mcfarlandpub.com

Table of Contents

Preface	1
Introduction	3
1—United States: Fascist Subversion and Sabotage Operations	17
2—United States: The Second Espionage Network and Operations Elster	84
3—British Theater	132
4—South American Theater	198
5—Southern African Theater	274
Chapter Notes	309
Bibliography	321
Index	327

Preface

This book examines the attempts by the Nazi high command and the German military to construct an international intelligence and counterintelligence service during World War II. A secret service community proficient enough to penetrate neutral and enemy nations beyond the Wehrmacht's reach was the Third Reich's goal, a capability notably absent from Field Marshal Keitel and Jodl's arsenal by the time Germany's troops entered Prague and Warsaw. The approach by this author is to examine the agencies and missions in their actions in the international arena and analyze the planning, execution and consequences. A central argument is that infringements by rival internal intelligence agencies and interdepartmental policy irreparably hampered decision making and damaged endeavors at turning this objective into realization.

The subject of this book covers the momentous years of World War II and forerunner events, but it is inevitably problematic to devote the amount of attention that is justified to military history on this scale. I have constructed a narrative focusing on continent-specific operations. The book begins with a discussion on the history of intelligence divisions in Germany from the origins in Prussia and an overview of the Nazi state foreign-intelligence structure. Each chapter is organized on an analysis of information gathering, covert action and counterespionage. Works from historians and research analysts traditionally have limited their coverage to Europe and America, but the theaters of South America and Southern Africa assessed in this book, unfortunately, suffer from insufficient recognition. An interesting side note is to acknowledge how recent the study of intelligence as a scholarly subject is. Indeed, until the 1970s the machinations of the belligerents' wartime secret services were still obscured, similarly SIGNIT and Magic were largely absent from the study of classic disciplines.

My experience of this subject stems from many years spent inhabiting archives and research centers and studying World War II-period German government texts and recently declassified files. A fascinating insight into highly secretive covert plans and missions was obtained, some of the episodes buried and ignored by researchers for decades. Intelligence operations by their very nature are often shrouded in ambiguity and misconception, and a multitude of issues relating to German secret services are still certainly unresolved. This interest was spiked by the release of a plethora of documents into the public domain and other Freedom of Information releases since 2001.

This text draws upon those documents that until recently were inaccessible; the declassified documents are drawn from intelligence agencies, government oversight committees and personalized accounts. The source materials can be found at several archive locations in the United States, Great Britain and Germany. This work also examines files released to national archives in the past few years from Mexico, South Africa and Argentina, among many other nations.

Introduction

The Abwehr department was originally founded in 1866 as the Prussian Army's intelligence arm and developed in ensuing decades into Germany's standing military intelligence division. Covert intelligence gathering had existed in manifold versions in Central Europe dating from the time Frederick the Great embarked on a program to recruit informants across the Continent from Spain to Russia. But minimal functional or conceptual development had occurred to invigorate intelligence culture during the remainder of the eighteenth and early nineteenth centuries. The Prussian chancellor Otto von Bismarck, in deciding to construct the Abwehr, observed that intelligence sources separate from the armed services would prevent authority from accumulating in the military ranks and he speculated that a personal adjunct department with these Machiavellian talents could prove immensely useful. This auxiliary division was founded in a climate of preparation for imminent armed conflict that had been advancing in Europe for many years. The Austro-Prussian crisis dominated contemporary national security policy matters. Bismarck's objectives in augmenting the standard military structure with an independent intelligence service were inspired by the dual necessities of defending the monarchy from political turmoil and a supplementary factor of state security matters in monitoring dissident groups. Bismarck recognized a utility beyond strategic or military intelligence instructing the primitive department under his command to concentrate on political opponents, including social democrats and communist parties. Other concerns were raised about influence of anarchists and nonconformist groups.

Later notable accomplishments during Austro-Prussian War and Franco-Prussian War resulted in military chiefs adopting a military intelligence division on a standing permanent basis and drafting additional offices and personnel. Agents and spymasters emerged, their stories forming almost a folklore myth within the embryonic intelligence community and the armed services. Early Abwehr commander Wilhelm Stieber became caricatured within the German intelligence field as one such departmental figure. He discovered revealing information about the French military defenses in the Franco-Prussian War that was assessed as playing a decisive element in a Prussian victory. His earliest major operation was concentrated on a rebellious political movement formed by the defeated Hanoverian monarch William V, honor bound to reconstitute the former defunct kingdom. Stieber succeeded in apprehending the deposed king's courier and confiscating his secret bank accounts, to the king's detriment.

Following the Franco-Prussian conflict's conclusion and the unification of Germany, Prussian governmental and military institutions were incorporated into the emergent new German state. The Abwehr department transferred into this updated incarnation, its designation consumed within the reconstructed German army.[1] After national unification, Wilhelm Stieber's agency instilled Imperial Germany with an intelligence capability that was dedicated to state security. The Abwehr was assigned exclusive responsibility for the combined spectrum of Nazi intelligence activities in the 1930s and initially attracted minimal interference from the political offices or SS agents. The organization's centralized structure in disseminating information to the Supreme Command of the Armed Forces (OKW) and General Staff oriented the department for becoming the foremost intelligence agency within Reich War Ministry. Bestowed capaciously with multiple self-contained jurisdictions encompassing counterintelligence, counterespionage, covert operations and intelligence gathering, it would develop into a sophisticated agency. Military intelligence accumulated and presented exigent information with both scrupulous accuracy and superior alacrity compared to the contending intelligence organization in the Third Reich. Even the traditional party apparatchiks inside the Gestapo and SD failed to develop capabilities rivaling the Abwehr agency until the closing engagements of World War II and internal consolidations of power.

Twentieth-century warfare was transformed into unprecedented militarization as battlefields engulfed continents and propagated new opportunities for strategic surprise and objective securement by exploiting mobility and rapid penetration. Command adapted itself by necessity to this emerging environment and impending advancements in ground warfare and general tactics. The alteration in intelligence perspectives was manifestly influenced by the twentieth-century innovation in military technology. Improved weapons systems, industry, railways, radio communications and mobile armor revolutionized warfare and, by extension, intelligence gathering. The response centered on establishing military divisions charged with supporting command decision making with the required strategic and tactical intelligence.[2] The content material was suitably refined to contain information that pertained to foreign military complements, topography and defensive systems, economic performance data and other factors relevant to the efficacious conduct of armed operations. Belligerent nations of World War II depended on intelligence reports, organized information and communications.

Walther Nicolai supervised the modernization of German intelligence and defensive security to accommodate the kaiser's ambitions during World War I. The Abwehr orchestrated intelligence and sabotage operations behind front lines and inside territorial perimeters of nations beyond the Wehrmacht's touch, the July 1916 "Black Tom" explosion in New Jersey (U.S.) being an example. Admiral Canaris, destined to be appointed the Abwehr chief and the agency's most famous commander, served on covert intelligence missions in Europe and the American continents as a junior officer. The Abwehr was terminated as a functional branch of the Wehrmacht and technically ceased all operations after World War I under Versailles Treaty provisions.

Despite constraints and restrictive limitations on military redevelopment the German military was rescued from its dissolution and reactivated in 1921. Surveillance of radical political associations and subversive movements was the central obligation delegated to postwar intelligence officers in the volatile Weimar landscape. The trade unionists and communists formed the prominent assemblies singled out for attentive monitoring, as did premature incarnations of the National Socialist German Workers Party (NSDAP). The Nazi Party, of course, later instituted its own independent intelligence service in 1931, known as Sicherheitsdienst (SD), translating to Security Service. The designation of military intelligence transformed many times after World War I. After demobilization of the German army the Intelligence Office became the Intelligence Group, attached to the Foreign Armies Branch of General Staff. National security requirements endowed on the reconfigured and adjusted intelligence departments were minimally altered and between 1918 and 1925 only perfunctory and domestic activities were permitted. The Intelligence Group experienced a designation realignment once more in 1921, and was then referred to as Abwehr [Defense] Group of T3. At a later juncture clandestine services would become a divergent branch of the Supreme Command of the Armed Forces (OKW).

A foremost development in modernizing the German intelligence apparatus into mechanisms tailored for optimizing warfare was the appointment to Abwehr chief on June 2, 1932, of Captain Conrad Patzig, who previously had directed the naval section. In April 1928 the Abwehr Group of T3 and the German navy's traditional espionage unit were amalgamated, and by October 1930 all the remaining quasi-independent service command intelligence agencies and connected departments were subordinate to the authority of a powerful defense ministry. By Conrad Patzig's tenure the three military branches—navy, army and air force—while prohibited from engaging in intelligence gathering installed qualified liaison officers for distributing intelligence requirements to Abwehr counterparts. Generally, they maintained a second capability specializing in intelligence for analyzing and reportage of field information.

Patzig's selection was in multiple contexts a radical transfer and generally not anticipated by the establishment of military or other intelligence agencies as they then existed. Patzig was the first naval officer to command military intelligence, discontinuing the intelligence community traditions that demanded Wehrmacht chiefs, and his tenure was embroiled in criticism and perfidious internal fissures. The chiefs of staff and Field Marshal von Blomberg, recently elevated to minister of war, provoked a challenging environment that irreparably hampered covert infiltrations and asset construction. Blomberg was aligned with the Fatherland's ideologically inclined Nazi Party factions, his proclivities sympathetic towards the party's in-house intelligence branches. In the Conrad Patzig era, Eastern Europe, Russia and Poland were identified as initial primary targets for counterespionage activity. The German rearmament phase was still embryonic, both Wehrmacht and Kriegsmarine merely beginning to resemble the military capabilities of other world powers. By 1934, the necessary funding had not materialized for intelligence services.

The Abwehr diligently conducted their surveillance operations across the Eastern European area as authorized, turning informants in Poland and Russia, but the scope and penetration achieved primarily basic results. Opportunities to engage in traditional espionage actions were exceptions and this generation of officers failed in obtaining substantive battlefield experience. The SS and Foreign Office technically comprised foreign intelligence briefs, but analysis reveals minimal development had occurred. Certain opportunities to uncover strategic information on nations or regions of interest were presented by cooperation and joint ventures with other foreign intelligence departments. An approach of pursuing relations with affiliated foreign agencies expanded the scope of domestic secret service operations. In Eastern Europe contracts for information exchanging and relationships of convenience were informally invested with intelligence agencies. Lithuanian state security, for example, disclosed information on the Soviet Union. The final 1930s period transpired to be the watershed moments for German intelligence, as a sophisticated evolution was mandated beyond the simplistic operations of 1934; decisive tactical and strategic intelligence on Czechoslovakia and Poland was now petitioned by the Wehrmacht from 1937 to 1939. In 1938, the Ministry of War, belatedly following another jurisdiction review process, was abolished, undoubtedly enriching the Abwehr's position. This latest reconstruction of internal institutions proved regrettable for Field Marshall von Blomberg who was unceremoniously removed at the instigation of Heinrich Himmler and his deputy, Reinhard Heydrich. The Abwehr now reported directly to the Supreme Command of the Armed Forces.

Admiral Wilhelm Canaris was appointed Abwehr chief, Germany's supreme spymaster, on January 1, 1934. Similar to his predecessor and the confirmed vexation of many observers he was both resolutely not the preferred selection for nomination and a senior naval commander. On the surface an introverted and intellectual character, Canaris was approaching retirement age by the time of this promotion, his career background history reflecting a distinguished service inside the navy and accomplishments as a military officer. Admiral Canaris's selection was unexpected because, despite his sustained years of commissioned naval and Abwehr service, he was not registered as a Nazi Party member and generally not construed as a party loyalist. Judging by SS and SD intelligence officers, Admiral Canaris's composed and intelligent approach was a conspicuous contrast to the otherwise violent techniques practiced in his industry. His reputation during the oncoming years developed into that of an individual inextricably associated with the shadowy cloak-and-dagger world of espionage. It was under the stewardship of Canaris that German military intelligence developed its specialty of instigating networks of agents and informants physically on the ground and magnified in scale and proficiency to its greatest extent.

In British intelligence circles Canaris was perceived as an individual who understood Hitler's self-declared historic mission with some skepticism, not that he relented in endorsing the reformation of Germany into a powerful European nation or the rearmament policies. In Canaris, similar to other military officers, nationalism formed inevitably as a byproduct of long-term service and, with the German World War I veterans, he bemoaned the decimation of the German navy and military following Versailles. Rearmament programs implemented within the Nazi regime appealed more to the spy chief than principles of national socialism or fascism. Between 1935 and 1937 Canaris bolstered the Abwehr's interior framework considerably; from an organization of 150 personnel the agency had developed to nearly a thousand in less than three years. The old guard persisted in traditional aristocratic officers, individuals who had encountered their first military existence in the kaiser's Imperial service. A modern generation from middle and professional social classes had voluntarily enlisted in the secret services after the war from academic, science, intelligentsia and civil service backgrounds. Within the intelligence community the officers advancing in promotion rapidly in Abwehr and SD or Gestapo commonly held discernible backgrounds in the Nazi Party.

The Abwehr, however, persuaded military chiefs on the undoubted productivity in guaranteeing retention of a degree of independence and routinely recruited from outside the party ranks, enlisting both non–Nazi Party members and operatives disinterested in Nazism. Consistently diversifying its assortment of domestic personnel, the section chiefs decided to fine-tune agents with specialist skills, language, culture and technical backgrounds. Admiral Canaris and his department heads preferred intelligence and highly skilled operatives with ideological predispositions taking a backseat. New personnel were posted either at headquarters in Berlin or transferred to substations in German regional districts classified under the insider terminology as Abwehrstellen (Ast) divisions.[3] While nominally independent ideology and party affiliation inevitably forcibly interfered in the streamlining recruitment processes, the SD's winning an internal battle was mandated an influence on selection. Recruiting an intelligence reserve was rendered obstructive because each individual candidate had to be rigorously screened by the Gestapo, and department commanders wanted to avoid being criticized for employing disruptive elements. Canaris's organization by 1943 was 30,000 strong, of whom 8,000 were officers, and its expenditure budget for that year amounted to 31,000,000 Reichsmarks.

Canaris simultaneously established the networks of Ast units and substation officials. His inner council of section chiefs (Sections I, III and III) were extremely dependable and primarily hand-picked. For the first three years of World War II Canaris ensured that Piekenbrock, Lahousen and von Bentivegni, the senior section chiefs, maneuvered independently, the bureaucratic arguments isolated if feasible from the command staff. Preparations for military engagement finally instituted a department format that endured from 1938 until the culminating twelve months of World War II. The umbrella canopy of the organization was combined from three distinct central departments: Section I—Espionage; Section II—Sabotage; and Section III—Counterespionage. Section I controlled substations, with command staff managing field operative networks engaging in espionage and counterespionage targeting foreign nations. Colonel Piekenbrock was appointed the chief of Section I and retained this official posting until his unfortunate transfer to the Eastern Front in 1943 and subsequent Soviet imprisonment. Abwehr I, the largest division section, consisted of nine subordinate groups: Army East; Army West; Army Technical; Marine; Air Force; Technical/Air Force; Economic; Communications and Secret.

Section II and Section III overlapped jurisdictions, with engagements in multifarious actions of sabotage and counter sabotage specialties. Missions of Sections II and III units were deliberately shrouded in ambiguous mystery.

Another division attached to Section III occupied a commission for surveillance of domestic industry in commercial and munitions factories. Other departments included the Naval Intercept Service (a former OKW organ), a structure transferred to the Abwehr in the late 1930s. Naval Intercept retained its function in signals communication. The Foreign section was an auxiliary administrative department operating as a liaison and dissemination station with the OKW and Foreign Ministry. Commanded by Vice-Admiral Buerkner, this department was traditionally external to spying operations. Abwehr headquarters delegated local functions expansively to field offices. As the Nazi empire expanded and encompassed new geographical territorial acquisitions an Abwehr substation was rapidly set up. The standing objectives seldom experienced any modification: providing the latest information to the Wehrmacht. In Germany and occupied countries the field branch substations were referred to as Abwehrstellen (Ast) and Nebenstellen (Nests) branches; in neutral countries the Abwehr officially designated substations Kriegsorganisation (KO). Under security procedures the KO substations acted in concealment as undercover attachments of the diplomatic missions, and the field stations reproduced the functions of the headquarters divisions in recruiting, training and dispatching espionage agents and informants. While in theory separation of geographical substations composed practical intellect the espionage business necessitated a significant amount of overlap, either resolved in combined missions or jurisdictional wrangling.

A second foreign intelligence and espionage service existed independently from the German military or OKW, the Security Service (SD). Originally introduced into operation as a security organ of the National Social German Workers Party, it ascended to perform a dominant and overbearing role as an intelligence department of the Third Reich. Structurally, the SD existed as a subsidiary division of Reichsführer SS Heinrich Himmler's powerful RSHA and emerged in greater importance under management and ceaseless applications to expand jurisdictions of Reinhard Heydrich. Unlike the Abwehr, the SD was not exclusively limited to military intelligence, focusing their attentions on diverse political and ideological functions in Germany and the occupied territories. SD Section VI was constituted as the Nazi Party's official foreign intelligence capability entirely independent of the Abwehr. It was the obligation within the RSHA framework to compile identities and background information on anti–Nazis to be summarily arrested and executed after occupation by the Wehrmacht. Individuals could be identified through the simplistic methods of analyzing media and newspapers or through pro–Nazi informants.

By March 1939 Heydrich had constructed a powerful and feared domestic spy service. He pulled minimal punches in capriciously resorting to blackmail and extortion to influence decisions by other Reich administrations. In 1935

Himmler first engaged the SD VI to assemble an international faculty to challenge the Abwehr. The premeditated objective was political intelligence, but as the war continued and the SS grew in prominence and standing, the SD acquired both economic and military intelligence functions. By the beginnings of European conflict in September 1939 the agency coordinated espionage systems in multiple international territories including South America, North Africa, Spain and Portugal. General Walter Schellenberg, who had attracted admirers due to a perceived expertise in counterintelligence operations, was recruited by Reinhard Heydrich and instated as VI commandant. He developed his profile sufficiently to become personal confidant to Reichsführer SS Himmler and deputy director of the Main Reich Security Office (RSHA). Schellenberg was immersed in many elaborate and notable German intelligence operations; for instance, he personally commanded the Venlo Incident on the ground.[4]

One of Schellenberg's wartime obligations was the masterminding of an occupation strategy for German police and administrative officials after the productive execution of Operation "Sea Lion," the planned invasion of Britain. As instructed, Schellenberg accumulated the Sonderfahndungsliste GB, or special list. This directory of British citizens was a guidebook of individuals considered generally ideologically unsound or classified as security concerns who would be incarcerated and executed after the invasion. The SS traditionally concentrated its attention on eliminating any opposition, existing or imagined, to the Third Reich. This function permeated and endured as a consideration within its entire intelligence structure, and Schellenberg ensured that the SD infiltrated other agencies wherever possible. In the late 1930s the Third Reich secret intelligence services were not legally authorized to undertake operations against Wehrmacht or other intelligence agencies. Regardless of that fact, Heydrich persevered in investigating and collecting surveillance evidence on the German officer core for detecting suspicious activity or simply to gather bargainable information on senior personnel.

In September 1939, within a brief matter of weeks of the hostilities commencing, the SD was reconfigured and combined with other state policing authorities inside the RSHA. This centralization of state security departments under the SS and Himmler's personal dominion blurred the boundaries dividing the Nazi Party and the central government. This powerful agency officially comprised the SD, Kriminalpolizei, or Kripo (Criminal Police), and Geheime Staatspolizei (Gestapo). Local independent state police forces disappeared as separate institutions and were relocated under the RSHA's auspices. Himmler and the RSHA connived to mandate that all Fatherland intelligence and police departments were jurisdictionally qualified for combating the national socialist enemies. Reinhard Heydrich later became Himmler's most powerful subordinate; with a standing admission to the Führer, he assumed presiding control over the new security service landscape. Institutional rivalries inside the German intelligence community dated back to 1934 when Heydrich and SD officials pronounced personally to Himmler their inventory of complaints and obstructive examples concerning Admiral Patzig. The Abwehr chief was accused of deliberately encumbering communication between military intelligence and SS security departments. In April 1934, Hermann Göring was forced to relinquish control of police as provincial police forces were classified as subject to centralization.

Many senior Abwehr commanders consequently recognized the SD irrefutably as a potential adversary detrimental to Germany's long-term interests. Colonel Piekenbrock and the future Supreme Command chief, Wilhelm Keitel, developed a distaste for the SD and perceived imminent friction and dissonance that threatened their own departments. In 1934, in conditions of ascendant internal Nazi Party opposition Hitler ordered a liquidation of prominent sections of the Sturmabteilung (SA) branch. Minimal moderation was displayed for former comrades as the SS commenced the "night of the long knives" massacres. This campaign of detentions and assassinations appalled many in traditional inner recesses of Germany's intelligence community, a definite contrast to Abwehr officers' reputation of pragmatic diplomacy and subverting agendas. Army and Abwehr officials eliminated in the purges included the former Abwehr chief Bredow, shot and killed at his home. Doubts about SS and negative institutional distrust fermented in the aftermath of the "'night of the long knives." Regular battles with Abwehr commanders and Canaris between 1937 and 1944 had critically incapacitated relations.

An attempt at triggering greater collaboration, the "Ten Commandments" agreement in March 1942, confirmed by the Abwehr and SS commanders, briefly soothed mounting tensions. The Ten Commandments defined foreign espionage as the Abwehr's jurisdiction, a provisional and impermanent reprieve preventing Nazi elements from muscling overtly into military intelligence territory. SD Department VI of the RSHA could be classified somewhat reservedly as a marginal foreign service division before 1942. By spring 1940 Himmler had adamantly conveyed orders that the fascist revolution demanded a foreign intelligence service attached to the Nazi Party while a framework existed the department was merely beginning to recruit highly skilled and appropriate personnel for overseas intelligence work. Schellenberg ensured that the SD oriented recruitment policies to select officers with experience of residing or working abroad, increasing population numbers from diverse national backgrounds and reprioritizing the selection of agents possessing multilingual skills. Other factors determined a progressive influence over international matters. The character of RSHA changed after the assassination of Heydrich, the irreversible accumulation of the security and police departments intensified and heightening national socialist paranoia reached a peak. Kaltenbrunner later succeeded Reinhard Heydrich as the security services chief. The von Stauffenberg plot and other conspiracies convinced senior SS officials of the essential necessity to unmask concealed enemies from inside.[5]

The Abwehr during wartime operations achieved notable results and developed a reputation for ruthless efficiency. Nazi agents uncovered a majority of The Netherlands underground resistance movement and for a time controlled its actions. The Blitzkrieg attacks in Poland and Czechoslovakia were effective because Abwehr operators had assiduously procured the allegiances of collaborating security personnel. National border defenses and security contingency plans were comprehended long before engagements had commenced by Wehrmacht commanders General Franz Halder and General Walther von Brauchitsch. Canaris's central policy upon taking command was dedicated to expanding the number of confirmed operatives abroad for the calculated purposes of delivering information on America and the Western Atlantic military. Commercial and industrial information, technical data and personnel records were delineated as fundamental intelligence requirements by General Lahousen, the commander of Abwehr II.

Concerning the United States, prior to the late 1930s period and the emergent European warfare the Führer's Germany had demonstrated minimal interest and failed to devote significant attention or realistic planning to the possibility of military conflict in the American theater. In March 1938 the Kriegsorganisation were assessed as insufficiently financed and fragmented, senior Nazi officials either discounting or overlooking the possibilities for deep penetration by clandestine networks in United States or Britain. Interestingly, a Nazi espionage network was in existence inside the United States dating from 1935 and Nazi Party manifestations originated in United States territory in 1933 with the assumption of power. But primitive and markedly limited covert operations appeared copiously deficient in specialist or military personnel and of course financial investment. German expatriates living in America, either as naturalized citizens or extraterritorial guests, formed the listening stations of Nazi intelligence services. Before the Wehrmacht forces summarily occupied Poland in September 1939, and before Pearl Harbor on December 7, 1941, the United States represented a frontier where most Abwehr commanders had repeatedly confirmed an exigent policy in treading circumspectly. At that time positive diplomatic relationships with North and South American nations were interpreted as being fundamental to conserve. The Foreign Office generally objected to exploiting embassies and legations as convenient cover and inevitable disruptions to their fusion of international ties.

In response to emergency conditions in the Pacific Ocean and Southeast Asia, with Japanese annexations now appearing to be contending inescapably with the U.S. and its Pacific territory, the Roosevelt administration became increasingly preoccupied with the Japanese question. Occupations in Asia and movements in the Central Pacific interpreted as concerted efforts to challenge United States naval hegemony in their own backyard caused significant alarm. In the aftermath of the Pearl Harbor attack and the United States' declaration of war the German military high command were compulsorily obliged to institute strategic attention across the Atlantic. In the previous three years Nazi Party officials had observed America with suspicion and plotted to prevent American participation or maintain an advantage in circumstances of open armed conflict. But opinion had differed wildly and Germany's military forces and intelligence services still remained critically in the dark about their newest adversary. The American zone, possibly arising from scornful attitudes concerning supposed decadence and "Jewish influences," had suffered from neglect by the party hierarchy. Core attention overlooked the United States as a national security hotspot and concentrated on Europe, the Soviet Union and surrounding territories.

A sabotage campaign could theoretically damage the formative U.S. mobilization efforts if targeted with sufficient intelligence and precision. The Nazi inner cabinet delegated this responsibility to German military intelligence; a new internal culture and profile of institutional priorities were being fashioned with new logistics specifically for wartime use against the United States. The espionage exploits leveled transatlantically—speculated on and debated inside the corridors of Abwehr II—were engineered to generate profuse military and propaganda benefits. From accounts of wartime meetings, elements within the German military dreamed of perpetual, aggressive campaigns of sabotage throughout the mainland United States. Comparable terrorist attacks, small-scale military assaults and incendiary bombings were envisioned for other non-occupied territories. The plotters expected the shock tactics to stimulate a domestic climate of immense trepidation and national hysteria. Industrial and military installations appeared in the initial proposals as principal targets for destruction. War was declared against the government of Japan by the United States on December 8, 1941. Germany and Italy issued corresponding declarations against the United States on December 11.

While Nazi Germany controlled a handful of operatives inside Britain, by mutual declarations of conflict their reliable personnel were unambiguously in diminishing supply. An Iraqi army officer on secondment was exposed prematurely in the conflict and other affiliated individuals appeared to be declining in the ratios of compiling reports, a deteriorating environmental landscape, certainly, for German intelligence. The Abwehr had considered strategies while being, to an extent, constrained by standing directives on avoiding destabilizing alliances with the British establishment. General Beck and others contested reckless interventions that had the conceivable capability of disrupting diplomatic associations with Britain or America.

After the eruption of mobilized combat in Europe and the collapse of France it became imperative for Germany to obtain intelligence on the magnitude of Atlantic convoys dispensing resources and apparatus to Britain, complements of the British Army, Royal Navy and border defense systems. Much of this information in 1938 and 1939 was plundered from open sources and otherwise publicly available media resources, and diplomatic personnel implemented an application as irregular "eyes and ears." But a counterintelligence and counterespionage aptitude required being assembled almost completely from a baseline condition. Instigation of massive military engagement and escalating confrontation on the front lines redoubled the German intelligence community's requirements for naval intelligence.

Geographical factors demanded an interjection of agents of influence and operatives into neutral territories to circumvent the Allied national security systems. Uncharted terrain for the Nazi expansionist policies dispensing institutional pressure and new personnel on Ast stations, military intelligence and the SS implemented intricate methodologies for detecting the European resistance movements. Strategies passed final approval for undermining and investigating anti–Nazi underground forces from Carte Organization in France to Pat O'Leary Network in Belgium. But an international intelligence network did not exist in this maelstrom, and neutral territories were in essence untouched by Germany's security services. The Nazis by September 1939 were compelled to construct a global intelligence infrastructure from the foundation up. Intelligence service declassifications from World War II have magnified in recent years, allowing new appraisals of German covert operations from this period. MI5 "Double Cross" files and Office of Strategic Services records, for example, and federal agencies from Chile, Mexico and South Africa have released informative sources on wartime espionage exploits.

Atlantic naval campaigns broadened to engulf previously unscathed geographical zones of the Caribbean and northern South America. The first order of business for Admiral Raeder's U-boat fleet was dismantling the British-controlled Atlantic blockade. The German Foreign Office descended into South and Central America from 1933 to 1935, with Nazi Party–affiliated organs and other diverse cultural associations enthusiastically being set up. On the guidance of Nazi cultural experts, many depicted South America as virtually an unspoiled wilderness with minimal apparent levels of cultural diffusion or external influences in many areas. Potential for colonial cultivation was envisaged, or at minimum ensuring Germany's government was the foremost integral accomplice for the insular administrations. With the entrance of both the United States and Canada into the European and Pacific theatres the SD VI and Abwehr Section I commanders, Walter Schellenberg and Colonel Hans Piekenbrock respectively, became conscious of tactical advantages to be had from sound intelligence operations in this distant territory, from isolating oceanic pathways of Allied convoys to photographing latest-generation military hardware under construction in Latin American plants.

The unproductive surroundings of 1939, with Germany reliant on embassy delegations and military or cultural attaché's for information, experienced a transition from March 1941 to June 1942. Brazilian, Argentinean and Mexican conspirators were installed and apprising handlers across the Atlantic in Berlin. A dialogue was brokered with the Nazi underground movements in the United States and personnel were exchanged. German commercial enterprises were desperate to acquire footholds in new markets and widened their economic and financial investments in Latin America. Lucrative investments inevitably cultivated collusion and co-assistance partnerships inside South and Central America, and scenarios were broadly debated for orchestrating revolutions targeting anti–Nazi governments.

Nazi intelligence from April 1938 to August 1941 constructed an underground movement in Southern Africa by embedding a diverse assortment of Abwehr, SD and former Gestapo operatives in German consulate networks. Italian delegations and collaborating informants from the Spanish and Portuguese districts were engaged in a conspiracy covering the strategically fundamental Cape area and nearby transportation routes, Vichy-controlled Madagascar and neutral Portuguese East and West Africa. Allied military forces in North Africa and Western Europe depended on the Southern Atlantic supply chain, with Japanese aggression now dissecting other Indian Ocean passages. From Rommel's major March 1941 offensive in North Africa to Operation Torch in November 1942, replenishing the Allied North African divisions was assuredly conditional on the Southern African theater. Admirals Karl Dönitz and Erich Raeder recognized that the African Cape and Southern Atlantic needed to be removed from the Allied sphere of influence and the relative freedom of movement annulled. South Africa, a commonwealth nation, was bitterly conflicted on the neutrality issues, with many Afrikaner sociopolitical movements and paramilitary organizations disputing any coalitions committed to by Prime Minister [and General] Smuts. Enemies from within demonstrated an unmistakable temperament to collude with the Abwehr intelligence agent representatives, with schemes envisioned for a jointly commanded Nazi coup d'état.

Subterfuge was required to ensure concealment and misdirection regarding the genuine identities of German agents.

British and South African security forces were desperately hunting for opposite numbers and evidence of Nazi infiltration. British intelligence countered the German incursions by responding with escalations of personnel from the Security Service (MI5), Special Operations Executive (SOE), Naval Intelligence and other agencies. In March 1943 a U.S. Office of Strategic Services (OSS) complement arrived, freshly engaged in the African conflict. Allied prosperity in Atlantic naval warfare, destined to become the deadliest maritime battle in history, and reinforcements for commodity supply chains were resting on preventing irreparable harm to their ambitions in this territory.

The German intelligence community endeavored to convene their various talents to meet the competing demands by collecting on a global scale the critical information interesting to the high command and service command branches subordinate to them. The concept of sending saboteurs to the United States was formulated inside the Abwehr II dating from mid–1940. Preliminary statistics and quantifiable data recovered numerous apparently compromised manufacturing and industrial installations to target. Missions were hatched to disable the New York water transportation systems and contaminate reservoirs, immobilize railways and communications infrastructure, dispatch political assassinations squads and divulge nuclear secrets. Many plans constituted a mathematically improbable gamble, and others qualified simply as incontestably unrealistic and were abandoned at early preliminary stages. But declassified files document that Abwehr military intelligence at Tirpitzufer headquarters and SD VI command based at Prinz-Albrecht-Straße were committed to opening their enterprises inside mainland United States and if possible establishing a permanent base of operations on American soil.

1

United States: Fascist Subversion and Sabotage Operations

The Roosevelt administration found itself in an increasingly untenable position following the outbreak of European-wide conflict in September 1939. The American public historically regarded European affairs with quantifiable indifference and generally opposed any expensive interferences in foreign conflicts, especially those occurring in distant geographical regions or in circumstances perceived as domestically irrelevant. The Czechoslovakia and Poland occupations precipitating the Anglo-French declaration of war moderately shifted domestic popular opinion, and prominent campaigns representing both pro- and antiwar lobbies emerged. Technically, the United States adamantly stuck to neutrality and professed impartiality; indeed steps were implemented by congressional representatives and business leaders not to alienate Nazi Germany or their Italian allies.

The U.S. officially at peace with Germany and a noncombatant in European conflict, industrial and commercial connections were unaffected and trade grudgingly continued with both factions. In private, Roosevelt expressed sympathy for the British and French stance, and the Lend-Lease Act was signed in March 1941. Under the provisions of the "Destroyers for Bases" accord on September 2, 1940, the Roosevelt government concluded a treaty to exchange 50 aging warships for military bases located on British overseas territories. Despite some controversy domestically in those early neutral years, the United States approved the distribution of armaments to Britain, and the Atlantic supply line to Western Europe increasingly represented an important naval front line for Germany and the other Axis powers. This Anglo-American industrial pact resulted in significant problems for Germany's military efforts. The Nazi Party high command and military chiefs began redirecting a renewed naval strategy outside of Scandinavia and the Mediterranean to restrict the Atlantic supply lifeline. Erich Raider and Karl Dönitz instigated their first Atlantic Ocean submarine campaign in February 1940 after the unfeasible winter period. The Kriegsmarine's main concerns became resolutely preoccupied with the Northern Atlantic convoys, and by March 1941 Admiral Raider had opened U-boat operations full time in the Caribbean. Plans circulated in military intelligence but it was Adolf Hitler's advisors and senior Nazi Party officials who delegated the instructions to engineer a serious effort to disrupt American industrial production, ostensibly from the inside. The purpose of incursion was twofold: to fundamentally reduce America's ability to manufacture military technology and munitions; and, as a propaganda device, to encourage heightened fear in the American civilian population. Nikolaus Ritter, who had been formerly employed in the manufacturing industry in America for several years, was selected to command the Nazi covert operations inside American territory. In 1937 he galvanized the mission of assembling an underground network of U.S.-based agents by posting himself, despite protestations, to New York.

Hitler, an Americanphobe by nature, observed the United States' potential as an industrial military power with dismissive skepticism. The prevailing advice of Nazi Germany's experts on U.S. battlefield prowess was that the American military-industrial machine required considerable time-consuming structural expansion to be converted into a dangerous and formidable adversary for the German armed forces. Many Nazi strategists analyzed the destruction at Pearl Harbor as a critical blow to American naval capabilities. In the 1920s, United States commercial interests had invested substantially in Weimar Germany, as the postwar conditions of reparations affected German cities and sluggish domestic economy was endorsed as an inciting environment for investment potential. Major companies demonstrated a discernible attraction to anticommunist and anti–trade-unionism rhetoric conveyed in the Nazi propaganda. Ford, General Motors and Standard Oil supplied Germany with important industrial technology, synthetic rubber and vehicles. Worldwide conditions in 1940, 1941 and 1942 prompted minor repercussions for U.S. industry, as trading embargoes and limitation on Nazi Germany lacked conviction associated with the 1943–45 strategy on economic warfare.[1] Public appetite remained ambiguous on intervention well into 1941.

The U.S. declaration of war on December 8, 1941, at first failed to motivate drastic alterations in domestic risk assessment. Secretary of war Henry L. Stimson, in a September 1941 report, evaluated the danger of Nazi infiltration and sabotage as remote. He demonstrated a greater preoccupation with Japan, commissioned several internal reports about the plausible threats of Japanese-Americans, and became a principle advocate of Japanese internment. While downgrading covert operations targeting America's East Coast, he vividly described possible threats of Japanese attacks on water supply stations and other critical public infrastructure in California, resulting, he predicted, in severe droughts affecting hundreds of thousands or sabotage designed to destroy war potential and slow down production.² Defending the national borders from possible Nazi secret service covert penetration at the beginning of formal military engagement in the war was still considered a distant priority. The battlefields of Europe had not yet encompassed directly continental U.S. territory, and Nazi Germany did not constitute a credible or realistic domestic security threat in the general perception. The FBI and its chief J. Edgar Hoover later stood accused of indifference and failure to institute appropriate security measures to protect Americans from espionage agents and collaborators. During the interwar years the State Department's attitude towards clandestine foreign-intelligence collection was not entirely dissimilar to that of the German Foreign Office. Many American diplomats did not regard espionage work as an appropriate or lawful method of fulfilling their ambassadorial duties, despite regular approaches from the Justice Department to inform the American government about regimes of interest and political developments. Personnel in the State Department commonly frowned on "aggressive" overseas espionage work.

In documents imparted to the U.S. State Department in December 1939 the diplomatic service reservations concerning their potential embroilment in intelligence operations were highlighted. A memorandum written in August 1939 by Vice Admiral Edwin Stark, the chief of Naval Operations, argued that naval attaches simply were not trained in espionage or qualified to be counter-intelligence assets. Furthermore, diplomatic status afforded to officers preordained that if they became implicitly preoccupied with secret intelligence work friction with the State Department inevitably resulted.³ The attitude of senior command structures was not sufficiently obliging or adaptable to a sustained intelligence undertaking. A standing federal expert cryptographic department did not exist and, in fact, attention to deciphering technology was invested in negligibly; institutions standard today including centralized intelligence, foreign intelligence and counterterrorism did not exist. The contained world of the U.S. military community had devoted minimal resources to intelligence matters. More abrasive perspectives towards foreign policy and national defense emerged during war conditions, precipitating changes in Cordell Hull and Francis Biddle, secretary of state and attorney general respectively, but that was twenty-four months away. The absence of national defense systems and the ensuing protocols is noticeable; the twenty-year environment of nonintervention policy encouraged minimal intelligence capability development. The inappropriateness of depending on the service attaches and diplomatic service personnel as the primary intelligence officers was becoming obvious.

The FBI was statutorily restricted to domestic activities throughout the 1930s. At this time nine other government departments were conducting operations that could justifiably be classified as "intelligence" in orientation. As the United States increasingly became embroiled in critical military developments in Europe and Asia-Pacific the need for coordination in intelligence analysis appeared mandatory.[4] Justice Department officials understood the necessities for launching investigations and surveillance details targeting self-proclaimed Nazi movements and fascist subversive activities. The assistant directors of the FBI interpreted a general obligation inside their standing operational remit dedicated to national defense as grounds for monitoring antigovernment political movements. But by December 1941 no specific counterintelligence department was designated with responsibility for protecting America from foreign covert action operations. The FBI, significantly, developed its internal organizational capacity after June 1942. The Law Enforcement Mobilization Plan for Defense and related policies established integrated networks and cooperative systems with FBI senior officials and the police executives in major districts. Stringent security and employee vetting examinations inside defense industries were implemented by the Justice Department, and a comprehensive network of over 20,000 informants existed by May 1942 posted to approximately four thousand industrial plants. The FBI expanded personnel during the war from 1,590 agents in 1941 to 4,880 in 1944.[5]

Closer connections with Britain prompted a renewed focus on America's counterintelligence and counterespionage security systems. Bill Donovan was instructed to conduct overseas missions as the special representative of the White House. He traveled to Britain in July 1940 to assess the capability of British military forces in resisting a German invasion and to evaluate Britain's vulnerability to German fifth column activities. The U.S., by mid-1943, from relatively moderate beginnings had progressively constructed a highly capable defense system. A presidential military order passed on June 12, 1942, created the Office of Strategic Services (OSS), with William Donovan appointed as the director.[6] Adolf Berle, assistant secretary of state, and J. Edgar Hoover, FBI director, conceived and implemented the Special Information Service (SIS) project, a Latin American counterintelligence agency commanded by the FBI in Washington. By December 1942 approximately 90 SIS operatives doubling covertly as legitimate legal attachés with diplomatic status operated from the U.S. embassies in 18 Latin American nations. These officers coordinated secret intelligence operations and information gathering inside assigned countries, collecting information and investigative sources from indigenous contacts and undercover SIS agents. The legal attachés passed data on to FBI headquarters in Washington and sometimes used the information to formulate local actions with embassy diplomats and armed services attachés.[7]

By December 1942 the domestic climate had certainly experienced profound modifications and cultural shifts, and a definite propensity for alarmist and sensational media articles started to appear in publications. The public was captivated by the possibility of German infiltrators and semi-mythical 5th columnists in U.S. cities. The American public's appetite for media articles and content about secret Nazi plots developed exponentially from 1942 to 1943. The Internment Acts rushed through Congress in the aftermath of Pearl Harbor embodied a degree of heightened popular anxiety regarding enemy attack. But legitimate risk assessment awareness about realities of coastal security requirements began to hit home.

Propaganda Efforts in the United States

The Bund organization was the disseminator in chief of pro–Hitler and anti-democratic propaganda in the United States, allegedly under complete Gestapo control from its inception. Publications similar in content to the Bund's periodicals and other pro–Nazi publications proliferated in the United States beginning in 1933. In Germany, theorists within the Reich Propaganda Office speculated that a persuasive content would be required to distract popular attention from the more traditional American attachment to both individualism and independence. The antiliberal and hierarchical social structure-oriented policies of national socialism were encouraged and permeated pro-fascist articles. Nazi strategists, in their concerted labors to cultivate devotees in the United States population to the national socialist cause, generally did not advocate manipulating or otherwise taking political advantage of an approach to racism shared by certain "white supremacist" cultures and movements. The thrust of propaganda excursions remained directed at German Americans. Hans Grimm, a high profile Nazi academic and best-selling author, toured the United States in 1936 and delivered lectures and speeches to German and American audiences, promoting the Führer's Nazi Germany. The Treaty of Versailles and other recent historical grievances were raised by Grimm among his audiences in an effort to generate maximum sympathy and a common alignment with Nazi Party messages.[8]

Heinz Spanknöbel founded the American Nazi Party in May 1933 and developed associations with the Friends of New Germany, a ubiquitous and influential character in American fascist circles. An immigrant originally hailing from Homberg, Germany, who settled in New York, Spanknöbel had accumulated an impressive portfolio of high-ranking personal connections in the German Nazi Party (Rudolf Hess, Deputy of the Nazi Party, permitted his investiture as leader of the American Nazi Party), and he ambitiously resolved to recruit well-connected Germans residing in the United States and embassy officials with potential utilization. Spanknöbel was the prime motivational factor in the inauguration of a second controversial and perceptibly visible fascist organization, the Friends of New Germany. The movement was established in New York City in 1934 and operated exclusively in that metropolitan area and the immediate surrounding districts. He convinced other prominent American fascists to merge two distinct and previously existing ideologically extreme-right organizations, Gau-USA and the Free Society of Teutonia, and constantly reinforced in persuasive rhetoric how combining resources profited all factions. Drawing inevitable comparisons with European fascism, participants dressed in a designated uniform: white shirt and black trousers for males, with a black hat and red symbol. Female members wore a white blouse and a black skirt. The FBI and the Dickstein Committee classified Spanknöbel as an intelligence agent employed by a foreign government.

The Friends of New Germany had convened assemblies and demonstrations, with Nazi storm troopers dressed in full traditional uniform, and its propaganda denounced minority groups, communists and Catholics at mass meetings. The leadership composed a somewhat unsophisticated official doctrine, preferring to punctuate their political demonstrations with rudimentary ideology and shock tactics. Visiting representatives of fascist movements in Europe appeared as prestigious guest speakers at the conferences to expound on national socialism and the European model. This period lasted for two to three years until a disagreeing wave of public resentment swept across the country, but pro-fascist militant campaigning across America from 1933 to 1935 continued unabated. The American Nazi Party and the Whiteshirts openly justified a pro–Nazi Germany stance and stoically defended Hitler's ambitious objectives and racist denunciations. Campaigns were launched to amend and refashion public opinion regarding Jewish boycotts of German goods, implemented after considerable lobbying following the Nazi succession to power. The Friends of New Germany engaged in numerous provocative awareness-raising stunts including storming the New York newspaper *Staats-Zeitung* and demanding that Nazi-sympathetic articles be published. They also actively infiltrated other neutral German-American groups and associations.[9] The Third Reich, it later transpired, had indeed invested substantive resources in attempting to influence U.S. domestic popular opinion through manifold covert methods, primarily centered on the German-American Bund movement, but the German government secretly subsidized other "front" organizations disseminating propaganda, including the American Fellowship Forum.

At many of these fascist rallies and meetings the organizers decided to adopt the promotion of anti–Semitic propaganda. Transparent racism and anti–Semitism were advocated more reservedly by a cautious Bund, which particularly encouraged moderation at exposed gatherings. The smaller defiant pro–Nazi groups wasted minimal exertion in delivering speeches reviling in demagoguery and drumming up suspicions on racial conspiracy theories. Any legitimate popular concerns about economic subjects, governmental issues or foreign affairs were rendered accountable to racist interpretation. Published literature and arranged public meetings discussed dogmatically the unparalleled evils of communism and Marxist ideology.[10] This expanding myriad of organizations and movements did not develop without inciting considerable internal friction and confrontation, and some German members had resigned membership and refused any involvement with Nazism. Order 76 was formed by an amalgamation of divergent nationalist groups in 1934; directed by Royal Gulden, the organization garnered a reputation of considerable notoriety. The Silvershirts, another pro-fascist political movement, was produced as a factionalized splinter group of Order 76 after unresolved incongruities isolated members. The FBI and Justice Department opened investigations on American Nazism with mounting trepidation about the internal threats or foreign infiltration raised in state and federal governments.

Nazi academics in Germany appeared in agreement about the possibility of promulgating the tenants of national socialism to an American audience. Propaganda subject materials should become more refined in subtlety and an acknowledgement was confirmed that ideological offensives were necessary to prepare the American population for a socially acceptable version of Nazism. The Nazi academic Bruno Steinwallner did not recommend that racial biology of Mein Kampf be adapted or subverted for the traditionally more liberalist focused market of America. Segregation legislation had existed in America in contemporary formats dating from the 1870s and in many states was condoned despite disagreement; but the 1935 Nuremberg Laws and eugenics conjecture were remote ideologically to American interpretation and perhaps too extreme in language for the audiences. National socialist theory as elucidated in their own propaganda matter had interpreted the rampant liberalism of America as inherently individualistic and decadent.[11] The newspapers and magazines transported back to the Fatherland from the United States heartland convinced many Nazi theorists that Roosevelt was governing under the control of other insidious forces.

U.S. presidential elections presented an immediate objective to attach to for both Nazis in Germany and their American counterparts. Nazis in both America and Germany perceived it to be axiomatic that Roosevelt's administration was an opponent of fascism; before the presidential election in 1936 the Bund and other pro–Nazi groups had channeled resources and campaigned actively within the anti–Roosevelt camps. The Third Reich agency, German Propaganda Bureau, directed its American theater investments into sustaining groups classified as suitably correlated with national socialism. Both the Nazi operatives and the American groups were dispatched considerable funding, which failed to pass unnoticed and resulted in congressional investigations and mounting controversy on the subject of American fascist movements and related organizations. The Special Committee on Un-American Activities, authorized to investigate Nazi propaganda, was formed in 1934 in response to a lamentable and now unmistakable surge in pro-fascist publications. A second federal investigation on the pro–Nazi movements amidst accelerating alarm was launched by the House of Representatives Committee on Naturalization and Immigration in 1934. The house committee was chaired by John McCormack, and Samuel Dickstein was appointed the vice chair. It was Dickstein who initially advocated this question as warranting the standing committee's attention, and he voiced his concerns about the substantial increase in immigration of pro-fascist supporters and growing anti–Semitism in the United States.

On the floor of the House of Representatives, Samuel Dickstein characterized the objective of the committee to Congress: "This special investigating committee should seek to accomplish three primary objects: First, ascertain the facts about the role of introduction into this country of destructive, subversive propaganda originating from foreign countries; second, ascertain facts about organizations in this country that seem to be cooperating to spread this alien propaganda to this country; third, study and recommend to the House the appropriate legislation which may correct existing facts and tend to prevent the recurrence of either condition in the future." Under Samuel Dickstein's administration the committee trawled through information on the Nazi organizations and a plethora of fascist literature being distributed in the nation. Throughout the remainder of 1934 the committee conducted hearings, bringing before its representatives most of the prominent and recognizable figures in the domestic fascist movements. Dickstein's investigation concluded that the Friends of Germany represented a branch of German dictator Adolf Hitler's Nazi Party in America.[12]

This proliferation of movements in alignment with Hitler's Germany emerged as undoubtedly a challenging national security environment in the 1930s. While the extremist groups probably did not attain sufficient power to realistically threaten the government, membership following was certainly capable of generating abundant public suspicion. The disclosed actions of implicated German cultural organizations were assessed as concerning because of the German-American Bund's apparent submission to instructions of a foreign government; postulation on international states collaborating with domestic radicals troubled many citizens. A majority of infiltrated cultural associations had in fact disavowed all contact with fascism. In February 1935, the Special House Committee released an official report on its investigations, proclaiming that the domestic-front Nazi infrastructure had directly targeted with propaganda 20 million Americans.[13]

The FBI's investigation report on the German-American Bund were released in 2001. In fact, from 1935 onwards the FBI retained open files on the Bund members, justified internally as pertaining to documented instances concerning possible "unpatriotic" activities or behavior adjudged to threaten national security. In 1939, according to the 2001 files, the FBI launched an official investigation into testimony raised at Dies Committee hearings, discovering substantial verification of serious allegations that members of Nazi Germany's legations colluded with domestic movements in engagement of espionage activities. Scrutinized groups most identified with connections to the Third Reich ministries included the German-American Bund and Silvershirts groups.[14] In a declassified letter dated March 15, 1939, J. Edgar Hoover disclosed that Attorney General McMahon had personally requested a detailed and rigorous investigation into the German-American Bund movement, precipitating the FBI's action.[15]

Personal files on all German-American Bund leading members were consequently produced. Ernst Goerner and Fritz Kuhn acquired confirmed identification as the most prolific and high-profile Nazi collaborators in the United States, practicing routine communications with contacts at the Reich Propaganda Bureau. Fritz Kuhn was the identical individual who in 1938 had filed a lawsuit against Warner Brothers, ineffectively opposing the production of an anti–Nazi movie, *Confessions of a Nazi Spy*. Evidence presented at the Dies Committee hearings disclosed that the Silvershirts of America organization was modeled deliberately on storm troopers of Nazi Germany and, more incriminating, had entered into communications with government officials in Germany. This movement was founded in 1933 by William Dudley Pelley, a prolific party organizer who instituted chapters of the Silvershirts traversing the United States; investigation observed his proclivities towards exercising the power of a dictator in his management approach. In a comparable configuration to other American Nazis he had elicited overtures from Nazi Germany's Foreign Ministry and other state bureaucracies agreeing to collude in whatever matters were determined necessary. The committee concluded that Silvershirts progressed beyond communications with Nazi state officials and cultivated interested coconspirators among pro–Nazi elements on German maritime vessels docked at the American eastern seaboard ports. Allegations were presented, with debatable confirmation, regarding chapters obtaining weapons, including firearms, and running drills.

George Sylvester Viereck was another contemporary American public figure who published pro–Nazi rhetoric. Rumor and speculation circulated in the U.S. and Europe for a considerable period of time accusing him of connections with either the German Propaganda Office or the SS. An audible public defender of Nazism and national socialism, Viereck obtained a controversial reputation and near-constant condemnation from the political left. A review of his publications reveals a protracted occupation disseminating pro–German propaganda in America. He edited the journal *Fatherland* in 1914 and encouraged U.S. neutrality with Germany and Austro-Hungary. Viereck had garnished a supplementary income financed by Third Reich paymasters during cover employment at the German Railroad Information Bureau and German Library of Information, both later confirmed as Nazi front organizations disseminating propaganda.[16] His observed propaganda activities progressed to writing articles for the *German-American Economic Bulletin* and *Today's Challenge*. From several accounts Viereck was predisposed to reminiscing and waxing lyrical concerning his personal encounters with Adolf Hitler, occasions which cemented his appreciation for the Fatherland. The initial Hitler meeting, a premonition perhaps of future circumstances, was a post–Beer Hall Putsch interview in 1923, this conversation sufficient to convert Viereck into an admirer. In 1933 he had arranged for a second meeting with Hitler a few months after his succession as Führer and visited Nazi Germany as a subsidized guest of Joseph Goebbels, the Nazi minister of propaganda. In European left-wing and socialist circles George Viereck was openly depicted as a propagandist or employee of the Hitler government.[17]

Viereck's policy appeared to involve remaining outside of the limelight and influencing news agendas from behind the journalistic and publishing scenes. He managed to convince pro-isolationist campaigner Prescott Dennett to inaugurate two organizations, the Make Europe Pay Its War Debt Committee and the Islands for War Debt Committee, and financially compensated Prescott Dennett for circulating articles advocating an isolationist stance by the Roosevelt administration and Congress. Viereck had dutifully assembled political contacts from the isolationist camp, including Congressman Hamilton Fish and his secretary George Hill; both individuals appeared routinely on public record consistently and ardently campaigning for noninvolvement of the U.S.

military in European or Asian affairs. Viereck's endeavors produced some quantifiable dividends, with the planting of numerous articles in the Congressional Record.[18] The publication of the *Preliminary Report on the Un-American Activities of Nazi Organizations* finally produced by the House of Un-American Activities Commission declared that Viereck was a compensated employee of front organizations operating on behalf of Nazi Germany. Evidence was uncovered documenting the financial transaction routes of the German Railroad Information Bureau and other companies.

In another, connected, conspiracy that recently declassified FBI files from 2002 illuminated, a group of New York business and professional individuals arranged a discreet conference at the Lexington Hotel and founded the American Fellowship Forum on March 16, 1939. The organization's stated purpose for existing was refocusing public attention on solutions to domestic social and economic problems. Appointed to be the national director of this forum was a Dr. Friedrich Auhagen, formerly a professor of German literature at Columbia University. Auhagen, as documented in FBI files, was a Nazi agent and former lieutenant in the Kaiser's army.[19] His occupation as an engineer resulted in advanced degrees in both engineering and economics subjects. This undeniably reputable background accompanied with eminent qualifications allowed the securing of academia positions at prominent American universities and served as an ideal cover for his propaganda work. In June the group introduced into media circulation a magazine entitled *Today's Challenge*; the organization extended its stated business of publishing articles supporting Nazi Germany and national socialist principles in general.

The conspiracy plot thickens further. FBI investigations on Dr. Auhagen and the American Fellowship Forum uncovered paper trails stretching from its New York office to Reich headquarters in Berlin. Dr. Auhagen and others associated with the shadowy circle received intermittent financial payments from Kurt Johannsen, a Nazi official in Hamburg.[20] The American Fellowship attracted substantial private benefactors including the noted American pharmaceutical pioneer and industrialist Ferdinand Kertess. Other political figures perpetuating standing connections with *Today's Challenge* and contributing article materials to the magazine were Senator Ernest Lundeen and Representative Hamilton Fish. Another journalist and propagandist, one George Sylvester Viereck, also developed alliances with Friedrich Auhagen.

The subversive behavior of Viereck was subjected eventually to review by a federal grand jury. Viereck admitted before a congressional committee to receiving a salary of $500 per month from Otto Kiep, the Nazi consul general in New York. He had received an additional $1,750 per month in remuneration from a front subsidiary company, the German Tourist Bureau. In late 1941 the grand jury concluded that he indisputably received considerable financial inducements from Nazi Germany's state officials, which culminated in his arrest in October 1941 for violation of the 1938 Foreign Agents Registration Act.[21] In 1942, Viereck was convicted and incarcerated, only to be released a year later after the Supreme Court overturned the original decision. He was convicted in 1943 for a second time and was temporarily imprisoned.

First Generation of Spies

A former German naval officer, Korvetten-Kapitaen Pheiffer, developed the first sophisticated Nazi German intelligence spy network in the United States. Pheiffer retired from military service after experiencing action in World War I but was reactivated by the Abwehr in 1935 and converted into an intelligence asset. The Abwehr recognized in Pheiffer the requisite circumstances for accelerating the military intelligence presence inside the Americas and for collecting comprehensive strategic information, a demand from the Wehrmacht and Kriegsmarine multiplying in volume daily. Conrad Pheiffer after 1936 would become a self-appointed hub of German intelligence in America. At least two other independent spy networks reported through him to the Abwehr headquarters in Berlin. Nazi espionage networks worked beneath the government detection radar for two years before FBI and Justice Department agents comprehended the proficiency of the underground operations. Pheiffer instigated a cover persona as representative of the Aussenhandelstelle, or German foreign trade office.

He had previously orchestrated the naval section of Bremen and exploited that function to cultivate contacts with international shipping interests at that port. The Aussenhandelstelle allowed convenient access to German business travelers returning from overseas. German regulations at that time required all citizens engaged in business enterprises abroad to be legally registered. Pheiffer interviewed returnees to uncover any pertinent information on foreign governments and their industrial interests. If possible, he recruited informants from business contacts, incentivized for either financial or nationalistic reasons. Other passengers of Bremen assessed as potentially informative—for instance, dockworkers and merchant marines—were targeted for recruitment.

German intelligence files had disintegrated into disrepair during the 1920s, with information either rendered obsolete or superseded by changing climates. When the military rearmament programs began in the early 1930s the international priority materialized of improving information obtained by foreign intelligence agents about the United States. By the time of Pheiffer's recruitment the Nazi high command was articulating displeasure at Abwehr and RSHA efforts inside America and complaints concentrated on intolerable and perceptibly high levels of inactivity. SD VI Foreign Intelligence officers did not supervise any undercover operatives and sustained zero contacts or informants in government and military circles. In fact, German information-gathering operations in America dated back to 1933 but were not sufficiently advanced in capability or well financed, Lonkowski and Griebl both had commanded independent networks. Pheiffer reactivated the earlier Griebl and Lonkowski espionage spy rings with the objective of converting the presently nondescript groups into formidable intelligence-gathering units.[22] Ignatz Griebl, despite operational naivety and minimal knowledge of security measures, was acknowledged as a valuable asset by Abwehr handlers. The German navy and air force were desperate for intelligence on their opposing counterparts in disciplines of technical design, armaments and specialist equipment. Griebl, over several months in 1935 and 1936, supplied Pheiffer with sensitive and classified blueprints, documents on U.S. aeronautic technology and research into methods of aircraft design.

Dr. Ignatz Griebl, another military veteran, had served as an artillery officer during World War I in the Wehrmacht. Disconsolate with unstable economic and social conditions permeating a deprived postwar Germany, he had emigrated to America immediately after demobilization. He studied at Long Island Medical College and graduated with an MD degree, temporarily investing his qualifications in the U.S. Army Medical Reserve Corps before employment in a financially comfortable private practice. Griebl established residence in New York and, content with the surroundings, became a long-term inhabitant. By introduction to Conrad Pheiffer, Griebl had assimilated into American everyday life and was a naturalized American citizen.[23] He earned the reputation as a transparent and ardent national socialist advocate even before Hitler's formal inauguration as chancellor.

By 1933 Griebl was such a prominent and recognizable character in American Nazi affairs that he and his wife were questioned rigorously by an accusative federal grand jury and later the Senate committee investigating subversive fascist activities. In November 1933, protests emanating from patients and anti–Nazi groups forced his unceremonious resignation as assistant clinical surgeon at Harlem Hospital in New York. He was indeed identified by the Special Committee on Un-American Activities as conducting personal relationships and speaking engagements with prominent individuals in Nazi Germany's government, including Hans Borchers, the German consul in New York. The attorney general's office had questioned Griebl after acquiring incriminating facts concerning his offering accommodation to a visiting press officer, a personal employee of Adolf Hitler. The State Department, through pursuing various investigations into the German press officer and his intentions inside America, discovered Ignatz Griebl's involvement. He was interrogated by State Department representatives who pressed him on the characteristics of his undisclosed association with this government official. Griebl's employment by German intelligence was speculated on, but at that juncture he was assessed as being merely an advocate of fascism. Any standard security procedures were not implemented to question his dealings further.

He later described traveling to Germany and having a personal meeting with Admiral Canaris in Berlin at the Abwehr's Tirpitzufer headquarters, the central command point inside the German intelligence community, and recounted his undisguised stupefaction and some trepidation at being in conversation with Nazi Germany's spy chief. Admiral Canaris personally demanded Griebl's redeployment back to America in the context of completing several objectives, despite evident reluctance and uncertainty that his prior American cover remained intact. Public associations with American Nazism had attracted the unwelcome and persistent attention of the federal authorities; indeed Griebl's FBI file dates to 1933. The content on Ignatz Griebl transparently describes the disposition of his association with the German-American Bund and other pro–Nazi groups such as serving as the Friends of New Germany's vice president. He frequently and without displaying much regard for security protocols arranged personal meetings with Fritz Kuhn, who was at that time the chief organizer of the German-American Bund and synonymous with admiration of Hitler.[24]

Griebl was sufficiently intelligent to employ some suitable clandestine methods to disguise his undercover actions, generally avoiding official titles or any unnecessary profile at demonstrations within the various pro–Nazi organizations in which he circulated. His FBI record documents that "behind the scenes" contacts and relationships with other high-profile Nazi supporters had forestalled paper trails. In November 1935 back in Germany, universal military service was officially authorized and another symbol of Versailles repudiated: the next phase stipulated open rearmament. Canaris increased the pressure on the Griebl and Lonkowski nets to uncover more advanced and prolific intelligence on the U.S. military, and instructions were issued to research and locate German-born engineers and scientists and individuals with strong connections working on American defense systems. The agents, relying on nationalist sympathies, payments or coercion, evolved the strategy of convincing these individuals to divulge sensitive security data. In April 1935 the Nazi operatives, in a formative operational success, managed to uncover information on aircraft in development for the U.S. military. Schematics for a Boeing bomber plane and a navy bomber aircraft being constructed for SBU-I carriers were couriered from the Farmingdale manufacturing center to Abwehr headquarters.

The Nazi operatives obtained a substantial proportion of their technical data from William Lonkowski, a German-American scientist employed as an engineer for a period at the Farmingdale facility and harboring other scientific community contact points. Pheiffer himself devised the covert system for delivering the purloined secret documents to Germany undetected. The dockyard area of New York served as an intermediary conduit for passing the information on to German commercial ships for transportation to headquarters in Germany. Pheiffer opened the network broadly to attract willing informants within the German-American or pro–Nazi movements, and it did not require lengthy persuasion to convince many approached targets to provide information.[25] It appears that patriotism more frequently than not provided the mitigating self-justifying factors in the psychological process of an individual committing to work undercover for a foreign government. One agent technically on the books transformed into a decidedly more uncooperative character, agreeing rather impulsively to clandestinely funnel intelligence for the Fatherland, but on reflection regretting this decision. He experienced difficulty in reconciling himself to working against the nation now regarded as his native land. Despite unexpected interruptions a network of cellular and self-contained groups formed, the analysis reveals, predominantly inhabiting the Eastern Seaboard but with corresponding satellite cells emerging across the nation.

Washington and New York formed the central coordination territories for operations and a convenient launching pad for a significant number of semi-independent informants. Spy ring networks were established by conspirators in Montreal, which later became the headquarters for all Canada and New England. Other cells were founded at Newport News, Boston, Buffalo, Bristol, Philadelphia, San Diego and Bath. The seriousness of espionage committed diverged to a considerable degree from the relatively mundane open source intelligence freely available to American residents and the opposite spectrum of scientists and engineers agreeing to obediently serve the Fatherland. Spy network cells were structurally calculated for a wide distribution and compartmentalized, and it indeed was possible that a deliberately restricted number of highly placed individuals acquired an awareness of only four or five cells. German military intelligence by 1936 employed the labors of hundreds of local-level employees, the part-time informants proving to be effective, albeit non-professional, tools in extracting data. Strategically placing agents on the ground had reduced operational needs on relaying information or waiting on other agencies.[26]

Pheiffer on multiple occasions rather too candidly discussed sensitive components of delicate missions with Griebl and other agents; infringement of compartmentalization was standard practice. The Pheiffer network in October 1935 planted a Nazi informant inside the office of an important naval architect, a center for conceiving and designing naval warships and other military defensive systems. Another celebrated counterintelligence breakthrough occurred when Pheiffer personally received the schematics of a classified anti-aircraft gun, primed for greenlighting, before the documents—formulated by technicians under great secrecy at Fort Monmouth—surfaced for final approval. Nazi headquarters in Berlin, according to postwar interviews with Ignatz Griebl, had continually pressed Pheiffer for intelligence reports on the latest developments in naval information and technology; the Fatherland's Kriegsmarine forces were still inferior to that of the other major powers. Rearmament programs of sufficient dimension to engender a tactical advantage for Nazi Germany in combat against the armed forces of Britain and France would not be totally finalized for two to three years. SD VI commanders from 1936 onwards expressly advocated for an expansion of information-gathering endeavors to encompass U.S. relations with Britain and European nations both militarily and economically.

Griebl, in his later testimony to the FBI investigators, explained the extent of his individual complicity and reported on other encounters with Pheiffer, his primary contact. On one occasion he recalled being guided forcibly by his associate into a discreet corner booth at a New York restaurant. Pheiffer passed under the table a documents folder containing an inventory of Abwehr and Reich War Ministry authorized targets, an audacious list by all accounts that contained blueprints of battleships, military research and industrial apparatus. Griebl declared in his own defense that any participation in undercover actions attributable to himself were assuredly limited, his expected standard operational duties pertaining merely to distributing messages and instructions to other members. In testimony to FBI special agents, Ignatz Griebl confirmed the enactment of cooperation and information exchange with Japanese intelligence services.[27]

In November 1935, sensitive naval information discovered by the Northwestern network, apparently originating from an informant in Seattle, was subsequently profitably sold to the Japanese. Japanese intelligence representatives expressed an interest in U.S. national defense plans and naval complement strength. Pheiffer said, "The Japanese consider the United States a potential enemy. They fear the Pacific Fleet. They are always most anxious for the naval and military secrets of the United States. But because of their appearance, they are marked, and find it impossible to do real espionage in America themselves. So they must operate through others, when we uncover anything of value to Japan, we sell it to them."[28] In time, radio communication would later be installed as a recurring strategy at the heart of the Abwehr's global espionage network. Werner Trautmann managed the more advanced World War II–era division that was designated to be oriented towards the United States. The operations center in Hamburg, fitted with the latest technology, developed into a massive complex; however, until late 1938 technological limitations prevented shortwave radio transmission from covert operatives in the United States to Europe. The first generation of Nazi foreign intelligence agents were forcibly dependent on shipping and human transportation.

Productive members of the Nazi spy conspiracy in America included Schluter and Schütz, who operated on the Eastern Seaboard. Schluter was officially designated as the New York liaison to Pheiffer and demonstrated sufficient application for assignment on several missions. His obligations were centered on smuggling through manipulating intrusion as a dockyard operator or impersonating legitimate employees from the German vessels and trafficking the sensitive appropriated documents originating from Pheiffer to their handlers stationed in Germany. Schütz performed a utility of U.S. quartermaster and connection point to the Berlin headquarters. Other agents with current or former occupational positions in aviation and the military were advised to concentrate on appropriating secrets—for instance, Guenther Rumrich and Otto Hermann Vos, the former individual being a discharged U.S. Army sergeant. In 1937 the FBI reported after an official case assessment that 30–35 operatives of Nazi Germany's foreign intelligence service had received official identification.

Otto Hermann Vos, a qualified engineer by profession, exploited his legitimate employment at the Seversky military plant. He fashioned an accommodating and mutually advantageous alliance with Griebl and another operative named Werner Gudenberg to smuggle documents confiscated from the industrial facilities to secret rendezvous meetings for information exchange. He worked conveniently in the experimental "dream department" at the Seversky company, a corporate subdivision delegated the role of researching advanced technology and a purview for examining data inside any sector within the massive establishment. Otto Hermann Vos, inspired with renewed impetus, practiced his commitment to national socialism by attending Nazi meetings and conventions in Long Island. A German-born scientist employed at a military facility who consorted with known Nazi Party members attracted the attentions of FBI agents. In Buffalo at the Curtis-Wright plant Werner Gudenberg was employed as a foreman in the metal works division. He was a squarely proportioned man with close-cropped hair, and any conspicuous behavior transpired unobserved by his unsuspecting coworkers. In November 1936 Gudenberg transferred to Hall Aluminum and Aircraft Company at Bristol, Pennsylvania.

The facility was contracted to manufacture bomber aircraft for the U.S. Navy. Gudenberg even applied for employment at the U.S. Navy Aircraft Plant at Philadelphia.

A Gestapo branch opened in America and Karl Herrmann was promoted to Gestapo New York chief in 1937; complicating matters, Pheiffer, as the Abwehr senior commander, was appointed Gestapo liaison. The new Gestapo detachment's operational directive was to pressure and intimidate German-Americans, individuals selected stemming from any disclosed associations with either anti-Nazi denunciation or a refusal to cooperate. Henchmen were recruited for this intimidation work, which largely required muscle. Left-wing and socialist groups exposed statistics of disturbing escalations in instances of physical attacks on their members.[29] A major operation in 1938 planned by Abwehr headquarters represented the most successful maneuver of Pheiffer's spy network. Admiral Canaris succumbed to substantial pressure emanating from the command of the Luftwaffe and consented to instructing his stateside agents to acquire the advanced Norden bombsight navigation technology. Major Ritter, a recent Abwehr recruit destined for promotion to the commander of operations in the United States, managed the proceedings. The mission being assembled in Abwehr headquarters centered on the Norden factory installation in Manhattan.

An old acquaintance of Canaris's appointed supreme head of Luftwaffe air ordinance, Ernst Udel, personally requested military intelligence expertise in obtaining the blueprints of the Norden bombsight. In fact, air force commanders for several months had persistently demanded from Canaris the information from his field operatives on this closely guarded American secret. The technology was classified as high value because it achieved general recognition as the latest premier advancement in gyroscope bombsight aiming devices. The Norden version was a sophisticated device connected to the aircraft's autopilot that calculated a trajectory based theoretically on real-time flight conditions; alterations to bomb trajectories were possible according to changes in the wind, altitude and other atmospheric effects. This technology was in long-term development by the American military; flight testing experiments had demonstrated impressive results enabling unprecedented accuracy from higher altitudes. The German version was not significantly far behind in sophistication, but without external expertise could potentially remain less advanced for several years. Questions were raised about the reliability and the maintenance of cover exercised by the U.S.–based operatives in a climate of several indiscretions, The Griebl and Lonkowski rings, while demonstrating occasional usefulness, were effectively redeployed to menial tasks and would be overlooked for this mission.

Nikolaus Ritter, later the adversary of British intelligence and a commander in the European theater, was another agent recruited by the Abwehr who had a background connected to the United States by occupation or residency. Born in 1899, Ritter emigrated to America in early 1924 and remained a resident until 1935. At first Ritter survived on relatively humble financial subsistence and rented an inexpensive apartment in New York City, drifting circuitously through several unstable occupations, working intermittently as an importer, factory operator and textile worker. In the textile industry Ritter finally encountered commercial success, establishing numerous profitable business ventures.[30] By the mid–1930s Nikolaus Ritter had an American wife and children, almost completely immersing himself in American culture and he officially announced his intention of becoming a naturalized American citizen. He adopted multiple contemporary trappings and insular customs that were associated with 1930s U.S. culture and manifested a passable American accent with only a persistent trace of German. However, the good financial times were somewhat impermanent. The Great Depression inflicted severe economic misfortune on Ritter's businesses, evaporating most of the assets he had meticulously accumulated during this tenure. He now, regrettably, found himself unemployed, verging on bankruptcy and in a financially precarious condition.

In 1935, Ritter turned his back on America and returned with his American wife and children to Germany. An opportune meeting with a German military attaché in Washington and promise of Hitler's supposed miraculous new Third Reich convinced Ritter that his former homeland supplied the most attractive future circumstances. He reenlisted in the Wehrmacht and was immediately transferred to the Abwehr, where he received a commission. Ritter returned to the Fatherland to find his perfect English assessed as valuable by the Abwehr and was appointed to positions originally in Bremen and then at air intelligence headquarters located in Hamburg. He was redeployed as the commander of U.S. operations and a primary agent on the Norden bombsight project. Inside America while undercover he adopted the pseudonym of Alfred Landing. The FBI would later unmask Ritter as a dangerous German government agent, but he managed to operate within the U.S. and avoid detection for over twelve months. Doctor Rantzau, a European theater military intelligence agent, was later exposed as a second assumed pseudonym of Ritter. Colonel Piekenbrock and Canaris both expressed reluctance at their new protégé's decision to appoint himself as chief of field operations inside the United States, but they acquiesced to pressure from the Luftwaffe regarding the subject of recovering the Norden bombsight. Ritter was instructed strenuously by the Abwehr strategists on the observance of operational security measures: under no circumstances should he initiate contact with friends and acquaintances or any previous relationships from his former life in America. Other important security protocols involved disguising his real identity and inventing a convenient cover persona for underground actions. Nikolaus Ritter was instructed to avoid meeting any German military and diplomatic personnel and to refrain from discussing operational aspects or spy ring operatives known to him. His mission parameters in New York, as delineated by his section chief, were to promote German diplomatic and economic influence in the United States. Another important member in the Norden conspiracy was Herbert Haupt.

The German-born Haupt spent his childhood living in Chicago's North Side, and extended family members similarly settled in Chicago and other parts of Illinois. He attained employment in West Garfield Park at a factory manufacturing components fundamental for the Norden bombsight. It was Hermann Lang, a scientist employed at the Norden plant, who managed to smuggle out and trace the blueprints; he was also a German citizen and self-confessed fascist who had participated in the Munich Beer Hall Putsch of 1923.[31] Ritter arranged a conference with Lang and assessed his capabilities as the inside man in the document extraction phase, finally authorizing execution of the critical junctures in proceedings. In smuggling the stolen Norden documents onto a waiting German commercial ship stationed at the harbor, the SS *Reliance*, Ritter would be commanding the operations. An improvised camouflage device involving adapting an umbrella permitted Nikolaus Ritter to surreptitiously courier aboard the blueprints creatively removed by Hermann Lang. The Norden saga was possibly one of the greatest feats of German espionage during this period.

Discovery of Pheiffer Spy Ring

Dialogue intercepted between an inconspicuous house in Dundee and the U.S. East Coast first revealed conclusive evidence pertaining to the existence of a complex and integrated Nazi espionage program. The case broke after MI5 (Security Service) detected and instigated monitoring of a secret Nazi controlled mail relay station in Dundee, Scotland in 1937. British Intelligence officers entitled to examine citizens' mail in national emergencies identified incriminating content matter in the letters emanating from the address. MI5 declassified file sections connected to the case in 2012, and the released documents include fascinating insights into investigations. After methodically sifting documentation and compiling incriminating data MI5 turned the information over to the U.S. War Department, which consequently discovered the damaging implications of the Nazi penetration. The Dundee inhabitant in question turned out to be an otherwise undetected local, Mrs. Jordan, a Scottish-born widower, from all accounts displaying perfidious loyalty to her now-deceased husband, a German citizen and former military officer. MI5 investigators determined other suspicious behaviors attributable to Jordan, with observation of her presence in marked proximity on multiple occasions to the British military and coastline defenses. Mrs. Jordan was placed under full-time surveillance order and observed covertly traveling to Berlin and meeting prominent German officials.

Late in January 1938, British authorities intercepted a letter from New York. The declassified files reveal that it contained a mysterious and possibly encrypted message printed by hand and signed "Crown." MI5 officers released the envelope and its contents back into circulation and tracked the movements. The letter had traveled from Scotland to Berlin, landing at the nondescript office of another unknown individual named "Spielman." Information gathered from informants and other sources indicated that Spielman was in reality Erich Pheiffer. Other intercepted documents that "Crown" submitted to "Spielman" had contained routine operational reports concerning his activities targeting the East Coast of the United States, the specific implication being Spielman was higher in the chain of command. All intercepted documents were examined by the U.S. War Department and FBI as the case rapidly unfolded and the multifarious divergent segments were gradually maneuvered into place. A more comprehensive picture of uncovered conspiracies and German-planned missions for infiltration emerged. The case files divulge some intriguing facts about other Nazi schemes in America.[32]

The Nazi government, desperate to obtain the latest strategic and military defense plans on the U.S. East Coast territory, commissioned the American-based covert operatives to formulate a strategy for extracting the documents by physical force. Analysis of intercepted communications disclosed the objective of kidnapping Colonel Henry Eglin, a commanding officer based at Fort Totten and apparently identified as holding sufficient personal clearance to secure possession of and remove the information. The kidnapping scheme entailed convincing Colonel Eglin through imprecisely defined subterfuge to attend a preselected New York hotel room, possibly orchestrating a honeytrap scheme to encourage cooperation, and persuading him to acquire the documents in question. At this juncture, other attending Nazi spy ring associates would intervene and overpower Colonel Eglin and capture the defense plans. Other clandestine initiatives were elaborated on. Nazi spies had collaborated in penetrating a military installation and stealing confidential codes and various geographical maps of U.S. Army Air Corps. Another improbable scheme had required forging President Franklin Roosevelt's signature to withdraw blueprints of the aircraft carriers *Enterprise* and *Yorktown*. This inspiration necessitated procuring White House stationery to assist the German counterfeit experts in reprinting their own fabricated versions, but this scheme was later abandoned.

The Justice Department now realized that German intelligence operatives were active inside U.S. borders. Strategies of counterintelligence and counterespionage previously unfavored inside the Departments of State and Justice were now being declared fundamental for ensuring national security; intelligence services marshaled their collective resources in preparing for combating the unveiled threat from within. In 1938, Germany and the United States were respecting peaceful relations regardless of discrepancies involving collaboration with British and French entanglements during the Spanish civil war, any previous observable encroachments on neutrality being relatively insignificant. The Abwehr's decision to instigate engagement in intelligence gathering and espionage developed complex and far-reaching implications for German-American relations. Ironically, Admiral Canaris had advised against covert penetrations or aggressive tactics on American soil, cautiously pessimistic in analyzing the potential for blowback in destabilizing relations or cause diplomatic incidents. But the Abwehr chief found himself countermanded by the Luftwaffe's interventions. Congressional representatives expressed shock and outrage as exposure of Germany's agents became general knowledge at the governmental level, the delicate balancing acts of citizens' political rights and the national defense and security policies once again fundamentally tested. The FBI investigation scrutinized exhaustively the disturbing minutiae uncovered in the "Crown" information depository, revelations concerning the planned kidnapping of Colonel Eglin and ensuing discussions of various locations. The real identity of "Crown" was discovered to be Guenther Rumrich, the prominent Pheiffer-Griebl spy ring operative.

On February 15, 1938, the FBI arrested Rumrich, arguably the most valuable German government agent in America at that time, and rapidly the Nazi espionage ring unraveled.[33] He was interrogated intensively by assorted representatives of U.S. military intelligence and the FBI. Major Dalton of G-2 had adopted preliminary obligations as primary interrogator. Dalton attempted to extract a confession that the obscure German captive was associated with a major foreign espionage network. Several days of intense questioning elicited informative specifics concerning Rumrich's coconspirators. The expanding contact list and the accompaniment of intercepted collated communications documents inevitably implicated Rumrich as a central figure in the conspiracy, so his continual rejections and denials were ineffective. FBI transcripts of interrogations depicted his initial attempts at resistance and to implicate merely a handful of personnel in the espionage ring to presumably restrict any negative repercussions on himself; but he eventually relented and consented to agreements in cooperating fully. The interrogations proved to be valuable in constructing an irrefutable criminal case against other detained agents, as physical evidence remained minimal. Within four days of Rumrich's arrest his statements had confirmed complicity in a covert underground conspiracy involving a foreign government intelligence agency.

Guenther Rumrich was twenty-seven years old by this time. His FBI record reveals that he was born in Chicago to Austrian parents: his father's diplomatic career had stipulated their deployment to the Austro-Hungarian embassy in the United States. Raised in Germany, Rumrich returned to America in 1927 and immediately enlisted in the army as a passage to fast-tracking citizenship; the majority of his tenure was devoted apparently to gambling and drinking in small-town establishments near military bases. An undistinguished record accompanied the future spy's service history in the U.S. military. He deserted in 1931 and pursued a relatively reclusive and undocumented lifestyle for the following 18 months while evading the MP investigators, finding temporary employment as a dishwasher and in other menial occupations. He decided on relocating to New York in 1936. Language skills perfected during his American travels had opened up alternative career opportunities. Rumrich was employed as a German teacher of American students at a language school in New York. He had discreetly inquired in cafes on East 86th Street in the Yorkville section of New York, premises even then synonymous with Nazi sympathizers and temporarily stationed crew members from the German merchant ships.[34]

East 86th Street had evolved into an unofficial headquarters for pro–Nazi Germans abroad. Rumrich, in a deliberate and concerted intervention to convince the powerbrokers of Nazi espionage of his talents, contacted groups with the suitable connections. He distributed an introductory letter to the *Völkischer Beobachter* (Public Observer), the official newspaper of the Nazi Party in Germany and Hitler's personal method of releasing information to the German public. He contacted Colonel Walthar Nicolai, the World War I-era intelligence commander, offering his nefarious talents as a prospective espionage agent in United States. Unfortunately, Rumrich's approach had generated some symptoms of confusion. Colonel Nicolai was no longer employed by German intelligence, and by this period Nicolai was engaged decidedly less auspiciously at the Reich Institute for the History of New Germany, a propaganda office certainly outside the purview of secret services. Abwehr commanders by February 1937 had heard the protestations of Guenther Rumrich. He was recruited by Pheiffer and his military connections transpired to be expedient in unearthing informants on military bases. Rumrich disclosed under interrogation that his original recurring contacts while undercover were the individuals Karl Schlueter and Jenny Hofmann.

It was the arrest of Ignatz Griebl in April 1938 that precipitated the total shutdown of the hidden Nazi espionage network. The confession he made to FBI Special Agent Turrou and the investigation teams was comprehensive in its exactness, recounting the Norden bombsight plot and other principal operations directed by Korvetten-Kapitaen Pheiffer, his former confidant in chief. Griebl's insider knowledge of Abwehr senior command in Berlin, the structure of highly restricted intelligence departments and Admiral Canaris's movements were declared to intently listening FBI investigators. He expounded on the capacity performed by German government representatives in supervising the espionage, and reports from Griebl's FBI interrogation clarified that naval program secrets were assessed in detail by analysts at Nazi headquarters in Germany. Griebl had informed investigators that the Nazi spy ring managed to infiltrate a coworker inside the premises of a clearinghouse for Washington loan offices for the purposes of reporting on army and navy officers and government officials needing finances. Nazi operatives could in theory approach financially compromised staff and offer bribes and other inducements to resolve debts.

Griebl informed FBI investigators on proposals to kidnap German-American citizens and secretly extradite them to Germany for "punishment"' in response to disloyalty towards the Fatherland, a terror tactic intended to curtail dissenting opinions. Further information on honeytrap schemes and ploys attempting to seduce German-born engineers and designers working in sensitive areas were exposed. FBI investigators checked the information uncovered with the Navy Department and other compromised agencies and concluded it was accurate.[35] Schlueter and a number of the Pheiffer espionage ring operatives were, unfortunately, either attending to business in Germany or otherwise outside U.S. borders during the arrests. Johanna Hofmann was detained and her confession appeared to corroborate the testimony of the other captured agents. Everything the FBI had initially suspected on examining the Spielman and Crown documents was confirmed: an espionage network extending insidiously inside the central infrastructure of the nation's state and industrial affairs had been under way. A somewhat diplomatic strategy was pursued by the FBI, which after deliberation decided against prosecuting Ignatz Griebl. On 10th of May Griebl managed to escape from the United States and stowed away on the freighter SS *Bremen* to Germany, disregarding his assurances to the FBI.[36] Special Agent Turrou later divulged how the ambivalent results of lie detector examinations administered in the beginning of May 1938 convinced the investigations team that Griebl did not propose a threat and vigilance was consequently relaxed.

The two weeks following Rumrich's arrest saw the entire Nazi spy network in the U.S. being dismantled and most prominent members imprisoned or inoperable as agents. In June a federal grand jury was convened in New York and duly indicted eighteen individuals on charges of violation of the National Espionage Act; however, many of the indicted individuals were at that time beyond the prosecutor's jurisdiction. In October 1938, a series of high-profile trial hearings opened proceedings with convictions being handed down. The accused Nazi espionage suspects were all convicted: Vos received a six-year sentence, Hofmann four years, and Rumrich and Glaser two each. The remaining collaborator was not forgotten. In Scotland Mrs. Jordan was sentenced to four years' hard labor.[37]

Operation Pastorius

The Wehrmacht had previously demonstrated success in training terrorists at a secret German army facility. This special operations division acquiring the designation zbv 800 Regiment accomplished many tangible battlefield results. Abwehr II, since modifications starting in January 1939, had refined sabotage as a formal military discipline and applied it effectively throughout Europe. In March 1941, as conflict with America appeared inevitable, Adolf Hitler and OKW high command secretly ordered the Abwehr sabotage program's attention to be turned to America. Plans for offensive penetration operation were slowly being hatched by Lahousen and Kappe of Abwehr II with the objective of covertly transporting sabotage units to the East Coast of the United States. German intelligence had produced strategies before for launching covert action operations on the opposite side of the Atlantic deep inside U.S. territory as an effective countermeasure to American industrial prowess. By December 1941 and Pearl Harbor, Berlin central command was hounding Admiral Canaris to launch sabotage campaigns with the aim of demoralizing public opinion, and the Abwehr commander turned this pressure on his subordinates. Confident in achieving mission success, Lahousen boasted of an American sabotage operation by summer.

At the core of this new espionage network would be German-Americans repatriated to the Fatherland prior to outbreak of World War II. A considerable number of German migrants to America had returned during the 1930s, after consolidation of power by the NSDAP and the supposed emergence of a magnificent new era for a rejuvenated Germany. Sections of the returning exiles complement were former German-American Bund members disillusioned with current prospects in depression-era America who nevertheless spoke impeccable English and had developed an intimate knowledge of American culture.

Under Abwehr II's mission the specially trained units were scheduled for assaulting defense plants, industry infrastructure and other targets assessed as critical vulnerabilities. In March 1942 military intelligence, after rigorous screening processes, selected 12 agents, all either naturalized American citizens or resident in the United States for lengthy periods of time. The Abwehr fashioned their hand-picked agents to be saboteurs, capitalizing on their capability in blending into American society and remaining unnoticed.

By April 1942 the preparations were concluded for the sabotage operations against the United States, the necessary tools and techniques ready. In active command of the project code named "Pastorius" was Lieutenant Walter Kappe, an Abwehr II of Intelligence II officer assigned individual accountability for coordinating the research and development from mission inception. The concept of depositing saboteurs on an American coastline was developed into a workable espionage program by Kappe in just over twelve months. His Nazi Party credentials, solidified by a general awareness of his enlistment in the early 1920s during the fascist movement's formative period, were considered an honorable accomplishment.[38]

He emigrated to Chicago from Germany in 1925. During the opening years of his residency Kappe had undertaken employment at an agricultural implement factory in Kankakee, Illinois, before setting up home in the suburbs of Chicago. In 1928 and 1929 he appeared on the subversive radar in America, emerging as a ubiquitous figure in national socialist politics and being affiliated with the front organization German-American Bund. By 1933 Kappe demonstrated a renewed interest in European politics and fascism and advanced as a prominent individual in many Nazi sponsored organizations in America connected with Teutonia and other pro-fascist groups. The Nazi Party loyalist conscientiously engaged in efforts to publish pro–Nazi propaganda in America and motivate stateside support for the Third Reich, and his patriotic sentiments for his homeland developed more strongly from this period onwards. A move to New York conveniently enabled the rising Nazi-American star to accept a position as senior official in the Friends of Hitler movement, based in the city. Encounters with dedicated Nazis and opportunities to hear directly about the fantastic vision embellished by Hitler's supporters had proved influential in Kappe's developing ideological attachment. As a leader in the Friends of Hitler movement Walter Kappe was assigned as press and propaganda chief.

In 1937 Kappe returned to Germany, after his industrious labors attracted the attention of senior Nazi Party figures, and was presented with respectable employment opportunities at Goebbels's Ministry of Enlightenment to serve in the Third Reich's Propaganda Office. The twelve-year American chapter had ended somewhat acrimoniously for Kappe, who was forced into repatriation after defeat in a power struggle with other American Nazis. He expended his time during the ensuing four years productively attending to unassuming functions at the Propaganda Office, delivering lectures and acclimatizing other repatriated Germans. By 1941 he had received promotion and transfer to German military intelligence. The first objective appointed to Walter Kappe by Admiral Canaris was the identification and training of operatives for the sabotage campaign in America.

The Abwehr had studied U.S. military production and key transportation lines in exhaustive detail for several years, and Lahousen extrapolated full utility of the resources in mission planning. The targets were meticulously selected by military intelligence with an obvious precedence oriented at observed bottlenecks in the U.S. military industry. Agents received instructions to award the foremost attention to disruption of light metals manufacturing centers.[39] The disparate fragments gradually formed a realistic and contiguous picture, with strategies for attacking a multitude of essential targets including bridges, power plants and factories and Jewish-owned businesses. To effectively disable and disrupt the light metals industry, critical in contemporary airplane manufacturing, Abwehr identified plants operated by Aluminum Company of America in Alcoa, Tennessee, and Massena, New York. In tandem with direct assaults on the light metals industry, disrupting reserves of indispensable raw materials in aluminum production was assessed as fundamental in tactical importance. The facilities selected in this assessment covered the Philadelphia Salt Company's cryolite plant.

The Abwehr researched plans to sabotage vulnerable waterway sectors; the Ohio River locks and hydroelectric facilities at Niagara Falls and in the Tennessee Valley were selected as targets. Transportation zones that represented realistic prospects for restricting communications and manufacturing were integrated into mission strategy, and railroad locations in Pennsylvania and rail lines in New England and New York registered on program agendas. The saboteurs, according to the earliest planning stages, would be instructed to attack with explosive devices Jewish-owned stores and businesses. Civilian attacks produced an added advantage of terror-inducing effects and weakening political resolve.

A British MI5 report produced in 1942 reviewing Operation Pastorius and declassified in 2011 revealed intriguing information concerning the Nazi strategy. Lord Rothschild, MI5's counterespionage section chief, was temporarily seconded to the United States to prepare a report on Nazi operation for the director-general, David Petrie. One factory recommended for sabotage was, after assessment, ranked as being so insufficient on America's vulnerable points itinerary that it had employed no permanent guards and in fact minimal security measures of any method. An inquiry was conducted into Abwehr II's accuracy in selecting this perceptibly unregarded installation, and it transpired that the location was of extremely high importance. Abwehr II anticipated that saboteur activities should result in considerable manpower being redirected towards guarding the vulnerable facilities, which would thereby generate apprehension and anxiety within the American population. For this reason, sabotage actions were not to appear accidental but clearly recognizable as sabotage.[40]

The Lord Rothschild MI5 report expands on Lieutenant Kappe's contribution to the program. Originally Kappe somewhat flagrantly imagined for himself a hands-on field operations role where he would personally return to his former hometown of Chicago and mastermind the operations. Much preliminary stage planning did not progress into more concrete objectives and had disappeared during tactical analysis. Kappe established the concept, in a draft paper produced in September 1941, of U-boats filled to capacity with German saboteurs arriving at the U.S. coastline and rotating every six weeks until the war's conclusion. Suicide missions were explored in the inner sanctum of Abwehr II, with Nazi commando squadrons instilled with instructions to assault American cities with rocket launchers and flamethrowers until they themselves were killed or captured.

The MI5 report expounds further on this theme's ambitious permutations. This first contingent of saboteurs were charged with a long-term function of establishing a permanent German espionage organization in the United States. Chicago was preliminarily selected as a national headquarters for this new organization, as returning German journalists characterized this city as particularly antiwar. Once members of the expedition had become sufficiently grounded internally in America and had adopted cover identities, another senior Abwehr agent, Reinhold Barth, was then to proceed directly to Chicago to command the expansion of operations. If and when Barth arrived and fulfilled the mission parameters, Kappe was scheduled, in these early planning segments, to embark for America to control all of the German sabotage activities. At least one saboteur was instructed to establish contact with individuals and organizations campaigning against participation in war and if possible to formulate new activist organizations.[41] Lord Rothschild confirms that the inspiration of sending saboteurs, if not the exact methodology, to America was first contemplated in German intelligence sections in a precursor study long before the United States declaration of war. On that basis a resident "sleeper" agent was planted inside America shortly before the Japanese attack on Pearl Harbor. The identity and address of the agent was supplied to the saboteurs written in secret ink on handkerchiefs.

Theoretically there was no shortage of possible candidates for Walter Kappe's initial crew of operatives. The Nazi Party had repatriated thousands of Germans living in the United States through offering the inducement of one-way tickets home. But the requirements were exacting. The mission's parameters demanded individuals who spoke English; demonstrated familiarity with United States customs; and had skills in a trade or occupation suitable for providing cover while living in America. Finding them proved to be a difficult task. Walter Kappe's previous appointment as an official assigned to Ausland Organization (Foreign Office of the Nazi Party) turned out to be pertinent. Prior to World War II the Ausland had ambitiously established Nazi Party affiliates abroad and encouraged all overseas German residents to enlist in respect for the national socialist cause. From Kappe's perspective this association had provided a broad spectrum of fascist sympathizers, an efficient forum unmistakably therefore in contacting ideologically inclined present or former German citizens who had either inhabited territory abroad or recently returned. Ausland and Bund sources provided a comprehensive catalog of potential secret agents for this undercover offensive mission. The operative recruitment strategy engineered by Walter Kappe developed into an active and aggressive campaign; with colleagues from Abwehr-2 of Intelligence 2, numerous labor-hours were consumed painstakingly examining thousands of personnel files from Ausland resources and other profitable depositories. Mandatory questionnaires submitted by Gestapo field offices to the returnees from overseas since 1937 had evaluated both ideological commitment and intelligence value, which fashioned another investigative intelligence database for identifying suitable candidates.

Kappe addressed the reunions and associations of former German-American Bund members around Germany. Most shortlisted contenders were selected via direct targeting strategies; some, like George Dasch, had approached the Abwehr on individual initiative inquiring into opportunities in foreign intelligence. The major contingency planning dilemmas and operations security indicators at this early juncture concerned methods of infiltrating members of the sabotage network into America; traversing the Atlantic represented a barrier and introgression into U.S. territory while avoiding detection was a second problem. The most obvious method was requisitioning a submarine. However, the German navy persisted from 1941 to 1945 in countering with reluctance its valuable U-boats being diverted for transporting saboteurs. In his departmental auspices the commander of the U-boat fleet, Konteradmiral Karl Dönitz, stood opposed to the landings as an unnecessary distraction. He declared his intention of focusing maritime resources on a single overriding goal of cutting the economic lifeline between the United States and Britain, an objective analyzed as feasible in the spring of 1942. German U-boats were inflicting damage on both American and British convoy shipping and industrial manufacturing worked overtime to construct replacements.[42]

The first six months of U.S. involvement and mobilization of forces in World War II resulted in the Western Atlantic experiencing an upsurge in instances and movement of German submarines. The Pheiffer spy ring net, with its complex underground of embedded informants and professional operatives, had been uncovered, with real identities understood by authorities. Therefore, former agents could not be securely reactivated. The Abwehr researchers were prohibited from recruiting as sabotage agents any operatives employed previously, all believed long since compromised. Indeed, the German foreign office and other departments remained disgruntled about Abwehr II's previous unsanctioned operations, and cooperation was only begrudgingly forthcoming. The more strenuously reinforced national security grid inside the United States, with the FBI and Justice Department rapidly installing counterespionage systems, fostered a complicated environment for the infiltration. The ability to resource mission teams sufficiently for maintaining the necessary level and duration of operational activity was a secondary logistical headache. Despite the impediments, plans on U-boat transportation began to take shape.

Early in 1942 Kappe contacted shortlisted contenders for interviews and selected the 12 individuals to comprise personnel for Pastorius. Each man consented to involvement willingly but was unapprised of the specific assignment. Four individuals, in a final decision on suitability, were quickly removed from the program, the remaining eight being divided into two teams under the leadership of George Dasch and Edward Kerling. Most trainee saboteurs needed to be compulsorily transferred from civilian occupations but two retained the distinction of serving as Wehrmacht soldiers. Herbert Haupt and Ernst Burger were naturalized American citizens. Burger, a long-term Nazi Party member, had participated in the infamous Beer Hall Putsch. His controversial past potentially representing an awkward and prohibitive obstacle, Berger was incarcerated by Gestapo officers as being implicated in serious allegations, but any indiscretions were apparently later forgiven. Four had associated with the German-American Bund and were theoretically sympathetic to Nazism during their time in America. Dasch, an early recruit, assisted in scrutinizing and appraising personnel and Ausland Organization documentation.

All eight nominated individuals were German by ancestry and had resided in the United States for substantial periods. Haupt had emigrated across the Atlantic Ocean as a younger child traveling with his family, and substantial numbers of his extended family inhabited the Chicago area. He attained U.S. citizenship legally as a byproduct of his father's naturalization in 1930. Quirin and Heinck returned to Germany immediately preceding the collapse of political negotiations and the outbreak of World War II in the European theater, and the six others were repatriated before December 1941. Any repressed admiration for their adopted nation was superseded by a primary allegiance to their country of birth. The two last mentioned individuals were both machinists employed in identical installations in the automotive industry for the Volkswagen company. Aged 39, George Dasch, the commander of the first ground-level group, had cultivated the personality of an unpredictable and ambiguous individual.

Internal Relationships and Background to Pastorius

During the U.S. neutrality period of September 1939 to December 1941, industrialized armed conflict raged in Europe and the Atlantic, but the Roosevelt administration remained an interested spectator. The German foreign office, believing preservation of cordial U.S. relations was a fundamental priority above lesser considerations, opposed sabotage actions inside America. The German foreign minister, Joachim von Ribbentrop, advocated that policy ameliorate a continuation of political and economic accords. However, satisfying Hitler's inner circle that this diplomacy was an advisable method proved challenging. Convincing the congressional representatives that German neutrality was indeed genuine, despite President Roosevelt's obvious disinclinations, and preventing U.S. naval forces from diffusing into the Atlantic Ocean were not sustainable if military intelligence campaigns to destroy American industrial factories were uncovered. Admiral Canaris staged concurrence with Ribbentrop's outspoken objections to sabotage as a defendable excuse for his organization's inaction.

He informed Adolf Hitler that the foreign ministry had forbidden military intelligence from launching covert enterprises against the continental United States that could be interpreted as sabotage or military action. The arguments against sabotage disappeared completely from the discussions as an outcome of America's entrance into the conflict and the official disintegration of her neutrality. Field Marshalls Wilhelm Keitel and Alfred Jodl, the chief architects of the Nazi military machine, adamantly demanded large-scale action against the American aircraft and military industries, comparable to tactics administered in the Poland and France invasions. Keitel informed Canaris that intelligence actions should change to fostering field combat advantages in the armed struggle against America. Renewed urgency gained momentum regarding assembling comprehensive sabotage nets in America. In this environment Operation Pastorius, the Abwehr's "ace in the hole," increased in institutional importance and Kappe received the green light.[43]

The Abwehr had desperately coveted a significant battlefield accomplishment to escape being swallowed by Himmler and the RSHA, a realistic pattern of events on the horizon as the systematic power consolidation accelerated a replacement of effectiveness. Canaris understood it was impossible to procrastinate indefinitely without jeopardizing his own imperfect position. Rumor had circulated already about the Abwehr chief protecting dissident staff under his express supervision and portraying him as a commander who retained divided loyalties. Hitler, on February 4, 1938, appointed himself war minister and assembled the OKW under his personal authority, but Field Marshall Keitel was the wartime superior officer of Canaris. Chief of Supreme High Command of the German Armed Forces Wilhelm Keitel did not prioritize intelligence matters in advance of any political contests infringing Wehrmacht objectives, but Canaris at least encountered personal security in this alliance. With the OKW appointed as jurisdictional authority for planning and directing operations between 1938 and 1940 the Abwehr enjoyed a luxurious position with almost complete autonomy of action.[44]

By 1941 conditions altered drastically in accordance with changing allegiances within Nazi power structures, the traditional monopolies of Prussian Imperial militarism being countermanded by fascistic politics. Himmler and Kaltenbrunner at the RSHA predatorily searched for an opportune moment or mistake to maneuver military intelligence under their control. The complex Nazi security structure and rivalrous nature of this conflicted assembly of departments inevitably loomed ominously within the background of Pastorius. The professional relationship between Heydrich and Canaris had deteriorated and contact reverted from fractured to nonexistent. Both Heydrich and SD VI chief Walter Schellenberg retained enviable positions in standing to gain personally from the internal transferring of department powers.[45] Negotiations were arranged between the Abwehr and the SS, continuing throughout the first quarter of 1942, and progress was at least discernible on the horizon. The parties reconciled temporarily, with agreements reached on the broader program of counterespionage powers being extended to the auspices of RSHA agencies, a compromise, the Abwehr accepting the premise of confining itself just to military intelligence. After dispatching his subordinates to SS headquarters for the purpose of negotiating on his behalf in preliminary discussions for approximately six months, Canaris finally held a personal meeting with his SS counterparts at Wannsee on March 1, 1942. The Wannsee conference inexorably became a watershed moment in redefining boundaries in the security services and attempts to resolve the disputes. A document was drafted in the aftermath of negotiations entitled "Principles Governing Co-operation Between the Security Police and SD and the Abwehr Agencies of the Wehrmacht," popularly entitled the "Ten Commandments."

RSHA obtained absolute control over political intelligence and the reformed Abwehr was rendered unilaterally accountable for "combating foreign intelligence services operating against the interests of the Reich." The SD and Security Police acquired sections of foreign espionage and new powers for investigating political actions relating to subversion and terrorism. Capacity for preserving logistical and financial resources necessary for coherent fulfillment of objectives now depended increasingly on RSHA authority. The Abwehr managed to ring-fence more restrictive functions; but deprived of singular authority for responsibility in counterintelligence, clearly the department would no longer possess the impressive potency it wielded at the beginning of World War II. This represented another stage in the continuous process of state security agencies becoming consumed by the Nazi Party. A degree of maneuverability was retained by the obsequious Abwehr after Wannsee, but the traditional standing formerly experienced by the Abwehr officers and commanders could never be matched. Machinations still unfolding resulted in the military intelligence chief's own survival appearing far from assured.[46]

On May 18, at a second conference in Prague, Czechoslovakia, the SS released its updated and self-aggrandizing version of the Ten Commandments document and after minimal negotiations this was reluctantly complied with by the Abwehr personnel, who were depleted of options. Heydrich fronted discussions for the SS, pleased at the vindication of his command this promotion demonstrated. Present representing the SS were Gestapo chiefs Nebe and Mueller, and Schellenberg. Supporting Canaris and military intelligence in attending the Prague conference were his loyal lieutenants, Bentivegni and Piekenbrock. Schellenberg's postwar recollection depicted the opening remarks. Heydrich came quickly to the point: "The security of the Reich demands a reorganization of the secret services on a centralized basis." The Abwehr had displayed its general incapacity and the agency needed to be replaced by the new, supremely skilled operatives trained intensively in SS centers answerable personally to Reinhard Heydrich. The reformed structures agreed in the modified Ten Commandments document practically achieved the transference of Abwehr sections into a unified service under SD leadership.[47] Canaris, in this amalgamated jurisdictional environment, reported to Heydrich, and the free hand enjoyed by the Abwehr was dissolved. Indeed, by August all independent security services functioned as departments within the centralized RSHA. Canaris tried his utmost to continue unhindered and produce realistic outcomes, despite departmental authority's now being countermanded by other agencies. Piekenbrock and other senior officials bemoaned profusely the disruptions in professional espionage, their traditional area of expertise, by the SS's jackboot thugs. Now national socialist ideological convictions formed precedent for future strategies.

This realignment of infrastructure within the Abwehr, Gestapo and SD introduced other senior commanders into the planning and oversight for Operation Pastorius. Future intelligence missions remained delicately in the balance, with the distinct possibility of SD personnel replacing the Abwehr on foreign operations, especially if any further blunders emerged. An environment of centralization and growing entrenchment of RSHA powers brought about a new climate and placed the Abwehr's senior staff in a position of restrictive scrutiny and review.[48] On the 27th of May, after Admiral Canaris and the other conference delegates had returned homewards, Heydrich was assassinated in an attack in the Prague suburb of Liben. The coordinated plot by Czech resistance and British intelligence inflicted mortal wounds on Heydrich, who died on June 4. This readjustment in power bases and recrimination following the assassination added to a precarious climate. Reinhard Heydrich's removal from the picture gave an advantage to Schellenberg, who subsequently advanced his position inside Nazi state security.

Preparations for Undercover Life in American

Despite the distractions and shifting jurisdictions at command level, preparations for Pastorius continued in relative isolation. Walter Kappe completed the evaluations and basic psychological tests. With the operation contingent finalized, the next segment involved training at a specially designed sabotage school for spies, the Quenz Lake facility. Kappe, from the accounts of his contemporaries, was depicted as a generally loud and gregarious character. In his early years he induced the perception in many quarters of an individual who immensely enjoyed social activities, being a regular patron of Chicago nightclubs. Pastorius represented the culmination of his diligent preparations in establishing a network of saboteurs.

The assorted collection of trainee foreign agents—without the majority of the group previously being acquainted or involved in preexisting relationships—arrived as scheduled at Quenz Lake camp school in April 1942, the establishment chosen for administering training in techniques of espionage essential for the mission. This espionage school, hastily assembled at the beginning of World War II, was constructed in close proximity to the German town of Brandenburg, forty miles west of Berlin. Quenz Farm had served previously as training quarters for a multitude of special projects involving foreign pro–Nazi civilians, and the prospects of using this exact location for a special American assignment would not require any extra preparations. A modicum of typically German industrial and manufacturing factories had relocated to Brandenburg in the past 10–20 years, but it still remained practically untouched. The Quenz Lake facilities incorporated a requisitioned converted mansion and the surrounding encampments. In the camp's grounds trainees were relatively unhindered in wandering about, and Brandenburg camp would be home for the remainder of the training period. Operation Pastorius agents, a diverse cross-section of characters and personal backgrounds, needed to establish personnel connections. Close-quarters accommodation engendered unavoidable friction and disagreements.[49]

Lahousen, Abwehr II chief and senior commander in mission planning, described the first weeks of Quenz Lake training in his wartime diary, which was recovered in the months following the climax of World War II. Each selected member was officially informed, without any prior operational knowledge, by supervisors that his presence was requested at the Quenz Lake site in April, the transfer and order documents quickly arranged by command staff and appropriate bureaucracies. The inaugural week sufficed as the standard agent meet-and-greet introductory sessions, which were purposely relatively minimal on training and complex operation matters. Internal team-working and camaraderie inevitably was essential in building a cohesive team that could function effectively behind enemy lines. At this juncture the possibility certainly existed of the agents surviving underground in America for several years; the accompanying provisions had accounted for two years without factoring in any replenishment needs. Pastorius members were introduced. A clubhouse situated in the camp's central residential building was specifically designated as the espionage group's social area for relaxation or break times. The facility incorporated several class and lecture rooms, a chemistry laboratory and a gymnasium.[50]

George Dasch had patriotically enlisted in Germany's armed forces as an adolescent (aged just 14) and served for 11 months as an administrative clerk during World War I. He was Kappe's initial and arguably most trusted recruit. A restless and impetuous young man, after discharge from the military he finished schooling prematurely and traveled Europe working at dockyards in Rotterdam, Hamburg and other locations. George Dasch found passage to America, an ambition harbored following his earlier positive experience of being treated in an American military hospital. He traveled to America in October 1922 as a stowaway on the American steamship SS *Schoharie*. After docking in Philadelphia Dasch began his new life in America. These formative years living in America were predominantly occupied with temporary employment in a multitude of professions; he worked in different periods as a dishwasher and waiter in Manhattan and Long Island.

In August 1926 Dasch was arrested twice for operating a brothel and violating Prohibition laws. Employed in the otherwise unfavorable conditions of a local New York hotel he romanced an American woman he later married (the couple remained betrothed at the time of Dasch's repatriation and she accompanied him to Germany). Later, the future espionage agent, convinced by economic opportunities following conversations with a former colleague, emerged in Chicago and commercially retailed sanctuary supplies for the Mission of Our Lady of Mercy. He settled for a sustained period in a German community in Yorkville, New York, but still sporadically transitioned through a number of locations. In 1927 he enlisted in the U.S. Army and received an honorable discharge after a year of service. He completed the required documentation and applied for national citizenship in 1939, but interruptions derailed the proceedings and he failed to attend the courthouse to be sworn in.[51]

Dasch, according to speculation in the 2011 declassified MI5 files, may have experienced a partial conversion to Nazism resulting from several conversations with his mother, herself originally a socialist. Repeated correspondence and personal dialogue during a family reunion in New York allegedly centered on attempts to convert Dasch to fascism. There is a definite suspicion, however, about the genuineness of his political outlook in either direction and the conversions could certainly be fraudulent. Dasch purportedly became anxious to return to Germany upon the outbreak of hostilities. After delays and repeated applications to the German consulate in New York and the German embassy in Washington, arrangements were finally sanctioned regarding his return. This passage was accomplished through the contrivance of traveling via San Francisco, Japan and USSR, as the British Atlantic blockade was preventing unauthorized shipping from crossing the Atlantic to Europe. The hesitations surrounding his applications were probably a byproduct of his background's being assessed as politically unreliable by German officials.[52] In May 1941 Dasch returned to Berlin. Debriefing and completion of the disclosure paperwork, mandatory for German citizens returning from residency periods abroad, had generated awkward and unwelcome questions. The Gestapo demanded an interview process for the vetting and evaluation of individuals, extracting intelligence from Germans reentering from nations that presented access restrictions and who had the potential for conferring informative leads. George Dasch's political interests and engagement history noted, the Gestapo requested that he attend a second interview for further questioning. He reported as instructed to an NSDAP headquarters office in Stuttgart and found that his movements in America and the Soviet Union had stimulated considerable interest. In Stuttgart, Dasch was shuttled between meetings with different Nazi officials and army headquarters.

Lt. Col. Warnecki completed Dasch's debriefing. He questioned Dasch intensively about his knowledge concerning Soviet Union matters and expressed interest in being apprised of any applicable intelligence. Dasch announced his desire to be a faithful employee of the Fatherland and to participate energetically in building the new Germany. He had stated in the interview, "Even if I have to work as a street cleaner and do my job cleaning streets right, I want to participate politically." Later, he contradicted this sentiment and insisted enlistment in intelligence services was a necessary mechanism for obtaining incriminating information against the Nazis. In his later statement, George Dasch explained the circumstances surrounding his recruitment:

> I spoke to Miss Leonhardt while working with her during the night. She told me that she was active in the Bund movement in the United States and she came to Germany on the same boat my mother did. She has been recently employed with Office of Espionage No. 3 which to her statement had charge of the censorship. I asked her at that time who this fellow Lieutenant Kappe was. She said, "Well, I know him from America where for a long time he has been a reporter with German newspapers in Chicago and also in Cincinnati and Philadelphia." Later on when we opened the question about his activities in the United States in regards to work, I approached her with the question whether he had worked for the New York German newspaper *Streets Zeitung*.[53]

This conservation in Dasch's own account served as an introduction to Walter Kappe. On 3, June 1941, Dasch was summoned to a meeting with Kappe, who cross-examined him on both his recent activities and his knowledge of the political atmosphere inside the United States. When Dasch divulged his inclination for reenlisting and serving in the German army, Kappe responded that in his estimation Dasch's talents could augment the Nazi movement in a different capacity. The new recruit was initially deployed to a Foreign Ministry propaganda office at Sonderdienst Seehaus, 24 Grossen Wannsee. He was being employed analyzing U.S. radio broadcasts, it transpired, a perfunctory position at a standard monitoring station for foreign media output. This was a minor posting, in professional advancement terms, that required expertise in foreign language skills, for which Dasch's English-speaking ability qualified him; but Dasch persisted in envisaging more personal glorification.

Destiny, he resolutely believed, had selected him for an important and history-making role, and he ambitiously inquired and spoke about his usefulness in correspondence to various prominent Nazi intelligence officials. Personal confidants, such as his cousin Reinhold Barth, and well-connected strangers to whom he imparted unsolicited advice were contacted—examples of the latter being a Lieutenant Kohle of Abwehr II and Captain Spies of Abwehr II's Central American division. He later confessed that he experienced a profound consciousness-raising transition as a propagandist at Sonderdienst Seehaus, which removed whatever illusions he had formerly subscribed to about Nazi ideology. He informed postwar researchers that he contemplated and incongruously debated at this time a preference for defection to the United States. Dasch had certainly caught the attention of Kappe, demonstrating ability and considerable American cultural expertise. Dasch impressed superiors at the Nazi Foreign Ministry propaganda office with his publication of reports on America and analysis of intelligence matters.

In November, Kappe organized a meeting with Dasch once again, this encounter serving as an assessment screening for the Pastorius mission. Kappe approached Dasch on the subject of returning to America and briefly summarized the outline proposal of an espionage mission requiring American-English–speaking agents to disperse behind enemy lines. He discussed a penetration designed to attack American industry and elaborated on the reasons why this mission could be imperative to Germany's military campaign. By mid–January, the original Pastorius recruit was now permanently assigned to Abwehr II. On March 1 Dasch reported to a secret Abwehr office to review the personal histories of several other individuals Kappe had tentatively selected to comprise saboteur teams. In a series of interviews George Dasch identified and omitted a number of individuals; some appeared interested simply in escaping the abrasive wartime conditions of Nazi Germany at any expense. He performed a prominent role in selecting the final team.[54]

Burger, another German spy with a record demonstrating long-standing residency in New York, had acknowledged Nazi Party connections dating back to the 1920s. The younger Ernst Burger, a committed and loyal fascist, spent his early twenties indulging in physical and ideological battles against rival socialists and communist factions on the streets. Enlisting in the NSDAP in 1923 at the tender age of seventeen, in Augsburg and Munich he endeavored to embroil himself completely inside local fascist politics and consorted daily with his Nazi Party comrades. In Germany, after returning to the heralded Fatherland in July 1933 with thousands of comparably enthused German-Americans, his disturbing personal experiences of this self-proclaimed glorious new movement did not constitute the positive vision he had anticipated. After a probationary period Ernst Burger was assigned to the SA chief adjutant's office headed by Ernst Roehm. He reported directly to Bergman, the second in command, and accompanied these officers in field matters across Germany. Burger was seconded to a different section, the SA Medical Division, in mid–1934, narrowly avoiding the June 30 Night of the Long Knives massacre orchestrated by Heinrich Himmler. He had resurfaced immediately after the June 30 purges and was transferred to a government bureau of propaganda. In spring 1940 he was jailed, supposedly for some content interpreted as being critical of Gestapo activities against civilians in occupied Poland. He was arrested by Gestapo officers and then incarcerated for seventeen months in a Gestapo prison facility. Without any injurious action on his part Burger was implicated in politically unfavored factions following Ernst Roehm's violent removal, his imprisonment certainly amounting to collateral damage.

Kappe discovered this candidate after hearing recommendations from influential supporters and long-term friends advocating for Burger, no doubt well connected after 20 years of service. In fact, a previous inconspicuous meeting had occurred during Kappe's lecture expeditions in America. Burger had waited amidst the audience to hear the German-American Bund representative speaking on the platform. In keeping with mission colleagues Burger spoke English fluently, his trace accent probably exceeding his colleague's linguistic skills. He had from the documented accounts acquired considerable knowledge of American contemporary language and professed awareness regarding U.S. sports and topical culture.[55] As with Hebert Haupt, another Operation Pastorius agent, Burger was a naturalized American citizen. Kappe arranged for Burger to be transferred from guarding a prison camp outside Berlin to the secret Brandenburg unit. The youngest of the new recruits, Herbert Haupt attended junior and middle school in Chicago and had served in the German-American Bund's Junior League. Concerned about heat from authorities, he departed for Germany in June 1941. Formerly an employee at West Garfield Park, he had previously performed integral duties inside an Abwehr project, assisting in Major Ritter's Norden bombsight operation. Herbert Haupt requested a temporary period of absence from his factory job and then disappeared from the streets of Chicago. It was subsequently revealed that he had traveled to Mexico City and presented himself at the German embassy, offering to conspire in intelligence work for Nazi Germany.

After securing financial assistance from the German embassy officials based in Mexico City, Haupt's circuitous and cumbersome adventures returning home required traveling aboard a Japanese freighter to Yokohama and later boarding a German steamer vessel that penetrated the British naval blockade of Germany. He aroused the attention of Stettin's local Gestapo department after a short while in Germany, which interfered with his attempts to persuade local companies about his suitability for employment. In March 1942, Haupt received a mysterious letter from Schriftleitung der Kaukasus, a cover designation for Abwehr II's activities at Rankestrasse. Walter Kappe invited Haupt to attend a meeting in Berlin to explain the episode surrounding his breaching the blockade. In the interview the rhetoric initially appeared concerned with Herbert Haupt's return voyage. Haupt was summoned a second time, and Kappe reminded him that two of his relatives were imprisoned in concentration camps and that his appearance had aroused unenviable suspicion in Gestapo agents. Continuing with these themes, Kappe adamantly insisted that without any employment prospects in Germany Haupt's only feasible option remained enlisting in military intelligence. Haupt agreed and on April 8 he was called to Berlin and transferred to Quenz Lake.[56]

Edward Kerling, born in 1909, was among the first 100,000 individuals to register for Nazi Party membership. He was the holder of the celebrated Nazi gold emblem, which signified his Nazi Party affiliation of long standing, he having enlisted at the tender age of nineteen; party membership records denote that he had maintained membership after emigrating to America in 1928. After working at smoking hams for a Brooklyn meat-packing company, he found positions as a chauffeur, handyman and laborer in Mount Kisco, New York, and Greenwich, Connecticut. Dasch later claimed that Kerling was an active organizer attached to the German-American Bund movement and had attended numerous pro-fascist demonstrations and lecture circuit tours. In 1940 he returned to Germany through Portugal and Rome. Immediately Kerling was assigned to Wehrmacht postings in France and dispatched to Deauville in an auxiliary capacity. The responsibilities covered transcribing documents at an army listening station, translating English language broadcasts. He diversified his occupational interests with involvement in monitoring propaganda shows in movie theaters.

In the spring of 1942 he was approached by Walter Kappe with the proposal of faithfully serving the Fatherland and returning to America with an appropriate remuneration. Impressing the assessors, Kerling was selected to command the second team. On April 8 he reported to Rankestrasse and from that destination he later went to Quenz Lake. Kerling would, during basic training, consistently demonstrate the validity of his reputation as exhibiting natural leadership skills and the strongest ideological commitment to Nazism. His compatriots indicated this character interpretation on several occasions. His selection as the mission commander for Jacksonville, Florida, was confirmed following brief deliberation.[57] Walter Kappe had not interviewed this candidate personally before March 1942, but the assessments revealed considerable intelligence and organizational skills. His obvious application to espionage and an almost immediate comprehension of mission complications affirmed Edward Kerling as a definite military intelligence favorite from the very beginning.

Werner Thiel was born in Germany and had emigrated to America in 1927 in search of improved employment opportunities. He was associated in the 1930s with Heinz Spanknöbel's Friends of Germany fascist movement, founding a local branch in Hammond, Indiana, in 1934. His profile in American national socialist and pro–Nazi circles was sufficient to warrant his identity appearing in FBI enquiries into subversive Nazi organizations and Dies Committee hearings.

Werner Thiel returned to Germany in 1941; in March 1942 he attended an Ausland Organization social reunion where he was introduced to and developed an association with Walter Kappe and George Dasch. The other Pastorius saboteurs included Heinrich Heinck, a 35-year-old former German-American Bund member. By January 1942 Heinck was employed, without a Nazi Party bureaucratic background or an observable political ambition, at a Braunschweig Volkswagen factory. He fulfilled his occupational designation as a drilling machine operator unassumingly. A month after the Ausland meeting he was instructed to rendezvous at Rankestrasse. The only operations personnel with a previous relationship were Heinrich Heinck and Richard Quirin, similarly employed at the Volkswagen factory.[58] Both Volkswagen automobile employees were technically exempted from military service because of their classification as essential wartime industrial specialists. Richard Quirin was recommended for the sabotage expedition to America by Heinck and he accepted. The final member, one Hermann Otto Neubauer, another former American Nazi, was conscripted into Wehrmacht infantry divisions upon reentering Germany, and by June 1941 he was stationed at the Russian front. He suffered battlefield injuries and was recuperating in a military hospital near Stuttgart when he received a couriered letter from military intelligence.

Classroom content at Quenz Lake was strictly divided between theory and practical sessions. The recruits settled into a routine of classroom time, private study and practical training. In his later statement, Burger revealed information describing recruitment and details of everyday life in the spy school. Each training day commenced with physical exercise in the morning, followed by lectures and seminars in morning and afternoon sessions. Regular breaks from the classroom were scheduled for social activities. Subsequently, saboteurs were escorted on outings to aluminum and magnesium installations, railroad shops, canals, locks and other facilities to familiarize themselves with the vulnerabilities of comparable targets they were destined to attack in the field. Orienteering and navigation techniques formed segments in the training programs to teach the agents to locate the decisive sabotage points for effective disabling. All instructions had to be memorized.

The expedition tours covered waterways and railway centers. A rail yard management facility and repair headquarters in Berlin were visited during the excursions. Under the meticulous guidance of several specialists, including a chief engineer, and accompanied by Reinhold Barth, the team were taught locomotive science and railway technology operations, in conjunction with possible sabotage methods. Lectures discussed the major terminals of the U.S. railroad systems, standard engines and technical components and average freight-train speeds; other briefings covered railroad bottlenecks where sabotage should theoretically inflict the greatest disruption.⁵⁹ At the end of May an aluminum and magnesium factory excursion was arranged for the trainees. First, a conference room discussion explained the specific importance of light metal installations, followed by brief technical lectures on the present production methods. Instructors Barth and Koenig accompanied the inducted Pastorius agents on the expedition. They were encouraged to inspect the facilities and received tutelage on sabotage strategies. Richard Quirin later explained in detail training operations at Quenz Lake:

> Kappe made arrangements so that we could get past the guard into the aluminum factory. Some fellow in the factory took us around and showed us the plant itself and we walked through it, looking at this and that, and then were taken to the power plant. They showed us the high voltage wires leading into the plant. They explained that if the power line could be cut off it would disable the factory. They said the power lines that come in were high voltage. Then they took us to some of the transformers, which were right there, and showed us these. They told us that if we would drill a hole in the transformer and let the oil run out it would put them out of order and make the plant shut down so that they could not get any power.⁶⁰

The saboteur training did not concentrate on subterfuge tactics in obtaining employment in installations at sabotage points; instead strategy for covertly accessing preordained targets was at their discretion in the field. Partially, this deliberate approach was motivated by a realistic understanding of evolving and unpredictable circumstances on the ground the saboteurs would inevitably encounter and the necessity of refining skills for rapid adaptation to opportune moments. Entry could be accomplished generally through temporary employment, breaking in or entering by stealth. Training exercises for movement by stealth did comprise segments in Quenz Lake's outdoor training facilities. Specific lectures were devoted to methods of identity concealment and blending into an American background while presumably undercover. The training contained mock scenarios and practical applications of the techniques under ground-level conditions adjudged feasible—from dead drops, transporting documents, and codes to forgery. The instructors tried their utmost in orchestrating mock exercises to simulate accurately the conditions saboteurs should expect to encounter in America. During the middle of May instructors finalized the preparations for assaulting America. The primary objective of infiltration, Kappe repeatedly reminded his students, was to inflict sufficient damage to impede production. He warned them against high-risk tactics of attempting to destroy major infrastructure, for instance large dams or iron bridges. That order of sabotage action was demonstrably too complicated for a relatively small team of agents; generally infantry commando were requisitioned for such actions. The agents were strenuously cautioned in the general avoidance of passenger trains. The Abwehr mission planners desired a minimization of civilian casualties or irreparable damage to Germany's reputation; the missions were expected to provoke disenchantment amongst the civilian population. It was anticipated that bombing attacks would result in the U.S. government's persecuting innocent citizens in America and encourage a popular revolt against government authority.

Pastorius's recruits were provided with lectures and laboratory exercises with instructions in chemistry, incendiaries, weapons, explosives and timers— the necessary techniques for perpetrating sabotage. A selection of the Abwehr's technical and engineering experts relocated to the Brandenburg camp as instructors and included Dr. Gunther Shultz. Training encompassed practical demonstrations and training in constructing explosives by exploiting household and commonly available ingredients. One technique trainees had accumulated during hours in manufacturing, and reproduced for the Allied authorities by Brandenburg observers, adopted the following paraphernalia: a glass tube device filled with dried peas and water, sealed with two elements of cork, each configured with a screw and two segments of wire to create a crude timing apparatus.[61] To ensure sufficient practical experience and test responses in the field the separately constructed testing zone at Quenz Lake was opened for exercises. Dry runs and real experiments drilled into team members the most efficacious methods of planting and detonating explosive devices. Standard training operations featured exercises in planting explosive devices at different precise coordinates on the secluded estate, determining, generally by trial and error, exact quantities of explosive materials required in a particular situation. Occasionally the instructors tested vigilance and reactions by launching surprise attacks.

The 1942 MI5 report into Pastorius analyzed the advanced technology to be delivered with the agents to America. Standard German methods of timer detonation generally supplied for sabotage actions involved a time clock system, a mechanism which theoretically allowed the saboteur sufficient laxity for departure before explosion. But this model had demonstrated an unreliability in earlier field operations, with devices failing to detonate. The Abwehr II team were allocated a distinctive improved version, a measurably more sophisticated and efficient weapon. The homemade delay mechanisms, however, would need to be constructed from merchandise, such as tin cans and razor blades, found in American stores. The teams were also provided with abrasives for interfering with the lubrication of different machine systems. The MI5 review document revealed other intriguing information hitherto unknown to Allied intelligence. Dr. Gunther Shultz, the laboratory employee of the Scientific Department of Abwehr and an instructor in the practical lectures at Quenz Lake School, was believed attached to zbv 800 Regiment, the military branch dedicated to special operations. As uncovered in earlier intelligence reports, zbv Regiment brandished purpose-built divisions for training personnel with expert foreign language skills for deployment within clandestine operations. Nationalities trained in zbv Regiment included North African, Portuguese, and Spanish, among others. Shultz was the same figure who visited Nantes in October 1942 to examine the British double agent Zigzag's proficiency in sabotage.[62]

Dasch, in concerted estimations of Quenz Lake instructors, did not properly psychologically attune himself to lessons or exhibit a constructive interest in practically any subject, content to amuse himself and occasionally perform as the comedian of the group. Other Pastorius members questioned Dasch's competency, concerned about the approaching precarious mission and impediments stemming from their compatriot's lack of dedication. His commitment as a full-blooded national socialist and Nazi Party loyalist was repeatedly called into question, as it was common knowledge at Brandenburg that Dasch had preferred avoidance of Nazi politics while residing in the United States and rejected participation in Bund and other fascist movements. Edward Kerling, an experienced member of the operations team, openly criticized Dasch to the Abwehr II commanders. Walter Kappe, for his part, never backed down from whole-hearted support and accreditation for Dasch. Minor frictions aside, the basic training passed relatively smoothly.

German military intelligence fabricated for each individual trainee an identity and life history, with necessary documentation including birth certificate, Social Security card and driver's license. Barth reinforced the fundamental basics of covert espionage by impressing on the saboteur teams that after disembarking in the United States the first mission objective, and the most important pertaining to operational security, involved fashioning disguises and accommodation for themselves. An undercover agent who had a well-prepared synthetic identity had adopted an effective system for avoiding detection and infiltrating a target. The agents were issued forged Social Security and Selective Service registration cards on May 22. Dasch and Kerling became George John Davis and Edward Kelly respectively, both born in San Francisco before the city's 1906 earthquake, precluding the possibility of anyone searching records to corroborate their credentials. Werner Thiel became John Thomas and was identified as a Polish immigrant in order to explain his still noticeable accent. Heinck, assigned a persona of Henry Kayner, was purportedly an inhabitant from Wilkes-Barre, Pennsylvania, a town he was consistently unable to pronounce. He now assumed a concealed identity, similar to that of his colleague Thiel, masquerading as a Polish immigrant who had resided in America from the age of 15 and was currently a New York City restaurant worker. Richard Quirin was now Richard Quintas, and Herman Neubauer became Henry Nicholas.[63]

The instructions to operatives advocated inventing a fictional story, describing the contrived personal backgrounds, and reminded them that cover stories should be rehearsed carefully. Kappe also cautioned recruits to practice using assumed names at Brandenburg in order to become accustomed to them. Herbert Haupt retained his original identity, as did Burger, due to their legitimate American citizenship and preexisting traceable records. Ernst Burger had worked sporadically as a commercial artist, and Walter Kappe suggested that Burger should exploit this background once arriving in Chicago. He was encouraged to launch into motion proceedings for inaugurating an art studio. By then inserting an advertisement for his enterprises in the *Chicago Tribune* at least bi-monthly this venture should garner Burger visibility and credibility. The team members, if this contrivance was managed correctly, would gain a convenient coordination point to exchange information. Saboteur trainees now verged on completing the preparatory training and progression to operations status.

On May 24 they received their respective assignments. George Dasch and his subsection were apportioned the task of damaging hydroelectric plants at Niagara Falls and aluminum factories in Illinois, Tennessee and New York. The cryolite plant in Philadelphia and waterway infrastructure on the Ohio River between Louisville and Pittsburgh were other targets allocated to Dasch's team I. Kerling's team II were instructed to perpetrate egregious sabotage against the Pennsylvania Railroad station in Newark, plus other vital railroad parts. Both teams were reminded repeatedly that critical damage should be inflicted on transportation, a resourceful strategy for causing disruptions and public anxiety. Team II were assigned responsibilities for attacking canal and waterway installations in Illinois, Cincinnati and New York City. Final preparations underway, both the team commanders were given handkerchiefs written, to avoid detection if the carrier were captured, in invisible ink that conveyed names of valuable contacts and mail drops in America. A recent invention by Nazi scientists, invisible ink had proved popular with the Abwehr commanders avidly researching the latest clandestine encryption methods. Invisible ink would later be utilized across the Nazi secret intelligence actions, including the European and South American theaters.

Dasch jotted down different addresses in invisible ink on a handkerchief he dutifully carried during the American expedition. The addresses included the false contact details of his brother as a location where Kerling could signal him if awareness of respective positions was lost. A second address contained the name of a Protestant priest he was advised to approach, and at least two other addresses were secretly encoded on the handkerchief, including an individual enabling contact with Kerling in emergency circumstances. Edward Kerling was similarly issued a handkerchief containing addresses and also a collection of four matches capable of producing invisible ink. The only individual charged with possession of this top-secret technology, he was duly informed that after becoming settled and accustomed to life in United States he was to communicate utilizing these matches with Kappe in Berlin. The communication was to be relayed by directing the correspondence, with Walter Kappe's reference details and the message in invisible ink on the document, through a drop station based in Lisbon. Each team was supplied with four waterproof crates for holding and transporting their equipment. Three boxes were packed with explosives and the fourth contained fuses, wires and acid.[64]

Most of the saboteurs decided against informing their families or friends about the assignment or the exact location of their posting. Some invented cover stories concerning being drafted into the military or simply redeployment for an unspecified, top-secret mission. The most candid was Burger, who informed his wife that he was traveling to America but not his purpose for being there.

Landings in Long Island and Jacksonville

On May 26, 1942, the first group of saboteurs departed by submarine from a German naval base at Lorient, France, and on May 28 the second group began their journey from the same base. Each voyage was destined for landing at prearranged coordinates on the Atlantic coast of the United States. U-202 transported the accomplices George Dash, Ernst Burger, Heinrich Heinck and Richard Quirin to Amagansett, Long Island. The second submarine, U-584, was requisitioned for the voyage of Edward Kerling, Herman Neubauer, Warner Thiel and Herbert Haupt, who crossed the central Atlantic and were deposited at Jacksonville, Florida. A short-term mission initiative demanded a rendezvous in Cincinnati in 6 weeks, but the Abwehr was still envisaging a longer-term strategy of Pastorius operatives scattering indiscriminately throughout America. For security reasons the U-202 and U-584 submarine crews did not engage in briefings describing the purpose of the mission and remained in the dark about the campaigns of espionage destined to happen in the United States. This ignorance appeared to be symptomatic of the standard Atlantic crossings—usually fraught with perilous risks—foisted on the submarine crew members. This was undoubtedly a dangerous time for a U-boat to cross the Atlantic. With antisubmarine tactics of the Allied nations and the Ultra program now beginning to reverse fortunes, mounting numbers of U-boats were permanently disappearing beneath the North Atlantic waves. The voyage to America in the confined conditions of U-202 lasted for about two weeks. The living quarters and general lifestyle on a German U-boat of this class were far from luxurious, but the agents resigned themselves to the situation onboard without complaint.[65]

As U-202 coasted discreetly 10 miles offshore from Long Island on June 12, the mainland lights clearly visible in the nighttime dark, preparations ensued aboard the submarine for imminent disembarkation. The coastline of Amagansett was now in touching distance, and within an hour personnel aboard the German submarine as it coasted parallel to the shoreline could distinguish hillsides and buildings in the background appearing out of dense fog. Lindner, the U-boat's captain, ordered his sailors to commence the preparations for unloading the mission's apparatus and landing craft. The German submarine's powerful engines stopped, and Lindner instructed his crew members to dispatch the vessel's rubber raft. Amagansett Bay was shrouded in the thick, impenetrable fog, which completely obscured the beach. The conditions required adaptations to landing, and a long rope was attached to their landing vessel with the opposite end connected securely to railings on U-202. Hesitantly the craft maneuvered towards the beach. Glancing behind them, the saboteurs, in less than a minute, saw that the U-boat had totally disappeared in the fog. The landing resulted in a drenching for the passengers as the strong waves uncomfortably buffeted their small landing craft. Finally, relief occurred all-round as they approached the beach and the Kriegsmarine oarsmen completed the journey's last stretch. Wading out of the surf, Pastorius's recruits set foot on American soil once again.[66]

Amagansett, New York, in 1942 was a small and quiet Long Island town, located 115 miles east of New York City (today the precise location of the landing is known as Atlantic Avenue Beach). The New York team landed shortly after midnight in the early morning (12:10) of June 13. Working rapidly, the saboteurs transported ashore the mission's consignments, which required several arduous excursions across the sand dunes. The Amagansett beach appeared deserted and initial preparations continued unhindered. The agents ferried resources and boxes containing the explosives, devices, primers and incendiaries. In terms of logistical responsibilities Lahousen and Abwehr II had not disappointed their brightest students: the supplies should, theoretically, be sufficient for an espionage campaign lasting a minimum of two years. The team were deposited ashore wearing German military uniforms, a strategy employed for their protection in case of immediate capture. Military uniforms in principle assured captured personnel would legally be classified as prisoners of war rather than spies, who were less protected by international statute. The men possessed close to $180,000 (equivalent to nearly a million dollars today). The German saboteur team, thus far proceeding according to mission schedule, were about to experience dwindling good fortune.

Burger, Heinck and Quirin were hauling the containers and other apparatus to a hiding place that was camouflaged discreetly in shrubbery on the beachhead while George Dasch attended to the submarine landing crew. The U-boat personnel had completed their assignment and now prepared for departure. Heinck and Quirin began changing from their saturated German army uniforms into their civilian clothing, and Burger concentrated on the apparatus burial and concealment. The tranquil silence permeating the sand dunes at this deserted hour was disrupted after Dasch observed another person on the beach, a searching flashlight moving definitely towards them. The unidentified figure evidently became aware of their presence and approached from across the sand dunes. It was a Long Island Coast Guardsman on night-watch duty. Seaman 2nd Class John Cullen, with the visibility practically nonexistent, had not observed any suspicious incidents until now. As the shape of several individuals materialized through the dense early-morning mist the startled Coast Guardsman instructed the strangers to identify themselves, Seaman Cullen observed the individuals with growing suspicion and questioned their business at the Amagansett beach so early in the morning.[67]

An intelligence report had been transmitted from the U.S. embassy in Switzerland on March 15, 1942, warning that German submarines were transporting groups of operatives to the coastlines of North America. At this point, direct assault on the American mainland by Nazi Germany or Japan was assessed as a remote possibility in most quarters. German U-boats in the beginning months of World War II had launched raids on American ports, but still the submarine landing threat, while considered, was largely ignored and overshadowed by competing national defense issues. Warnings from Switzerland did instigate a modicum of reaction at the highest governmental levels. The report was discussed by the Joint Chiefs of Staff on March 30, and President Roosevelt and others had forwarded proposals and new coastline defensive systems had been discussed. However, none of the interventions passed the planning stage and the whole matter was dropped.

Dasch described the Amagansett landing and encounter in some detail during recollections in later statements. Recently declassified documents from the Nazi War Crimes and Japanese Imperial Government Inter-agency Working Group (IWG) and FBI (2001) have revealed further information on Operation Pastorius reports and FBI statements. Dasch assumed personal charge of this unwelcome and precarious incident, proclaiming this assorted collection of strangers to be local fishermen who were the unfortunate casualties of a maritime incident. Dasch elaborated on this narrative of misfortune and explained to the Coast Guardsman that his partners were nothing but stranded fisherman from Southampton. That attempt at an explanation quickly unraveled under further questioning by Cullen: the disoriented saboteur team were unconvinced of their present location in relation to local geography and the coordinates quoted by Dasch regarding their journey did not add up.[68] Cullen responded that it was four hours until sunrise and suggested everybody accompany him to the coast guard station. When Dasch refused the offer of guidance, recuperation, and spending the remainder of the early morning back at the station the situation unraveled. Dasch panicked and seized the guard by the jacket collar, threatening violent actions and simultaneously stuffing $260 into Seaman Cullen's hands in an attempt at a bribe. At first the guard appeared reluctant to accept the payments. In Dasch's own account he had asked the Coast Guardsman, "Do you have a mother and father? Well, I don't want to have to kill them." He then continued with negotiations: "Forget about this, take this money, and go have a good time." Cullen, realizing this might be an opportune moment to extricate himself from the situation, decided to accept.[69]

Cullen reported the strange encounter to his superior officers immediately after returning to the station. By the time armed coast guard patrols returned to the scene the Germans had vanished. Within a brief time a probing survey of the immediate surrounding beach area by the coast guard teams unearthed the hidden apparatus. A search identified freshly constructed holes with obvious indications of deliberate concealment and the four wooden munitions crates, accompanied by a duffel bag filled with German military uniforms. The mysterious and unidentified individuals from the beach lamentably slipped beyond the search teams. But through the dissipating fog in Amagansett Bay the Coast Guardsmen observed the departing German submarine. (In an unfortunate incident, indeed, the U-boat had obliged the passengers by maneuvering dangerously close to the shore and, touching bottom, had inadvertently become ensnared on a shallow sandbank. For almost three agonizing hours Lindner desperately utilized every naval strategy in the Kriegsmarine book to dislodge the submarine perched perilously close to the beach. Eventually, U-202 embarked on the return journey.) Back in Amagansett, confusion reigned. The coast guard officers were uncertain about what circumstances to expect, and reports of suspicious figures on the beachhead and possible U-boat sightings were troubling.

The Rothschild report on Pastorius produced for MI5 described in detail the problems that rapidly engulfed landing operations. The submarine found itself in difficulties because it hovered at a distance exceeding safety parameters, in theory preventing the mission's landing craft containing the cumbersome sabotage supplies from traveling a long distance and risking submersion. Upon inspection, this technique was remarkably similar to strategies employed in landing the German agent Jankowski in Canada in 1941. The complexity of striking a balance between the submarine's integrity and the security of the landing team was the subject of acrimonious discussion between German military intelligence and U-boat high command on the submarine's return from the expedition.[70]

Dasch and his team had decamped from the local beach and walked adjacent to a minor coastal roadway. The conditions gradually became lighter as the hours progressed to a more reasonable morning period, and approximately one hour later the saboteurs cautiously ventured into the town of Amagansett and took advantage of the opportunity for stocking up on provisions. They then purchased tickets as unobtrusively as possible, having intelligently decided on adopting a circuitous route to New York. In accordance with their security measures they divided into two groups and traveled separately. The coast guard managed the first six hours of the investigation, and branch commanders were rapidly informed and orders delegated to the coastline.[71] The New York office presided over the unfolding events until around midnight. Captain John Baylis, the New York coast guard commander, called the Federal Bureau of Investigation. An examination of the initial reports arriving at Baylis's office still did not reveal the exact conditions of the incursion at Long Island. Fears heightened of a German invasion, but this notion quickly proved inaccurate and implausible. On the first day George Dasch and his men arrived behind enemy lines the FBI was formally appointed by the Justice Department to direct the investigation into their appearance.

FBI agents immediately seized possession of everything accompanying the German agents during the voyage. Except for the clothes and money, all the other deposited equipment, including explosives, was now in FBI hands. In Washington, FBI director J. Edgar Hoover imposed a media blackout to avoid alerting the saboteurs and ordered the largest manhunt in the bureau's history. Attorney general Francis Biddle, in a memorandum to Roosevelt on June 19, described what was known to the American government at that time about the perplexing scenario following the landing at Amagansett: "Cullen discovered two men placing unknown material in a hole. One of the men covered the patrolman with a gun. Returning Coast Guard patrolmen discovered clothing similar to those adorned by the German submarine personnel with signature markings." Investigations escalated as the accusative speculation focused on Axis interference. The Eastern and Gulf Central Coast Guard Commands were cautioned on maintaining a constant vigilance by the U.S. Navy and Army on the potential alarming dangers of additional landings by German agents. Unfortunately, the FBI and Justice Department still did not comprehend the picture unfolding and had no awareness concerning the location of the intruders. The Nazis had placed on enemy territory a sabotage division highly competent in the techniques of terrorism.[72]

J. Edgar Hoover appointed the assistant director, Earl J. Connelly, to direct the investigation. The $260 Dasch had impulsively produced in endeavoring to bribe Coast Guardsman Cullen was sent to the FBI laboratory for fingerprint analysis. No immediate prints or physical evidence of any real value were found. The money stimulated inquiries to every banking institution on South Long Island from Riverhead to Montauk Point, the island's eastern frontier. Local banks had not registered any unusual or incriminating transactions in the previous 24 hours and the assessments uncovered no records of withdrawals or deposits that could be connected with the bills. The Federal Reserve Bank in New York was drawn into the investigation but offered minimal feasible ideas for streamlining tracing the money. A clothing article was recovered, a raincoat bearing the manufacturers label "Crawford Clothes," and early indications amounted to a positive lead. Possible information to be ascertained by researching the origin of the coat had dissipated within hours. Management at Crawford Clothes explained to the FBI investigators that the garment was manufactured by a New York company by the thousands and the jackets had no identifying marks to indicate the store address. The possibility that a resident or residents of Long Island had colluded or consorted with the individuals from the beach could not be overlooked.[73] Agents analyzed FBI and police records for possibly related criminal or subversive connections, and known Nazi sympathizers in the vicinity were questioned.

Kerling's team had departed from the submarine base at Lorient, France, aboard U-584 two days before U-202 and the New York unit section. On the evening of May 26 the U-boat exited from the harbor docking clamps to start its transatlantic journey, destined for Jacksonville. Group II landed at the beach of Ponte Vedra on June 17, 1942. The commander, Edward John Kerling, was still a relatively young man (33) and his team's complement were generally considered to be the less experienced. Similar to their compatriots, the saboteurs wore complete or partial German uniforms during landing to ensure treatment as prisoners of war if they were captured. Team II was charged with the objective of infiltrating from the landing zone to northeastern American regions, which required traveling a lengthy distance. Moving from Jacksonville to Pennsylvania presented some serious obstacles, and the language barrier undoubtedly would be encountered. Penetrating the industrial heartlands depended on the most critical factors of capability in camouflaging presence, blending into the surroundings and traveling unnoticed. Kerling was confident in his English language skills and those of Herbert Haupt, but the remaining agents, training not withstanding, spoke with unfamiliar accents. Haupt convinced the others to bestow him responsibility for handling encounters requiring conversation.

U-584's crossing and landing stages unfolded without the complications of their coconspirators to the north, and they completed the journey to Florida untroubled by any enemy naval presence. Fortunately as forecast, weather patterns in the region proved hospitable. The landing and apparatus concealment phases passed by unnoticed, and the border defenses and local security remained unaware of incursions in their midst. Two of the team journeyed the distance to Jacksonville Beach without, as expected, having observed either civilians or law enforcement. At about 11:00 a.m., after recuperating in the warming morning, the four changed to civilian clothing and walked to the highway beyond the beach. At a nearby gasoline station Herbert Haupt, with his youthful appearance, certainly did not project the demeanor of a dangerous or suspicious character. He inquired about the bus schedule to Jacksonville and returned to the group satisfied: local buses were conveniently scheduled at this station. About forty-five minutes later the four Operation Pastorius agents were standing in the center of Jacksonville. Accommodation requirements and security protocols motivated the decision to lodge at different hotels, as moving in smaller numbers attracted less attention.[74]

The spies reconvened that evening more comfortable in their progress thus far; excellent spirits were evident and lively conversations took place. A temporary furlough preparing for the ventures ahead was scheduled in Jacksonville. Perhaps as a method of relaxation, this 24-hour period was spent frequenting restaurants and bars. FBI and law enforcement remained completely unaware that four Abwehr spies were dining in Jacksonville restaurants, discussing their next movements and the days ahead. Mission Stage 2 was a rendezvous with their comrades in Cincinnati the following month, on July 4, and the establishment of new fabricated identities. While divisions surfaced internally in the New York team immediately upon arrival, the Florida infiltrators advanced without any major unexpected developments or internal disagreements. The mission commanders and team members were apportioned money. Kerling personally possessed $50,000 for living expenses, travel and materials. For comfortable everyday usability the bills were divided into high-value and low-value denominations; lower value currency could be depleted without attracting attention or being too easily traced. For Haupt, Neubauer and the other would-be secret operatives this represented a handsome allowance and was certainly beyond their standard expectations for remuneration.

Nazi Spies in Manhattan and Florida

Four of the Operation Pastorius saboteurs engaged in this precarious mission reestablished communications and consorted with relatives and former acquaintances, contravening their original instructions. Apart from a solitary instance, the civilian relations cognizant of the strange German agents' clandestine arrival by submarine declined to notify authorities. Haupt displayed minimal inhibition regarding reappearing in Chicago. Initiating contact entirely against orders with family members, he looked up companions and friends in Chicago, his home base during the majority of his adult life. Inventing elaborate stories to justify his strange disappearance and subsequent return, Herbert Haupt talked about his adventures to anybody willing to listen. His parents were astonished to be reunited with their long-departed son, whom they presumed had been forcibly living abroad and incapable for the foreseeable future of crossing the Atlantic. Hermann Otto Neubauer, after journeying separately, contacted Haupt and informed his coconspirator of his presence in Chicago. Haupt and Neubauer attempted to mingle discreetly in American society as the former's local connections concealed their movements. On Sunday, Theil and Kerling convened independently in New York. With time on their hands, Theil and Kerling embedded themselves in the hustle and bustle of sprawling New York City. Traveling the crowded streets, they visited famous sightseeing locations. Kerling could not resist looking up his American wife in New York, as their marriage was still legally valid.[75]

Dasch and his team had succeeded in finding their passage to Manhattan without further obstacles. The trainee terrorists were settled in New York, preparing for the adventure ahead. They had approximately $80,000 in mission funding to furnish the basic operational necessities and, comparably to their compatriots, they partook in the comforts and distractions of New York's nightlife. Without any information in the newspapers, Dasch and his companions remained completely oblivious to the discovery of their buried paraphernalia. They thus remained unaware that the combined powers of the U.S. Justice Department were now hunting for them. The FBI and Justice Department investigation into the incident on Amagansett Beach by this juncture was classifying the incursion as an enemy infiltration. Visual identification by the Coast Guardsman of the submarine U-202 departing from Long Island had been verified, and the New York FBI field office comprehended completely that German agents were at large in the United States. Judging by the estimated time frame and probable traveling distances, the FBI theorized that New England or other points in the Northeast still harbored the missing enemy spies. That afternoon the saboteurs purchased suitable clothing at Macy's and other department stores and detached into two groups for the night. With Quirin and Heinck checking in at Hotel Martinique, Dasch and Burger registered at the Governor Clinton. That evening Dasch and Burger began discussing their reservations about Germany and apprehension for family members. Slowly, they realized they shared an inner conflict about the mission as well as the prospect of betraying the operation.[76]

Unexpectedly from Dasch's perspective, it was Ernst Burger, the Beer Hall Putsch veteran and SA stalwart, who opened the conversation and expressed ominous misgivings about the mission. Burger's experiences of denunciation and incarceration at the hands of the Gestapo had cultivated a latent bitterness towards the Third Reich. Dasch and Burger examined their interpretations of life in wartime Germany and the national socialist project. Further, Burger's story of misfortune included being compelled on Gestapo directives to endure seventeen months in the Nazi prison system. In their Manhattan hotel room Burger confessed that other members of his family were detained by Nazi security officers and a relative deported to a concentration camp. Burger's wife, emotionally distraught about the imprisonment of her husband, her own interrogation and the intolerable pressures placed upon the family, miscarried their child. Shortly after the close call on Amagansett Beach, George Dasch's nervousness concerning the mission had now irrefutably amplified. He was tentatively contemplating turning himself in to U.S. authorities, and this would presumably facilitate escape from the severest possibility of a later arrest.

The two individuals during that 24-hour period explored famous historical and cultural sights of New York as the self-introspection continued in earnest. It was George Dasch's turn to deliberate on his disillusionment. His expectations restored during nearly a decade of propaganda on the new Germany were abruptly dispelled by the reality of living in Hitler's paradise. The relative comforts of food and high-quality social conditions in New York functioned to alleviate the harder edges constructed in the more difficult environment of wartime Nazi Germany. An understanding between the two Operation Pastorius agents gradually formed. Quirin and Heinck were still unaware of their comrades' surfacing reservations and waited, avoiding attention, at another hotel on the opposite side of Manhattan. Not having the second thoughts and mitigating concerns of their compatriots, Quirin and Heinck still followed their operational instructions as ordered.[77] Neither man expressed reluctance or hesitancy concerning commitment to terrorism and sabotage behind enemy lines that appear on record or, for that matter, alignment with national socialist politics. Dasch was still conflicted about jeopardizing the assignments and the matter of resolving to contact the U.S. authorities and manifested symptoms of psychologically deteriorating under the extremely high pressure. He reacquainted himself with a former drinking establishment, and friends recognized their drinking companion and acknowledged him warmly. With the mission continuing unabated, Dasch, drinking heavily, amused his mounting audience with extraordinary and fantastic stories about sinister spies. He hinted at his engagement in espionage missions for Russia and insinuated that he had infiltrated a sabotage school in Germany for the purpose of uncovering information about the Nazi Party.

Both the reluctant German assets both expressed discernible paranoia about contacting the FBI. During sabotage training at the Brandenburg school Kappe had bragged to his recruits that safe passage in America was guaranteed because the Gestapo had infiltrated the FBI. Dasch concluded that the approach with the minimum negative fallout was an anonymous phone call placed to the FBI and arrangement for further contact. On June 14 he called the FBI regional office in New York. Agent Dean McWhorter answered the anonymous call and was notified of important information for Director J. Edgar Hoover. The caller purported that it was absolutely imperative that he personally deliver this information to FBI headquarters and requested that somebody alert Hoover. The caller apprised the agent McWhorter that his importation from Germany had occurred recently, but he neglected to clarify the insertion method. Based on FBI internal records, this confusing message was assessed preliminarily as a hoax. Dasch then telephoned other information lines and applicable departments. Dasch, a colonel in the Military Intelligence Division, attempted to be connected with attorney general Francis Biddle. U.S. military intelligence had advised George Dasch to contact the FBI.[78]

On Monday the 15, Dasch and Burger formulated their next contrivances for presenting themselves to the American authorities. As a bargaining chip in their favor, a supplementary scheme was invented to persuade FBI officials about their inclinations to cooperate by composing tantalizing documentary intelligence "for a propaganda campaign" against Germany. Both individuals possessed the relevant backgrounds for conniving in Allied psychological warfare campaigns. Dasch argued that implied sincerity was corroborated by not requesting monetary reward and the exculpatory materials at the beach. He commented positively on the viability of convincing the FBI. The plans confirmed, it had been decided Dasch would travel to Washington to advise power brokers on the exigency of a personal conference with Hoover in which he would divulge everything associated with the mission. As a protective measure Burger's immediate course of action was to return to their hotel building to pacify Heinck and Quirin. In his later recollections George Dasch at this critical intersection had analyzed the various permutations for turning himself in and beginning negotiations. He registered at a Washington hotel in preparation; certainly paranoia at this stage was a motivating factor in the decision making.

A telephone call was received at the FBI's Washington office on the morning of Friday, June 19, from George John Dasch. He alluded to the code name "Pastorius" and proclaimed an association with incidents connected to national security and attempted to arrange an immediate face-to-face dialogue. He concluded in his rationale that simply announcing overtures of intelligence knowledge should set the correct alarm bells ringing. An FBI vehicle arrived outside his hotel in due course and transported him to headquarters. Entering the Washington, D.C., FBI headquarters on the 19th of June Dasch turned himself and the Pastorius team in to American authorities. This strange-appearing, self-proclaimed foreign agent was dismissed by numerous agents, apparently, as a crackpot. Agent Traynor, with some knowledge of D.M. Ladd and Hoover's manhunt, supervised the initial interview with the mysterious individual. At this point George Dasch was interrogated for several hours, but he was not classified initially as a trustworthy source and FBI special agents examined him very suspiciously. He endured a 13-hour interrogation and debriefing. This operation, he disclosed to FBI agents, was the inaugural mission in a program of sabotage planned by German intelligence to inflict critical damage on American industry. Traynor listened, astonished, as Dasch's confession had explained the projected schedule of further landings every six weeks. Dasch produced accurate statistics on the targets selected for disablement and the techniques of destruction that had been drilled into the saboteurs. He also admitted where the other remaining saboteurs were residing and the New York team were promptly arrested on June 20.

As Dasch unveiled the intricacy of his espionage experiences to agent Traynor, the skepticism prevailing among a diminishing section of bureau colleagues rapidly dissipated from his own mind. The significance of this individual who was still claiming to be a foreign undercover intelligence operative while sitting nervously in the FBI's interrogation room became apparent. Traynor was in all probability the first person in American law enforcement to recognize a connection between the Long Island disturbances, the sightings of a German U-boat a short distance from U.S. territory and Dasch's incredible story. Calling investigating teams working at Long Island, Dasch's description definitely matched reports by the coast guard. Ernst Burger was apprehended at 5:00 p.m. on the June 20 at the Governor Clinton Hotel. With assistant director E.J. Connelley present the FBI agents removed a compliant Burger on suspicion of conspiracy to commit sabotage acts. The hotel room was searched after Burger consented to signing a legal waiver, and other articles were recovered. This included a cap which was identified as being adorned with an emblem of the German marines, operational materials and $3,500 in cash.[79]

The interrogation of Burger lasted from June 21 to June 23 and was attended by special agents Lamman, Fellner and Rise. Burger had admitted arriving in America through surreptitious methods and undertaking prior military training in Germany, identifying George Dasch as principal commander of his division and indicating this person had the most awareness of the practical matters. Under examination Ernst Burger confessed that his Social Security card was a forgery and disclosed that he had completed a blank registration certificate before departing Germany. The detection and capture of the still-unaccounted-for second spy team was a more difficult objective to accomplish since Dasch understood only that the detachments were scheduled to rendezvous in Cincinnati. The current whereabouts of Kerling and his accomplices was a mystery to the German agent, but he did supply to the FBI the handkerchief listing German contacts in America. During the ensuing several days he was meticulously interrogated and he furnished other information on the saboteurs, possible locations and data that could aid in their more expeditious apprehension.

The handkerchief contacts transcribed in invisible ink, which the FBI's laboratory discovered could be, intriguingly, reproduced by the application of ammonia fumes, were tracked down.[80] One by one the missing Nazi military intelligence agents were detained, Neubauer being the final Pastorius saboteur arrested. From the Florida group Kerling and Thiel were apprehended in New York on June 23, while Neubauer and Haupt's unshackled stateside trajectory was concluded after their arrest in Chicago on June 27. By this juncture of living behind enemy lines many of Germany's operatives had reportedly started developing a profound sensation of paranoia regarding the FBI tailing their movements. When all seven operations team recruits had been incarcerated the FBI officially arrested Dasch and placed him in a holding cell with his colleagues. To Dasch's disappointment it was distinctly a prospect that the United States government intended to prosecute their chief informant without any distinction from his colleagues. After protracted questioning Kerling reluctantly agreed to cooperate; initially he refuted harboring knowledge pertaining to a Nazi controlled sabotage plot or being under the employment of Nazi Germany's military intelligence, retaliating with effusive counterclaims. But with the information provided by Dasch and Burger the FBI possessed sufficient incriminating details. Kerling's available options evaporated as evidence mounted up.

In addition to the sizable quantities of materials brought ashore by the saboteurs they had received $175,200 in U.S. currency to finance the activities. A total of $174,588 was recovered by the FBI. The saboteurs had expended $612 for refreshment, essential needs, accommodation, travel and the ill-advised bribery attempt. Burger and Dasch later insisted they held anti–Nazi convictions with the intention of impairing the mission from the moment they were recruited. In Dasch's case his general antagonistic behavior and encounter with the Coast Guardsman somewhat validated his statement. It is equally possible both individuals rationalized that incarceration was inevitable and thus the only conceivable option for avoiding execution was to confess everything. There is no concrete evidence prior to the Manhattan hotel conversations that either man rejected their allegiance to the Third Reich. But both men did independently conclude the existing mission was unsalvageable and that they would double-cross their German employers.[81]

As media reports filtered the dramatic articles on exposures of undercover foreign operatives back to Germany, Lieutenant Kappe was compelled to watch passively as his illusions disintegrated. The elaborate training program and laborious selection of eight covert specialists had failed. Concerns about George Dasch had been evident from the very beginning, but Abwehr II's screening and psychological evaluation stages had apparently misinterpreted his prominent character flaws. Insufficient ideological conviction exhibited by the mission team was abundantly evident and was another factor in their demise. The Abwehr chief, Admiral Canaris, inevitably stood to be judged with the harshest criticisms and repercussions; his reputation as commander of an independent military intelligence personally rested inescapably on the success of operations in North America. When the news of the failure of Operation Pastorius was announced General Lahousen wrote a brief commentary in his diary: "Since early morning radio reports continue to come from the United States ... that all participants [have been] arrested." Lahousen was doubtless a casualty of relentless Gestapo-Abwehr rivalry, but he survived to testify for Allied prosecutors at the Nuremberg war crimes tribunals. Walter Kappe survived the war. It appears probable that the collapse of his mission resulted in his reassignment to less glamorous duties than intelligence.[82]

The Nazi operatives turned out to be highly ineffective as saboteurs or spies. A combination of inadequate and incorrect training, defective mission parameters and other incidents of insufficient professionalism resulted in sustained failures. Once the Pastorius program began unraveling the coconspirators were rapidly tracked down and unmasked. The Abwehr II hierarchy failed to effectively input compartmentalization or select agents with appropriately clean records. Recruiting U.S. citizens might in retrospect have jeopardized the mission during its early stages, with past fascist and political group proclivities documented in government records and openly available to investigators. German intelligence had conceivably miscalculated the prudence of dispatching long-term and naturalized residents to commit assault against a previous homeland. The language barrier, despite an emphasis on naturalized American and English speakers, still inconveniently reared its head. Heinck's command of English did not go beyond rudimentary. He was unable to recollect or pronounce correctly the name of the fabricated hometown of his persona's cover story.

Dasch on the outside appeared to be a perfect agent for Operation Pastorius. His linguistic skills and American accent would permit movement under the enemy radar without attracting undue suspicion. A former German soldier and believed to be trustworthy patriot, in fact Dasch was military intelligence's very first recruit, hand-picked from the foreign broadcast monitoring section inside the German Foreign Ministry. The previous December he had composed a long memorandum outlining techniques of sabotage and vividly indicated promising targets in America. The report had greatly impressed Walter Kappe, who summoned Dasch to assist in reviewing files of German-American returnees in order to isolate suitable candidates for the planned mission. Dasch's intimate knowledge of American customs was a fundamental advantage in Abwehr II's perspective. For example, both he and Burger were thoroughly familiar with baseball, in contrast to Kerling, who had not attended a ball game during his eleven years in America. Lieutenant Kappe had acknowledged that Dasch showed minimal propensity for applying himself to the training lectures, and one instructor complained about his egregious disinterest and lethargy. Kappe enquired with Dasch to investigate the origin of this resounding assessment criticism, and his protégé replied that he was preoccupied with his responsibilities as group leader. He protested constantly that technical details represented an irrelevant capability in field conditions and explained his preference for instinct. Kappe had accepted the explanation. As for Burger, Kappe conceded that earlier contentious trouble with the Gestapo produced an unavoidable impediment; former SA officers were classified as persona non grata and generally ostracized in national socialist circles. But this regrettable incarceration controversy was not synonymous, he commented, with disloyalty, Kappe was adamant about not pronouncing judgment on the matter from the framework of SS and SA rivalry.

The Pastorius review prepared by Lord Rothschild, head of MI5's counterespionage section, directed to director-general David Petrie presented an analysis of the mission's planning and execution. Lord Rothschild noted that Operation Pastorius was extremely well planned: "This sabotage expedition was better equipped with sabotage apparatus and better trained than any other expeditions of which the Security Service has heard." From criticisms of the mission execution, Lord Rothschild described how, during a holdover in Paris awaiting transportation to the Lorient submarine base, an operative displaying inadequate discretion became inebriated at a hotel bar and "told everyone that he was a secret agent." Generally the operative's espionage tradecraft and the adherence to contingency planning was not appreciated. Fraternization with compromised contacts and traceable addresses, the report assessed, may have contributed significantly to time saved in detecting suspects and, ultimately, to the "failure of the undertaking."

In another damaging setback to the German intelligence analyzed comprehensively in MIS's review, the incarcerated agents, with the primary offenders being George Dasch and Ernest Burger, exposed classified and sensitive information to the American authorities. The tangible elements were assuredly relayed immediately to counterintelligence operations. Dasch had examined files about the Abwehr II programs in Europe, Belgium, Holland, Denmark, Poland, Norway and Yugoslavia. Intelligence data surfaced on Hans Ritter's 1942 operations inside Spain, insinuating that Ritter was the principle operative in a Nazi-controlled underground espionage network. Ritter's vocations and sphere of influence were revealed to Allied intelligence concerning the perpetrations for sabotage assaults against Allied shipping in Mediterranean ports. Burger confirmed the existence of a secret POW camp specifically for Moroccan citizens complete with a mosque. The interned population were intended to be suborned into various clandestine undercover activities as German agents, a concept that appears to have been discontinued at a later date. Recovered information enabled the Allied investigators to determine that complements of German saboteurs were being deployed to Egypt, Suez and Turkey. Rothschild's report concluded: "It is believed that a decision had been reached not to send submarines on pure espionage missions, but to include two or three saboteurs among the normal crew of a submarine on occasional trips." He confirmed that Pastorius's failings diminished the possibility of future attempted infiltration via submarine landings. He proposed that next-generation saboteurs not be deposited with large quantities of apparatus if the program was ever resurrected, but instead that they be given instructions to purchase their materials in the nation of operation.[83]

U.S. Authorities—Reaction and Prosecution

J. Edgar Hoover forwarded a memo to Marvin McIntyre, secretary to the president, on June 22 at the White House with this statement: "The lack of protection of our beaches and coasts is making it possible for these groups to enter freely and with minimum possibility of detection and presents a very pressing problem warranting immediate consideration." After the announcement regarding the capture of saboteurs, the public was informed that enemy infiltration remained a serious problem. Hoover was the loudest of those clambering for tightened border security, and he privately lobbied for a sustained media blackout on all but perfunctory issues. A secondary motivation for Hoover appears to be a propensity for ensuring maximum credit for FBI personnel.[84] In Hoover's presentation to Roosevelt of the FBI investigations and related melodramatic events, reference to saboteurs denouncing and informing on colleagues was omitted and their intervention in detaining other conspirators was also downplayed. In Hoover's account Dasch had been apprehended two days after his accomplices, with the chronology reversed. This sequence of events implied that Dasch's unmasking was predicated on the detainment of other suspects, and an impression was therefore deliberately fostered that the FBI special agents themselves uncovered the Nazi saboteurs rather than investigating evidence from informants. This reframing of circumstances surrounding the detainments does not reduce the valuable contribution of FBI and other investigators. Congress and other senior government departments by the end of June were generally clear in their understanding of the details of Nazi landings.

The sensational accounts were finally released to journalists on June 27 in a substantively redacted form. With inevitable leaks, speculation had indeed mounted in newspaper circles about a supposed law enforcement manhunt for Nazi saboteurs. A reporter from the Associated Press inquired about conjecture that the FBI had arrested German agents in New York who had landed on the East Coast by submarine. Legal injunctions prevented public disclosure and editors were advised against publishing any sensitive allegations that had circulated. With approval from Roosevelt and the attorney general, Hoover personally released the story at a press conference. A media sensation then erupted, with worldwide coverage, in the following days, and a shocked U.S. population discovered that a terrorist plot had secretly operated at home. The information promulgated at the press conference was a concise and brief explanation of the agents' capture; the Justice Department refused to discuss any details concerning the investigation, defending that decision by quoting national security. The American public was informed about the installations scheduled for attack—the magnesium factories and railway bridges. Photographs and descriptions of explosive materials and equipment discovered on Amagansett Beach were also released to the media.

For both Dasch and Burger their incarceration allowed them only moderate departure from the predicament of their former mission collaborators. The judgment to contact the FBI New York office and appoint themselves catalysts in the mission's downfall had not dissuaded the American authorities from arresting them. In private Traynor and other FBI agents assigned stewardship reassured them that their cooperation, ostensibly dating back to an early period of the investigations, automatically strengthened their standings. Agent Traynor reminded them that the FBI had two priority subjects to consider: defensive in detaining the saboteurs and protecting the United States from other infiltrations. George Dasch expressed doubts about the nature of his incarceration and future outcomes that did not inspire him with confidence. Complaints were registered against various FBI guards or personnel Dasch purported treated him as a criminal and objecting to his imprisonment. He persistently requested an audience with either Hoover or Roosevelt or an intervention from their direction for an improvement in his present fortunes. He claimed he deserved recompense for his integral participation in capturing the other saboteurs. With reference to Dasch and Burger's continuing status as defendants, FBI agents Willis, Donegan and Traynor were present for discussions on June 29. The undeniable possibility of endangerment to cooperating German agents' immediate families if German intelligence discovered their complicity was understood. One scenario had Dasch and Burger entering the courthouse to be indicted without any deviation in treatment from the other defendants, thus forestalling premature information disclosures to the enemy. A strategy was agreed to by the FBI agents of convincing Dasch to enter a guilty plea. Dasch, however, decided that he would plead not guilty and resisted efforts to persuade him otherwise.

According to the existing legal statutes the saboteurs should technically be prosecuted under Title 18, Section 88, of the U.S. Code, which dealt with conspiracy. But President Roosevelt pressured attorney general Francis Biddle to find an alternative outcome.[85] On examination the penalties contained in Title 18 were relatively moderate in comparison to the perceived context and national security implications—a maximum sentence of two years' incarceration and a $10,000 fine. Roosevelt believed it necessary to send a clear message about the ineffective reality of clandestine sabotage against America. He contended that two years' imprisonment was insufficient for such a dangerous crime and although the saboteurs were arrested prior to terrorist attacks occurring, without preventive detainment they would assuredly have enacted their assignments as intended. The FBI and Hoover concurred, adding that national security policy during military engagement should not be undermined by statutes designed for peacetime scenarios. The government's chief lawyers advised Roosevelt that prosecution by military tribunal was turning into a feasible alternative; harsher punitive measures on the statute books notwithstanding, proceedings were manifestly more controllable in the sanctity of military court. To discuss the multifaceted legal ramifications of prosecuting the eight men, Roosevelt convened a series of meetings with attorney general Francis Biddle and Henry L. Stimson, the secretary of war. On June 28, 1942, Major General Cramer wrote to Secretary Stimson commenting that a civilian court was incontestably an incorrect trial venue for the German saboteurs because "the maximum permissible punishment would be less than is desirable to impose." Federal and district courts patently demanded a higher evidence burden and other disclosure orders. Cramer forwarded his assessment that a conviction could be problematic to obtain in civilian courts.[86]

Biddle succinctly informed the president on June 30 that a military tribunal was eminently preferable to a standard civilian trial for handling the proceedings and pointed out that it would assuredly be a briefer hearing; laxer regulations on secret evidence and disclosure violations existed; and the death penalty could be imposed with a two-thirds majority. Biddle speculated that if the eight defendants were prosecuted in a federal or district court the jury decision might be impeded by the inconvenient reality that no sabotage had been committed and the Pastorius accomplices given the minor sentences allowed under conspiracy statutes. Another possibility was examined: that of jurisdiction being assigned to civilian courts and prosecuting the German intelligence agents under the existing espionage laws. An obvious advantage associated with the espionage legislation was that of decidedly harsher sentencing guidelines: a maximum imprisonment of thirty years or the death penalty. But this was also rejected, similarly based on the possible outcome of not guilty verdicts because no sabotage incidents had occurred.[87]

In a dialogue with President Roosevelt, Francis Biddle elaborated on the jurisdictional and legal precedent, stating, "This is not a trial of offenses of law of the civil courts, but is a trial of the offenses of the law of war, which is not recognizable by the civil courts. It is the trial, as alleged in the charges, of certain enemies who crossed our borders.... They are exactly and precisely in the same position as armed forces invading this country." Roosevelt concurred in a document distributed to the attorney general's office on June 30 consolidating a summary of persuasive arguments to his compatriot on the full extent of the legal system being applied to the captured German spies, including the two American citizens, Haupt and Burger. He reminded Francis Biddle of the infamous incident of Nathan Hale, a Revolutionary War solider and intelligence operative who was captured by the British. Stimson and Biddle emerged as vocal exponents and influential driving forces behind transferring the hearings of the Pastorius members to a military tribunal.[88]

Hoover, after undertaking a comparable progression of deliberation and alternative searching with assistant director Connelley, declared personal support for a military tribunal prosecution. The military establishment expressed unmitigated delight at this prestigious trial's transference to their auspices. Publicity surrounding the investigation had induced considerable disagreement and several expressions of frustration from Cramer and the other military officials who preferred restrictions on transparency to be mandatory at upcoming prosecution proceedings. The military tribunal alleviated any considerations about the unwelcome openness of media and freedom of journalists to document events. Prospects of damaging information on security, coastal and interior defensive systems being publicly disclosed partially motivated this decision. President Roosevelt, in a memorandum sent to attorney general Biddle wrote, "Surely they are as guilty as it is possible to be and it seems to me that the death penalty is almost obligatory." In further discussions on sentencing, he professed "the death penalty is called for by usage and by the extreme gravity of the war aim and the very existence of our American government."[89] Debate regarding suitability of the death penalty continued.

The U.S. administration, committed to demonstrating the total failure of Germany's intelligence operation, demanded that justice be expeditious and unyielding. Roosevelt ordered the formation of a military tribunal. The Nazi conspirators were formally accused of the following: Violating the law of war; Violating Article 81 of the Articles of War defining the offenses of corresponding with or passing intelligence to the enemy forces; Violating Article 82 of the Articles of War defining the offense of spying; and Conspiracy to commit the offenses alleged in the first three charges. On July 2, less than a week after the men had been captured, Roosevelt issued a proclamation to the nation:

> I, Franklin D. Roosevelt ... do hereby proclaim that all persons who are subjects, citizens or residents of any nation at war with the United States or who give obedience to or act under the direction of any such nation, and who during time of war enter or attempt to enter the United States or any territory or possession thereof, through coastal or boundary defenses, and are charged with committing or attempting or preparing to commit sabotage, espionage, hostile or warlike acts, or violations of the law of war, shall be subject to the law of war and to the jurisdiction of military tribunals; and that such persons shall not be privileged to seek any remedy or maintain any proceeding, directly or indirectly, or to have any such remedy or proceeding sought on their behalf, in the courts of the United States.[90]

The defendants were prosecuted before a specially convened military commission appointed by President Roosevelt as precedent dictated. The hearing dates spanned July 8 to August 4, 1942. The prosecution section was directed by the army judge advocate general, Major General Myron C. Cramer, and attorney general Frances Biddle. A defense counsel team was appointed comprising Colonel Kenneth Royall and Major Lausen Stone. The accused German spy operatives were housed in the basement jailhouse section of the Justice Department building and awaited instructions. Defense counsel Kenneth Royall realized that the most efficacious legal strategy for defending his clients amounted to nurturing the tribunal's awareness of the hesitation of Pastorius's complement in carrying out the mission. Royall noticed converging themes repeatedly conveyed in the accused's' statements.[91]

Haupt, Burger, Dasch and even Kerling had divulged their stated intentions to double-cross the Abwehr commanders in the FBI interrogations and their unbounded refusal to participate in espionage offensives once inside

American borders. It sounded partially convincing on the surface, whether legitimately authentic or not. A standard explanation portrayed in the defense testimony argued that the defendants, while misguided, anticipated defecting to the United States, concealing this intention during mission training stages. Operation Pastorius therefore transpired in this interpretation as nothing more significant than a desperate attempt to escape the detested environment of the Fatherland. Due to his unique circumstances Dasch was defended separately. His legal counsel protested competently that FBI and police investigations conceivably may have consumed weeks without his client's full cooperation. Obligations emanating from the FBI's assurances of leniency for Dasch were disclosed to the commission, in conjunction with his legal counsel's assertion that he showed an undeniable inclination to betray the mission.[92] With the trial in progress attorneys for the defense filed a Supreme Court motion that concerned the military trial's legality and demanding it be declared a violation of the defendant's constitutional rights. This argument was based on a landmark Supreme Court decision from the Civil War era, *Ex parte Milligan*, which pronounced military trial of civilians unconstitutional. Colonel Kenneth Royall had dredged up this controversial 76-year-old legal precedent. The defendant in question, Lambdin Milligan, historical records confirm, was a resident of Indiana and an outspoken opponent of Abraham Lincoln.

Milligan was prosecuted for allegedly conspiring with the regular Confederate military forces and threatening conflict against the government of Indiana, distinguishable by these conditions from any traditional civilian legal jurisdictions. The charges accused him of conspiracy against the government of the United States, affording aid and comfort to rebels against the authority of the United States and violating the laws of war. A military commission tribunal was convened in 1864 that originally and unceremoniously resulted in a guilty verdict and a sentence of death. The U.S. Supreme Court determined that hearing an appeal was indeed justified and in April 1866 unanimously granted him habeas corpus.

The judges concluded that the judicial rights of American citizens concerning trial in civilian court were inviolable and permissive suspension of habeas corpus unconstitutional unless "ordinary law no longer adequately secures public safety and private rights." The Supreme Court decided that it was appropriate to hear the Pastorius petition, *Ex parte Quirin*, which subsequently has formed an important legal precedent. *Ex parte Quirin* is a much-discussed test case in contemporary law and a standard citing in arguments regarding legality of military tribunals in adjudicating cases centered on terrorism. Beginning on July 29, arguments were presented to the specially convened Supreme Court sessions from both contingents. The prosecution insisted that foreign terrorists employed by an enemy combatant must comprise a military action. Royall argued that Long Island and Florida beaches should not be characterized as "zones of military operation," as no episodes of armed combat and no plausible threat of invasion existed. Civil courts were functioning adequately without martial law's being declared or presidential decrees and under the existing circumstances were appropriate venues for the hearing.[93]

Biddle responded that the United States and Germany were enemy nations at war, and cited a law passed by Congress in 1798 that stated, "Whenever there is a declared war, and the President makes public proclamation of the event, all native citizens, denizens or subjects of the hostile nation shall be liable to be apprehended ... as alien enemies." The Supreme Court unanimously denied the appeal and upheld the jurisdiction of military court on July 31. In his summary rejection of Royall's petitions Judge James Morris remarked, "It seems clear that the petitioner comes within the category of subjects, citizens or residents of a nation at war with the United States, who by proclamation of the President ... are not privileged to seek any remedy or maintain any proceedings in the courts of the United States. The military commission was lawfully constituted ... [and] petitioners are held in lawful custody for trial before the military commission and have not shown cause for being discharged by writ of habeas corpus."

Within a month all eight accused had been sentenced to death and six executions had already been carried out. Authorities finally acknowledged the remaining defendants' (George Dasch and Ernst Burger) collaboration with the U.S. government and commuted their sentences respectively to thirty years and life imprisonment. After the prosecution and defense attorneys rested on August 4, all the defendants were found guilty. Attorney general Biddle appealed to President Roosevelt to commute the sentences of Dasch and Burger, and both were instead remanded to sentences in a federal penitentiary. The treachery of Dasch and Burger was not entirely academic, as Roosevelt's intervention spared their experiencing a similar treatment to their comrades. The six condemned individuals were executed at the District of Columbia jail on August 8, 1942; outcomes of the contentiously assembled military tribunal were predetermined and reservations surfacing pertaining to successful convictions failed to materialize. Stimson and Biddle both agreed that powerful and unambiguous messages needed to be sent to the German military intelligence and Wehrmacht commanders. Verdicts by the military commission further represented efforts to contain public apprehension about espionage attempts or domestic threats. The American public, outraged after reading about the enemy incursions, endorsed the death penalty ruling.[94]

The president had demanded the death penalty from the beginning and sustained a proactive interest in this element of judicial proceedings. He contended, "Offenses such as these are probably more serious than any other offense in criminal law. The death penalty is called for by usage and by the extreme gravity by the war aim and the very existence of the American government." In April 1948 President Truman granted executive clemency to George Dasch and Ernst Burger conditional on deportation. They were released from prison system custody and immediately transported to the American Zone in West Germany. Unexpired portions of their sentences were suspended under agreement of multiple conditions related to employment and affiliation with subversive organizations. Both individuals were prohibited from entering the United States again. But they gained their freedom.

The uncovering of the Operation Pastorius conspiracy resulted in a major propaganda coup for U.S. authorities and the FBI. Reporting of the law enforcement prowess in apprehending an enemy sabotage network substantively improved the career prospects and reputations of many who were involved.[95] The bureau basked in the triumphant media attention for several years afterwards. After Pastorius other allegations of sabotage and enemy assaults were investigated during World War II, but zero incidents were officially corroborated. The mission represented an unmitigated disaster for Abwehr Western Atlantic operations, and department chief Admiral Canaris received a significant personal and irreparably damaging rebuke from Hitler. A final attempt to infiltrate U.S. borders with saboteur divisions occurred in late 1944. In an approximate replica of Pastorius, U-boats once again deposited undercover agents on the American coastline.

2

United States: The Second Espionage Network and Operations Elster

Landing saboteur teams on American shores seemed a distant possibility back in 1937. German intelligence culture preceding the later remilitarization and modifications presided over by Admiral Canaris persisted in functioning primitively. The chief was resolved upon his appointment on amending the institutional culture he encountered at Tirpitzufer and initiated a program for removing any structural impediments to obtaining the intelligence requirements. In modernizing the regime the Abwehr station commanders were instructed to commission supplementary Ast and Kriegsorganisation (KO), or Combat Organizations, subsidiary networks and to recruit diversifying portfolios of agents. Substation staff received new assignments for focusing departmental energies on expanding fields of intelligence activities and existing departments relocated permanently to different cities.

Hamburg Ast and its designated substation in Bremen concentrated resources predominantly on naval operations against America and Britain. The station formed an important management hub and coordination point for the Abwehr's intelligence penetration operations nationwide in the United States. Observing a peacetime code of conduct then under War Ministry direction the Abwehr was still permitted intervention by engagement in nonmilitary tactics and instead were authorized in relatively benign information gathering. The wartime version required an in-house development of considerable impetus for another two and a half years. But gradually the organizational re-forming did inspire an increase in institutional competence.

The jurisdiction of Hamburg Ast station comprised the administration of operations in the geographical territorial zones of South America, the Iberian

Peninsula and Greece, amalgamated with its responsibilities for America and Britain. The Dresden, Stettin and Breslau stations supervised coverage of military activity throughout Europe, the Soviet Union and the Middle East. The KO, as discussed, conspired in neutral territories with either diplomatic or economic cover, representing a complex challenge for penetration. KO substations were established at different occasions in Sweden, Yugoslavia, Finland, the United States, Turkey, Morocco and other nonoccupied European territories. Spain and Switzerland, both theoretically neutral states in the conflict, transitioned into veritable hotbeds of espionage activity as German, Allied and Soviet Union agents descended on Madrid, Lisbon and Geneva. The respective intelligence communities understood fully the strategically valuable counterespionage opportunities.

KO substations were generally attached covertly to the German embassies and consulates if possible. Operators managed networks of domestic informants and professional Abwehr intelligence officers engaged in the more complex missions to retrieve information. The informants recruited in foreign nations tended to be either German immigrants, naturalized or permitted residency, and various other domestic citizens agreeing to cooperate with Third Reich handlers for financial incentives. Agents customarily operated outside any cooperation and awareness of the host governments; therefore training in subterfuge and countersurveillance techniques rapidly became mandatory. In the neutral territories the unavoidable risks surfaced of diplomatic blunders and damage to important relationships with independent nations. Traditionally, German military officers were not expected or specially trained to direct attention towards political circumstances or to become involved in counterintelligence machinations. These underhanded activities offended the personal codes of honor according to sections of the Wehrmacht, lineal descendants of the Prussian Imperial military who had also refuted such obligations. Another hindrance in developing a credible military intelligence capability was ongoing jurisdictional conflict with other Reich departments such as the German Foreign Ministry's intelligence service. From 1935 onward the Foreign Office had fomented discord by lobbying for restrictions on security service personnel movements in theaters perceived as its own jurisdiction.

Informal intelligence-gathering sections augmenting other German political departments were content to restrain military intelligence and limit their remit to conventional targets. Admiral Canaris intended to cultivate new alliances and improve communications on all fronts. He established cordial links with the Foreign Ministry personnel through eliciting the comradeship and fraternity of a former Kriegsmarine officer and colleague, von Weiszäcker. At this present occasion Weiszäcker was a state secretary, but he was destined to execute ubiquitous functions and was seconded to the Vatican as official German minister. Later, during the height of World War II, secretive pathways to engage in communication with London and Washington would be transmitted through the Vatican. Canaris and Weiszäcker restored, to a degree, working relations. The Tirpitzufer and Reich Foreign Ministry subsequently confirmed bilaterally, on the surface at least, a standing commitment to overcome a decade of thorny relations. But this new cooperation was endorsed at expense. The Abwehr was evolving into a fundamental building block amid the totalitarian architecture, the agency's traditional culture of independence dating from its reformation. In the aftermath of World War I there was no priority of Nazi Party officials. The perceived lines of engagement separating the intelligence machine comprising the Abwehr and the excessively brutal objectives of the Nazi bureaucratic structure became increasingly blurred. In his inaugural speech as Abwehr chief, Canaris observed that he expected the atmosphere of resentment towards the SS and Heydrich to change. His speech was characterized by observers as pro–Nazi and Canaris referred to his desire for "comradely cooperation."[1]

In the emerging climate of impending international conflict and preparation for the Blitzkrieg operations targeting Germany's borders in January 1939 the efforts promoting foreign infiltration in Europe were stepped up. Abwehr and SD clandestine actions escalated and the intelligence budgets spiraled commensurate to expected results, the Abwehr experiencing a deluge in funding to refine its intelligence work overseas. In further comprehensive reforms the Ast and KO substations controlled another section of subsidiary departments. The specialist groups were assembled for activation under the new frameworks dependent on either deteriorating political conditions or preparations for military engagement. Entitled Spannungsagenten and Kriegsagenten branches, the attached subdivisions were configured with structures for mobilization with a rapid response capability, agents after confirming delegated orders and receiving a specific code word traveled to a specific predetermined location. The mission parameters from this point converged on obligations for identifying positions on the ground and reporting on any observed military actions. Spannungsagenten were expected to disseminate to the Abwehr commanders all information on observed enemy mobilization, while Kriegsagenten units conducted covert intelligence assignments within enemy territory.

Analysis consisted of intelligence assessments researching the adversary's capabilities and vulnerability, selecting insufficiently defended or extremely fragile resources that were requirements for sustaining a prolonged military conflict. Launching espionage operations to discover technical military information and any engineering advancements or intelligence on naval bases and Luftwaffe airfields manifested a propensity for uncovering critical weaknesses that could be converted into decisive tactical information for the German battlefield ambitions. Still deficient in the necessary numbers of highly skilled agents, by September 1938 the Kriegsagenten was investing significant resources in recruitment.

The Abwehr strategy to prioritize expansion of domestic and international offices and expand their cooperation with other colluding foreign intelligence organizations, pursued since 1937, produced dividends. By the time major European conflict irreversibly erupted Canaris reportedly commanded Abwehrstellen substations in 21 military districts domestically. Germany had constructed a capable military-industrial machine. The Third Reich continued to maneuver without a centralized intelligence structure, exceptional within standard state intelligence apparatus. Nevertheless, in 1940 and 1941 Abwehr commanders were persistently ordered to be vigilant in containing missions in neutral America to a minimum. Hitler realized the damage that would result if the U.S. entered the conflict in opposition, and he had no desire for other exposures of Nazi Party dilettantes challenging American interests this early in the conflict. The German military and Nazi high command wanted to concentrate all efforts on Europe, as France and Britain opened up as principle fronts.

Walter Schellenberg became more preoccupied with ruthlessly striving to expand the SD's foreign intelligence services and in recruiting international agents. Reinhard Heydrich and his later replacement, Ernst Kaltenbrunner, as senior directors of RSHA understood the preeminent advantages of cultivating a separately controlled intelligence network and agents of political influence. By 1939, SD VI had experimented and invested financially minimally in U.S. and any wider North American operations. More effective infiltration occurred in South America. Schellenberg formerly managed a portfolio of European covert operatives and did not respect the ongoing numerically unproductive circumstances as tolerable.[2] Demands concerning the expansion of the agency's profile in the United States and other international theaters partially represented motivation for constructing an effective intelligence organization, but it also embodied a functional method of ensuring that Schellenberg himself was commander of the most powerful state security agency. Institutional rivalries within the political structure continued permeating the foundations of government structure. Wrestling control of military intelligence from the Wehrmacht resulted in instigating a prominent conviction within the SS, as it explored strategies for further ventures in America.[3]

Nazi Germany was not the only foreign power with the intention to covertly plant substantial numbers of agents in New York and elsewhere in the United States. The British SOE formed a subversive warfare operation to counter Nazi Germany's influence in America and to advocate to an American audience for intervention in the European conflict. From 1941 onward hundreds of British agents were deployed to New York City. Designated SOI Department of Special Operations Executive (SOE), this clandestine section was commanded by William Stephenson, a Canadian national and later an important figure in British intelligence. The predominant sphere of activities of the covert operations appeared to be the delineating of propaganda and influencing public opinion. UK time-limited declassification released the SOE official case documents in 2014, opening a renewed interpretation. Sidney Morrell, an agent stationed in SOI, claimed that 20 individual rumors per day, at a minimum, were released. The British agents employed a pattern of propaganda techniques extending to planting newspaper stories and maintaining contacts in the foreign language press for the reasons of filtering back information from international articles. Respected and highly regarded journalists were cultivated as friendly sources, including Dorothy Thompson and Edgar Mowrer, while *PM* and *New Republic* publications covered subject matter leaked by SOI.[4]

Other media outlets assenting to collusion were the *New York Times* and its Jewish owner, Hays Sulzburger, publishing articles disclosing anti–Nazi information dispensed from SOI. A register of U.S. industrialists, damagingly from a reputation perspective, associated with Nazi Germany and infractions in domestic trading embargoes was reproduced without omission by the *New York Times*. The FBI financed the Friends of Democracy movement, and liberal campaigners and other associated prointervention advocates emitted highly vocal condemnations of America First. Stephenson's SOI unit administered a joint campaign against Nazism and noninterventionist organizations, colluding with a plethora of anti–Nazi movements by distributing instructive information and financial assistance. An undercover operative was concealed within America First for the implicit purposes of amassing intelligence and destabilizing the neutrality group from the inside. In September 1941 Adolf Berle, in a confidential memorandum to secretary of state Cordell Hull, complained that inside South America "Britain had been active in making things appear dangerous."[5] He cautioned for the State Department and FBI to be prudent in reviewing intelligence. On a notable occasion MI6 passed along a geographical map displaying an Axis strategy for remodeling completely the South American borders after invasion. President Roosevelt publicly denounced the Nazi-produced document as a blueprint for aggression.

Espionage in America

Before Major General Lahousen had ordered the Operation Pastorius undertaking, an earlier infiltration had been endeavored ambitiously, through very different methods, to establish a long-term presence in the United States. This military intelligence-controlled intervention was instead oriented towards espionage and information-gathering actions rather than sabotage or combat operations. An American front offensive evolved from institutional pressures industriously remolding Kriegsagenten and Spannungsagenten security services. Effective infrastructure was installed within Nazi occupied Europe, and corresponding sophistication became an essential priority in noncombat zones and neutral terrain. By January 1941 and the origination of preparations for Pastorius, the Duquesne Spy Ring encompassed prominent sections of the northern and eastern United States, a close second to the Griebl-Pheiffer network when comparing the numbers of active personnel and the volume of information consumed. The purpose of Duquesne primarily centered on assembling and protracting information collection apparatus and the communications systems; the Tirpitzufer headquarters speculated this could be accomplished through a variety of hard and soft techniques. A stratagem was developed of embedding the German agents within industries and occupations of high intelligence value inside the United States, and informants were carefully selected to be lucrative sources of strategic and sensitive information, forming Canaris and Piekenbrock anticipated highly valuable components of military planning and military action during impending conflicts. This advancement of covert underground cell networks gained momentum in early 1940. Major Ritter, now the commander of U.S. operations, demanded a more substantial repositioning within the re-formed bureaucracy at Hamburg Ast. The station was gradually reoriented as a management structure to ensure the Abwehr's ability to maintain the necessary level and duration of operational activity in achieving objectives in the United States and other territories.

Intelligence missions inside American society during a peacetime environment, while benign in comparison to the sabotage intervention, represented a hostile action against a neutral government. Foreign Office and most Nazi high command personnel remained committed before Pearl Harbor, in public conversation at least, to maintaining the neutral and impartial relations. Any postulated breaches to neutrality obliged the compulsory and meticulous weighing of conflicting demands. The Abwehr's containment in balancing the feasibility of unsanctioned missions encouraged rather less controversial tactics in information gathering. Admiral Canaris advised against any disruption to the "non-hostile strategy" and implied resonant concerns about the repercussions on expanding the European conflict. Griebl and Ritter had demonstrated the feasibility of U.S. intelligence-gathering infiltration in 1935, 1936 and 1937, becoming the inspiration for a rejuvenated effort focused on comparable repetitions of nonviolent methodologies. The United States still unequivocally represented a major threat to ambitious Nazi expansionist policies. Dating from January to June 1940 the Duquesne spy ring experienced a massive increase in funding, with a centralized impetus for an active penetration network to replace Griebl-Pheiffer. Undercover agents attached to Duquesne managed to infiltrate a restaurant where the proprietor exploited his position to obtain information from important customers, while an airline worker located on the Eastern Seaboard enabled real-time reporting on movements of Allied merchant and naval shipping.

Many of the covert infiltrations targeted mundane-appearing professions, but Ritter remained convinced that agents embedded inside this unassuming directory would demonstrate their usefulness. One profession in America targeted was that of delivery worker. According to Nazi spy chiefs, members of this occupation were suitable for cultivation as assets for intercepting covert messages. William Sebold, a naturalized American citizen who had emigrated from Germany after the nation's economic collapse and ensuing turbulent national climate following World War I, was a hand-picked selection by military intelligence planted in the Duquesne spy ring. Simultaneously he fulfilled a dual existence as an informant for the FBI. The Justice Department and FBI's uncovering of the Duquesne espionage operation was significantly influenced by Sebold and his accomplishments in covertly penetrating deeper inside the conspiracy. William Sebold had cultivated sufficient trust and comradeship with fellow operatives and the Abwehr spymasters for an appointment as controller of the mission's radio transmission station, falling under FBI control. Located in Long Island, New York, this intrusion maneuvered the United States into the enviable position of intercepting almost all the information transmitted from the espionage ring back to Germany.

Sebold was solicited for recruitment by German intelligence in September 1939 and immediately went to the American consulate in Cologne, proffering the convenient excuse to his Gestapo contacts of obtaining a new passport. Sebold informed the consulate personnel without Gestapo awareness about the circumstances of the approaches at Hamburg and Münheim and attempts at recruitment. The consulate officials were unreconciled about correct mechanisms for handling this delicate situation and advised that this American citizen return to Cologne in exactly two days, once again espousing the pretense of a passport collection. When he reappeared at the Cologne consulate American officials informed William Sebold that the U.S. diplomatic service had abrogated jurisdiction, and other Washington government agencies had now announced an interest in his predicament. Information concerning this case had circulated in the Justice Department, which delegated the investigation to the FBI. The American intelligence authorities immediately comprehended the potential for a systemic counterespionage coup on their watch. During the ensuing conversations William Sebold was persuaded after some procrastination to cooperate with the FBI after he returned to America. His life as a double agent was about to begin.[6]

Sebold returned to the Dusseldorf Gestapo office and confirmed his acquiescence to their earlier demands as instructed. Complying with the communications protocols Gestapo field operatives forwarded details of this latest acquisition to their opposite numbers in military intelligence. William Sebold was officially integrated into Major Ritter's multiplying network of overseas operatives in October 1939. Continuing to conspicuously exhibit a willingness to follow the instructions imparted by superior officers, Sebold reported to the Hamburg station as ordered. He participated in induction training programs, completing the final phases at a specially designed facility for foreign espionage operatives.

A native of Germany, William Sebold had experienced combat as a soldier on the European battlefields of World War I. After departure from Germany in 1921 he worked in manufacturing and aircraft production throughout the continental United States. On February 10, 1936, he finalized the proscribed immigration documents and legally adopted U.S. citizenship. In early 1939 nostalgic sentiments clamored for his attention regarding his former life in Germany, and on deliberation he resolved to petition for a temporary leave of absence from his aircraft company employer in San Diego. Looking forward to the welcome occasion of visiting his family members in Münheim, he proceeded with the Atlantic crossing in February of 1939, with the initial destination of Hamburg for attending to personal affairs. Briefed about Sebold's impending arrival, personnel were transferred into the appropriate positions before the SS *Deutschland* docked at Hamburg. Gestapo officers awaited his presence in Germany. A 24-hour surveillance detail had received authorization on William Sebold's movements from the very moment he arrived. While navigating through customs clearance he was approached by a detachment of local Gestapo. Sebold later recollected his astonishment at this encounter with the Gestapo and the cloak and dagger manner of their methods. The agents confronted Sebold and adamantly demanded a private conversation before bundling him into a vehicle stationed outside.

A German-American working for a prestigious American aircraft company was of special interest to the Nazi intelligence services. The Gestapo, after discovering his previous employment at the Consolidated Aircraft Company, enterprisingly decided to sound out recruitment opportunities. This intriguing background of expertise in an American industrial sector presented multifarious pathways for exploitation; if it turned out he was not susceptible for handling as either as a permanent field agent or an informant, the briefing sessions could still prove illuminating. Sebold was transferred to the Gestapo headquarters in Hamburg, where a Colonel Kraus interviewed him. Kraus briefly questioned the recent arrival from America about his awareness of technical information that was potentially profitable to the Fatherland before proposing that Sebold consent without presenting any complications to enlisting as an informant. Sebold was not persuaded until the Gestapo reminded him of a temporary period of incarceration on smuggling charges before he emigrated to America. Neglecting to divulge this pertinent and compulsory information on his U.S. citizenship application reappeared to haunt him. If Sebold declined to cooperate the Gestapo assured him this violation of immigration statutes would be supplied to the Americans. At the meeting with Colonel Kraus he was further threatened with the not unrealistic scenario of deportation to a concentration camp.

Sebold exhibited symptoms of reluctance from the beginning and attempted to protect himself behind his American citizenship. He was granted some extended time to consider the Gestapo's proposal, but warnings directed at he himself and his family members were beginning to appear persuasive. His interrogator in Hamburg, Colonel Kraus, had stated, "Your family lives in Münheim, not in the United States. If you do not cooperate, we cannot guarantee their safety." Next the Hamburg Gestapo agents informed Sebold that an obligatory second interview was being scheduled and he should wait until being contacted again before he was finally permitted to continue on the journey to Münheim. In examining his reemergence in Germany the returning migrant had originally contemplated remaining in Münheim and finding employment and financial security locally, but this now appeared improbable. Sebold convinced himself he had few options besides complying with the threatening orders. At the appointed time on July 8 he was greeted in the Duisburgerhoff Hotel lobby by a man who identified himself as Dr. Gassner.[7] This unknown but presumably senior officer interrogated the candidate about his knowledge of military aircraft and technology in America. The officer directly requested that Sebold forget his protestations and advised that conditions would measurably improve after he accepted their offerings. The mission apparently involved returning to the United States and becoming embroiled in espionage as an undercover operative. Sebold's subsequent dialogues with Gassner and a Dr. Renken, later identified as Major Ritter of military intelligence, had finally persuaded him to cooperate with the Third Reich.

Discussions began regarding their intention for deployment of Sebold as a foreign operative inside the United States.[8] Ritter explained in detail the existing espionage and sabotage apparatus presently in operation throughout America, discussing informants allegedly planted inside the American armed forces and government agencies in Washington. Major Ritter for three to four months had experienced growing pressure from his Abwehr superiors to implement measures for expanding internal communications practiced by espionage systems under his control and streamlining the more expeditious trafficking of information. The Gestapo offered a promising candidate, William Sebold. World War II had begun with the invasion of Poland and Ritter planned to deliver essential intelligence from his American network and spies buried within the commercial and defense industries. Both, military intelligence and the Gestapo remained completely unaware of Sebold's prior visit to the consulate during his deliberations and conversations with the American authorities. Sebold later revealed his reticence in accepting the Abwehr's offer and anxiety regarding reprisals against family members whether he acquiesced or not.[9]

Admiral Canaris personally selected Nikolaus Ritter to coordinate the Duquesne mission. He was responsible for perpetrating Germany's most serious infiltration of America and supervising a productive spy network. After cutting his operational teeth masterminding the Pheiffer spy ring Ritter was now exposed to the United States authorities, but fortuitously escaping apprehension he found himself redeployed to Hamburg Ast, Germany. Respected in Nazi intelligence circles as an American theater expert, by autumn 1939 his centralized career was advancing. During a previous life Ritter had resided in America and New York for thirteen years. He endured difficult circumstances but cultivated financial stability in textile manufacturing sectors, becoming by all accounts largely accustomed to American life.

Ritter eventually repatriated to Germany following financial setbacks and bankruptcy threats, and by September 1939 he was the senior Abwehr commander of espionage against the United States and Britain. In America by the time of the Duquesne operation Ritter was a recognizable figure associated with German intelligence and could no longer independently maneuver stateside. He had opted for assuming a pseudonym while stationed underground in America, the persona of Alfred Landing. Now this identity would undoubtedly be well publicized and Ritter depended on spy ring commanders remotely operating. Admiral Canaris instructed him to develop contact with Fritz Duquesne, whom he remembered personally from his background inside South America during World War I.

Undercover in America

Abwehr documents reveal that both Piekenbrock and Ritter professed remarkable enthusiasm for the observable progress demonstrated by William

Sebold at the Hamburg spy school. As mission commander Ritter insisted on personally directing their recent addition's induction and guiding him through procedures; Ritter and the other command chiefs assessed Sebold as exhibiting significant potential. Ritter followed reports intimately on Sebold throughout the training and indoctrination process. Colonel Hans Piekenbrock, Abwehr I chief and technically the highest managerial connection preoccupied with North American operations, ordered the Duquesne plan's implementation. He monitored closely the planning for U.S. operations and developed into a somewhat cumbersome interference for Ritter, who resented the pressures for intelligence information increasingly being placed on him. "Tramp" was the Abwehr code name selected for its ace operative, William Sebold, the final segment in the American jigsaw puzzle. Colonel Piekenbrock reflected that Sebold's turning represented a valuable and exigent augmentation to the Duquesne operation activities and complimented Major Ritter on his personnel selection.[10] Immediately after final training, Sebold was given his official travel documents and fabricated ID in preparation for posting to the United States. He received final instructions, sailed from Genoa, Italy, and arrived in New York City on February 8, 1940.

The Abwehr advised their newest recruit that financial and other material necessities would all be available after he instigated contact in the United States. William Sebold was ordered to purchase radio components and establish his own radio transmitter station for communicating with Hamburg Ast substation. His spending allowance upon departure amounted to a thousand dollars, provided by the Abwehr, stuffed in his jacket pockets. Before departure from Germany Sebold had utilized a secret contact for notifying the U.S. consulate in Cologne about his transportation details and destination. The FBI thought it distinctly possible that the Gestapo had arranged agents at the dockyards to observe passengers disembarking from the vessel and, if possible, anyone waiting in anticipation for the arrival. The federal agents confirmed that the German intelligence asset should travel from the harbor directly to his sanctioned hotel in Yorkville to avoid suspicion. The first debriefing interview about the American voyage was undertaken later. He introduced himself in America under the assumed name of Harry Sawyer. FBI teams were assembled on the ground and apprised of Sebold's mission combined with the intention of controlling him as a counterintelligence agent. An important objective was to manipulate the unfolding conditions and diverse permutations at ground level to identify other underground German agents in the United States. Under the guidance of special agents Sebold established a residence in New York and the FBI ensured the capacity to observe every meeting taking place. Federal Bureau of Investigation agents aided William Sebold in locating a professional office in the city.

An appropriate commercial property was selected following comprehensive vetting at the Knickerbocker Hotel, Times Square. His artificial persona of Harry Sawyer existed complete with a fantasy background as a diesel engineering consultant concocted by Major Ritter and the Hamburg operations team. The office served an important function in the deception as a business headquarters. A primary concern to the FBI was installing the surveillance team's equipment, and the Knickerbocker Hotel rooms were consequently outfitted with elaborate hidden microphones and two-way mirrors. Ritter's front company, Diesel Research, was frequented literally within days by Nazi informants in possession of intelligence concerning U.S. defense industries. FBI surveillance of the 42nd Street building advanced to the extent of installing a secret room next door, where agents observed and recorded events through the two-way mirror. The two-way room was soundproofed and used by the FBI teams to monitor the microphone listening devices and for recording visual content using a 16 millimeter motion picture camera.[11] The unwitting Nazi agents apparently still remained unaware of the sophisticated surveillance increasingly surrounding their activities.

In 1937, Fritz Duquesne was 60 years old and a resident of New York, eluding police by disguising himself under one of forty different aliases he adopted during his lifetime. Implicated in subversive incidents in America dating back to the beginning of the 1930s, and garnering a comparable reputation in territories extending to South Africa and South America, he was contacted in New York and recruited as an intelligence-gathering operative by Ritter. Duquesne, a native of South Africa, was deeply Anglophobic and had devoted many years in attempting revenge upon Britain for political and military actions targeting his homeland during the Boer Wars. This hatred motivated him to confer his services as saboteur on Germany and undertake military activities during the First World War. There is evidence that Duquesne was a prime instigator of sabotage against British targets in South America from 1914 to 1916. He had developed the personal reputation of an individual with a marked tendency of exaggerating his own stories, but deciphering the fact from fiction in Duquesne's background is difficult. In April 1934 he secretly accepted an intelligence officer role for Order of 76, an American pro–Nazi organization, discussing at that time a merger with William Dudley Pelley's Silvershirts.[12]

An early unmasking of Duquesne's occurred in October after an investigation by John Spivak, a writer for the left-wing newspaper *New Masses*. Spivak enlisted Duquesne's Jewish girlfriend to apprise him of the South African's activities. A detailed FBI file on Fritz Duquesne is still in existence that depicts in comprehensive detail his participation in the later events.[13] On January 26, 1940, while Sebold was in Hamburg undertaking final orientation, an individual calling himself Hugo Sebold, connected to Germany espionage, handed William Sebold a consignment of microphotographs and addresses of contacts living in New York with instructions to acquaint himself with these people after allowing a certain period of time to elapse after his arrival in America. The identical surnames of Sebold are coincidental and the persona Hugo Sebold was uncovered as a pseudonym for Henry Sarou. One of the microphotograph contacts was Colonel Fritz Duquesne of 17 East 42nd Street, New York City. Recommendations for contact advocated mailing a prepared letter of introduction. The document in question was contained in a packaged microphotograph, serving as an operational security measure convenient for verification of identity. When Sebold returned to United States territory in February 1940 Duquesne was operating a business known as the Air Terminals Company in New York.

After establishing his first communication with Fritz Duquesne by mail as instructed Sebold, using the pseudonym Harry Sawyer, organized a meeting at Duquesne's New York office. During the meeting Duquesne appeared extremely concerned about the possibility of electronic surveillance devices being present in his office. Possibly demonstrating symptoms of paranoia, the South African indicated that the sensitive dialogue and exchange of information should happen elsewhere. Duquesne then furnished him with a secretive pink-colored fragment of paper, on which lettering printed in English stated, "We will go out. Cannot talk here." For posterity William Sebold decided on retaining this note and turned it over to FBI special agents. Duquesne said nothing more but changed his outer garments, wearing his winter jacket as they walked on the main street. The Air Terminals Company office was apparently not a sufficiently reliable environment for covert discussions, and he instead suggested reconvening to a local automat as it should not be crowded at that hour.

On the journey to the automat Duquesne inquired precisely how William Sebold had surreptitiously entered American territory, probing whether his doubtless circuitous route included China. Duquesne continued that a document mailed from China had apprised him that an individual called Sawyer would imminently be contacting him, and Sebold responded that he embarked from Genoa on the SS *Washington*. The South African then inquired whether he experienced any trouble crossing the borders or with the immigration authorities, to which Sebold replied that he had not. Introductions settled and remembering his orders, Sebold then informed Duquesne that he couriered microphotographic messages and other sensitive documents for delivery to him. The two spies compared notes about the members of the German espionage system, establishing pedigree and ascertaining respective levels of intelligence experience.

Duquesne bragged that he was an expert saboteur and the inventor of several new types of explosive devices currently being deployed to Nazi espionage teams throughout the United States. He declared his ambitious plans for destruction in the coming war between U.S. military forces and Nazi Germany. In the course of their conversation he confessed to Sebold on the subject of previously facing prosecution for murder in New York. Fritz Duquesne adamantly cautioned his apprentice to refrain from consorting or generally maintaining the company of other German nationals, as every German "in America was a squealer," and reminded him to uphold security discipline by "burning everything." On this last comment William Sebold was assured that any incriminating documents or evidence should be dispatched or burned immediately upon application being concluded to avoid leaving traceable matter for the police or FBI. He discussed at considerable length an important criminal case that was reported on extensively in February, the conviction of Fritz Kuhn, an American fascist leader. Duquesne proclaimed that the evidence was planted by Jews. The conversations were finalized by the spy ring chief's reassuring Sebold that he would be notifying Hamburg about the rendezvous and subsequently be in touch. Sebold received funding from the Abwehr to support the espionage operations as his individual assigned mission gradually developed throughout March and April 1940.[14]

On April 24, William Sebold telephoned the espionage commander and arranged another appointment in front of 84 West Broadway. Meeting at their designated location, Duquesne had recommended holding their conference at the nearby Horn and Hardart. A mutual agreement was then reached to attend regular meetings on Wednesdays at 2:00 p.m. in front of 84 West Broadway. Duquesne reiterated his conviction that somebody was following him and explained that for security reasons he was transferring his nefarious operations to 120 Broadway, sustaining his business enterprise subterfuge under the personality of a managing director of Security Service Company. He stated that he had obtained designs on airplane wings from an informant and had mailed them to the "other side."[15] Duquesne submitted information intermittently from April 1940 to July 1941, the highest volumes of trafficked intelligence centering on U.S. national defense, movements of shipping destined for British ports and industrial technology.

The FBI conducted surveillance and monitored covert operations during this entire period. Sebold progressively unraveled how the spy ring members routinely received financial payments from Germany in exchange for assiduous complicity. Penetrating the espionage network and managing an effective countersurveillance operation delivered a virtual treasure trove of information on network activities. Intelligence orders communicated by Hamburg Ast to the

American operatives intercepted conveniently for federal investigators by William Sebold allowed a glimpse into the Nazi priorities for information gathering. Piekenbrock and Ritter filtered information and transmitted instructions to the front lines, generally in response to the Wehrmacht or other military branches submitting internal requests. Sebold reported on orders to discover whether AT&T had invented a secret energy ray to target aircraft bombs; whether the U.S. Army had in development a uniform for repelling mustard gas; information on antiaircraft shells guided by electronics; and research on chemical and bacteriological weapons to be released from airplanes. The overriding thrust for intelligence requests transmitted from Major Ritter to America between May and November 1940 was obtaining the latest tactical picture relating to U.S. military mobilization and movements.[16]

Agents of the Duquesne Espionage Ring

Prominent agents in the espionage network that William Sebold encountered in New York during the initial unpredictable weeks included ubiquitous enthusiasts Lilly Stein and Everett Roeder. The second individual was employed as an engineer at the Long Island Sperry industrial plant and had previously conspired in a Nazi espionage network as an accomplice in the Norden bombsight theft. In a relatively short time Everett Roeder evolved into a senior, well-connected operative and cultivated a considerable reputation within German intelligence circles. His professional competencies as a qualified engineering draftsman were useful operationally as was his evident knowledge of industrial design. Roeder was selected to complete technical drawings of uncovered aeronautic and industrial technology blueprints as required. On May 24, 1940, during a standard West Broadway conference and a Jersey ferry excursion, Duquesne unwittingly relayed his awareness and preceding acquaintance with Roeder to U.S. authorities. He mentioned two German spies that resided on Long Island hastily departing for Germany on the *Bremen* and leaving their wives behind. He admitted he was acquainted with Roeder and supposed that this individual had performed a crucial role in smuggling the bombsight to Germany.

Sebold had instigated contact with Everett Roeder two weeks earlier and informed Duquesne that in conversation the agent had insinuated he now possessed large quantities of schematics and prints but refused to pass these doubtless influential documents along unless he received higher compensation. Duquesne suggested injudiciously that Sebold purloin the planning texts and burn Roeder's house down. Fehse and Bante informed Sebold about shipping and naval information. Much of the information gathered by these individuals was classified as open-source intelligence that was available in industrial sector magazines or the product of enterprisingly approaching experts who unwittingly had passed intelligence to foreign government agents.[17] The FBI official case file on the Duquesne espionage ring explained the valuable functions of Paul Fehse and Paul Bante inside the covert operations. Bante, another disillusioned World War I veteran, had relocated to the United States in 1930 and adopted naturalized citizenship in 1938.

Formerly a German-American Bund member, Bante later confessed to FBI special agent investigators that military intelligence bureaucrats in Germany controlled a second operative he consorted with, Paul Fehse. In earlier occupational endeavors assigned as a German government asset, following initial recruitment by the Gestapo, Fehse was assigned directives to establish himself as an agent provocateur and foster discontent among union workers. His record demonstrates a previous marginal association with Pheiffer's intelligence network in March of 1937, and he had developed a convivial acquaintance with the accomplices Griebl and Rumrich. Both individuals were implicated in spying for Nazi Germany and convicted of espionage charges in 1938. Bante had escaped exposure due to his assuredly less integral function. He was identified as a prominent individual in reestablishing the covert penetration operations that in theory should replicate Pheiffer-Griebl in magnitude. Bante was assisted by Paul Fehse in identifying sources of information about merchant and naval shipping containing munitions and supplies.

Sebold was introduced formally to Paul Bante at the Little Casino Restaurant in New York, which was patronized by members of Military Intelligence's espionage ring. In the German-populated town of Yorkville, Richard Eichenlaub and his wife, the proprietors of the Little Casino Bar on 206 East 85th Street, quietly and unobtrusively continued their undercover activities and adapted the premises into the ipso facto headquarters for the Duquesne Nazi spy ring. Richard Eichenlaub also reported to the Gestapo and ensured the restaurant was remodeled into a fertile platform for retrieving information from unassuming patrons. He collected intelligence from any customers engaged in national defense production or otherwise conveniently useful backgrounds. Located in a bustling district, the venue was apparently popular and widely attended by the local community. The schedule of this clandestine meeting was recorded by FBI surveillance teams, according to the extracted contemporary field reports, as of June 24, 1940. Fehse by June 1940 had received an internal promotion and his formerly perfunctory role was transformed into that of an influential driving force inside the covert community. He arranged underground meetings, directed members' activities, and collated batches of information and arranged for its transmission to Germany, chiefly through William Sebold.

He was reputedly trained in espionage work in Hamburg and claimed to be commander of the Marine Division in the American espionage system.

Paul Fehse, upon initially meeting William Sebold, barely concealed his distrust and questioned the circumstances behind his recruitment and his awareness of prominent intelligence figures in Germany who presumably could impart the satisfactory verification. He demanded some precise information for authenticating the radio operator's supposed background and status. Fortunately, Sebold's contact list was genuine and he was sufficiently convincing to satisfy Fehse. The "drop" arrangement for Fehse and Bante generally entailed a handwritten message personally handed to Sebold at his commercial office. Their unrestricted New York dockyard presence returned on many occasions to procure some intriguing assets; in collaboration both individuals routinely appeared in the FBI surveillance and intelligence reports surfacing at the Knickerbocker office. Fehse divulged harnessing a secured address in Philadelphia which had not previously been disclosed in July to the FBI's still-undetected inside man and therefore presumably difficult to trace. This location Sebold had expeditiously divulged was a backdoor channel for relaying intelligence materials without interruption and opening dialogue with Hamburg in emergency situations. The FBI instructed Sebold to investigate and uncover everything possible relating to this channel.

In July 1940 Fehse attended Sebold's downtown Manhattan commercial office and informed his supposed comrade about an upcoming mission: a reliable informant planned to retrieve data about rubberizing, self-sealing airplane fuel tanks and a new braking device from an associate employed at a shipyard.[18] Deeper into the investigations Sebold discovered that a hitherto concealed accomplice, Alfred E. Bokhoff, an American naturalized citizen since 1929, was the resourceful inside man who enabled Fehse to obtain the sensitive intelligence on the transportation itinerary and cargo of vessels. Bokhoff had been a mechanic for the United States Lines in New York City for 15 years prior to his recruitment as an informant. Because of his occupation on the dockyards he became an acquaintance of practically all informants in the illicit community working as seamen on various ships.

Carl Reuper, a mechanic working for the Air Associates Company in Bendix, New Jersey, was an industrious coordinator in the underground network and commanded a espionage ring quasi-separate from Duquesne. He communicated sensitive information using a shortwave radio transmitter originally under his express control rather than accessing Sebold, which presented a dilemma for the FBI's counterintelligence program. In a misguided effort to augment operations, Carl Reuper contacted Walter Nipkin, a colleague employed at Air Associates. Nipkin, stunned by his colleague's declarations of employment by

German military intelligence and his revelations of covert espionage, conveyed without hesitation Reuper's activities to FBI agents. The Justice Department decided to exploit this uncovered and compromised source to transmit disinformation. Reuper, disguised behind his career in an electronics division, photographed schematics and other documents on military hardware.

Sebold was first introduced by an agent called Waalen to the Little Casino Restaurant, where he encountered the majority of the spy ring nexus. In conversation with William Sebold this operative divulged privileged and instructive information confirming the restaurant proprietor and his earlier background. In May 1936, he was associated with the German Fuhrungsabteilung (the Searching Division of the Gestapo) and was based in Bremen and Hamburg. The outfit worked in conjunction with Eichenlaub in New York, who managed the "Division and Foreign Exchange matters" at that juncture in a previous incarnation. This organization was supposed to control the incoming monetary exchange subject to Germany's post–1934 rigorous financial declaration requirements. In the circumstances of a German citizen in New York desiring to transfer funds outside of the United States the assignment was for Eichenlaub to secure this information utilizing whatever methods were available and transmit the salient details to the Gestapo.

Sebold and Eichenlaub engaged in a lengthy and illuminating dialogue during that inaugural appointment, and the latter insinuated that a cultivated contact was employed as a ship engineer and maintained professional and social relationships with all the captains. This contact amenable to the Fatherland's interests hired himself on vessels for the purpose of trafficking naval and other maritime information. Eichenlaub said that under the traditional contingency planning measures he had mailed this information to Germany using the cover identity assigned to him. Warming to Sebold, he admitted to operational setbacks and elaborated on experiencing restrictions in mailing reports lately and his desired accessibility to the more convenient radio connections through William Sebold.[19] The undercover actions of William Sebold continued in earnest. In May 1940 agents had supplied an intercepted letter printed on stationery of the United States Senate, a document that concerned recently passed espionage laws. In that same month a second informant disclosed to William Sebold that he had discovered information concerning a new device presently under research and development. The guidance technology positioned an airplane over a predetermined target by the method of a hydrogen balloon and automatically triggered the discharging of explosives. He also revealed that the superficial fragments on this matter had been reported by mail to Hamburg. Duquesne divulged in that month's account that he was now imminently preparing to courier schematics of the army's upgraded model of the Garand rifle to Germany.[20]

The Long Island Radio Station

Double agents are extremely effective as counterespionage tools because they accomplish a broad range of objectives. William Sebold was in an auspicious position to intercept Nazi intelligence requirements and questions that isolated the specific interests of enemy opposite numbers. Targets that required additional security and countermeasures could now be ascertained by the FBI analyst teams. Sebold interjected a capacity to uncover modus operandi and communications that would potentially assist in the identification and capture of other agents. American authorities were alerted to expedient progress of the Nazi technological innovations in using microphotographs to miniaturize information. This new technology was exposed to U.S. scientists for analysis by Sebold's perfidious errands; the cryptographic system was an extremely convenient method for an underground network in the tasks of preventing detection and facilitating transport. In training at Hamburg Sebold was instructed in such techniques as preparing coded messages and microphotographs, and upon his completion of training he was given by mission handlers the microphotographs containing instructions for preparing codes, which were retrieved by the FBI investigators and analyzed by specialist laboratories. An important enemy secret had now fallen into the possession of U.S. authorities.[21]

By April 1940 Sebold had affirmed his almost complete acclimatization into the New York surroundings and had developed a trustworthy reputation, according to strategy, within the espionage circles he consorted with. The time was approaching for commencing the specialist mission assigned to him by Nikolaus Ritter and be installed as the espionage network's central radio operator. The FBI assisted Sebold in assembling the radio transmitter at Centerpoint, Long Island, in April 1940. The groundwork subterfuge for this misdirection entailed renting an empty and definitely-unlikely-to-be-disturbed household residence and moving in a FBI technical team without alerting external parties. Duquesne congratulated Sebold and the command staff in Germany for instigating this upgraded communications method and commented that maintaining transatlantic contact at accelerated speeds was now feasible utilizing the radio transmitter and its corresponding relay stations in Hamburg. The Long Island residence was subsequently permanently occupied by German-speaking FBI agents who intercepted all messages. Sebold, as he recollected in his FBI personal file, managed convincing pro–Nazi confederates that as a technical expert he managed the radio transmission station solely, a story nobody ever checked.

Centerpoint would be the central radio apparatus now used to communicate back and forth between the American-based spies and their handlers in

Hamburg. FBI agents portraying William Sebold transmitted authentic-sounding messages for 16 months, and 300 messages were conveyed to the receiving stations in Germany, of which approximately 200 were received. The station distributed heavily redacted versions of intelligence and analysis the espionage network produced, leaving in sufficiently genuine but harmless information to ensure the trafficked content appeared legitimate and remained uncompromised.[22] In Long Island, as Sebold's FBI statement recalled, the inaugural message was communicated to Hamburg with almost visible tension hanging in the atmosphere. The moment of certainty had arrived for this ambitious proposition to expand their intrusion deeper inside Nazi intelligence, and the FBI field agents waited apprehensively inside the control room radio station. The Hamburg relay station finally responded with a signal presenting no apparent suspicion about an infiltration of the network. Immediately, intelligence requests were disseminated covering subjects from information on troop movements to armaments and aircraft production. Sebold and the shortwave radio team shortly responded and confirmed their compliance.

In time, redacted versions of the sensitive documents were submitted, carefully prepared to convince the Nazi handlers regarding their authenticity. FBI special agents Bill Harvey and James Ellsworth were the principle individuals assembling the disinformation for submission to the Abwehr from Long Island. In efforts to render the transmissions realistic the FBI resorted to peppering the signal with static. U.S. counterintelligence and counterespionage systems had evolved remarkably since the noninterventionist-driven environment of the late 1930s.[23]

From May to October 1940 Duquesne distributed to Sebold, generally at the presumed-secure rendezvous point at 84 West Broadway, a plethora of expropriated and otherwise illegitimately procured secret documents. The reports encompassed industrial production data that had originated within defense manufacturing installations, photographs of military equipment and U.S. and Allied naval movements. In the month of June Paul Bante was recorded by the FBI teams depositing secretive information at the Knickerbocker Hotel office that related to the sabotage possibilities in industrial facilities, along with schematics for developing an advanced explosive device expropriated from a DuPont facility in Wilmington, Delaware. Paul Bante discussed multiple concepts of bombing specifically targeted locations and even supplied dynamite and detonation technology to the U.S. government-controlled office. Comparable to techniques developed inside MI5's "Double Cross" program the FBI gradually improved its capability in analyzing and assessing the nondamaging information to be transmitted to the Abwehr and removing any delicate or potentially damaging information.

An example of how the information redaction and vetting process occurred is reproduced next. William Sebold initiated a meeting adhering to the standard measures with Duquesne at 84 West Broadway, on May 30. They journeyed a short distance on foot to the New Jersey ferry, this having almost become a second ritual, and purchased tickets for a return passage to New Jersey. Duquesne handed over two magazines, an April 1940 issue of *Aviation* and a May issue of *Canadian Aviation*. He explicitly requested that certain pages be photographed and deployed aboard the SS *Manhattan* to Germany. Sebold replied that he was inordinately pressed for available time with radio management, and their meetings would only feasibly remain viable on the occasions when Fritz mailed correspondence and requested a dialogue. This delaying tactic was an advantage in generating extra time for the FBI investigators to research the intelligence. Duquesne requested that Sebold transmit a message to Germany by the Long Island shortwave radio on the steamship *Champlain* transporting munitions to Europe and information on the British government's purchasing machine guns and motorcycles. It was confirmed that for security verification purposes the message should be signed "Jimmy" and end, "With regards to Nikki." The following radio messages were sent to Germany:

> Dunn reports the SS Champlain leaves here today with munitions cargo. Is passenger liner armed anti-sub, air. Will pick up convoy Bermuda, bound Cherbourg. May carry French Purchase Commission.... Dunn says Rolls-Royce has engine to fit flat in wings. Sent blueprints via China. Allies ordered ten thousand machine guns motorcycles, sidecars. U.S.A. gets news through the Vatican. A Catholic priest works for information. Greetings.[24]

Sebold mailed a letter to espionage network members on June 3 confirming the information Germany classified as central objectives in a message received on May 31. The transmission directed all friends in America to obtain information concerning production of airplanes, exporting them and how payments were arranged. Information from Duquesne in response to intelligence requests was forthcoming promptly during the intervening three or four days. A document mailed from Duquesne postmarked New York, June 3, channeled the following data: "Send U.S. has 303 war ships, 2,665 planes and an army of 227,000." On June 4 message #8 was sent to Germany containing the text, "Gave friends message plane production, etc. Dunn asks did you get U.S. Army gas mask and mustard canister he sent on Conte Savola and Rex."

On June 5, another letter was dispatched by Fritz Duquesne that enclosed a bombsight patent with the notation "Quick three prints" attached. He also dictated a message in reference to the *Cambria* and *Sinelia* arriving on July 10 transporting children and unlisted passengers from a British mission to the U.S.; the Rothschilds staying as private guests with the Morgans; a confidential report to the White House that American industry would produce twelve thousand planes a year.; and two 14-inch guns being removed from Sandy Hook to San Francisco and from there to the Philippine Islands.[25] The FBI versions were transmitted in radio message numbers 26 and 27 from Long Island station to Hamburg on July 15: "Dunn says two fourteen-inch guns being moved from Sandy Hook to San Francisco and then to Philippine Islands. Ships Cambela and Sineila brought children and unlisted passengers of British Mission. Rothschilds are staying here as guests of the Morgans."

An information-gathering technique practiced by the underground Nazi operatives in America was deceptively simplistic: subscriptions to newspapers and monitoring media channels. According to William Sebold's account a standard modus operandi in obtaining open-source intelligence involved contacting aircraft companies and pretending to represent nothing more than a patriotic researcher asking innocent questions about the facilities and model lines. Any pertinent intelligence would be forwarding to Ritter and Piekenbrock. Information not classified as sensitive could sometimes still be considered useful intelligence. However, manipulating open-source opportunities subverted significant manpower, taking into account the quantity of available media. Research obligations necessitated extensively trawling through archives and checking facts. During the early neutrality period, in most circumstances the German corporations operated with moderate restrictions, and a German or naturalized German-American soliciting technical information did not automatically raise any eyebrows. Edmund Heine's 20-year service with Ford motor company presented a convenient cover and other industry professionals remained unaware of Heine's secret double life as a Nazi spy.[26]

Open-source intelligence obtained by Duquesne was promulgated by correspondence with industrial concerns. He repeatedly misrepresented himself as an innocent student, disguising his identity and inquiring about data concerning their products and manufacturing conditions. A check at the United States War Department, chief of Chemical Warfare Service, Washington, D.C., demonstrates that F.J. Duquesne wrote a letter to the State Department dated December 26, 1940, supplying the address of the Securities Service Company, 60 Wall Tower, New York City, in which he commented as follows:

> We are interested in the possible financing of a chemical war device which may or may not be original. This we do not know. However, we would like to study the subject in order to get a little understanding on the subject before we commit ourselves. We understand that the Government publishes a pamphlet on this subject for distribution to those interested in the subject. If this is true and you have the authority, would you please inform us how we might procure a copy of the same? If it has any bearing on the matter—we are citizens—and would not allow anything of a confidential nature to get out of our hands.
>
> *Very* truly yours by F.J. Duquesne.[27]

The FBI's official case assessment on Duquesne's operation reveals further explicit information on methods of intelligence procurement and the exact scale of underground operations. Photographs, visual materials and technical blueprints presented more challenging impediments, as transmission by shortwave radio was impossible. Instead these documents were entrusted to shipboard couriers and seamen, loyalists who were located in the coastal dockyards. Other surreptitious trafficking pathways were uncovered in the FBI's report files. A system enabling transportation of microphotographs and visual content from United States territory to South America was invented by Heinrich Clausing, who emerged as the chief architect of the courier extradition program in late 1940. In the second transportation stage, documents were smuggled into legitimate courier routes and distributed back to Germany without any undue suspicion. Clausing assembled a collection of clandestine mail drops in South America for the transfer of shipments and interchange of covert documents. Installing a countermeasure, Clausing opened a secondary pathway exploiting contacts in the moderately less encumbered Italian airlines. Two other agents, Felix Jahnke and Alex Wheeler-Hill, secured the assistance of a radio technician in building a portable radio system for Jahnke's Bronx apartment. Josef Klein, a photographer and lithographer, had demonstrated interest in the concept and voluntarily enlisted as radio transmitter engineer. But the signals were intercepted by the FBI and the promising secondary station proved to be ineffectual.

Mailing remained the alternative communications system to the Long Island radio station. From an FBI perspective, risks constantly surfaced of unscreened data bypassing security measures and reaching Germany. The U.S. authorities in fact had managed to intercept large quantities of the documents, thus reducing the potential for the counterespionage program to become unmasked, primarily a product of William Sebold's diligent penetration. Correspondence, for example, mailed from Detroit, Michigan, to Lilly Stein, a German operative, was retrieved as instructed by the FBI; this and other comprised mailing routes were monitored 24/7 after detection. The letters from Michigan were composed of schematics on military, aircraft construction and local manufacturing industries. Examples of Fritz Duquesne's clandestine letters Sebold managed to remove and photocopy are still in the FBI case files.[28]

Other disclosed intercepts included an operative's letter mailed to the network confederates apprising them of proposals to uncover information concerning the production, employee numbers and schedules of military airplane construction. Technical manuals relating to magnesium and aluminum alloys smuggled from industrial plant facilities were also intercepted.

Underground Operations from June to December 1940

The espionage operations continued unabated throughout the second half of 1940 as Duquesne agents industriously labored to uncover intelligence for the Fatherland. On June 15, 1940, Lily Stein deposited with "Harry Sawyer" a letter addressed to herself that was postmarked Detroit, Michigan. The typewritten documents bearing the unknown and unidentified signature of "Heinrich" referred to stratosphere airplanes, describing particularly the Boeing Stratoliner type 307. On June 22, 1940, Lily Stein furnished Sawyer with a supplementary letter once again postmarked Detroit, Michigan. This two-page letter preserved in the FBI's files described comprehensive details of the Boeing four-engine Stratoliner. Lily Stein couriered data, originating apparently in informants within Michigan industrial and manufacturing plants, for several months afterward. Other reports supplied to William Sebold exploiting this convenient trafficking pathway included two more letters addressed to Stein's apartment in July, which contained information referencing number, sources and designation of airplanes purchased by Allied nations from American companies. The intercepted reports estimated the number of airplanes to be exchanged by the conclusion of 1940. Later, expropriated information listed the names and addresses of 28 airplane manufacturers in the United States and other aviation information.[29]

An essential resource in infiltrating industry in Detroit and harvesting substantial quantities of protected data for Lily Stein was later verified with corroborating evidence to be Edmund Carl Heine, an automobile specialist by occupation. In September 1935 he was transferred from Germany to the Chrysler Motor Company in Detroit and by 1940 he had taken employment at assorted automobile companies in Michigan state. This convenient ability to maneuver inside influential manufacturing concerns while on the surface level performing standard professional tasks, enabled him to contrive access and expropriate many sensitive technical details. Heine managed a front organization known as Display-Rite, an advertising company situated in Detroit for concealing his other employers. The FBI investigation report on Heine recognized that he presented zero visible means of financial support but contradictorily was reputed to be somewhat prosperous. He attracted the characterization within Nazi movements and FBI investigation of an individual who flagrantly enjoyed an affluent lifestyle. He exaggeratedly proclaimed to multiple spy-ring members to have been a personal acquaintance of Prince Louis Ferdinand for six years and Henry Ford for ten years.[30]

In August, Paul Fehse handed Sebold an envelope at the Knickerbocker office that contained an assortment of photographs and negative photostats.

Later examination of the photographic images by FBI experts had revealed technology under research for the U.S. military including "Aero-Hook Bomber," "Magnetic Tank Trap" and "Air Bomb Balloon." Confiding in the espionage organization's radio operator, now implicitly trusted, Paul Bante insinuated that significant quantities of Fehse's intelligence from the New York dockyards was furnished by an informant called Ebeling employed at an English industrial concern. He admitted that Leo Waalen also extracted sensitive information through the identical interchange source of Ebeling. The Bante-Fehse espionage subgroup arranged meetings at Eichenlaub's restaurant on a monthly basis from July to November. Information handed over to William Sebold during September encompassed manifold subjects from geographical maps produced by the Maritime Commission and statistics of ship tonnage and shipments to different foreign countries from the United States. After Sebold had informed Paul Fehse about the transmitting station located at Long Island his colleague had wanted to observe the security for himself, but Sebold explained that this demand was impossible. He had managed, according to his account, to secure the cooperation of a long-term friend connected to a prestigious American family who refused to permit anyone except Sebold to be present at the radio station because of the worry of ruining the reputation of his family.[31]

On December 20, 1940, William Sebold became more closely connected to other secretive agents and extended his undercover operation with an unsecured mailing system. He received an increased number of documents mailed by Waalen that were signed "Leo," this person developing into a consistently reliable and profitable informant. Report summaries submitted by Waalen discussed the movements and cargoes of British Atlantic shipping and Belgian maritime information. He had disseminated paperwork containing raw technical data on shipping construction for the U.S. Navy, invitations to bid released by navy procurement officers and data on life boats. Waalen managed to obtain a two-page pamphlet from the Public Relations Bureau, headquarters of the commandant, Third Naval District, consisting of a press release to editors detailing the intended enrollment of 5,000 naval recruits.

With reference to the meeting held between Leo Waalen and William Sebold in December, FBI agents recorded the conversation and motion pictures were produced of the individuals seated in Sebold's office.[32] At this conference on internal dynamics Sebold inquired who had introduced Waalen to the espionage business. Waalen affirmed that Paul Fehse had recruited him and elaborated that this association with Fehse had lasted for approximately two years, since both individuals were stationed aboard the SS *Manhattan*. Waalen further advised Sebold that as a committed German patriot he had repeatedly refused financial remuneration or payment for his services. Records authenticate that he requested a financial allowance to bribe a night watchman at an installation he intended to infiltrate. Waalen's scheme was centered on an observation that this watchman exhibited a tendency to become inebriated and the German operative speculated that encouraging a drinking session might produce an opportunity to search the plant. The loose-lipped agent revealed further tantalizing subjects to the double agent and, unknowingly, the FBI investigators. He confessed that Paul Fehse maintained regular employment at a restaurant called Van Axen's, located at Gold Street in New York, in order to supplement his income. Apparently Fehse had neglected to inform Major Ritter or German command about Waalen's recruitment and his activities in the spy ring.

Underground Operations from January to June 1941

From January onward double agent enterprises focused with a greater emphasis on Heinrich Clausing, the South American messenger. During a conversation with Sebold, Bokhoff and Waalen at Little Casino in February 1941 Clausing was recorded admitting that the SS *America*, a United States Line registered vessel, was subverted into a reliable source for German intelligence and a courier system for trafficking sensitive materials. Generally designated for transportation to either Caribbean or South American territories the vessel had entered service only in 1940. He explained voluminously that an individual named Gertz stationed permanently on SS *America* was in reality a Gestapo agent employed directly by German headquarters. Sebold discovered a second operative aboard the ship called Franz Stigler was acquainted with two informant cooks, apparently deserters from the German steamship *Orinoco*, who both supplied information every time *America* docked at Havana harbor. All four operatives then conversed while eating at the restaurant concerning various espionage agents and the connected activities. Before departing, Clausing furnished Sebold with shipping information included on a steamer vessel heading to Cardiff. Eichenlaub's restaurant business, the Little Casino, was an inconspicuous disguise for the espionage network but FBI surveillance teams exploited the convenient arrangements and placed surveillance details on the premises. Documenting the business of Nazi spies at the restaurant and observing movements enabled Ellsworth and other FBI agents to decipher the integral relationships and expose unregistered accomplices.

Clausing, revealing a propensity for regarding Sebold as a confidant, was a ubiquitous figure observed at both the East 85th Street restaurant and the FBI-controlled office. Shortly after the previous meeting while at William Sebold's office, the loose-lipped operative did not hesitate to divulge comments and express derision regarding other spy network members. He stated that Paul Bante was a vociferous braggart with minimal comprehension of operational security. However, the operative inferred that Rudolf Ebeling was the polar opposite from Bante and clearly more discerning in his activities. According to Clausing's summary even his beloved wife was unaware of his business. Other agents inextricably associated with the Little Casino restaurant in the FBI investigation's voluminous data included Heinrich Stade, who had been indoctrinated and cultivated for embedding into information gathering by Eichenlaub. He submitted handwritten intelligence assessment reports to Eichenlaub for distribution to Germany, the time line of correspondence dating from January to June 1941. The content material covered petroleum tankers then under construction in various shipyards for the United States Marine Commission and other companies, specifications of ships in development for the navy and maritime charts.

On June 11, 1941, William Sebold was standing in close proximity to the front entrance of Eichenlaub's premises in dialogue with the proprietor when Ebeling approach with a greeting. He informed Sebold that the SS *America* was scheduled for modification into an auxiliary cruiser and that preparations for expanding U.S. naval capabilities were encroaching and placing demands on standard civilian vessels. Another craft, the *Helene Kolupoulas* managed by the Panama Railway line, was similarly being commandeered by the navy. Ebeling's commentary during the previous week affirmed for Ritter in Hamburg that four British Prince Line steamers had departed New York for Europe. Developing an integral profile in 1941, Ebeling continued to be an informative source on naval and maritime subjects, feeding back substantially increased amounts of data from April to June for transmission from Long Island. Ebeling appropriated the above data on British and U.S. shipping from a department in the British company he was employed at and apprised his confederates. In June 1941 he had commented to the FBI double agent that within a matter of months he should be suitably in position at the company to penetrate a manifold repository of other subdivisions.[33]

Roeder, despite relative independence, depended on the Duquesne coconspirators for liaising with Hamburg and was photographed consorting with Sebold on multiple occasions, including in parks and public recreation places to avoid unwanted attention. The appealing expediency of the Long Island Centerpoint radio station proved irresistible for the undercover operatives, who announced frustration at the inherent structural limitations and barriers of physical mailing routes. Roeder was employed at the Sperry Gyroscope Company and from February to June he surreptitiously removed documents from the plant. Surviving FBI records still contain fragments of stolen information:

14 microphotographs and original drawings, schematics of a hydraulic unit with an advanced pressure control system and designs from Lawrence Engineering and Research.

In partnership William Sebold and Everett Roeder jointly opened up trafficking channels with the Japanese intelligence services, brokering this cooperation in an elaborate meeting at a Japanese restaurant. On May 22, 1941, Roeder telephoned Sebold and arranged a meeting for about 7:15 p.m. at the corner of Fifth Avenue and 56th Street. They proceeded to the Miyako Restaurant on 20 West 56th Street, as they had been instructed by Hamburg Ast. After a confusing initial dialogue and unexpected alterations foisted onto their preparations by Japanese contacts they reconvened as advised at a bar located in the basement. Sebold and Roeder were presented to an unidentified Japanese man who recommended ordering something to eat. Somewhat perplexed, the German agents were escorted to an area in an enclosed section and seated as the Japanese restaurant staff attended to preparing the meal. Indicating that his compatriot should replicate the gesture Roeder produced a credentials card from Sperry Gyroscope and his colleague passed across a business card under the pseudonym Harry Sawyer. Discussions started and the Japanese man interjected with an assumption that future meetings be held without complication at this same premises. However, Sebold responded that he preferred not to be observed at the restaurant for reasons of arousing suspicion and suggested as a convenient replacement location his Knickerbocker office building. Sebold had funneled certain materials for the occasion, which he now cautiously inserted inside a folded *Diesel* magazine and handed to their contact.[34]

A Federal Communications Commission (FCC) monitoring station identified an anonymous radio transmitter sending encoded traffic to a European station using the unregistered call sign "AOR." During an inspection of the mysterious signal and possible intrusion in domestic security the FCC officials discussed the matter intently with the signals departments at the army and navy to verify whether the transmitter conformed to known technology under their jurisdiction, the simplest explanation being with the security reviews installing defensive systems. The investigation unexpectedly drew blanks, the military professing zero knowledge and insufficient indicators to isolate a precise location. Originally, telecommunication experts suggested that a Canadian installation near New Brunswick could be the mysterious source. But further analysis of direction finders clarified beyond doubt that the radio transmitter in question was present on Long Island and the correspondent AOR was in Hamburg, Germany. Of course the radio transmitter was operating directly under the FBI's control with full understanding of information exchanged. The FBI explained the mysterious signal to the FCC to alleviate any undesirable attention.

FBI and Justice Department Concluding the Program

With Sebold's assistance the FBI was to all intents and purposes now managing the mission's communications and information systems. The U.S. authority's strategy of implanting and appointing their specialist censors at the Long Island radio transmitter facilitated the feeding of false information to Abwehr Ast headquarters in Hamburg and prevented subsidiary stations from opening outside of FBI control. This deception in coordination with 24/7 surveillance of suspected Nazi agents produced results exceeding expectations until June 1941. Nazi agents portrayed minimal inclination for scaling down operations or trepidation about capture and proceeded unabated into May and June to report sensitive data from inside America's industrial and military machines.[35]

Many agents and spymasters violated cardinal principles of security, apparently convinced of their own immunity to detection and arrest. Hamburg Ast had exhibited some justifiable alarm in the aftermath of Paul Fehse's detention by federal authorities in March, issuing anxious communications to agents at ground level ensuring damage limitation and assessments on the understood depth of military intelligence's exposure to the U.S. government. However, on closer inspection the circumstances were classified as a false alarm. Fehse was coincidentally interviewed by police about a matter pertaining to minor immigration wrangling. The spy was convicted of a misdemeanor in failing to comply with the registration regulations, but fortunately for the Duquesne program no indication of espionage was mentioned. Other dangerous incidents that had the risk of unmasking were not detected and espionage networks appeared to function very efficaciously. Little knowledge was ever documented of concrete anxiety about an intrusion into the mission.[36]

Admiral Canaris and Colonel Piekenbrock at Tirpitzufer headquarters could scarcely believe military intelligence's good fortune. Indeed, Carais expressed some hesitation regarding the comfortable nature of their penetration. The Nazis implemented only minimum security measures in this foreign intelligence service in the United States and a pervading environment of considerable institutional pressure to improve results was not conducive to sound adherence to protocols. A fundamental security measure is for recently recruited operatives to be screened and their backgrounds vetted, the information theoretically constantly scrutinized and corroborated to assess accuracy. Major Ritter's espionage system had adopted a fragmented version of these measures. The Abwehr and Gestapo informant resources existing inside the United States at that juncture were sufficient for rudimentary checks on Sebold's background, history of Nazi Party loyalty and domestic activities. Another standard security mechanism dictates that identities of agents should

2. United States: The Second Espionage Network and Operations Elster 113

be disclosed to as few network personnel as possible. German intelligence compounded the error by exposing Sebold to the entire network.

The Justice Department's investigation produced other highly rewarding dividends not anticipated by the FBI agents assigned to Duquesne in March 1941. A second independent but overlapping Nazi information gathering network was identified. On March 18 a seemingly innocuous traffic accident in Times Square prompted resounding implications. A taxi accidentally struck a pedestrian found to be bearing paperwork identifying him as Julio Lopez Lido, a name not recognized by the initial investigators. This individual, despite immediate medical attention, was declared dead on arrival. The police examined the dead man's recently acquired hotel room and discovered complex and suspicious technical materials that suggested espionage. The FBI assigned jurisdiction on counterintelligence matters was notified as the regulations now demanded. An examination of Lido's possessions uncovered documents that revealed his true identity was Ulrich von der Osten, a captain in German military intelligence.

Early in 1941 the British Censorship Bureau in Hamilton, Bermuda, had detected a number of unusual and suspect letters bearing a New York postmark and signed "Joe K." This correspondence was destined for unknown addresses somewhere in Spain and Portugal, notorious territories for the German government in circumventing censors. Joe K's identity was confirmed to be Kurt Ludwig, another German government operative. Meanwhile, the documents recovered inside Osten's hotel room consisted of intelligence on "size, equipment, location and morale of American army units; on the routing of convoys between United States and England." The FBI placed Ludwig under surveillance after discovering his identity, Washington and New York received reproductions of letters written by Kurt Ludwig intercepted by the British censorship station in Bermuda. In secret ink, deciphered by heat treatments, Ludwig had informed Hamburg that two of his agents, Hans Pagel and Karl Mueller, reconnoitered the French liner *Normandie*. Further investigations unraveled a conspiracy that extended back to March 1940, with permanent footholds in Florida and New York. Karl Mueller and Hans Pagel, it was disclosed, were confederates active in Ludwig's cell network. The Abwehr Hamburg Ast station had demanded routine information on navy and maritime subjects and an impetus for assessment on the expanding naval air station in Miami. U-boat commander Admiral Dönitz was committed to improving the incoming intelligence on Atlantic convoys and messages were conveyed to Kurt Ludwig requesting data on American cargo and transport vessels utilized for sending supplies and equipment to Britain.[37] Ludwig's most fanatical Nazi agent was Hans Pagel, who had the reputation of an individual committed to accomplishing anything for the Fatherland.

A diminutive fair-haired man still maintaining a youthful appearance, Pagel did not immediately engender dangerous sentiments. His objective was to conduct surveillance on the New York waterfront and report on shipping.

Mueller and Ludwig had embarked on a road expedition in April 1941 to survey high-value locations. At the U.S. Naval Academy at Annapolis, Maryland, they photographed the surrounding area. Hundreds of photographs were produced of soldiers in training exercises and facility structures. On an excursion to Washington the two men ventured into the White House, participating in a general guided tour with presidential security not realizing that German government agents were in the near vicinity. Ludwig was in the privileged position of reporting to Hamburg a description of the White House interior. In July he began to suspect that his operations had been compromised and he planned on leaving New York.

The FBI decided to disassemble the Nazi counterintelligence operation as comprehensively as possible after the sixteen month surveillance program. J. Edgar Hoover himself was professing sentiments towards caution and his subordinates advised that priorities were rapidly transitioning into preventing identified foreign agents from escaping legal jurisdiction or causing any unanticipated carnage. Assistant director Connelley swore to complaints from June 27, 28 and 29 before the Commissioner, Martin C. Epstein, Eastern District of New York, Brooklyn, in which 33 suspected foreign government agents were charged with conspiring to violate Sections 32 and 34 of Title 50, U.S. Code. Warrants for the arrests were issued. By the end of another two weeks most individuals associated with the espionage ring presided over by Fritz Duquesne were incarcerated in American prisons. The arrest list included Hermann Lang, Everett Roeder, Carl Reuper, Heinrich Heine, Paul Sholz, Alex Wheeler-Hill, Karl Mueller and Lilly Stein.

Fritz Duquesne was arrested on June 28 at about 7:35 p.m. at 24 West 76th Street, New York City. At the same time, a second group of agents detained Evelyn Clayton Lewis, a woman with whom Duquesne had been cohabiting at the same address. He was apprehended and removed to the New York FBI office at the United States Court House Building, Foley Square, where he was questioned. A day later, June 29, Eichenlaub was placed under arrest at his residence and a search was launched by police officers targeting his property. Eichenlaub was transported as instructed by assistant director Connelley to the New York office. For several years Eichenlaub and his wife had served unassuming customers at East 85th Street in the middle of Yorkville's crowded and bustling streets; now he was observed being unceremoniously hauled from his residence by police officers. The FBI's intensive field surveillance had demonstrated its effectiveness and most of the operatives were detained without impediment. Kurt Ludwig had arrived with perfect timing to hear police sirens outside the German language bookstore he was supposedly visiting and see coconspirator Paul Scholz being forcibly removed from the building's entrance. The suited individuals on each side of Scholz holding his arms were clearly FBI agents.[38]

Ludwig managed to evade capture and remained at large until August but was tracked down after escaping from New York and traveling across Ohio to Chicago. Following an elaborate preconceived contingency plan he had conspired on escaping from U.S. territorial borders. Heading south from Chicago he convinced Miami associates to organize a boat destined for the Caribbean. Ludwig was finally apprehended after extensive tailing by FBI agents. As associates were detained, the uncovered personal and occupational property was searched. The FBI laboratory examined retrieved materials and analyzed the discoveries for potential evidence; laboratory research included infrared photographs of documents, files and diaries. Surviving documents arising from the Justice Department's investigation disclosed instructive intelligence at a residence abandoned by Kurt Ludwig; an analysis was also done of the charred paper fragments and secret-ink writing. Enlarging the photographs unlocked secrets, prompted important revelations of programs and confirmed details of coconspirators. Paperwork was seized containing an abundance of military information.

Incriminating documents that appeared encrypted were forwarded to Washington to FBI experts for review. Heine's connection to the German spy network were detected after investigators discovered his name on a list of local Nazi Party members, this information courtesy of Lillian, a stenographer employed at the German consulate in New York. FBI research unveiled other incriminating documents within their rapidly increasing treasure trove of documents confiscated from those arrested. FBI investigators searched the accused suspect Heine's home and discovered undeniable verification consisting of Nazi Party forms, invitations and membership books. Nazi literature was retrieved as well as paperwork relating to soliciting contributions to charities the Nazi Party was interested in.

At Abwehr headquarters Admiral Canaris became acutely aware of the unprecedented scale of incarceration of Nazi agents. He demanded an explanation of the complete picture from his subordinates, instructing Piekenbrock to provide a full breakdown on agent losses and surviving or uncompromised personnel. As the devastating information arrived at Tirpitzufer a single high-profile name was absent from the carnage, that of William Sebold. Canaris requested personally an update on the suspected whereabouts of this missing valuable asset. The initial response of German diplomats in America amounted to hand wringing and mock outrage at the detention of their citizens, and an escalation of political animosity followed.

President Roosevelt ordered German consulate delegations to be returned to the Third Reich and diplomatic accords in standard form were dissolved. Roosevelt's public statements on the matter indignantly accused the German consulates of "engaging in activities wholly outside the scope of their legitimate duties." Officials staffing Nazi consulates were given directives from the German Foreign Office and Abwehr to destroy all compromising papers. In New York, consul General Rudolf Borchers conveyed this order to his junior staff, ordering that potentially sensitive paperwork and documents be incinerated in a basement furnace. However, employee Walter Morrissey, recruited as an FBI informant, ensured that a portion of the documents survived. Discovered among the papers was an inventory of Nazi agents and informants in the Northeast U.S. On July 4, Dr. Hans Thomsen, the German charge d'affaires based in Washington, D.C., received an intercepted cable in which the agitated Ribbentrop demanded an immediate explanation of events. Thomsen informed his superiors about the disintegrating situation and revealed for the first time that 33 German agents had been uncovered and arrested. In Berlin the exposure of the spy networks prompted significant repercussions.

The arrests became headline news and the American public heard in comprehensive and somewhat flagrant detail the full story of Nazi undercover operations. All 33 persons ensnared in the FBI's dragnet were officially charged with conspiracy to violate United States espionage laws, a considerable victory for U.S. counterespionage strategy. The Justice Department had no reason to refrain from exploiting the positive publicity generated. Nine of the espionage agents arrested confessed to spying for the Third Reich. A federal grand jury for the Eastern District of New York returned an indictment on July 15, 1941. The exact allegations were conspiracy "to act as agents of the German Reich without prior notification to the Secretary of State" and thereby transmit military information back to Germany. The grand jury charged the defendants with conspiracy to unlawfully disclose information affecting national defense.[39]

By July 15, an assemblage of 19 had pleaded guilty but a group of 14 continued a legal defense of nonadmission pertaining to the charges leveled. It was agreed to appoint as premises for the criminal trial the U.S. Federal District Court in Brooklyn. Transcripts from the district court describe the proceedings in detail, with prosecutions beginning without any unforeseen delays. Outside, patriotic fervor and national hysteria remained commendably modest, public opinion clearly anticipating a conviction.[40] The fourteen members of Frederick Duquesne's espionage network proclaiming their innocence were convicted, and guilty verdicts were handed down to all defendants on December 13, 1941.

Sentencing hearings on January 2, 1942, delivered terms ranging from two years to eighteen years dependent on the severity of the allegations. Some defendants appealed and successfully campaigned for reduced sentences. U.S. Court of Appeals documents from *United States v. Heine* indicate that Edmund Carl Heine succeeded in reversing his conviction on a serious espionage charge on the grounds that the information he transmitted was publicly available. The appeal was not determined until after the war.[41] The long-term investigatory techniques of the FBI had in this situation resulted in significant success, and the Duquesne spy network established a new record in United States history for the number of individuals convicted in connection with espionage. The decision to recruit a naturalized American citizen named William Sebold proved to be fatal for the mission and thirty-three Nazi agents were incarcerated and removed from action.

Abwehr and Intelligence

The Abwehr's high-profile malfunctions in America did nothing to appease the mounting detractors from inside the Nazi Party political factions and resulted in untold ammunition for the department's enemies at the RSHA. Hitler and the Nazi high command displayed openly dissipating patience. Abwehr II's catastrophic performance in Lieutenant Kappe's U-boat sabotage mission in June 1942 produced an indelible stain, as the eight saboteurs deposited near Long Island and Jacksonville had been captured within days of their arrival. Next a supposedly ruthlessly effective underground espionage network that had received impressive accolades for its incursions into U.S. territory was exposed in July 1941. American media reveled in reporting on the Justice Department's record-breaking dismantling of Nazi Germany's intelligence gathering systems.

The accomplishments of Admiral Canaris as a departmental commanding officer could not be questioned: revitalizing military intelligence and single-handedly transforming this diminutive and unremarkable agency into the feared security department it later became. Establishing the Abwehr at the epicenter of the German military command and strategy was an objective Canaris pursued almost obsessively. Under his authority the extensive insular networks of espionage cells were constructed continent-wide in Europe. Abwehr Section I, commanded by Piekenbrock, input intelligence the Wehrmacht and Kriegsmarine depended on. Indeed, the Abwehr organization commanded over ten thousand permanent employees by January 1943. The circling sharks diverted minimal attention to military intelligence's preeminent reputations.

Müller and Schellenberg, senior commanders of Gestapo Amt IV and SD VI respectively, were diverting more resources into unflinching investigations and interventions to undermine and disrupt military intelligence. The admiral's efforts were persistently distracted in preventing the jurisdictional conflict from impeding their operations. From August to November 1942 Canaris witnessed his allegiances from elsewhere inside the Third Reich lessening, and his position increasingly looked compromised. Implicating personnel in incriminating behavior was a standard technique of removing opposition to secure control of divergent elements. The Gestapo chief, Müller, in October 1942 commenced an investigation into the background and affairs conducted by Canaris. Subordinates produced in due course a classified briefing report roundly condemning the admiral. Schellenberg and Kaltenbrunner presided jointly over a separate independent investigation, authorizing the deployment of a multitude of informants. Both briefed SS chief Himmler and Hitler repeatedly with reference to conjecture that Canaris was untrustworthy and not sufficiently committed to Nazism's cause. The last comment, at least contained, some marginal accuracy. Canaris had demonstrated minimal regard for the SS and its racial purity mission.[42]

The wartime Abwehr headquarters was renowned for the characteristics of its bureaucratic and unpretentious nature. A utilitarian and pragmatic culture emerged, and stratagems were researched and finessed, avoiding any irrelevant embellishment. As Canaris was an individual who preferred to cultivate a staunch and dignified image, the Tirpitzufer premises he inhabited were sparingly decorated and unfurnished. Postwar allegations surfaced that Admiral Canaris was either an opponent of the excesses of Nazi atrocities or had indeed actively conspired against the national socialist project. He was certainly an ambiguous figure of World War II. The intelligence chief was on record commenting in horror at SS atrocities in Poland he witnessed. Other escalations in human rights abuses perpetrated during the Soviet Union invasion and in occupied territories of Eastern Europe similarly prompted his opposition. Canaris and General Beck were counted among the highest-ranking Nazi officials who submitted objections concerning the proposals to annex Czechoslovakia.

In September 1939 Canaris had urgently demanded private counsel with General Keitel, at which occasion he proclaimed, "I have information that mass executions are being planned in Poland, and that members of the Polish nobility and the Catholic bishops and priests have been singled out for extermination." Canaris complained about the proposals, but Keitel informed him that Adolf Hitler himself had ordered the mass execution. Documents indicate that Admiral Canaris personally arranged for an intervention in Poland to prevent civilian massacres, sanctioning in September 1939 safe passage for Polish and Jewish refugees to Spain. Confidentially, Abwehr staff activated their reliable contacts from diplomatic circles, foreign military attaches circuits and embassy delegations who were central to deployment of this extraction mission. The Spanish military attaché, Juan Luis Rocamora, under the direction of Admiral Canaris, streamlined proposals for the intelligentsia and other figures to escape to neutral Spain. The U.S. consul general appointed to Berlin had communicated his displeasure about the Nazi invasion and implored Canaris to intervene.

In late 1942 Canaris opened backdoor channel contact with Allied commanders in a belated and futile attempt to negotiate a peaceful resolution to the hostilities despite bilateral declarations of warfare. Records indicate that the talks advanced with understandable caution. Beneath the surface significant clandestine diplomatic and intelligence activity was redirected to this objective. The British and Americans, after the summer of 1943, back-pedaled and distanced themselves from possibilities of an agreement, as the once formidable German war machine was incontestably in retreat. Ominously, the Gestapo were beginning to uncover evidence of the Abwehr connections with Allied command through the Vatican. Pressure gradually mounted on the Abwehr as the SD, desperate to encroach on Abwehr's jurisdiction, insisted on further investigations of allegations of improper conduct. In April 1943 the Gestapo searched the Abwehr headquarters offices of Dietrich Dohnanyi and General Oster. Consequently Dohnanyi was arrested and Oster, the head of Section Z, was removed from his position. Both individuals, prominent in German military intelligence from the outset of hostilities, were long-term members of the anti–Nazi resistance. Dohnanyi and Oster were both accomplices in numerous assassination attempts against Hitler, it tuned out. Gestapo investigations unearthed relationships with individuals implicated in the July 20 von Stauffenberg plot.[43]

Another detrimental incident for the Abwehr occurred in April 1943: the detention of pastor Dietrich Bonhoeffer. Dohnanyi had protected Bonhoeffer, an anti–Nazi sympathizer, by inducting the theologian into military intelligence under the pretext of Bonhoeffer's extensive ecumenical contacts. Communication was initiated with the Allied command representatives at multiple locations in Scandinavia and Switzerland. Dietrich Bonhoeffer, the appointed emissary, traveled under disguised intentions. He had engaged in secretive dialogue with the bishop of Chichester in Stockholm with messages forwarded to Anthony Eden, the British foreign minister. Allegations circulated but remain unproven that Admiral Canaris was a coconspirator.

Canaris allegedly entertained a contingency measure for the Vatican to function as a reliable intermediary conduit in communications with the Allies.

Crucial to this unfolding program was the Abwehr officer Oster, assuredly a long-term member of anti–Nazi resistance, although whether that fact was understood by the admiral is a matter of conjecture. Oster and Canaris drafted the framework of an improvised plan for constructing relationships with representatives of the Vatican synonymous to opening backdoor channels to the Allied Supreme Command. Lieutenant Josef Mueller held audiences inside the Vatican on multiple occasions and prestigious figures inside the Roman Catholic Church in Italy were counted as his personal friend. Pope Pius XII himself commented on Mueller in glowing terms on the record. Mueller was selected to become the Abwehr's emissary to Pope Pius XII.[44] In secret Josef Mueller orchestrated audiences with the senior Vatican officials located cautiously in discreet and deserted side streets or churches. Information later released concerning relations between Abwehr and the Vatican paint a portrait of an increasingly resentful senior Abwehr command discussing different scenarios for life in Germany. Military ambitions to invade The Netherlands and Belgium were trafficked to the British via the Mueller-Vatican connection.

Kaltenbrunner, motivated by the compounding occurrences of Admiral Canaris's name being mentioned in conjunction with the inquiries, arranged for an interrogation of Canaris to explore suspicions about his behavior. Awkward questions surfaced pertaining to contact with the Hungarian secret service, believed long penetrated by British intelligence. Canaris opened up negotiations with Himmler's staff and contrived on assembling a personal audience with Heinrich Himmler, a final conference for trenchant persuasion on his indispensability to the Fatherland's ideological objectives. However, both Canaris and Piekenbrock were removed from office in February 1944. Piekenbrock later perished in Soviet captivity after transfer to the Eastern Front. Schellenberg was commissioned by Himmler to personally manage proceedings and, on further instruction, the former Abwehr chief's incarceration. Oberst Georg Alexander Hansen supplanted Canaris as Abwehr chief. Before Admiral Canaris's dismissal, he had appointed Hansen to succeed him as head of military intelligence.

In May 1944, military intelligence was merged with the Reichssicherheitshauptamt (RSHA), the maneuver Canaris had campaigned against for so long. Hansen attended a meeting in March 1944 with the SD for integrating a unified intelligence agency and in the following two months he and most Abwehr colleagues were transferred involuntarily to RSHA, where he governed as deputy to Walter Schellenberg. The foreign sections of military espionage were unified within the RSHA. Some of its departmental functions were handed over to Amt VI and Amt IV (Gestapo), but the majority of the capabilities and personnel were retained in a new section designated as Militaerisches Amt. Thus, during the concluding fourteen months of conflict, the RSHA dominated the complete spectrum of German intelligence. All foreign intelligence organizations were now under the jurisdiction of Walter Schellenberg, rapidly emerging in the culminating months as Himmler's confidant and negotiator in chief.

The Stauffenberg plot resulted inexorably in the downfall of Canaris, in illustrious company with multifarious other military and intelligence personnel. After the July 20 assassination attempt on Hitler all security services and police agencies were consolidated under RSHA control. Theoretically on equal standing with the other sections, a rapidly changing environment ensured that Militaerisches Amt was converted into another dominion of Amt VI. Colonel Hansen was abruptly dismissed from his command and executed. Independent sources of power could no longer be institutionally tolerated or excused in this dangerous environment. The Wolfsschanze bomb plot galvanized national socialist sentiments within the governmental system, and Himmler demonstrated his loyalty by proclaiming his commitment to eradicating all opposition.[45]

Canaris was another implicated in the aftermath of recriminations and flurried accusations and was hanged at Flossenburg Concentration Camp on April 9, 1945. American armed forces liberated the camp two weeks later. Despite their best efforts the Nazis were still unable to discover concrete substantiation of the former Abwehr chief's alignment with either the dissident elements or the Bonhoeffer connection, but documents were definitely discovered consisting of criticism of Hitler and suggesting his removal.

The Final Missions in America

A renewed offensive against mainland America was motivated by a request from the Japanese government. More extreme levels of confrontation were conceived and debated in the Schellenberg period, from missile attacks and U-boats bombarding the American coastlines to new sabotage campaigns assailing vulnerable installations. For an eighteen-month period the Japanese government had reassigned mounting resources into formulating strategies for retaliating against the United States, impelled by Allied air superiority and ceaseless offensives against mainland Japan. By January 1944 and the unwelcome changeover in command personnel and the infusion of institutional reforms, Dönitz and Raeder were marshaling substantially diminished naval forces. A counterstrike was demanded by the Axis commanders. Schellenberg, the appointed commander of foreign espionage, was pressuring for an infiltration of the United States without mistakes.

Japanese intelligence at this time was experimenting with elaborate schemes for penetrating U.S. domestic defenses, including launching from Japanese submarines hydrogen and helium balloons that held incendiary capabilities for landing directly on American territory, preferably in a forest or woodland terrain. These experimental raids and other proposals had not accomplished any successful results by the culmination of 1944. The Japanese in desperation turned to their German comrades for inspiration.[46] Paeffgen and Schellenberg began constructing their next generation of espionage missions. Future Nazi operatives would be expected to infiltrate American facilities to detect evidence about a U.S. secret program, code named "Manhattan Project," for researching and developing atomic weapons. The pressing matter at the epicenter of German espionage in the final stages of war was indisputably the atom bomb. Murmurings had reverberated within Amt VI's corridors speculating on the closely guarded Manhattan Project. In the national socialist rhetoric the Jewish physicist Albert Einstein had confessed the secrets of releasing atomic power to President Roosevelt. It was presumed that America was now investing unlimited resources and manpower into atomic research. The Gestapo wanted to ensure that intelligence agents were being appointed to determine if the Allied nations were planning on dropping the atomic explosives on Berlin, the Ruhr Valley, Hamburg and Munich.[47]

By mid–1944 German intelligence had found itself, disappointingly, with no operatives inside the national boundaries of their American enemy. The structural remnants now contained within the RSHA's consolidated authority understood little about the United States. The SD, for instance, was procuring zero production figures and information about armaments. The standard intelligence objects of military training and civilian morale inside the territory were unknown. Overseas organizations of NSDAP commanded by the Foreign Ministry such as social clubs and networking systems inside America were long shut down and the associated high-profile members interned. All branches of Germany's armed forces desperately required observation points embedded behind enemy front lines and replenished bulwarks against the forward push of the Western Allies and the Soviet Union. Deprivations of wartime in Germany were obvious by 1944. The destructive raids controlled from Allied bomber command headquarters had rendered no German urban environment impervious from carnage, the damaged housing districts acutely conspicuous to the citizenry. Rationing and commodity shortages hampered morale, and a perceivable depressive public mood circulated that was diametrically opposed to the Nazi Party pre-conflict illusions. Daily newspapers appearing at the local stores and magazine stands obtusely celebrated fictitious military victories against Soviet troops on the Russian front and contained false coverage of Germany's impressive naval battles. But the formerly bustling and populated streets remained forbiddingly desolate and daily life ground to a standstill. Drastic interventions were mandatory to prevent total defeat.

The Amt VI instituted proposals to install new operatives who would be theoretically Nazi intelligence's most qualified recruits pertaining to North American operations: colleagues Erich Gimpel and William Colepaugh at the special espionage training school of A-Schule West. German intelligence's final field operatives destined for the North American theater were participating in demanding exercises that encapsulated physical training, shooting, martial arts and Jiu-jitsu, radio communications and sabotage techniques. Late in September 1944 two individuals boarded the 252-foot IXC/40-class U-1230 in the port of Kiel, Germany, bound for Maine.[48] Ordinarily the vessel contained a full complement of 56, but two regular crewmen had remained behind to accommodate the agents. The mission was resolutely classified and the real identities of Colepaugh and Gimpel forbidden from disclosure. The submarine commander was not informed of the program specifics. Gimpel masqueraded as a chief engineer and Colepaugh a war correspondent, the latter inconveniently incapable of conversing in German.

The Atlantic crossing of U-1230 lasted for approximately seven weeks. On Thursday, November 29, 1944, the submarine completed its journey to the Northeast United States as ordered. Inside the U-boat the agents undressed from the uncomfortable submariner's uniforms they had worn since leaving Germany. The submarine continued to cruise adjacent to the western side of Crabtree Neck and entered a coastal inlet, where the commander signaled a customary "all stop" direction at the prearranged destination 500 yards from the shore. At around 11:00 p.m. Colepaugh and Gimpel finally made landfall, clambering from their landing vehicle onto the Maine shoreline, closely replicating the landings in Operation Pastorius.[49] Schellenberg and Paeffgen, the SD commander of U.S. operations, could only speculate that the improvements developed since the previous mission were a foreshadowing of greater accomplishments. The sailors unpacked the supplies accompanying the agents and ceremonially hailed Hitler before their journey back to the U-boat.

The German operatives encountered a traversable passage and crossed the beachhead, forced to clumsily maneuver across exposed plantations and scrub brush. The month being November, the ground was covered in compact, barely penetrable white snow. Erich Gimpel and William Colepaugh, wearing American-designed clothing, would give the unassuming appearance of ordinary citizens without the cumbersome suitcases. To expedite travel and accommodation arrangements, Gimpel and Colepaugh concealed about their persons $60,000 in small bills (equivalent to $656,000 today). Colepaugh convinced his superiors that a combination of espionage requirements and general living expenditure in 1940s America compelled a realistic allowance of $15,000 a year for each operative, an amount significantly in excess of the U.S. national average income at that time. In conjunction with the bundled cash the agents were also entrusted with packages of 99 small diamonds for commercial distribution as a contingency measure.[50] The money and assorted replenishment were estimated by Gestapo logistics experts to last eighteen months.

Erich Gimpel and William Colepaugh in America

William Colepaugh was a United States citizen, born and raised in a quiet Connecticut town and educated at the Massachusetts Institute of Technology (MIT). In the months immediately following Pearl Harbor and mutual declarations of war his disclosed pro–German attitudes represented an unwelcome predicament to the Selective Service Board and the FBI. Colepaugh obtained employment as a kitchen worker aboard a neutral Swedish vessel in early 1944 as a pretext for escaping across the Atlantic. He abandoned ship in Lisbon and presented himself to the German consul. Unable to communicate in German he announced in English that his motivation was triggered by a commitment to serving the Fatherland, escalating to a willingness to contribute by any method necessary to a German victory in the European conflict. The Lisbon consul officials were definitely not the last Nazi bureaucrats to seriously consider that Colepaugh was an American double agent. William Caldwell was the pseudonym chosen for William C. Colepaugh and appeared on his false ID documentation. He spent most of his childhood years in Niantic, Connecticut. The younger Colepaugh in his teenage period, from all accounts, earned a disreputable reputation for delinquent behavior in the Niantic local community. His father, frustrated and losing patience, decided to transfer William to the Admiral Academy in Toms River, New Jersey. Later, William studied at MIT but demonstrated little appetite for academic life.[51] It was not Colepaugh's parents who had emigrated from Germany but his grandparents, and in his adolescence years he apparently understood little about German culture or his personal family ancestry.

His interest in German Nazism stemmed from reading and digesting media broadcasts about the Third Reich, and he was inspired by Blitzkrieg attacks launched by the Wehrmacht in the beginning months of the war. An obsession with Nazi Germany and the homeland of his ancestors developed in Colepaugh's mind. Regular audiences at the German consulate cemented the philosophical awakenings of this ideological convert, and he established a relationship with a father figure in the consulate general. It did not require a long period of time for William C. Colepaugh to express a commitment towards aiding the Fatherland. He traveled from western districts in Germany to Berlin The Nazi authorities had observed his movements extremely closely. Upon appearing in the German capital he was intercepted by RSHA representatives and interviewed by officers who assessed his capabilities and desirability for recruitment. A consultation was arranged with SS major Skorzeny, by reputation Hitler's favorite commando. In June 1944 Skorzeny determined it imperative that Colepaugh be transferred to an SS training school he himself lectured at in the German-occupied Netherlands. At The Hague, Colepaugh was introduced to Erich Gimpel, who later recalled his initial optimism upon discovering that he was instructed to be partnered with this individual.[52] Erich Gimpel was German born. His first opportunity to experience life outside the confinement of national boundaries was in 1935. Seduced by an exported imagery of tropical climates and sophisticated nightlife, he was attracted inexorably to Latin America. As an electrical engineer he had applied speculatively for a radio technician post at a prestigious German company in Peru and was surprised to be accepted.

In Peru, Gimpel first demonstrated his applicability as an intelligence agent. He reminisced in a postwar autobiography about the patriotic enthusiasm that undeniably ignited in him regarding a triumphant German victory after he read newspapers in Peru confirming the outbreak of hostilities. He was recruited as an intelligence informant and assembled a clandestine radio transmitter, passing on his observations from Lima, the Peruvian capital, to German U-boats waiting several miles offshore. Gimpel had endeavored to educate himself on the complicated science of distinguishing specifications of vessels and cargo ships. He managed with ingenuity to manufacture his own intelligence coup, reporting accurately on the restricted purposes of confidential discussions between secretary of state Cordell Hull and the Peruvian government officials. He discovered the subject of the deliberations and informed his superiors; as predicted by his observations Peru severed diplomatic relationships with Nazi Germany. A relatively inexperienced agent, his industrious labors in extracting meaningful facts from public officials and corrupt police officers had not progressed entirely unnoticed. A Peruvian criminal police officer appeared at his residence and accused Erich Gimpel of unspecified suspicious infractions and demanded to search inside the property.[53] Gimpel's residency status was now placed in considerable jeopardy and his episode in Peru appeared to be limited. In June 1942 Gimpel, along with hundreds of other German citizens, was deported and barred from returning again. Options in Latin America were egregiously diminishing and in August 1942 he returned to Germany, traveling home passing through Sweden.

In July 1943, Amt VI contacted Gimpel and, following brief negotiations, he confirmed recruitment to that organization. German intelligence recognized immediately the inherent advantages of securing Gimpel's services: technical ability in radio communications; English language speaking abilities; experience in undercover espionage and surveillance; and lastly, previous experience in the United States and South America. The prospective operative described tantalizingly the interior of Tirpitzufer during his inaugural visit. The cavernous and dimly lit inner corridors were distinguished by minimal official markings and a utilitarian façade, according to Gimpel's recollection, and he reported on an exceeding silence in the "fox hole" headquarters. He summarized the building's interior paradoxically as sufficiently "old fashioned to be classified as a modern structure and too new in appearance to be old fashioned." Perhaps surprised at the unexpected proposal, Gimpel originally transpired to be unwilling as a participant and declined Paeffgen's advances. Paeffgen was not prepared to tolerate this matter's being unresolved and administered a diatribe of counterarguments and vague threats. He eventually convinced Gimpel to enlist.[54]

Dr. Paeffgen explained that the Fatherland's naval difficulties were mounting, whereas the American naval fleets could alternate their position and redeploy complements practically instantaneously. In other words, he continued, for instance if the U.S. naval forces combating Japanese forces needed reinforcing the Americans were competently mobile to maneuver shipping in the Pacific Ocean as strategy demanded. But if Germany simultaneously launched an offensive in Europe it remained possible for America, with its flexibility, to redirect its naval forces to that secondary theater. Erich Gimpel found himself deployed to the SD's Operation Pelican scheduled for completion in Autumn 1943 and referred to as a mission the world had never seen before. The mobility achievable by the U.S. Navy in transferring military strength was facilitated by the Panama Canal. Dr. Paeffgen theorized that with Panama Canal transport removed the American fleet would instead be compelled to navigate Cape Horn and expend valuable time. An engineer from Breslau, a leading technical expert in the Panama Canal's construction, was enlisted as a specialist adviser.

On a deserted lakeside bordering Wannsee an exact replica model was constructed of the Panama Canal to test experimental theories for inflicting irreparable damage. The Gatun spillway, an installation section of the canal, was selected as a sensitive and vulnerable target. Ten or twenty times a day Erich Gimpel's assembled sabotage team attempted to destroy the spillway. He was even seconded Luftwaffe pilots and the use of two U-boats. Training operations drilled into the sabotage team an extraction strategy that guided the coconspirators to reconvene at a neutral South American nation and either intern themselves or return by U-boat. At the last moment, with the mission apparatus and submersible vehicles stockpiled onboard the waiting submarine in preparation for departure, Operation Pelican was canceled. Reliable field information attested that the mission was compromised. In early 1944 Gimpel was informed about Operation Elster, an alternative mission in the groundwork stage, this time refocusing on mainland United States.[55]

Military advantage was expected to be proffered for Germany's armed forces in the aftermath of Operation Elster. In postwar investigations some intriguing technicalities were uncovered concerning the American mission. The U-1230 submarine was contrived originally by Amt VI for being shadowed by a second submarine equipped with advanced V missiles; the technology developed from Werner von Braun's latest designs could logistically be maneuvered into appropriate range for launching at the New York and Washington, D.C., areas. European cities had experienced V missile attacks and the effectiveness of the weaponry had been incontestably demonstrated. In the end, the mission proceeded according to schedule without added the complication of the rockets, but the proposal achieved reinstatement as a fundamental priority for any future transatlantic missions post–Operation Elster. In this culminating episode of World War II, German naval presence that distant across the Atlantic was increasingly rare. The movement of U-1230 in close proximity to the American coastline had not occurred unnoticed; during this time American intelligence had detected an increase in German radio activity in the North Atlantic. The FBI was informed and suspicions were instantly raised concerning attempts to deposit enemy agents and the alternative risks associated with a German U-boat that close to landing territories.

The Crabtree Neck region was selected as an appropriate landing venue by the Amt VI mission developers; it was suitably remote, with minimal local population and urban development. The two espionage agents hitchhiked on the highway before, fortunately, managing to unobtrusively summon a passing taxi and persuade the driver to transport them to Bangor, Maine. Acclimatizing to American culture in reality proved to be more difficult for Gimpel than he had previously anticipated and basic requirements of ordering food in restaurants and purchasing clothing generated precarious exposure risks. The agents boarded a train from Bangor to Boston at approximately 7:00 a.m. Boston presented a possible impediment as it was a former hometown of William Colepaugh, but avoiding the city—with the chance of recognition—was not feasible. Minimal contingency appeared plausible, and the two individuals reasoned the appropriate course of action was to remain persistently on their guard and alert. On the train to Boston, Gimpel was almost culpable of incriminating the undercover duo. He managed to order breakfast collectedly enough and displayed only residual accent in conversation with the buffet vendor, but he was rendered speechless when the employee responded by inquiring on the specialty of bread he preferred. Traditional custom in the Northeast had been neglected as any element of the mission training. The men departed from Boston and Massachusetts immediately the following day and completed the journey by railroad to Grand Central Station in New York City on December 1. It was now three days into the American expedition and the intruders were in downtown Manhattan.

The Episode of Nazi Spies in New York

Colepaugh and Gimpel had successfully reached New York, the initial penetration stage effectively accomplished. The accommodation rented by the German operatives was a deliberately nondescript apartment at 33 Kenmore Hall Hotel, Manhattan. The American accent and demeanor of Colepaugh allowed his undisguised free movement and dialogue with any relevant personages who proved necessary. Renting accommodation and their remarkably expedient negotiations with the landlord had not presented any serious dilemmas. The first objectives in New York were concerned with reading newspapers and attending theater shows to achieve full acclimatization and in developing reciprocal relationships with connected individuals such as waiters, couriers, bartenders and stewards. Gimpel rehearsed his knowledge of America, aware of his own cultural limitations compared to his informed American colleague. He practiced immediately recalling baseball and sports information, the location of famous landmarks and natural geography.

They expended a majority of the next week searching for a second apartment not constructed with reinforced steel, a unique specification because the steel hindered radio transmissions. Locating a suitably manufactured apartment complex at Beekman Place, they rented the accommodation for $150 a month and paid two months' rent in advance.[56] A radio transmitter for broadcasting on rapidly instigating the assembling of a radio transmitter system after discovering Beekman Place. An important security measure from his perspective, he said later reminiscing in Peru about his exposure, was that apparatus parts should be of American origin. It was not an uncommon amateur hobby to maintain an interest in radio transmitters, but wartime American authorities were tracking the purchase of suspicious technology, including radio components. Gimpel traveled to multiple radio shops in different districts of New York to evade detection. A close study had been produced of American POWs and their family connections, and the analysis of methods of communicating messages to Germany had recommended fabricating letters purporting to be mailed by family members of POWs in the United States. But transatlantic censors were notoriously efficient at recognizing any encrypted messages. Mailing documents exploiting the Red Cross or alternative mailing routes would take several weeks.

Both individuals were taken aback at the perceived ebullience of New York and the relative nonchalance of New Yorkers conducting everyday business in conditions of wartime. The devastating impressions of conflict in Europe and Asia were very evident in the nation's newspapers, but the U.S. population was to an extent shielded from the deprivations and horrors of warfare, an inescapable contrast from general living conditions in Germany. Colepaugh increasingly displayed symptoms of detachment from the mission. While his colleague focused on assembling the radio transmitter relying on his Peruvian training, the American citizen encountered numerous entertainments in local bar establishments and the company of women. In a single day he managed to expend $1,500 in mission funding, receiving lectures and admonishment from Gimpel about the importance of not attracting attention. He constantly warned that individuals spending significant amounts or tipping employees above the average inevitably created an impression. An undaunted Colepaugh insisted that he was integrating into New York and the inhabitants of Manhattan respected people with financial influence.

However, the earlier conspicuous journey in Maine returned unsatisfactorily to haunt the two agents. The FBI's probing of evidence implied the definite possibility of another submarine landing and sabotage team infiltration. Two days after the operatives' arrival in New York U-1230 reportedly engaged in naval action a comparatively short distance from the Maine landing zone. The authorities, regional FBI chiefs, were checking into the prospect that the submarine comprised a mission for deposited enemy agents. Boston's field office discovered witnesses who had indeed encountered suspiciously behaving characters on the Northeast coastline. After questioning local sheriffs and law enforcement agents, the FBI was positively convinced another enemy infiltration was underway. Boston FBI agents redrafted northwards exercised their professional investigation techniques and discovered 29-year-old Mary Forni and her next-door neighbor, 17-year-old Harvard Hodgkins. Both were residents of Hancock who remembered driving past irregular individuals walking in the desolate highway snow and they were able to provide descriptions of them.[57]

The radio transmitter was finally completed on December 21, Erich Gimpel, enthused by this realization, was beginning to generate confidence about the mission. He evaluated his language skills as having much improved and now routinely engaged in conversation. In Germany coded documents had been entrusted personally for his stewardship as the more experienced team member and he commenced decrypting them. A New York address of an unknown Mr. Brown was standing out amidst the unscrambled content. This individual was identified by Amt VI as an extremely valuable contact who had demonstrated loyalty previously to the Fatherland. The reachable address was listed as being on 41st Street. Gimpel decided on a proactive approach and explained to his companion his decision to temporarily leave to become acquainted with the mysterious Mr. Brown. The address transpired to be a stockbroker business in a small-scale tower block. Unfortunately, Mr. Brown was indisposed and not expected to return for an extensive period.

Deciding that espionage actions were less appealing from the perspective of being embedded inside the maelstrom, Colepaugh abandoned Operation Elster during his comrade's absence. On December 21, the American exited their Beekman Place apartment building with both of the suitcases and the mission's entire financial reserves, stashed in cash bundles. Erich Gimpel returned to the apartment to discover that everything had been removed.

In New York Colepaugh had been reluctant and disinterested in performing the most perfunctory of tasks, not the least of which was communication with their home base. Reality was exacerbating the reservations circling around him. Four days before Christmas, Colepaugh had snatched the suitcase containing the espionage devices and cash amounting to $48,000. He contacted a woman, having developed a relationship during their expedition, and they jointly checked into a midtown hotel. Uncertain about the appropriate course of action, Colepaugh looked up an old school associate still living in New York and explained the predicament, mentioning that the situation carried serious repercussions. The friend surmised that Colepaugh must be fabricating the scenarios, but on realizing this eccentric-sounding narrative was indeed a genuine account he insisted on telephoning the authorities. After a postponement during which he resided with his childhood friend through the Christmas holidays, Colepaugh turned himself in to the FBI on December 26.[58]

Meanwhile, Gimpel, without any indication of his partner's present circumstances or location, deduced correctly that William Colepaugh had traveled through Grand Central Station. He managed to retrieve the suitcases from the station baggage room after some anxious moments. Erich Gimpel had participated as a trainee at military intelligence during Operation Pastorius planning, and in an earlier visit to Germany he became vaguely associated with several of the volunteer agents, including Hebert Haupt and Edward Kerling. In his postwar autobiography Gimpel expressed a dismissive attitude towards the strategy and execution of Operation Pastorius, referring to the command personnel as "amateurs." He described a sentiment of empathy towards his American predecessors and recalled the newspaper articles covering the convictions and enacting of death sentences with horror. American newspapers had recorded with precision the macabre details of execution by electric chair, which had produced an indelible imprint on Gimpel.[59] The images were now returning to him.

A manhunt for Gimpel immediately centered on Manhattan and was guided by his former comrade. Erich Gimpel was captured by FBI agents on December 30. In February 1945 Gimpel and Colepaugh stood trial before a military commission, accused of conspiracy and violating the 82nd Article of War. The hearings were concluded with minimal elaboration, the precedents of prosecution by military tribunal and *Ex parte Quirin* having now been established. Both men were convicted and subsequently sentenced to death. The attorney general followed a procedure similar to the Pastorius prosecutions, but this time a Supreme Court appeal was not forthcoming. The American military establishment persisted in demonstrating paranoid tendencies about the unwelcome possibility of further border incursions and committed to projecting an uncompromising image. The executions were scheduled for April 15 but were postponed by President Roosevelt's sudden and unexpected death, Germany surrendered in June 1945 and President Harry Truman commuted the death sentences to life terms in prison. Colepaugh was paroled in May 1960 and Gimpel was repatriated to West Germany and released in 1955.[60]

3

British Theater

The German Foreign Ministry and intelligence agencies in the years preceding World War II were dependent on the German émigré communities for foreign intelligence collection and developing more elaborate espionage rings in British territory. In the environment before the conflict, with remilitarization an incomplete project, most of the German command staff at political and military levels proceeded cautiously in relations with Europe's major powers. Intelligence agencies were prohibited from operating extensively in Britain and direct employment of agent provocateurs was similarly denied. Not recognized as an enemy either politically or diplomatically, Britain was a territory where the Nazi Party high command wanted to avoid embarrassment.

Comparable to other emerging battlefield fronts the German government had failed on investing heavily in developing sound strategic or analytical intelligence gathering during the 1930s, and in these instances significant gaps certainly existed in the contemporary assessments of Britain's military strength. His Majesty's Navy and Air Force both persisted as closed books, and before 1937 the War Ministry and the Abwehr had failed to insert a single valuable secret agent inside Britain. An understanding of the senior military and intelligence sector chains of command, a basic and exigent security requirement, and other fundamental intelligence necessities did not yet exist.[1] Wehrmacht commanders plotted with their respective officer complements in preparing for the tactical operations eastward, apparently not anticipating a conflict against Western Europe before 1937 or 1938. Initially all intelligence work targeting Britain was forbidden wholesale and only in 1936 was this obstructive conditional rule marginally relaxed and a measure of covert activity permitted. In 1937 the removal of restrictions began to accelerate.

The political movements of Britain and France in reaction to Nazi Germany's transitions and the territorial expansions was a matter of intense debate within Hitler's command staff. On March 12, 1938, German military forces invaded Austria, resolving a long-standing fascist objective of uniting the two nations. This gesture represented another critical juncture in a substantial and growing list of treaty infractions and other actions perceived as inciting hostilities. The German foreign office was determined to discover the British cabinet's tactical position following the aggressive southern annexation, as full-scale warfare at this premature time for the national socialist project could prove destructive. Many figures within the Abwehr prophesied scant rewards in openly provoking a conflict with Britain and displayed anxiety about disrupting diplomatic relations. Reports from German diplomats in London indicated that the Neville Chamberlain government was reluctant to defend Czechoslovakia and interference generally was unpopular in Central European affairs. Ribbentrop, believing himself in touch with power brokers in London, reported to Berlin that his conviction was the British government harbored zero intentions to engage in military action against Germany.[2] German military intelligence was not so easily convinced, and Admiral Canaris pressed Piekenbrock and his other subordinates to attain empirical evidence of British and French government's perception of the unfolding conditions.

General Keitel, the future chief of the Supreme High Command of the German Armed Forces, inherited by default the position of military intelligence's emissary to Britain following the Austrian annexation. Military intelligence, meanwhile, remained hopeful that communication lines would continue open for as long as feasibly possible. Hitler ordered a succession of delegations to discuss the matter with representatives of the Chamberlain cabinet, imparting a trusted personal adjutant in Captain Wiedemann with full authority for leading the tense negotiations with foreign minister Lord Halifax. Wiedemann was in fact the same individual who had arrived in America in 1935 accompanied by considerable financial support and Hitler's personal backing in establishing the American Fellowship Forum with Dr. Auhagen. Lord Rothermere's contact with his former mistress Stefanie Hohenlohe and Adolf Hitler arranged the clandestine meeting between Hitler's adjutant and Lord Halifax in July 1938. Hitler assured Halifax that Germany intended to obtain a revision of her frontiers by peaceful means, but the unfolding environment and the future apparently circling on the horizon were appearing difficult to predict for all parties.[3]

Twelve months before, the Abwehr had lobbied Nazi Party high command for permission to cultivate a renewed espionage network internally in Britain, and a reprioritizing of counterespionage services targeted Western Europe. Sections of the senior command within the intelligence community resisted Nazi Party radical ideological convictions concerning Lebensraum and provocatively inciting mobilization from Europe's major powers in this premature environment. But the distinct prospects of future warfare and the necessity of understanding the latest information could not be neglected. Canaris's request, endorsed by Keitel, was granted and he consequently introduced the first systematic investigation of Britain's military capability and structure since World War I. The department chief of Abwehr I, Piekenbrock, furnished Canaris with reports on Allied rearmament programs from August 14, 1938, onward, which, based on initial accounts, was proceeding slowly at this critical point but commanded greater resources than Germany.

Nazi Germany and Britain's government both instantly recognized the mutual intelligence gap that had been growing since the 1920s. The designation and internal structure of the Secret Intelligence Service (MI6) and other security agencies in Britain were unknown and the extent of any penetration in Germany was similarly unquantifiable, although not generally perceived as a realistic security concern. In 1939 telling documents produced by MI6 indicated that on Britain's side the intelligence chiefs could not identify the official title of German military intelligence or commanding officer. An MI5 assessment from June 1940 on the Wehrmacht advancements into France concluded that British intelligence was disadvantaged in evolving on the battlefield methods of detecting opponent agents without concrete knowledge of German espionage structure or methodology. Between 1937 and the outbreak of armed conflict German intelligence officers did succeed to a degree in recruiting and handling a small contingent of agents. The Abwehr interviewed members of German communities in London to identify prospective converts. By August 1939 most existing operatives had expired in terms of functional usability, the operatives either compromised and on authority radars or their information simply insufficiently relevant. Recruitment and activation of German citizens and other nonnationals residing in Britain proceeded relatively smoothly in the 1936 through 1938 climate, but this strategy proved more problematic in terms of infiltrating highly protected military or other establishment circles. Insufficient funding and distracting attentions to Eastern Europe resulted in inattention to the British theater and only moderate achievements of intelligence penetration. The first generation of intelligence missions at the beginning of the conflict would encounter numerous setbacks and unexpected complications, a result of the unproductive prewar conditions. Training programs and strategic planning required considerable research and institutional development to stimulate the intelligence breakthroughs required by the German military.

A notable Abwehr-handled asset in the prewar environment was a well-connected Iraqi army officer, Captain Mahomet Salman. Due to an undeniably reputable background and influential familial relationships he finessed access to prestigious British and Commonwealth military circles. The content matter he returned to his controllers conveyed the distinct impression of an individual well informed about the developments inside British armed forces. Captain Salman had studied armored warfare at Sandhurst and other military bases in an exchange program with cooperation from the British army. He was reassigned to the classified Mechanized Warfare Experimental Establishment (MWEE) and obtained admittance to secret research on mobile armor. Captain Salman pursued congenial social relationships with senior British army officers. The information quantifiable as being valuable, the German panzer command supplied with it was more informed about capabilities of British tanks and engagement tactics.[4] An information trafficking scheme was constructed, and Salman communicated this information utilizing an official diplomatic bag disguised as harmless letters addressed to his brother, a Major General Salman, another Abwehr agent and commander of the Iraqi air force. As the Abwehr had appointed a resident officer in Baghdad, it was not difficult to transport information back to the Tirpitzufer.

Another reliable undercover agent in military intelligence's otherwise minimal portfolio was Arthur Owens, whose disgruntlement with the British government was supposedly fueled by his ardent Welsh nationalist politics. An electrical engineer by trade and an employee at a family technology firm with business interests and prospective clients in Germany, he customarily had legitimate reasons for journeying to Berlin and Hamburg, beginning in 1935. Owens divulged transparently to local acquaintances anti–British sentiments and agreed without any visible reluctance to register in German intelligence as an informant, with not insubstantial financial reimbursement. His proficiency in supplying naval information was of particular appeal. Owens had exploited his business journeys to Germany equally in passing on information to British intelligence. By January 1940, he had declared his genuine loyalty to Britain and assumed the position of a double agent.[5] He recruited a network of agents inside British territory, all nothing more substantial than figments of his imagination.

Germany's remaining resources for discovering information on he British government's perspectives and military strength derived from a plethora of divergent and not entirely coordinated routes: aerial reconnaissance, wireless intercepts and embassy staff. Postwar Allied analysis revealed a more prominent role of the Research Office than earlier suspected. Investigations indicate that this relatively small German intelligence agency under the nominal supervision of Hermann Göring was a highly valuable intel source. Responsible for signal interception and wiretapping, the Research Office monitored sensitive Nazi operations directed at their own personnel and those of Allied forces. Examples of archetypal activities are recording conversations of the Nazi state officials suspected of disloyalty or mismanagement and foreign diplomats with residences in Berlin.

Early infiltration efforts had not constructed the intelligence capability desperately needed by the Wehrmacht. German military intelligence was restricted by the internal machinations and thus far had failed to interject personnel inside the British military infrastructure or political sector. Strategic plans were hastily assembled by Abwehr I chief Piekenbrock to deposit agents on the British coastline to embed themselves in British society. With the imminent annexation of Poland—which was assessed by virtually all commentators as a definitive prelude to expansion eastward—and the opposing united block of Britain and France forming pledged to defend Polish sovereignty, the neutrality discussions appeared in serious jeopardy. Hopes for rapprochement dissipated with the realization that conflict against Britain and neutralizing the Western Europe Theater was mandatory before launching an attack on Russia. By August negotiations on the Western frontier had ominously extracted abortive responses. Lord Halifax was no longer reassuring the German ambassador about peaceful coexistence. Chatter from Canaris's sources formerly in dialogue with their British counterparts was silenced.

German Intelligence Ordered to Prioritize British Front

Military intelligence demonstrated foremost efficiency in battlefields during the invasions of Poland and Czechoslovakia. Domestic senior military chiefs and police officers from nations selected for German appropriation were persuaded to exchange loyalties and work for the Wehrmacht; assets on the inside distributed to their Abwehr handlers documents containing strategic army plans and blueprints of defensive systems. The national state security offices in Prague and Warsaw were raided immediately after annexation and relevant secrets or military information removed. Abwehr mobile units descended rapidly into freshly occupied territorial zones to prevent the accidental destruction of useful information. The immaculately conceived and executed operations targeting secret service and intelligence headquarters unearthed numerous cases of sensitive documents, all of which were shipped to Abwehr headquarters. Now the Reich intelligence chiefs were ordered to reorient the full attention of their respective agencies on a British offensive. Hitler issued General Wilhelm Keitel, chief of Supreme High Command, with instructions for formulating the essential strategies for Operation "Sea Lion." The Nazi war machine finalizing the French campaign authorized the deployment of Wehrmacht divisions and resources necessary for Operation Sea Lion; correspondingly, intelligence missions were ordered to give the Wehrmacht and OKW information for directing the invasion.[6]

Preparations were earmarked for final completion by September at the latest. In fact, Admiral Raeder, the driving force behind the Scandinavian actions, had prepared an alternative document depicting the preliminary phases for a seaborne invasion of Britain in November 1939 even before Hitler had asked. At the Wolfsschanze conference on June 20, 1940, chiefs declared that Atlantic coastal bases must be at the disposal of the navy for warfare against Britain. Raeder issued a report on the classification of vessels available and geographic areas where it was proposed to land Keitel's forces. He requested assurances on the interjection of overpowering air supremacy from the Luftwaffe to support ground troops, described as indispensable, and further outstanding technical details were outlined. The Hamburg Ast substation would focus its attention on the British theater and subsequently developed into the largest intelligence regional station located in Germany. In the period preceding the invasion of Poland and outbreak of war, the Hamburg Ast station oriented towards continental European matters and prioritized tracking intelligence in France, Spain and wider Mediterranean region. The geographical jurisdictions shifted as circumstances evolved and Hamburg station was converted rapidly into a productive clearinghouse for all information retrieved from Britain. Hamburg, a relatively short distance from Britain, also served as prime location for Abwehr radio listening stations. From this discreet location, in fact, conversations transmitted from across Europe were monitored.[7] A precise time scale for the imminent cross-channel assault was still undecided. Hamburg Ast and the other intelligence agencies proceeded with launching preparations by training covert operation teams and enlisted individuals of interest determined suitable for penetrating enemy defenses or counterintelligence. Subjects identified as immediate priority concerns spanned supplying intelligence on estimations of strength and capability of the British forces and the extent to which replacements could be deployed to reinforce front lines. The remaining subjects of fundamental intelligence interest were the Royal Air Force, industrial information and surveys of landing zones. The declaration of hostilities had vastly increased the Abwehr's commitments.

The rapid expansion experienced by MI5 in the new climate after September 1939 created an immense degree of institutional strain and, in this break from tradition, inevitable confusion. Continued growth in recruitment of new personnel witnessed a six-fold increase in staff membership, with the MI5 staff contingency amounting to 868 by the first months of 1941. In the British intelligence structure, MI5 (Security Service) had standing jurisdiction on counterespionage domestically and MI6 (Secret Intelligence Service) was oriented for gathering intelligence outside of Britain. The veteran director Vernon Kell was replaced by David Petrie in June 1940. Numerous internal reviews, including the Hankey review, published between 1938 and 1941 were highly critical of MI5. Major General Stewart Menzies had achieved promotion to commander of the reinfused German section at MI5 in 1932, but minimal solid advancement occurred in spite of his diligence. By 1939 intelligence services, in the considered estimation of in-house experts, had not regained the venerated and integral position it had in World War I. Gradually, Section V department of MI5, a counterespionage division, was restructured during the opening months of World War II.

British intelligence during the interwar period had suffered from similar insufficiency in investment that had disadvantaged the Abwehr. With the collapse of Poland, Scandinavia and France, thousands of continental refugees proceeded to Britain searching for sanctuary. MI5 recognized the potential security risks and the concealed opportunities for Germany to penetrate security systems, Sir David Petrie reasoned it was necessary to implement meticulous vetting procedures for assessing new arrivals.[8] Another evolving objective disseminated to staff the monitoring of conditions in territories classified as neutral in order to identify enemy operatives and Nazi sympathizers. Arrivals from Spain, Switzerland, Portugal and Eastern Europe continued to materialize in unsustainable numbers at Britain's borders. MI6 increased the monitoring of German activity in other international theaters. In terms of resource cultivation Britain has historically depended on the importation of raw materials and foodstuffs from Africa, India and the Western Pacific. In both categories of intelligence work a powerful weapon in the locker of British intelligence became the Intelligence Section (ISOS), a cryptography division responsible for decoding German traffic headed by Oliver Strachey

The Home Office, in conjunction with MI5, distributed coded telegrams nationwide to regional police chiefs authorizing the detention of enemy aliens whose names appeared on a secretly compiled government list. A total of 880 individuals assessed as being dangerous to national security were scheduled for arrest and internment, the names methodically selected by MI5 researchers in identifying possible insular candidates as security risks; by November 470 individuals were confined.[9] Mass internment of enemy aliens, from the perspective of British security services, reduced complications associated with foreign intelligence agents remaining at large domestically. Churchill and the War Cabinet exhibited general support for the internment of inhabitants from enemy states and ideological confederates.

The German intelligence agencies of the Abwehr and RSHA had indeed developed programs to infiltrate spies into Britain disguised as refugees, of which British intelligence had some awareness. New reception centers were installed by MI5 at entrance points as improvised locations for vetting new arrivals. Migration of European refugees from neutral territories gained momentum and existing customs and immigration services buckled in managing the masses of incoming people, MI5 continued to pronounce concerns about potential hazards of German agents slipping through the immigration net and protested the inadequacy of reception center facilities. Defending dockyards and harbors from enemy infiltration expanded as a priority into 1941, and observations about management of vetting motivated the implementation of a new system. A central organization with the purpose of processing new migrants officially opened for business in January 1941. The London Reception Centre now assessed incoming traffic from Europe with MI5 controlling the screening process. A total of 31,000 migrants traveled through British borders and the London Reception Centre. This immigration control system proved undeniably efficient in preventing Axis agents from penetrating routes of entry and formed a crucial element in the tracking of Nazi operatives.[10]

The Abwehr primed operatives for rupturing border defense regulations and inhabiting the UK at considerable expense. They had trained their promising personnel in countersurveillance and counterintelligence techniques to circumvent MI5's restrictive measures on newly arrived migrants at reception centers. Nighttime curfews were instituted for non–British citizens and the Home Office introduced specific ID documentation. Controlling movements of citizens from other European countries in theory rendered espionage actions of enemy agents deliberately problematic. In Britain the domestic climate was concerned about the prospect of Nazi saboteurs descending into formerly protected and sheltered communities. An outbreak of public scares emerged in reverberation of the Low Countries and other territories falling to the German forces, and newspapers published articles and commentaries by people convinced that a fifth column existed secretly in Britain. Suspicious observations and multiple witnesses reporting "Nazi spies" circulated habitually, and police and home guard received accounts daily of various sabotage incidents and anonymous "bizarrely and incongruously behaving" strangers who were imagined to be undercover agents. Devious characters, according to speculation, stood accused of secreting articles in newspapers to transmit encoded signals to Germany, poisoning chocolate, recruiting lunatics from psychiatric hospitals as suicide squads and implanting assassins into the British countryside.[11] More accurately, by this period the German intelligence commanders had without mitigation failed to construct an espionage network and in fact controlled zero senior-level contacts.

As Operation Sea Lion was morphed into the determining and final patterns for mobilization and duels between the RAF and Luftwaffe intensified, the reality of German intelligence ambitions differed from stories contemplated and digested following declarations of war. Military intelligence was more preoccupied with engineering conspiracies that were grounded in integral strategic and tactical military objectives. Piekenbrock and the Abwehr Section I operations teams postulated with definite alacrity that depositing agents equipped with advanced radio transmitters behind enemy front lines could generate superior disorder and confusion to either poisoning or assassination squads. Abwehr divisions once entrenched in forward positions were destined for instructing how to observe troop movements, isolate installations exigent for defense and prepare the groundwork for further engagement.[12]

An assiduous and unexpected source for Nazi intelligence in Britain, harvested in the opening phases of hostilities, was Tyler Kent, an American cipher clerk employed at the U.S. embassy in London. Kent reproduced copies of Churchill's and Roosevelt's correspondence by accessing the U.S. State Department's "grey code" and other sensitive documents beginning in October 1939 and conveyed the expropriated intelligence to German government representatives he was acquainted with. The documents comprised a volume of secret data—for example, details of the "destroyers for bases" agreement. The British government had traded 99-year leases on maritime bases for 50 U.S. Navy destroyers, Kent revealed. The telegrams and draft documents exposed insights on strategic concerns of the War Cabinet and preliminary planning for the U.S. Navy to cooperate with the Royal Navy in combating German surface raiders. The Security Service case reports, declassified in October 2001, portrayed a comprehensive picture of the damage perpetuated by Tyler Kent's intelligence breach and the characteristics of the information passed to German intelligence. In March 1940, Kent showed some fifty of these classified telegrams to an attractive Russian woman called Anna Wolkoff, who rerouted them to the Abwehr via the Italian embassy in London.[13] These cables, according to a Security Service assessment, delivered to Canaris important specifications on the strength and disposition of British forces in France and raw deliberations on future military strategy.

The 29-year-old Tyler Kent officially entered State Department employment in 1934. Denied promotions in diplomatic fields, an ambition harbored since graduating from college, he developed a discontented and resentful attitude towards his employers. He regarded working life as a code room technician his unjustifiably operating below his deserved station. Kent believed his impressive academic qualifications and family connections inside the diplomatic service were sufficient to open doors for him. He was detained in May 1940 on suspicion of improperly conveying information derived from his U.S. government employers to Anna Wolkoff, an active member of the Right Club organization and in correspondence with British fascist leader William Joyce (latterly known as Lord Haw Haw). This assortment of strange coconspirators was unmasked and encompassed various Italian diplomats based at London's embassy and Captain Maule Ramsay, former Member of Parliament and founder of the Right Club.[14] Francesco Maringliano, an official at the London embassy, masterminded the transfer of the documents from Right Club contacts to Rome. Hans Mackensen, the German ambassador, then ensured the materials landed on Joachim von Ribbentrop's desk.

Anna Wolkoff was the daughter of respected Russian aristocracy emigrating to London with remnants of her family to escape repercussions during the Russian revolution. The Bolsheviks repossessed almost all the family holdings, and the formerly prestigious Wolkoff family was unendurably banished from returning to their homeland. In London political circles Wolkoff fostered an association and mounting fascination with anticommunist organizations and right-wing movements, The Right Club, a fascistic amalgamation of comparably discontented individuals, shared Wolkoff's perspective of blaming contemporary European dilemmas on Communism and Freemasonry. Captain Ramsey, the Right Club's founder, remained convinced that Britain was becoming incrementally occupied by an international Jewish conspiracy. Wolkoff and Ramsey persuaded their recently acquired American friend, employed at Grosvenor Square's U.S. embassy, to supply the secret communications dossiers to German intelligence.

Kent's diplomatic immunity was withdrawn by Ambassador Kennedy and an official search of his apartment uncovered prohibited and unsanctioned copies of classified materials amounting to hundreds of embassy documents and internal membership records of the Right Club entrusted to Kent for safekeeping.[15] In October 1940 he was prosecuted on five charges under Section 1 of the Official Secrets Act and two under the Larceny Act and sentenced to seven years. In secret trials conducted at the Old Bailey the other convicted individuals were sentenced to 7–10 years of imprisonment. The British government found in the embassy scandal the exact provocation necessary, and the oncoming week witnessed a substantial roundup of British fascists and extreme-right members. Incidentally, codebreakers at Bletchley Park first detected signals of inappropriate behavior inside the U.S. London embassy. Cable intercepts indicated that sensitive documents concerning Britain's strategic military policies were transmitted from the German embassy in Italy directly to German Foreign Office headquarters.[16] In time, Bletchley Park analysts decrypted transcripts of personal communications between President Roosevelt and Winston Churchill among the intercepted files.

Operation Lena and a First Attempt at Penetration

On 22 June Abwehr Ast and KO stations in Germany and occupied Europe were primed for the imminent cross-channel invasion and advised that all operations should be integrated into German military strategy for Operation Sea Lion. The broad-front expeditionary force was destined for landing at designated sectors between Ramsgate and the Isle of Wight. In preparation for the invasion on 19 July Canaris contacted Piekenbrock and Lahousen and advised the Abwehr I and II commanders that all operations targeting Britain must now be coordinated on an emergency basis and ordered the implementation of Operation Lena. The inaugural group of German covert operatives who arrived in Britain in September 1940 were known as "Invasion Spies," and the flow continued unabated for several months.

The position of commanding officer for the training and insertion of agents was assigned to Major Ritter. In a later autobiography discussing the events Ritter recalled, "There was no handbook to follow, and no time to lose." The hands-on developmental phase was expressly under his departmental remit. In his capacity of managing counterintelligence operations concentrated on the British theater he had been producing residual and perfunctory information for over six months. Arthur Owens, the darling of German intelligence, had unfortunately reduced frequency in feeding back intelligence. Ritter's request to discover data on coastal defenses, landing grounds and other defensive fortifications had encountered only ominous silence. Ritter commented on the matter: "Johnny [code name] was unable to gather all the intelligence required ... and some of it was stale by the time it filtered through." Owens had disappeared from the Abwehr's radar. Calculating whether this unwarranted transformation proved temporary or permanent was impossible to predict. Hamburg Ast station, commanded by Ritter, was instructed to dispatch new reporting agents with minimum delay.[17]

Germany's reservoir of trained covert operatives in this preliminary stage were undoubtedly a diversified community. Some, of course, were committed Nazis harnessing political party affiliations, but the background history extended to criminals, con artists and drifters. In orchestrating Operation Lena, adventurous and committed personalities capable of being trained as saboteurs and espionage operatives were preferred as recruits. All agents enlisted in preparation for the impending invasion of Britain were deliberately selected from amateur ranks with minimal experience of any professional intelligence work. A major dilemma became identifying high-caliber foreign agents with a strong understanding of the English language and the ability to disguise their own accents and remain undetected. Each Abwehr agent transferred to clandestine field operations, as declared in planning documents and manuals, received the necessary identity cards, clothing and food ration cards and purchasing coupons expected of British lawful inhabitants.

Once grounded and commencing the perpetrating of mission objectives, agents were trained on assimilating and procuring suitable accommodation and financial support. Military intelligence had previously embarked upon campaigns to furnish the OKW with invasion intelligence requirements, but the intelligence community had historically never invested in creating a credible agent training program. The insufficient funding before 1939, which continued until the weeks immediately preceding the outbreak of conflict, was definitively responsible for innumerable intelligence failures. Keitel had recognized the prevailing dilemma of insufficiently competent or qualified operatives suitable for covert actions or survival once they arrived in Britain.[18] Field Marshall Keitel ordered Canaris to develop a semi-independent but complementary scheme to Operation Lena. This training program code named "Lobster" purportedly was an integral augmentation to the military intelligence strategies. Canaris assigned supervision of exercise fulfillment to Captain Wichmann, senior commander at Hamburg substation. Lobster indeed produced on its veritable assembly line a number of sharpened individuals destined for transferring into Operation Lena.

Standard procedures for embedding and concealing operatives in neutral or hostile territory with unpredictable resupply points entailed a command structure of cellular networks and personnel handlers to case manage and impart assignments to agents. Covert infiltration is frequently employed in prevailing conditions where an open presence would endanger operatives or otherwise be assessed counterproductive to their objectives. Undisclosed intelligence maneuvers inside a neutral or enemy territory violated domestic legal frameworks and prompted risks of compromised diplomatic accords, the cellular structure needed to protect the anonymity of agents. Case handlers theoretically developed a one-to-one relationship as a form of representative liaison, thereby reducing potential exposure of other network agents. The mission complement contained 21 agents, and 5 of Operation Lena's personnel were entrusted with radio transmitters and converted into operators. During the later, advanced, stages of the incursion, shortwave radio operators were destined to become valuable chains in relaying intel. Ritter recognized and advocated to his colleagues the policy of attending to the general welfare and sound psychological performance of individual agents; the complexity of life surviving behind enemy lines according, to Ritter's school of thought, demanded this approach. German intelligence, from early 1940 until the Invasion Spies era, found that the practice of handling and controlling operatives was a profoundly difficult and error-prone occupation.[19]

From September onward a total of 21 agents were dropped into Britain under Operation Lena. Transportation to shorelines along Britain, for German agents, inspired marked ingenuity inside Hamburg Ast and experimental tactics. The manifold intrusion methods included parachutes, sailing vessels and U-boats. The first group landed on the South English coast near Dungeness on September 3, 1940. Two separate teams, rather than use parachutes, had depended on passage aboard a German naval ship and slipping ashore by transferring to rubber dinghies closer to the beachhead perimeter. Abwehr switched from naval strategies to planting operatives behind enemy positions to aerial attempts towards the end of 1940. Hauptmann Gartenfelt was appointed commander of the parachute operations to coordinate and assure productivity in line with the high expectations, and under his supervision an itinerary of aerial missions were deployed. In the following year, from March to May 1941, records show that Gartenfelt had launched four parachute missions over the border defenses of Britain. The physics of dropping agents via parachute presented numerous challenges including avoiding enemy radar and other advanced methods of detection; the packing and transportation of cumbersome equipment such as radios transmitters; and landing the operatives close enough to predetermined drop zones. Aeronautics technology this prematurely in World War II, as bombing operations had demonstrated time and time again, remained relatively unsophisticated.

The German agents' insufficient backgrounds in counterespionage training transpired to be problematic from the moment the operatives had landed on the ground and encountered civilians or ventured to acquire accommodation and resources. It became apparent the individual personalities of Operation Lena were unqualified for intelligence work, jeopardizing the mission's effectiveness from the outset. Elements of military intelligence's assembled plan attested to the unrealism in the field and rapidly the mission disintegrated. A series of blunders exposed the inadequate preparation, and recurring problems had surfaced with inaccurate counterfeit documents, which resulted in almost complete capture by British authorities within days. The German agents were assigned incorrect or outdated ID documentation for example. By December 1941 all 21 German agents from this initial counterespionage incursion had been either captured or were otherwise officially accounted for. The primary rationalization for Operation Lena's demise can feasibly be traced to Arthur Owens. His unparalleled expertise as a double agent was critical in uncovering Operation Lena's existence, as he disclosed to the British government precise information concerning the names, drop-points and mission orders of the approved contingent of undercover operatives.[20] From the beginning the operation was compromised and irreparable. Major Ritter had spent several months planning the Abwehr's boldest mission yet to circumvent Britain's defensive perimeter but to no avail. The ensuing investigation for British intelligence was rendered transparent after Bletchley Park had decoded the German Enigma transmissions. The first decrypted documents were produced by Alan Turing's codebreaking team simultaneously with the German invasion of Norway in April 1940, and within twelve months Bletchley Park understood the deciphering systems of virtually all German encoded networks and were reading messages in real time. Transcripts detected information corresponding to Owens' accounts.

Investigation case documents associated with Operation Lena personnel recently passed declassification and were released to public viewing, offering informative content from the contemporary British and Nazi senior commanders and case officers. A renewed assessment of the strategies and tradecraft techniques employed by the Abwehr commanders and cellular networks is now possible, and insights into Nazi establishment's future intentions are presented. On September 3, Waldberg and Meier landed near Dungeness in Southern Kent, while their mission companions Kieboom and Pons accomplished landfall farther north at Dymchurch and Rye. This detachment was scheduled for an inconspicuous maritime crossing of the English Channel. When the German invasion started they were ordered to disappear into the civilian population and continue reporting from behind enemy lines. Kieboom reported later that he imminently expected a German invasion force. Jose Waldberg, a long-term associate of the German Nazi Party, exhibited a pronounced commitment towards the ideological tenants of Nazism. In contrast, the Dutch citizens Pons and Kieboom were for all practical purposes press-ganged into servitude. Spending the duration inside the unwelcome confines of a concentration camp was offered as an alternative to recruitment as an invasion spy operative.[21]

Pons and Kieboom landed on the coastline seemingly undetected and immediately dragged their supplies onto the beach. They decided after a consultation that crossing a nearby coastal road and traversing the seemingly deserted secluded field beyond appeared pragmatic. The second intention of undertaking a journey to a local village identified in mission planning was agreed upon. But without warning police headlights appeared from the beachhead darkness followed by a squadron of police vehicles evidently expecting their arrival.[22] The police immediately detained the two accomplices and confiscated their apparatus and radio devices. During investigation at the local police station Jose Waldberg's collection of notebooks and false identification credentials offered clues for the reason behind their presence in Britain. Meier, flustered under questioning from interrogators, admitted he did not possess a required ID card, a sufficiently incriminating circumstance. In an ill-advised attempt at a mitigating cover embellishment he claimed to be an undocumented European refugee. Meier had landed Waldberg in a compromised position and his hastily assembled explanation unraveled under interrogation. Both men were detained at the police station while the inspector awaited confirmation from his superiors. The four spies were reunited at Seabrook Police Station and transferred to MI5's secret interrogation center in West London, Camp 020.[23]

The MI5 file covering the period January to December 1940 was released in 2005 and contained interrogation transcripts and a detailed analysis of the attempted covert penetration. Pons divulged his understanding of the mission and pronounced his dissatisfaction with background arrangements and attentiveness to the venture by his commanding officers in German intelligence. Kieboom also required minimal persuasion in confirming cooperation and declared during questioning that Jose Waldberg was an insufferably loyalist Nazi and ringleader of the group. All four individuals received training in Hamburg for a short-term operation in reporting on enemy military forces, airfields, antiaircraft defenses and civilian morale, assured by their handlers that the Wehrmacht's impending arrival guaranteed their rapid extraction. According to intelligence sources contained in MI5's file, Kieboom had consented to contacting his German handlers to impart disinformation; the fabricated incident report stated that the landing elements transpired successfully and the team were presently concealed in hiding, made necessary by Pons' involvement in a shooting incident. Waldberg refused the persistent endeavors to stimulate any cooperation with interrogators, convinced that a Wehrmacht detachment would arrive to liberate him from incarceration. The German agents were arraigned for criminal trial and prosecuted at the Old Bailey courthouse under the Treachery Act. The wartime British government was anxious to avoid circumstances of complacency and ensured that three of the convicted men were executed, while Pons escaped with a life sentence.[24]

Swedish national Gosta Caroli and coconspirator Wulf Schmidt, a Danish citizen, were two of Operation Lobster's earliest inductees. Dr. Praetorius, an Abwehr commanding officer, recruited the Scandinavian agents, theorizing that non–German citizens would be examined less suspiciously by British authorities and in fortuitous circumstances even be treated as comrades. Both had previously associated with fascist organizations in their respective home nations. Caroli's personal background information contained in the MI5 files describes accounts of this operative formerly serving briefly without distinction in Sweden's military before traveling to Argentina and West Africa. Schmidt, by all accounts an ardent loyalist Nazi, found himself inside a Copenhagen hotel room with two Military Intelligence agents pitching an honored role in the

Third Reich. Both individuals had obtained invitations to attend the Hamburg substation and upon entrance there were introduced to the mysterious character of Dr. Friedrich Praetorius, an officer stationed in the economic section of Abwehr I. Enticed by the glamour of undercover work and his ideological beliefs, Schmidt agreed without hesitation.

He was recruited nearly simultaneously with fellow Danish citizen Bjornson, and the two posted together during introductory training. After relocation to Hamburg, Caroli and Schmidt were informed of their partnering and experienced training in espionage, radio operating and the necessary spy skills. Briefed thoroughly on the mission in a training center with walls covered typically with images and maps of landscapes, the agents were expected to maneuver covertly within the facilities identified for infiltration.[25] The two individuals were advised by military intelligence training officers about the inherent risks correlated with the dangerous occupation they had volunteered for participation in. According to standard procedure, once underground in England the contingency measures were constrained to the extent of the agents primarily operating remotely. In Hamburg, mission training seminars had centered on imparting teachings regarding aircraft recognition and meteorology, and they received demonstrations explaining the complex subjects of recognizing the designation of antiaircraft guns, reporting on airfield operations and identifying specifications of aircraft. Schmidt and Caroli were driven on excursions for field radio transmission and receiving tests to a deserted area in close proximity to Cologne. Ritter personally attended to maximizing the facilities and specialist auxiliary support delineated to training and development of Operation Lena's recruits. The mission's transportation aircraft was a stripped-out Luftwaffe bomber plane, expressly converted for espionage missions. Painted entirely black, the aircraft deliberately retained zero military markings or insignia in an attempt to obscure identification. The bomb-release mechanisms had been completely removed to reduce weight and increase speed.

Men parachuted from Luftwaffe aircraft on 15 August, and the drop stage, frequently the most concerning phase, occurred without interruption or atmospheric delay. Radio communication, as prearranged, was opened with Abwehr receiving stations. Therefore, operational security could assuredly be classified intact. The first stage of underground activity featured Schmidt and Caroli traveling to Winchester and sheltering temporarily at a protected safe house. Their contact was code named "Johnny," the Welsh nationalist Arthur Owens, who of course was unknown to the two Scandinavian agents as a double agent. Awaiting police arrested Gosta Caroli and narrowly missed simultaneously sweeping up his still-unaccounted-for associate. Caroli was transferred to Camp 020 on Saturday 7 September. The circuitous story he unveiled to MI5 investigators described landing not by parachute in August but entering by Danish fishing trawler he had charted for depositing himself on the northern coastline in July. From there, Caroli summarized to interrogators, he desperately had ventured south, subsisting primarily on bread and chocolate in attempting to reach the destination of the Danish consulate in London. This journey implausibly had necessitated living completely on the road for the remainder of July and throughout August. Schmidt was still at large. With search teams expanded in close proximity to the safehouse, it later transpired the Swedish national was motivated in his initial decision in exiting Hamburg to avoid marriage and various other personal circumstances. The opportunity for relocation had provoked in that period a positive inducement; now suddenly the bleakness of his present situation behind enemy lines was hitting home. He endured the next 24 hours concealed in foliage in countryside areas, but a nighttime rainstorm was not a conducive environment for camouflage. His appreciation for the mission bestowed on him by the commanding officers at Hamburg Ast diminished. According to a personal account contained in the British intelligence files he was experiencing profound reservations and contemplated abandoning the mission. Schmidt reminisced on his former carefree days in the prewar conditions of Denmark and Hamburg, and analyzed the present circumstance. This previous life appeared little more than a fantastical vision.[26]

Caroli insisted that relocation to Britain embodied a plainly understandable desire for self-preservation in escaping ravaged Scandinavia, this decision finalized only two months before. But he admitted residing in England previously for intermittent periods while employed as a journalist for a Swedish press agency in 1938 and 1939. The definitive factor incriminating Gosta Caroli was in fact the counterfeit identity documents, the reproduction standards for which were undoubtedly impressive and at surface inspection not distinguishable from the genuine article. However, serial numbers of Operation Lena personnel had been forwarded by Arthur Owens some weeks before their border penetration. Excerpts from the interrogation transcripts indicate the techniques exploited by Major Stephens, the commander at 020, to extract information from Caroli. The exchanges record how the British verbally dissected any contradictions and obscuration, particularly original justification for unlawfully entering Britain.[27] The interrogations extracted identities of other influential Abwehr officers in Hamburg, his controlling station. Caroli was perceptibly reluctant to betray his mission colleague, Schmidt. A camaraderie had developed during mission training for Operation Lena; both had resided in the same accommodation during espionage training. However, his information ultimately resulted in Schmidt's arrest. Pressure on Caroli and Schmidt subsequently mounted, their complicity demonstrated beyond any reasonable doubt.

Major Stephens now insisted that the captured Abwehr operatives disclose all information concerning other agents in Nazi Germany's espionage network and the Invasion Spies personnel.[28]

The psychological pressure included the threat of imprisonment and execution. The two men confessed in exchange for a promise by MI5 to advise against institution of the death penalty. Tommy Argyll "Tar" Robertson, a senior officer, realized an advantageous and hitherto unconsidered possibility for counterintelligence. Incarceration long-term and capital punishment were originally employed for controlling the epidemic of enemy spies, but a tempting proposition of turning agents with valuable intelligence on enemy security services could not be overlooked. Caroli and Schmidt were understood to be committed long-term Nazi affiliates and proclaimed misgivings about allegiance to Abwehr military intelligence were only expressed after negative turns in the mission.

Despite these barriers both operatives confirmed their cooperation with British intelligence in a double-cross program. Safeguards were constructed under the auspices of Robertson and Guy Liddell for the Scandinavians to complete scheduled broadcasts to Hamburg using their assigned transmitter and codewords, as instructed by Abwehr commanders during training but now unexpectedly under the control of British intelligence. Gosta Caroli accessed his shortwave radio transmitter to connect with Ritter in Hamburg Ast station and confirmed the agents' arrival. An intermediary period expecting a forthcoming response ended fulfilled as Abwehr handler's replied according to procedure. Ritter conferred in encrypted information caches supplied to Caroli the future destination routes on British territory of other Operation Lena agents, unwittingly delivering into MI5's hands the precise details of sanctioned missions and landing zones. Agent V-3725 was revealed by Hamburg to be imminently waiting to parachute into Britain, and a designated landing point was divulged. Caroli and Schmidt continued to faithfully send transmissions to the Abwehr command in Hamburg over the next eighteen months, to the perception of German intelligence. Reports contained information on British and Allied armed forces complements, civilian news output and the British orchestrated Dieppe raid. Converting the enemy personnel into intelligence assets was an insightful idea and a profound cultural transformation in the campaign against the German intelligence system.[29]

Tor Glad and Helge Moe, both Norwegian citizens, agreed voluntarily to enlist in Nazi Germany's latest counterespionage scheme destined for assaults on mainland Britain. The agents were later code-named respectively "Jeff" and "Mutt" by British intelligence from the monikers of well-known American cartoon characters. MI5 declassified the wartime reports in October 2002. Glad, documents reveal, had previously experienced military service as a Norwegian army sergeant and was recruited by German intelligence while he was a resident in Norway in 1940. He became personally friendly with a Dr. Benecke in the tumultuous months preceding the German invasion; in private conversations both men discussed without pretense an attachment to pro–German and fascist sympathies. Motivated by an admitted disposition to cultivate favor with the factions governing Norway after the conflict he accepted Dr. Benecke's declaration of employment at the Abwehr. In the days immediately before German Wehrmacht troops landed on Norwegian territory Glad perfidiously entered active duty in military intelligence. Later, he repeatedly insisted, with debatable sincerity, the mitigating circumstances of deferring to his own self-interest and desperation to survive German occupation. In 1941 Tor Glad was persuaded by his Abwehr superiors to enter Britain and act as saboteur and embedded informant.[30]

His mission objectives in collusion with compatriot Helge Moe, defined in MI5's analytical review, contained instructions to engineer damaging fires in food storage depots and factories, to disrupt electricity power lines and generally to instigate panic among the civilian population. The two men were ordered to report by shortwave radio exigent information on locations of airfields and the effect of German bombing. They were initially trained in Norway, and their inaugural lessons were centered on Morse code transmission delivered by a German naval officer called Pavlowski. Another identity was discovered by MI5 when their chief controller and training supervisor was understood to be a Dr. Muller. The preparation in the manufacture of explosive and incendiary mixtures for the purposes of sabotage was inserted as a training segment. Mutt and Jeff eventually arrived by rubber boat off the Aberdeenshire coast on April 7 1941, delivered by German seaplane.

The immediate mission plan required their traveling first to the northern Scottish city of Aberdeen and then Edinburgh. Their instructions were to transmit protracted communiqués by wireless over the next month, their handlers demanding at this stage content on troop movements, the discernible impact of bombing assaults on civilian morale and meteorology reports. Sabotage action missions were predetermined by Hamburg, with the locations and targets specified for assailing with extreme prejudice. Germany's misguided understanding of British culture at that time had depicted chaotic conditions internally, with people migrating northwards en mass and arterial roads left uncontrolled. Muller informed Mutt and Jeff that exploration by roadway in their assessment produced minimal possibility of their presence being detected by authorities. The seaplane touched down in Murray Firth and a dingy transported the duo shoreward; their first decision on the ground in Aberdeenshire was a rejection of their training and commitments by contacting police and surrendering.[31] They adamantly maintained their genuine sympathies to be exclusively with the Allied nations and declared themselves at the disposal of authorities. Jeff entered into a hunger strike in protest at his injudicious incarceration and was removed to Liverpool prison, where he proved to be a troublesome internee. Case handlers transferred both individuals to Camp 020.

Both men had coincidentally applied for membership in the Norwegian National Socialist Party in 1937. Mutt reaffirmed under interrogation that his reasoning for involvement in Nazi Party circles before the conflict and in German military intelligence was to penetrate German security services and obtain information important to the Allies. However, MI5's analysis report confirms that Jeff was definitively a proven German counterespionage agent in Oslo, being inducted before Norway entered the conflict. In further condemnation he had actively conspired against the Norwegians during the military campaign and occupation. It was assessed by MI5 sources that Jeff "only decided to throw in his hand with us afterwards when he considered a German victory no longer assured."

A manifold detachment of Invasion Spy agents crossed Britain's borders between September and December 1940. Vera Erikson, Werner Wali and Karl Drucke arrived in a combined section on September 30; meanwhile, Hugo Jonasson and Gerald Libot had been deposited in the southern coastal territory a week earlier, traveling unobtrusively by a cutter ship to Plymouth. Another party landed near Narn on October 25 comprising Otto Joots, Legwald Lund and Gunnar Edvardsson. Jan Ter Braak endured longest behind enemy lines: the Operation Lena member displayed some enterprise in circumventing the initial search patterns and other police operations. Ter Braak landed at Amersham in Cambridge and persisted in eluding authorities while staying primarily this region. He was assigned the mission of assassinating government leaders and reputedly followed Winston Churchill on wartime expeditions to factories throughout the United Kingdom. The body of Jan Ter Braak was discovered on April 1941 inside a bomb shelter in Cambridge, where he had committed suicide. The at-large German spy was discovered to have been afflicted by financial constraints and psychological stress, and the Nazi agent had hastened his demise by placing a 6.35 mm Mauser automatic to his temple. At first glance Jan Ter Braak, was an unremarkable Dutch refugee, but his identification documents and other paperwork were decidedly illuminating. His credentials were consistent with the serial numbers revealed to MI5 by agent Snow. A concerning thought emerged at Camp 020 centering on the potential threats from other unknown German agents who had possibly slipped through the defensive systems.

The Culmination of Operation Lena

Most German agents from these intrusions intending to preclude a Wehrmacht invasion force had been captured by December 1941. Once transferred to Camp 020 at Latchmere House, Richmond, Major Stephens and interrogators relentlessly dissected the full picture surrounding the individually assigned missions. Tar Robertson had managed to convert several of these incoming agents into MI5 assets. In 1940, Robertson received promotion to the rank of flight lieutenant in the RAF's Intelligence and Security Department and was subsequently seconded to MI5. By January 1942 Britain controlled 19 former German government spies collaborating with Robertson and Liddell as double agents; most of them complied under threat of execution and consented to MI5's circumscribed programs against their controllers. Among the 19 surviving agents cajoled and persuaded into obligingly cooperating were the two Norwegians, Moe Helge and Tor Glad, who had disembarked on Aberdeenshire's coastline. Their exclamations of harboring no inclination to spy for national socialism and relinquishing their anonymity immediately after landing undoubtedly saved them from an unfortunate ending. During the next three years the German assets, threatened into changing allegiances, endowed British intelligence with indispensable information. Despite impressive success, 16 German operatives had refused to cooperate and were executed. The method of capital punishment remained hanging, most of the spies meeting their fate in Wandsworth prison.

The German agents captured in the aftermath of Operation Lena had elucidated to interrogators prime intelligence that encompassed senior officers and upper echelons of Nazi hierarchy, including the OKW in Berlin and Hitler's inner circle. In attempts to reduce their own culpability, Caroli and others downplayed their prospective espionage activities—which conceivably without impediments or arrest might have continued—but they informed on the other Abwehr operatives, even betraying Ritter and personnel linked to the planning stages. Important lessons were learned. Controlling enemy agents, British intelligence realized, should—if correctly orchestrated—enable apprehending other concealed networks and foster information collection on working methods of the German secret services.

Another successful British intelligence double-cross operation has come to light in recent years. An agent code-named "Jack King," his details only recently revealed, demonstrated a productive track record in identifying hundreds of domestic British residents who were prepared to supply national secrets to Germany. In investigating a potential fifth column that threatened Britain's internal security, MI5 increasingly focused its attention on organizations classified as suspicious, such as the British Union of Fascists and pacifist or other antiwar movements. All individuals uncovered by King were committed national socialists with a long-term substantive connection to fascist political groups. A declassified intelligence report in 2014 discussed many aspects of "Jack King's" penetration.[32] He utilized contacts inside the German community and fascist movements, primarily in southern England and London, to circulate within the community of inner sympathizers with links to Nazi Germany. His methodology for covert infiltration involved posing as a legitimate Gestapo agent and convincing targeted individuals of his identity.

The released data in MI5's report indicates he identified hundreds of Nazi sympathizers at large. His undercover actions managed, without generating significant outward awareness, to neutralize an extensive network of pro-fascist individuals plotting to assist Nazi Germany, supporters who zealously pledged their allegiance and physical support during a future German invasion of Britain. Individuals uncovered by Jack King included Edgar Whitehead, Hilda Leech and Marita Perigoe. The latter, a Swedish national, was a longtime associate of diverse extreme-right European political movements. After brief flirtations with the British Union of Fascists she dismissed the movement as overly moderate and not in synergy with the tenets of her national socialist interpretation. By 1944, Jack King was handling six senior level pro–Nazi operatives who believed the information supplied to him was distributed to Germany.[33] Regulation 18B granted Home Security powers to detain people deemed risks to national defense. In reacting to the propensity within fascist movements for treachery, the security measures deployed for internment were applied to extreme-right movements. Some organizations campaigning for appeasement or a nonviolent foreign policy in the mindset of MI5 presented potential pro–Nazi collaborators. The Peace Pledge Union and the British People's Party were among the principal pacifist groups calling for nonviolence regarding Germany in the 1930s; without doubt, evidence confirms relationships existed with the German Ministry of Propaganda and officials in Nazi Germany.[34] Direct communication with foreign intelligence agencies or behavior amounting to treasonous conduct was apparently not discovered. The Internment Acts generally applied to suspiciously behaving individuals with a proven fascist background, rather than to appeasement groups.

British Intelligence and the Double-Cross System

An agreement to cooperate obtained from captured German agents opened up the distinct opportunity for switching allegiance and opting for alternative future employment as double agents in British intelligence. If determined by MI5 that individuals might cultivate conceivably useful information or demonstrate suitability at leaking false intelligence back to Germany they were selected for the chance to turn double agent. After recruiting the first cohort of Operation Lena agents, MI5 was now obtaining advanced warning of infiltration. The potential applications of extending this new program appeared axiomatically decisive in intelligence battlefields, and competing ideas for exploitation approaches began to surface within British intelligence. John Cecil Masterman was appointed the inaugural commander of the "Double Cross" program. This sudden expansion of the asset processing system motivated Guy Liddell to form a small steering group to streamline management under Masterman in January 1941. Comprising senior officers from MI5, MI6 and the Wireless Committee, this group became known as the XX Committee or Twenty Committee. Further investigations by MI5 in the aftermath of Operation Lena's spectacular failure focused on British media's reporting surrounding the German spies' arrests.[35] In one incident three different versions explaining how the agents were detected were published by newspapers.

Facts suitable for printing or mass consumption were limited because of classified material and the trials had been conducted in secret at the Old Bailey court. Press organizations consequently filled in missing, incomplete or insufficiently accurate explanations of how the foreign agents were discovered. It transpired after the war that a substantial volume of wartime reporting was completely false. Controlling reams of information delicately as required was incontestably challenging. The publicity devoted to capturing parachutists and other secret agents was intended to divert German attention away from other operatives. In different instances cases were handled behind closed doors because MI5 intended to maintain the pretense that the espionage operatives remained at large and uncompromised. As the war progressed the British developed the initiative into a highly sophisticated and adaptable system.[36]

The captured Operation Lena and other Axis agents were complemented inside the Double Cross program by more professional and experienced cohorts (in most instances originating in Allied nations) who had volunteered of their own individual accord to become double agents. Arthur Owens, code-named Snow, continued his counterintelligence activities on both sides of the English Channel as an undercover specialist. Others had volunteered their services to British intelligence from the furthest corners of Europe, including Poland, Yugoslavia and Spain. In postwar recollections John Cecil Masterman stated, "We did much more than practice a large-scale deception.... Britain actively ran and controlled the German espionage system in this country. This is at first blush a staggering claim, and in the first place we could not bring ourselves to believe that we did so. Nevertheless it is true, and was true for the greater part of the war."[37] German postwar sources have confirmed that Masterman was in essence correct: no German intelligence agent escaped the British net or operated independently on British territory after 1942. The Twenty Committee held weekly meetings from its original formation until May 1945 inside the MI5 office located at 58 St. James's Street. Its essential purpose became the instrumental issue of deciding on the information to be securely permitted for dissemination to German handlers; as a secondary function the committee compared and assessed the divergent agents' reports to guarantee a reliable measure of consistency.

Protecting the double agents by assuring authenticity was unquestionably the most important factor in preventing exposure. The double-cross system at ground level was coordinated by Robertson, whose diversified profile extended to overseeing the case management of assets, exploring new deception plans and formulating tactics for delivering the most damaging information to the opposition. In the reorganization Tar Robertson was now redeployed as chief of B Division's Section B1a, a department dedicated to the management and administration of agents. Guy Liddell was in overall command of B Section, the branch of Security Service responsible for counterintelligence; he monitored defectors, suspect refugees, Nazi agents and double agents.

The controllers of the "Double Cross" system quickly realized that false information being disseminated by different agents to the Germans had to correspond generally and the transmissions by necessity should contain elements of realism sufficiently accurate to justify the Germans' confidence. But of course the content material should not be valuable enough to compromise the Allied effort or their intelligence sources.[38] In reorganizing the secret operative's new undercover life story it was sometimes necessary to construct a false depiction of reality. Agents therefore needed case handlers, radio operators and, on many occasions, guards. In situations involving captured enemy personnel the code books and wireless systems were commandeered and manipulated to transmit disinformation and assist the British cryptanalysts decoding enemy ciphers. One of the fundamental advantages in evaluating the program was the Bletchley Park codebreaking facility, which converged saliently in tracking the German assessment of information leaked by Double Cross to determine the response.

The process of running double agents implied the double agent must communicate a great deal of accurate information. Masterman commented that an assessment of this method could only be implemented with the cooperation of those with intimate knowledge of the agent's potentialities and technical knowledge of the subject in question. A team of case handlers, analysts and administration staff would, during the next six months, inflate the departmental inner ranks of Section B1, Liddell and Robertson resolved to place scrupulous attention to the handler relationships with agents. The Double Cross system developed into a program for thwarting and distracting the German war effort at every possible juncture. Twenty Committee output contrived to motivate both German intelligence and the Wehrmacht to remain critically unbalanced, diverting the enemy's attention to less dangerous sectors. Furthermore, the Abwehr, pleased with the seemingly valuable information produced by its controllers, regarded minimal advantages in dispatching more operatives to Britain. This reduced the dangerous prospects associated with any further insertions and agents operating undetected inflicting irreparable harm. By 1942 the Twenty Committee was using all available double agent resources in deceiving the Third Reich intelligence community.[39] These double agents provided information to their German counterparts in several meticulously orchestrated deception missions, transitioning into critical efforts to persuade military strategists to reach the intended conclusions. In 1942 and 1943, this was a strategy employed in preparation for military operations in North Africa and Sicily.

Arthur Owens was one of recently promoted Colonel Ritter's and German intelligence's most important agents inside the British frontier. He demonstrated an uncanny and confidential knowledge of British air force defensive systems. Ritter himself personally had recruited Owens in Lisbon back in 1935 and the Welshman had demonstrated his credibility virtually immediately. Owens was disguised behind his identity as a double agent completely until the war's conclusion. Doubt surfaced in British intelligence about Snow's enduring loyalty, with accusations of trafficking nonsanctioned information; but Snow had a fundamentally important role in determining the future of Allied landing in Sicily and Normandy. With the opening of expanded military frontiers Snow was indispensable in deceiving the Germans with intricate details about supposed British and American military plans. The Double Cross agents would prove increasingly decisive from 1943 onward as momentum of the European conflict shifted in the opposing direction.

An artificial source representing a massive puncture in northwestern European coverage was a Nazi agent code-named "Hektor" by the Germans. From 1943 to the end of 1944, Hektor from the German perspective passed on sensitive information on RAF aircraft production and manufacturing, and latest statistics on aircraft development, intelligence requests periodically appeared concerning aeronautic engineering and industrial equipment. The Abwehr was convinced that Hektor or Kramer was a window inside the British interior from Stockholm, funneling key strategic planning documents originating inside the Royal Air Force. He informed his Abwehr handlers about realistic-sounding developments of further connections in Sweden; indeed, Kramer garnered the little disputed reputation of a consummate asset. His contacts diligently conveying information to senior commanders stemmed from Lufthansa and personnel based at major airports. The trafficked subject materials in reality were fabricated by Kramer himself.[40] His deception maintained the illusion of relevancy by his reproducing hearsay and rumor from newspapers. Feeding back publicly available information was another standard technique.

A whole series of secretive methods were practiced by the Double Cross program and Twenty Committee to disseminate fabricated evidence to German intelligence that confirmed the information trafficked by agents. Elaborate deceptions were concocted with manufactured counterfeit documents, and "leaking" information on radio frequencies understood to be monitored by Hamburg was another route for ensuring consistency. Other agents demonstrating mastery at supplying either ineffectual or artificial content to German intelligence were Zigzag, Artist, Brutus and Hubert.

Eddie Chapman

Eddie Chapman was a British citizen recruited by the German secret service following his discovery by German military troops languishing in a Jersey prison. Developing his vicarious talents in the criminal underworld during a misspent adolescence, Chapman became a proficient thief and safecracker. In fact, during an illustrious criminal career he engaged himself in all manner of illegal exploits, from petty crime to fraud. Chapman had originally traveled to the Channel Islands for his own respite and to find a destination to lower his profile.

He was born on November 16, 1914, and was a native of Burnopfield, Durham. Chapman relocated to Soho, London, after receiving a discharge from military service, and this district would form his primary location for criminal enterprises. Joining the Coldstream Guard regiment at 17 years of age, Chapman quickly developed a reputation as a delinquent and troublemaker, spending 3 months in military prison for absconding without permission. Most of this post–armed forces period was spent working sporadically in casual occupations, from bar tendering to film sets. His gambling and alcohol problems would return to haunt Chapman, an individual who enjoyed social life in London, as his lifestyle soon outstripped any income. Chapman's history as a criminal in the underworld of prewar Britain is well documented and, unsurprisingly, his record demonstrates that he was no stranger to the police, with numerous arrests and serving a two-month sentence in Wormwood Scrubs Prison for forgery. Chapman arrived in Jersey as a wanted fugitive on the mainland, but he was inopportunely recognized by a Jersey policeman and forcibly taken into custody. The local police service received word from Scotland Yard that Chapman should be detained pending the arrival of their escort officers.[41]

Chapman still languished in a Jersey prison as German troops landed on the Channel Islands. As the departure time back to Britain neared, Chapman had reflected on his situation and imagined a different future for himself. He spent numerous hours while incarcerated studying literature and a multitude of subjects and teaching himself French and German. He befriended an inmate, Faramus, who collaborated in composing a letter after the invasion addressed to the German command post in St. Helier and General Otto von Stülpnagel, the officer in command of occupation forces in France and the Channel Islands and to whom the two prison compatriots candidly offered their services to the Third Reich. Chapman listed the various criminal offenses he practiced, emphasizing an expertise with explosives. His first maneuver after release was to approach the German command center on the island and inform an officer, "I would like to join the German secret service." He was questioned and the Nazi officer produced a written record documenting the encounter and apprising his superiors. It was the first of several interviews, at each of which Chapman repeated the same story: if the Germans wanted him to become an espionage agent and informant for them, he was capable and willing to do so.[42] The prospective German convert backed up his arguments by presenting press clippings of his criminal past.

Chapman explained to the multiple German officers he congressed with during the evaluation proceedings his eagerness in inflicting disdainful revenge on Britain's government because of his prior, bitter personal experiences. It was undoubtedly an engaging account: a poverty-stricken childhood and inadequate education, Chapman the victim of circumstance and falling into a life of crime. He continued to persuade regarding his case, informing the Germans about a long-term prison sentence hanging over his head in England. After a transfer to Paris he confirmed an agreement to commence training as a Nazi spy. The Abwehr chief in the Nantes region, Captain von Gröning, managed Chapman's formative indoctrination and training and evolved into his assigned spymaster and mentor. Recollections later by Chapman portrayed a genuine camaraderie forming between them. An espionage school was installed by the Germans outside Nantes. Speculated on ambiguously within British intelligence's analysis reports, the facility comprised this latest recruit's residence and training center for the intervening twelve months. Gröning and Abwehr commanders practically coveted Chapman, considering him a prize asset and requisitioned investment in training to develop the necessary talents for espionage behind the enemy fronts, spanning explosives to parachuting. Patriotic rumblings were surfacing, and unbeknownst to his handler Chapman seriously doubted his own intentions to act as a German spy.

German specialists trained Chapman in transmitting Morse code, invisible ink techniques, sabotage arts, and encoding and decoding ciphers. He was taught how to dynamite munitions trains and petrol dumps, ingenuous subterfuge methods of packing an attaché case with explosives, and covering contents with pajamas or towels. Later Chapman described in precise detail how Ackerman, a technical instructor at Nantes, constructed elaborate diagrams depicting mechanisms for connecting explosives with dynamite wire. Ackerman recommended schemes for purchasing the ingredients necessary in manufacturing the explosive materials over regular store counters and in pharmacies; he extrapolated on how potassium nitrate, a fertilizer product, and other chemicals such as potassium permanganate and ferric oxide were conveniently available in standard stores.[43] After the possibility of a maritime crossing was rejected it was decided that Eddie Chapman would indeed be returned to England by parachute and he received a course in parachute jumping.

During a practice parachute session, one of six preparatory and feasibly hazardous jumps, he dislodged several teeth; the consequent dental services left him with a smile that revealed two gold front teeth. At La Bretonnerie training center von Gröning informed Eddie Chapman that a challenging and fallible operational field experiment of his capabilities had been developed. He was commissioned to place a fabricated explosive device inside the Battignolles locomotive factory, an act that required him to surreptitiously clamber over protective barbed wire fences and maneuver past patrolling guards. Gröning had apparently conceived of this difficult secret operation after a discussion and the extra incentive of a financial wager with Major Meier, the person responsible for security over industrial factories in the region. Chapman managed to achieve his mission objectives with aplomb.

In June 1942, the Abwehr finally presented their British asset with a contract, in essence exchanging financial remuneration for collaboration with the Nazi government. For the amount of 100,000 Reichsmarks he was disposed by the contract's articles to return to England and perpetrate a sabotage assault. The target was a strategically crucial airplane factory producing Mosquito fighter bombers—the De Havilland works in Hatfield, north of London. After reviewing aerial photographs of the industrial installation, Chapman was imparted with diverse paraphernalia: a wireless set, twenty-four electric detonators, an American Colt .32-caliber pistol, a British entrenching tool, an illuminated wristwatch, a cyanide capsule in case he needed to commit suicide and £1,000. The return passage to Britain did not progress smoothly. A combination of cloud density and minimal visibility impeded navigation when it was absolutely necessary to avoid the enemy radar and defensive system. The pilot, on separate instances with navigation restricted and unaware of his location, managed to drift off course, completely losing the ability to determine the aircraft's bearings. Ischenger and Schlichting, aircraft personnel, both later recalled how Chapman retained an observable demeanor of calmness throughout the crossing, whether genuine or not.[44]

On December 16, 1942, Eddie Chapman—following months of intensive training by Abwehr Nantes and assumed by handler von Gröning to be converted into an accomplished and committed Nazi—parachuted onto English soil. Overshooting somewhat the preconceived drop zone but landing relatively safely at Lilleport in Cambridgeshire, a few hours after his jump Chapman surrendered to local police. MI5 moved in and took custody as lawfully entitled, and Chapman almost immediately offered his services. MI5, Section B1A, had discovered important elements of Chapman's mission since the parallel detection of suspicious information contained in decrypted German radio communication messages by Ultra. Section B1A implanted a countermeasure strategy, apprising RAF Fighter Command to continually track the German plane's movements and intercepting this alleged intelligence operative on the ground. After his parachute landing and hiding out temporarily inside a discreet wooded area, Chapman's first decision was contacting the nearest police station. He had to trenchantly overcome the local police officers' doubts about this obviously incredible story, but the officers reluctantly agreed to contact MI5. The officer who accompanied Chapman to MI5's headquarters coincidentally recognized him. On handing Chapman for questioning to Tar Robertson the policeman informed the MI5 officials about his own prior service with Chapman in a Coldstream Guards platoon. As was standard protocol for all captured spies Eddie Chapman was transferred to Camp 020 for further interrogation, and the camp commander, Major Stephens, drafted an assessment report classifying Chapman as confident and bordering on arrogant.

The German spymasters were adamant that Chapman had reiterated once than more to MI5 that he establish communications with his former criminal associates in Soho. He was instructed during other briefing sessions regarding visiting London and other cities for the express purpose of reporting on troop movements and defensive measures. John Masterman and the Twenty Committee decided to escort the cooperative Eddie Chapman on these expeditions in reality in attempts to interject accuracy and believability into the intelligence submitted post-screening to the handlers. In due course, Chapman indeed instigated communications with Hamburg by shortwave radio, as Gröning had expected, and sent the message containing "FFFF landed two miles north of Ely and buried gear. Took train next day with transmitter to London and later contacted friends. All OK. Fritz." He was then instructed by Hamburg to submit a perfunctory description of his landing and exploits in the immediate aftermath. In 2001 MI5 released a substantial collection of Eddie Chapman's wartime documents, or "Zigzag," as code-named by British intelligence. The information documents how extraordinarily potent an asset the Abwehr assumed Chapman to be. He was awarded an Iron Cross, Nazi Germany's highest decoration of honor, the medal pinned on during a ceremony in Berlin. Chapman received financially lucrative payments for his espionage activities. The greatest achievement of Chapman's double-cross career was convincing the Nazis of the authenticity of the fabricated bombing raid targeting the De Havilland production facility.

Chapman, in conjunction with MI5 and the Double Cross program, concocted a sabotage assault on the De Havilland factory at Hatfield, a major manufacturing center for the advanced RAF Mosquito airplane. German reconnaissance aircraft had subsequently photographed the designated Hatfield targets, and the realistic appearing but totally artificial damage convinced Eddie Chapman's German controllers regarding the assault's success. The Mosquito was essentially a reconnaissance plane with multiple capabilities to perform as both fighter and bomber aircraft. The technical brilliance was produced by an extremely lightweight aerodynamic design that permitted the Mosquito to attain maximum acceleration and high speeds—for that time. The German Air Defense chief and military high command became infuriated with this new technology. Göring's fighter planes and defensive systems were powerless to prevent deep penetrations.[45] Eddie Chapman was selected as the perfect operative for the De Havilland mission. The most promising industrial target for damaging Britain's ability to continue production was theorized to be the special lightweight wood. Abwehr agents had consumed months investigating an ideal weaken spot. A factory storing this component appeared to be just that.

Further elaborations by the Twenty Committee engineered sequences of imaginary incidents, notifying Hamburg controllers of Chapman's exploration and reconnaissance of Hatfield facilities. Chapman decided that the most effective strategy for damaging and irreparably restricting production long-term was destroying the main power plant. From a deserted location in Kent he radioed his superiors with positive developments and annotations on obtaining the explosives needed for covert operations. On January 29, 1943, Zigzag's message commented, "Will attempt sabotage this evening at six o'clock." Later that night a second message from England arrived: "Mission successfully accomplished." He digressed into an intricate rendering of the circumstances he had encountered at the De Havilland installation, recounting for the benefit of the radio operators in Hamburg an improvised technique of combining two separate explosive devices with timers. He finished the construction by attaching wristwatches to practical lessons guidance and demonstrations during sabotage training in Nantes. Gröning pronounced his elation with his protégé's accomplishments, vindicating the considerable investment and hours expended, not to mention fundamentally his professional reputation. Superiors back in Berlin demanded unequivocal proof and orders were conferred to Luftwaffe commanders to arrange reconnaissance flights for deployment over the Hatfield site. The aerial photographs appeared convincing. Without obscurement they documented visible dents in the power plant's roof and debris from the explosion, including smashed generator sections and heavy apparatus scattered covering a wide area. Military intelligence reported zero doubtful contentions about having severely restricted the future production of the Mosquito.

The MI5 camouflage experts had arrived at Hatfield the previous evening and industriously finished the contrived simulations by 11:00 p.m. despite the inky blackness. Chapman's MI5 file described the techniques employed to reconstruct a convincing but artificial image for German reconnaissance aircraft. The camouflage was excellently staged and the impression obtained by MI5's technical analysts predicted that aerial photography from any height above 2,000 feet would depict with dependable accuracy considerable devastation and forestall the fostering of any reservations. Four replications of the sub-transformers had been constructed of wood, with all the authentic transformers covered by netting and corrugated iron, which was painted to convince the aerial photograph analysts that bomb damage had been inflicted.[46] On returning to Germany, Chapman, despite the reconnaissance evidence, would be summoned for a debriefing session. The double agent, MI5 advised, needed to finesse the burgeoning relations with his German handlers and be persuasive on the mission's success, with minimal photographic documentation by himself from inside the De Havilland facility to demonstrate his case. Wartime documents indicate considerable debate within MI5 on the question of permitting Zigzag to return to Germany. He did, as encouraged by his handlers, travel back to Germany with security concerns outweighed by potential for a counterintelligence coup. Initially, in debriefing sessions as speculated by MI5, von Gröning was becoming impatient and frustrated at the vague reassurance Chapman was feeding him. His explanation and the cunning fabricated display at De Havilland were sufficient to satisfy interrogators, and the Nantes commandant deemed no further verification was worthwhile. In fact, the questionnaire submitted by German intelligence was highly educational in indicating the key intelligence requirements of their corresponding numbers. A recurring theme referenced England's southeast coast pertaining to the geographical locations of divisions and brigades, and specific interests mentioned antitank guns and other weapons.

For his next Abwehr mission Eddie Chapman adopted an artificial backstory and identity, the assumed persona of Hugh Anson. Gröning temporarily relocated him to Lisbon with a naval sabotage mission in the preparation stage. Chapman enlisted as a crewmate on the *City of Lancaster*, a Liverpool-based merchant ship that routinely traversed the Portuguese coastline transporting commodities. His assignment's first objective was to board the vessel while disguised as a legitimate crew member and discover the entrance to sensitive areas. Following his instructions Chapman then planted explosive devices onboard the *Lancaster* before slipping inconspicuously ashore, the ensuing detonation resulting in the merchant ship's destruction. This incident was another elaborate fabrication by MI5, and the dual machinations of contrived media reporting and propagating misleading information engendered the desired impulses within enemy intelligence networks. The *Lancaster* survived Chapman's "attack" and was removed to an unknown location. Upon his return to Germany, Zigzag's reputation as a premier undercover asset inside military intelligence circles ascended higher, and he was now quantified as essential to manipulating a competitive advantage against the Allies.[47] He was once again transferred and spent the next 15 months in relative luxury, selected for appointment as a training instructor at an Abwehr espionage school in occupied Norway. The Nazi intelligence system's brightest prospect was awarded the Iron Cross for his appreciated exploits in damaging De Havilland factory and the *City of Lancaster*.

In 1944 Zigzag was reposted to his former homeland for an espionage mission. He brought with him a sizeable quantity of information covering the German Secret Service. MI5's Double Cross team obtained critical intelligence on the inner workings of their opposition and capabilities. This rejuvenated introduction of Chapman was organized for selecting viable targets from inside domestic territory for the V-1 flying bomb technology. To inflict maximum devastation on the Germans was becoming a priority. The final segment of his wartime undercover activities was a deception operation to misdirect the V-1 missiles and disrupt the enemy aerial assault strategies in the culminating months of conflict. Chapman justifiably garnered the reputation of being among Britain's most successful double agents, and for the remaining months of the war he operated undercover without being unmasked. Following the end of World War II Chapman was released from his commitments to MI5 and pursued a number of business interests. He remained friends with von Gröning, his former Abwehr case handler, with mutual attendance at weddings. Chapman died in 1997.

Intelligence supplied by agent Zigzag to the Twenty Committee and MI5 case handlers is found in multiple transcripts from interviews with Lord

Rothschild, head of the B1C Section of MI5. The revelations provide an illuminating picture of an assortment of sabotage techniques in development by the Wehrmacht, photographs of sabotage technology and data concerning prospective sabotage sites. The debriefing sessions revealed hitherto unknown details on the training of IRA dissidents by Germany. MI5 released additional documents in 2012 from the Chapman case. During debriefing interviews with Section B1 staff Chapman announced his desire to return to Germany, adopting the disguise of his Abwehr service employment, to assassinate the Führer.[48] He postulated about how this implausible-sounding scheme could be accomplished by exploding a bomb at a Nazi ceremony, explaining that his German spymaster had promised to escort him personally to a Nazi rally and arrange an audience with Hitler. Further plans documented in the files included Chapman dressing in a Nazi uniform and infiltrating a podium adjacent to Hitler. The handlers, however, were definitely not in agreement, believing the scheme unworkable.[49] They dissuaded Chapman from taking the assassination scheme further.

Juan Pujol García

Spanish national Juan Pujol García, code-named "Garbo," was definitely a multitalented double agent with exceptional influence inside the Allied deception program. He infiltrated Nazi intelligence with formidable diligence and formed personal associations with multiple Third Reich consulate and bureaucratic officials with connections. He offered his services cautiously, presenting himself as both fervently anti–British and a committed fascist sympathizer. A background record existed for Garbo as an undeniable volunteer within a pro–Franco militia during the Spanish Civil War and a Republican deserter in another period. Announcing himself to the German embassy staffers in Madrid, he proposed to become an espionage activist for the Third Reich burrowed inside either neutral Lisbon or the United Kingdom. Rebuffed at first, Juan Pujol García persisted stubbornly until he procured a personal audience with a secretive Abwehr official, code-named Federico, with the real identity of Friedrich Knappe-Ratey. At the meeting Juan Pujol presented a distorted image of himself as a committed national socialist and combat veteran on several battlefields in support of General Franco.

In May 1941 Juan Pujol appeared at the Abwehr Madrid headquarters and expressed an outline proposition and his much deliberated personal contention on traveling to Britain and orchestrating the dissemination of covert information to Berlin. Karl-Erich Kuhlenthal, the intelligence officer assigned to perform the appraisal duties, was initially unenthusiastic and failed to recognize much advantage in using Pujol's services. At this time Kuhlenthal was the senior Abwehr officer stationed in Madrid and commanded significant connections in Berlin.[50] Juan Pujol, in the Nazi assessment, harbored genuine hostility for the British and simultaneously a profound admiration for Hitler. As enticement he mentioned to interrogators his relationships with allegedly prominent contacts in Spanish security services and foreign office. He concocted a scenario for maneuvering in geographical locations that were problematic to access without attracting suspicion. Pretending to be legitimately traveling to Britain as a correspondent for a Spanish newspaper removed obstacles. He devised a second scheme with a coherent excuse of investigating the financial transactions at a bank for a business associate. His persistence rewarded, the Spanish volunteer was recruited and thereafter controlled in Abwehr intelligence by Karl-Erich Kuhlenthal.

Pujol participated in briefings and training programs developed for the orientation of agents. Kuhlenthal delved into the Nazi intelligence system and its objectives relating to opposing security services in Spain. Code-named Cato by the Madrid Abwehr station, Pujol gradually, as understood by his appointed handlers, developed an integrated network of underground informants. Using earlier civil war linkages, he ambitiously targeted for recruitment nationalists from Britain and Ireland to expand the conspiracy beyond Spanish borders. He had managed to be succinct and suitably discursive in recording content and scenarios associated with the informants, assuring Kuhlenthal that his contact repository was embedded deep within the military and establishment structures in Spain and Britain. From Lisbon he transmitted fictitious intelligence reports to the Germans, pretending he resided in Britain. This supposedly high-value covert information was not authentic and in actuality was plagiarized from guidebooks and magazines resourcefully borrowed from local libraries, geographical maps, newsreels and English language vocabulary books. Pujol had no prior experience of visiting Britain and occasionally it showed.[51]

The Twenty Committee and Section B1A of MI5 converted the double agent program into an art form. As Double Cross system and Masterman organized an appropriately meticulous assessment of Garbo's feedback, the impressive magnitude associated with the Spanish agent's fictional characters became digestible. His hidden network contained at its peak complement 27 illusionary informants. He steadily submitted intelligence communiqués to spymaster Kuhlenthal discussing intimate facts in a plethora of interconnected circumstances and, if necessary, personal minutiae of the operatives he was pretending to control. The artificial informant list included military deserters and disgruntled commissioned officers, dockyard workers, a Welsh Aryan supremacist, students and disaffected civil servants.⁵² One typical corrupted official was purportedly an informant inside the Spanish ministry of information. Suddenly Pujol became an eminently desirable asset, so desirable an acquisition that British agencies disputed who should manage this evolving case.

MI5 smuggled Pujol from Lisbon via Gibraltar on April 24, 1942. He was then escorted to London and resettled in a safe house in the North London suburbs of Hendon. He was awarded the code name of Garbo in recognition of his ability to assume an assortment of characters, and Tomás Harris became his designated case officer. As Masterman had noted, "He came to us therefore a fully-fledged double agent." During the next three years Garbo transmitted 1,399 messages and 423 letters to his Abwehr handlers in Spain, Tomás Harris and two other full-time MI5 case officers were deployed to process his traffic and the 27 fictional individuals in Garbo's network. The complicated and diverse array of nationalities was absorbing enough, with operatives hailing from Portugal, England, South America and Greece. The highest point of Juan Pujol García's career would manifestly be connections with the counterintelligence activities in preparation for the Allied invasion of Normandy in 1944.

The deception plan covering the invasion was code-named "Fortitude," and its principle objective was to persuade the Nazi high command that instead of attacking Normandy the main thrust of Allied advanced expeditionary forces would be Pas de Calais. To this end, fabricated United States military divisions were constructed entirely from thin air; false radio transmissions disseminated misleading information; and other controlled deceptions were released into motion with precise timing. Fortitude was essentially a countermeasure to ensure divided German armed forces were encountered on the ground by the D–Day troops. The Double Cross program convinced the OKW and Hitler that the D–Day invasion force was destined for the alternate location. Garbo proved himself immensely valuable during Fortitude, submitting large quantities of communiqué's to stimulate his Nazi handlers about the deception.⁵³

Arthur Owens

Arthur Owens specialized, as the manager of a family-owned business, in the manufacture of battery accumulators. As discussed earlier he was, fortuitously for British intelligence's purposes, a frequent visitor to Nazi Germany, beginning in 1935, because of business transactions. The British Admiralty had requested that Arthur Owens hold conversations with their representatives and divulge any pertinent information about expeditions to Berlin and other cities and to retrieve, if possible, technical and defense information as demonstrations of his loyalty. During a 1936 foray to Germany, Owens was introduced to a Luftwaffe lieutenant, Nikolaus Ritter, who adopted the pseudonym of Dr. Rantzau and was seconded to Abwehr's Hamburg station concerned with aviation intelligence.

Operational security measures observed at that time attempted to ensure that Owens should never discover the genuine identity of Rantzau. Ritter treated Owens to a luxurious dinner in Hamburg, no expense spared, and they ended the evening in a succession of attractive local nightspots. The campaign of recruitment had begun. Ritter appealed to Owens' apparent Welsh nationalist bitterness toward the English as appropriate reasoning for turning as a secret agent for Germany and reneging on prior commitments or sentiments towards his resident government. He outlined fully the lucrative financial reimbursement Owens should anticipate receiving for collaboration with military intelligence. That was a satisfactory incentive for Owens, who resolved to confirm his agreement. In conversations with Ritter during that Hamburg sojourn and on subsequent occasions Owens revealed his own personal reasons for the purpose of authenticating trust, with considerable synergy to Ritter's own comments regarding his staunch willingness to become a spy. Financial motivations and various other personal experiences were implied as explanations for his treachery.[54] His double life as an Abwehr spy began in 1936 after being inducted as an agent. For eight months previously agent Snow had engaged in sporadically passing to the British Naval Intelligence Directorate (NID) information obtained on routine business excursions to Germany's interior as advised. This mutually favorable and generally unhindered arrangement commenced after Owens was introduced to the deputy director of naval intelligence and during lunch at the Army and Navy Club found himself invited to furnish the Admiralty with any useful fragments of information should the appropriate sources be acquired in Germany.

Seduced by adventurous notions of secret agents and their lifestyle Owens' first undercover mission occurred in January 1936, when he returned with information of value on coastal motorboats operated by the German navy. Having requested to be classified as a regular agent he was transferred to the Secret Intelligence Service (MI6), which evaluated Owens as deserving of further scrutiny for missions abroad. SIS assigned Owens a case officer named Colonel Edward Peal and welcomed the Welshman into the closeted espionage world with minimal reservations or doubts expressed. His business credentials theoretically, from Peel's perspective, provided a convenient and unobtrusive entrance into sensitive regions on the European mainland. Agent Snow's next assignment was a discreet journey to Holstein and Kiel, where he clandestinely photographed several Kriegsmarine warships.[55] Owens admitted with full disclosure his ongoing relationship with Abwehr officers and Dr. Rantzau. For the ensuing three years agent Snow voluntarily passed information to MI6 and Special Branch while engaging simultaneously in the identical relationship with German intelligence.

In September 1939 he traveled to Holland accompanied by a second operative former police officer, Gwiylm Williams, both assuming identities of disgruntled Welsh nationalists. Fellow Welsh double agent Williams earned the distinct reputation of an effective by-the-book operative while undercover. As supposed collaborator MI5 Double Cross records confirm he accompanied Owens to Germany and Portugal on several occasions. A meeting was arranged with Abwehr senior commander Nikolaus Ritter, who in the aftermath of British and French declarations of war demanded subordinates expand their networks of agents. Owens and Williams reported to MI5 concerning the conversations on their return, presenting to controllers exigent information including encipher keys to various Abwehr radio codes. Owens' greatest accomplishment as a double agent was the uncovering of "Operation Lena." The entire mission was essentially doomed from the beginning, its misfortune being that documents delivered faithfully by another of Owens' coconspirators, McCarthy, had been carefully doctored and altered by MI5 to include a number of telltale mistakes.[56]

The identification card, for instance, was a counterfeit machine-folded version. Ration books were definitely nonstandard, deliberately altered to resemble documents issued to travelers and nonresidents. Owens had convinced his German counterparts to disclose the designations and strategies devised for each Invasion Spy, and all necessary sensitive data was disseminated to Owens, supposedly to enable the artificial paperwork to be produced and for other operational matters. British police and intelligence personnel were deployed to exposed landing sites and awaited the imminent arrival of the intruders. The Invasion Spy period and the remainder of 1940 and 1941 incited intense postulation about the predicted location and target of a German expeditionary force. Nobody doubted that an impending assault should be expected. Owens and Williams, under the direction of MI5, endeavored to misrepresent and deceive their contacts about the strength of Britain's defensive capability, division complements and armed forces overall. The information in reports that Owens routinely transmitted to Ritter are a fascinating insight into Double Cross's strategy for misdirecting their opposite counterparts, and many fragments survived in the Security Service files. The Snow files were declassified in 2005, and wartime assessments feature an intricate explanation of the Welsh agents' exploits.

Sufficient quantities of information concocted by Robertson and Masterson were original and these partially verifiable reports had inspired confidence.

Intelligence content was produced by field expeditions and operations, combined with a network of fictitious subagents that worked for him. Comparable to Garbo's prodigious achievements, one informant in his account worked inside the Air Ministry, and others subverted authority detection at RAF depots. He informed headquarters in July 1940 that a total of 38 agents had been recruited. The story fabricated by MI5 formulated the image of Owens targeting other individuals in the Welsh nationalist movement. Ritter pressed Arthur Owens, or "Johnny," his Abwehr code name, to investigate airfield positions and collect intelligence data on RAF airplanes. Requests accumulated on obligations for gathering information on shipbuilding data and authoritative estimates on the Atlantic convoy system and the armaments industries. On a society level, the Abwehr priority requests were centered on food rationing, Ministry of Food initiatives and information on the repercussions from blockades or industrial unrest. Other inquiries concerning developments in food prices and the details of commodity shipment destinations were delivered to Robertson's clearinghouse. Gwiylm Williams was allotted extra freedom of movement to enable suitable mobility in searching for information. Because of his supposed pronationalist feelings he presented himself as committed in resorting to any method possible to discourage the manufacture of military equipment in factories in Wales.

After their initial conferences with nominal controller Dr. Rantzau, Snow was introduced to another operative code-named "Charlie," a German photographer believed to have been coerced into working for Nazi Germany under undoubted duress. Threatening language of endangerment against his brother and other family members residing in Germany were difficult to discount or ignore. Charlie was employed for producing photographs on shipping and microphotography for sending the intelligence reports prepared by agent "Johnny." He evolved into a cooperative and valuable asset for British intelligence in submitting the negatives and copies of photographs, as these conduits inside the inner workings of German intelligence were critical. He competently assisted Owens in several missions, not least by confirming and vouching for his elaborate cover stories. His involvement was ended in 1941. Snow's infiltration of German intelligence continued from September 1939 to April 1941 and had opened permanently an unfettered conduit into the enemy's insular strategies and objectives.[57] He gathered information for MI5 on the Nazi chemical weapons programs, invasion plans, infrared technology and senior counterespionage personnel.

The code breaking work at Bletchley Park was ameliorated by the fact that messages prepared by MI5 on behalf of Snow were relayed to Berlin on an Enigma-generated code. Comparative analysis of these intercepts with the original MI5 text was crucial to the complete understanding of the German Enigma-based communications. An appreciably more accurate understanding of methods of German wireless codes and procedures emerged from the Snow case. Contacts firmly established and finessed in Nazi Germany by this infiltration proved fundamental in obtaining a more comprehensive picture of the enemy's tactical positions. The Twenty Committee's outlook asserted that every agent should be under the control and continual escort by British security personnel. Arthur Owens was appointed a case officer and his own team of MI5 specialists, a radio operator for transmissions expertise, round-the-clock bodyguards, a chauffeur and a housekeeper. A methodology adhered to, if plausible, in order to guarantee Arthur Owens portrayed realistic experiences, was an accompanying escort to RAF bases and other locations to imbue the necessary authentic-sounding qualities to the Ritter transmissions.

Problems were definitely encountered. Agent Snow disliked—and voiced his displeasure about—the constant MI5 presence and the restrictive 24-hour guard. Whenever Robertson or a case officer pressured him sufficiently complaints were forwarded about being treated like a prisoner and multifarious other resentments. A potentially disastrous incident nearly occurred and was narrowly averted in 1941 when Major Ritter, after summoning Owens to Lisbon, almost uncovered the divided loyalties present in their agent following a mission failure. In defending himself against the accusations, Owens gambled by divulging a long-standing dialogue with MI5 but at the same time proclaiming profusely to be committed to his German employers. He managed to convince Ritter that his affiliation with MI5 was a deception for obtaining secret information from inside Britain's intelligence system. At this exact point in time another double agent, Walter Dicketts, on a separate and semi-independent mission to Germany, was perilously unaware of Arthur Owens' present movements or revelations. Shortly after arriving he was arrested and forcibly taken into custody. With minimal awareness of the extent Owens had incriminated himself, selecting the appropriate course of action was a difficult prospect. For two weeks Dicketts was subjected to an intense and aggressive interrogation, which he survived. Major Ritter and the Abwehr chiefs found the agents convincing, and both were immediately reactivated and dispatched without hesitation to Britain with renewed cash funds. German intelligence commanders assumed incorrectly that Walter Dicketts was probably unaware of involvement between his associate and MI5.[58]

The contrasting accounts of Owens and Dicketts on the unfolding events were analyzed by the Twenty Committee in London and showed some contradictions but fortunately held up. The MI5 files on Arthur Owens include interpretive documents about his reliability as a double agent. Tar Robertson questioned Snow's enduring loyalty and implied a greater than perceived attachment might exist to his alternative employer in Berlin. Paperwork refers to his estranged wife, who contacted MI5 to inform authorities and openly accused him of treacherously being a German government agent. Owens' personal life continued to generate awkward problems and MI5 officers in 1944 issued a detention order for Snow's girlfriend "Lily." A second challenging and ambiguous situation occurred in 1940, prompting British intelligence to reassess their operative's allegiances. Abwehr intelligence in May 1940 advised on directives for transporting Owen to the Third Reich for further training. Ritter personally ordered a U-boat for this expedition. With maritime traffic on the northern Europe front at virtually saturation levels and the conflict engulfing Scandinavia and France, this amounted to an undoubtedly complicated venture. German naval command refused permission for secondment of a submarine; alternatively, following considerable wrangling, a viable twin-engine seaplane was selected as a vehicle for extracting the agent.

Requisitioning accomplished, Ritter scheduled for Owens and an unknown accomplice subagent to be removed from the Grimsby coastline on May 20. MI5 discovered the planned operation and decided to manipulate this promising opportunity in order to deposit another double agent into Abwehr's midst. Former confidence trickster Sam McCarthy was selected for the mission, in essence performing the character of Snow's partner. However, the proceedings experienced an unexpected alteration. Onboard the intermediary transit vessel charting a course towards the rendezvous location in Grimsby, McCarthy and Owens each became convinced the other was a legitimate German agent. Genuine motives became obscured and McCarthy, his paranoia manifestly growing, locked Arthur Owens inside his cabin and waited until the trawler returned home. MI5 determined upon investigating the circumstances that Snow had possessed unlicensed classified documents not officially subject to authorized clearance. Explaining his motivation, Owens protested in his defense that these "nonessential" documents would be necessary for demonstrating his capabilities to Major Ritter. He digressed on his suspicions that a Gestapo double agent had penetrated the operation and placating the confidence of his German intelligence contacts was therefore of profound importance. Ritter, aboard the seaplane, circled the coordinates at the confirmed rendezvous point for the trawler, but the mission ended unfulfilled. The pilot advised that reserve fuel supplies were dangerously low and Ritter called for the extraction to be abandoned.

The Lisbon confrontation transpired to be Owens' final overseas mission. By the end of 1941 his case was largely discontinued. The revelations in Portugal persuaded the Twenty Committee that agent Snow had attracted too much exposure and overseas missions would rapidly become counterproductive utilizing this pathway. Snow was interned for the remainder of the conflict, as rigorous security measures applied to all Double Cross personnel. He continued to serve British intelligence while interned at Dartmoor Prison, and he developed acquaintances with German POWs and reported on observations and dialogues that revealed facts.[59] The arrangements so carefully constructed by Owens and the Twenty Committee would be reactivated one last time, Snow's previous capital was exploited in the grand misdirection strategy of Operation Fortitude. Owens was a notable source of fabricated intelligence carefully disseminated in this counterintelligence operation, and his exertions proved crucial in reducing the ground defense forces encountered by D–Day troops in Normandy.

One senior British MI5 personnel charged with accompanying agent Snow and appearing in numerous debriefings stated that Owens was the most prolific source of information concerning Nazi security service opposite numbers. At times, Abwehr II or another intelligence agency within the Nazi hierarchy or military would discover information that transpired upon analysis to be erroneous or at least highly suspect. In intelligence circles, receiving ineffective data is a standard scenario; the Abwehr trained handlers to prioritize drawing information from the informants or agents who demonstrated a high level performance. But coordination in the agent "Johnny" case within the nexus of German intelligence agencies failed to identify the most critical evidence indicated by its various divergent departments. This coordination breakdown had facilitated agent Snow in repeatedly passing through security nets.

Popov and Jebsen

Dusko Popov had navigated in respected Yugoslavian diplomatic and business circles for many years, and these relationships later facilitated dialogue with European political and establishment figures in wartime. He was supervised as a dual operation with long-term friend and associate Johnny Jebsen; in fact, he dependably volunteered for an alliance after Jebsen approached him in May 1940 and announced his involvement as an espionage activist for the Abwehr since the war's beginning. Popov's charisma and connections with powerful people were advantageous in his efforts to become not only a spy but also a double agent. The two individuals had originally become acquainted while studying at Freiburg University, Germany, in this early formative period developing into trusted companions. Popov was originally, records reflect, a native of Titel, Austro-Hungary, now Serbia, and settled in Dubrovnik. Both he and

Jebsen were descendants of prestigious and wealthy families, Jebsen's parents were prosperous from business dealings in Germany and Denmark. The younger Jebsen had adopted somewhat upper-class mannerisms, wearing expensive dinner jackets and a monocle. This background proved immensely useful in convincing German intelligence of the value of the two men. Both undoubtedly also harbored a distinct animosity towards Nazism.[60]

Popov and Jebsen both opposed Nazi Germany and colluded in their determination to inflict permanent blows from the inside on fascist intentions in Europe. Any outward manifestation of Dusko Popov's political aspirations were not interpreted correctly by Reich bureaucrats. He was sufficiently credible to persuade Jebsen's influential Nazi contacts that he was passionately supportive of Hitler's Fatherland. Jebsen's recommendation was not the final obstacle to his acceptance into the German secret service underworld. In early 1940 Ernst Menninger, the handler of Jebsen, requested an analysis report on the French theater and possibilities for collaboration with the Wehrmacht.[61] The report impressed Menninger and the Abwehr leadership in due course, as his predictions occurred almost without caveat. The French occupation was immediately followed by Pierre Laval's treachery in the Vichy government just as Popov intimated. Consequently, their self-promotion obviously producing solid dividends, in the summer of 1940 Jebsen and Popov were cordially invited to dinner with Menninger, then a senior official in the Abwehr Belgrade office.

The dinner was a sociable affair, but Popov was unmistakably participating in an assessment and screening process for other unknown interventions. Menninger appeared to enjoy the company of both individuals. By this time Popov had confirmed, in the midst of fervent deliberation, a prior agreement with British intelligence undisclosed to either Menninger or the Nazi infrastructure. He had contacted the British embassy in Yugoslavia, and apprised Clement Hope, an embassy official, of the recent negotiations and his research assignments. The Abwehr Belgrade commander was enthused about Popov's report. Popov's social connections were obviously assets that could be harnessed by skilled intelligence officers. Jebsen and Popov's detectable associations with neutral and questionably loyal individuals in France, Yugoslavia and neighboring Eastern Europe would be constructive assets, but Menninger was contemplating a different field of operations. In July 1940 he proposed that Britain be the nation selected for infiltration and officially invited Popov to volunteer for induction into German military intelligence. The Abwehr registered the code name Ivan. At this juncture the former university friends ended up becoming double agents working as espionage exponents for both the Abwehr and British intelligence. In the negotiations various inducements and substantial financial reimbursement were assured in exchange for confirming cooperation.

Dusko Popov presented a consignment of research documents compiled in his precursory relationship with Abwehr officers to the British embassy in Yugoslavia. That was his first major instance of treachery. Jebsen and Popov continued to ensure that critical information destined for the Nazis was diverted into British intelligence's possession. Uniquely, this appropriated content had inspired interdepartmental cooperation between the Secret Information Service and the Security Service in working domestically in both Britain and pan–Europe. Popov's legitimate import-export business subsequently afforded coverage for recurrent expeditions to Lisbon, where he imparted an assortment of secretive intelligence to the Nazi representatives, albeit that perception of events was purposely cultivated. Intelligence agency presence in Lisbon was practically at saturation levels, but Portugal still was a satisfactory destination for many methods of undercover activity. Popov's Lisbon business transactions were periodically accessed for a convenient excuse if he or Jebsen were located in Portugal or Spain and had acquired information for distribution to handlers. British intelligence encouraged Jebsen and Popov to factor into collaborations any chance of progressive intrusions to maximize the penetration. Much of the intelligence report content exchanged with their Security Service handlers referred to inner Abwehr politics and decision making.[62] Both assets were exploited for trafficking misleading information back across the channel to the Abwehr.

Dusko Popov's personal file was released by Security Service for public viewing in 2002. The firsthand accounts and commentary by the case handler describes how the information Popov supplied to German intelligence was filtered through MI5 and the Twenty Committee. He reported on military and political developments, German rocket manufacturing and assaults and indication of the later Japanese attack on Pearl Harbor. This infiltration was classified as sufficiently important for meticulous dedication to be employed by the British intelligence handlers to determine what attractive and convincing subject matter should be leaked through the Serbian, now code-named "Tricycle." The Security Service maintained significant institutional momentum in proliferating alliances with anti–Nazi political movements and opposition organizations in Europe. Informants were also coordinated from within supposedly pro–Nazi movements, determined to be crucial in fostering dissent against the occupying forces throughout Yugoslavia. These connections were assessed by Security Service as fundamental to protecting their assets Popov and Jebsen.[63]

Case files on Popov portray with greater clarity his reassignment for action in the Americas on August 10, 1941. The Yugoslavian government's overthrow in 1941 and the escalating German military assaults inside national boundaries rendered the fortunes of the Serbian operative difficult to predict. German intelligence (evidently their internal machinations encountered a similar dilemma) decided on the prudence of redeploying him to the United States to establish a German spy network. While residing in the United States the double agent reputedly lived the extravagant lifestyle he had previously been accustomed to. He rented a New York penthouse on Park Avenue and invested in expensive motor vehicles and vacations spent at luxurious ski resorts. The German plans for an espionage network rapidly failed to advance, intense concerted U.S. authority and FBI "heat" being a prominent interrupting factor. His erstwhile mission for Nazi intelligence firmly on the back burner, Popov improvised from Twenty Committee's perspective as an unofficial British intelligence liaison officer, advising the FBI on his undercover activities and conveying relevant information on Nazi strategic and military objectives. Dusko Popov had procured through surreptitious means and delivered to U.S. authorities a classified list of intelligence targets produced by German secret service personnel, a combined total of three pages. Disputed claims indicate that Tricycle informed J. Edgar Hoover about matters pertaining to a Japanese planned attack on a U.S. navel base, Pearl Harbor being mentioned, before the culmination of 1941. Hoover and others consistently denied this discussion happened.[64]

As a now senior Abwehr field operative Popov was instructed on several occasions to travel to Brazil and obtain pertinent information from August to November 1941. He generally engaged in covert conferences with Gustav Engels, at that juncture acting commander of the Brazilian Nazi operations. This provided illuminating reports on Nazi–South American operations for both the FBI and MI5. A rendezvous with Engels at his AEG office was arranged in November, and Popov was ordered to instigate advanced preparations for constructing a radio transmitter in the United States and to organize collecting information on Atlantic convoys, war production and technical developments in antisubmarine warfare. The Abwehr were proposing that Popov should eventually assume control for the Portuguese operations in Atlantic radio transmissions. But delays were emerging, partially branching from unforeseen political culture shifts and complaints about Popov's insufficient productivity.[65]

On the return section of his journey heading back to Europe Tricycle's luggage contained details of Nazi operatives and safe houses in South America. It was observed by the FBI personnel assigned to "babysit" agent Tricycle that his egregiously excessive spending was causing unwanted attention and had stimulated alarm as a propensity for opening security risks. Dusko Popov began an illicit romantic affair with a Simone Simon while on secondment. The FBI discovered this personal entanglement and organized a surveillance detail for Simon. From contemporary accounts the FBI indicated concerns about his romantic attachment's Italian heritage and the possibility for divided loyalties. The American authorities expressed doubts indeed regarding Dusko Popov's legitimacy and investigated his movements for suspected infringements.

The Abwehr was experiencing an enhanced period of considerable reshuffling in early 1942, motivated among other factors, by the expanding marginalization of military intelligence and the intrusion growing daily from Himmler's RSHA. Popov's primary supervisor in Abwehr was the reasonably amenable Major von Karstoff; that connection, however, was terminated with prejudice after Karstoff, accused of unacceptable operational failures, found himself deported to the Russian front. The Gestapo officially were given the authority for handling Popov. The Serbian had prior entanglement with the Gestapo and justifiable reasons for observing this transition with disquiet. During an abortive earlier venture at Freiberg University to enlist within Nazi bureaucracies he was deviously ensnared under the false pretenses of supposedly meeting with Abwehr recruitment officer Major von Karstoff. The anticipated Abwehr personnel were absent and instead the young student encountered a group of Gestapo agents who proceeded to instigate a serious physical assault. An intervention was necessary to prevent more sustained or life threatening injuries.

British intelligence was not optimistic about this unpredictable development or the changing environment of their high-performing plant. Dusko Popov was questioned extensively by the Gestapo officers assigned to him, suspicions still circulating after his reemergence from America and for other irregularities. Reviewing Ivan's intelligence contributions since recruitment, according to the Gestapo, documented minimal valuable data or reportage of genuine sophistication appropriated to handlers. But credibility remained to observers intact and, despite the Gestapo interference, undercover covert operations persisted unabated. The traveling expeditions to Lisbon also continued. In 1944, Tricycle performed a prominent segment of Operation Fortitude's campaign of elaborately conceived misdirection by submitting the fabricated data judiciously to his handlers.[66]

On April 29, 1944, Jebsen was captured in Portugal by a suspicious local Abwehr station during the planning stages of Fortitude. He was imprisoned at the Oranienberg concentration camp but loyally refused to divulge sensitive information exposing Tricycle, Garbo or Operation Fortitude. It is believed that Jebsen was killed towards the end of World War II, probably in March 1945. Popov was not unmasked in the environment stemming from this incident's precarious and unpredictable fallout. According to Twenty Committee's reports, after Fortitude he did not experience any impediments in continuing to disseminate the data produced by Security Service personnel. The female double agent code-named Gelatine, Friedl Gaertner, was introduced to German secret services by Tricycle in 1941 and formed a synergy with his operations. Born in Raithern, Austria, in January 1911, she had departed for Palestine in 1934 and traveled sporadically in Europe before settling in Britain in 1938. Gelatine began informing the authorities on the activities of German organizations in Britain.

Contemporary case files recorded the techniques associated with Gelatine's accomplishments as an informant and the organizations penetrated, including the Anglo-German Fellowship and the Link. Documents examining and probing this undercover surveillance mission describe the Security Service intervening with the metropolitan police to ensure that standard movement restrictions under the Aliens Act were temporarily rescinded. After an introduction to Dusko Popov, Gelatine was enlisted, by all accounts, willingly to distribute messages written in advanced secret ink to her German intelligence contact in Portugal. The Nazis demanded the procurement originally of political and military content. By 1942 MI5 case officers started to circulate extra misinformation into Gelatine's letters. An informal network was constructed to ensure mission compartmentalization that encompassed Tricycle, Jebsen, Gelatine and other agents focused on the Iberian Peninsula. A secondary objective of MI5 in assembling this separate network was to interject multiple independent human sources to authenticate the leaked intelligence.[67]

In early 1942 a case summary by Masterman proposed that Friedl Gaertner's case should be examined to scrutinize the prospect of abandoning or discontinuing activity because the once-prolific Nazi handlers no longer appeared to be responding to messages and activation requests were ignored. The regulatory of Gelatine's communications consequently reduced, as her conduit pathway was only utilized intermittently by the British. Her identity was mistakenly almost revealed in 1943 while she was on a personal vacation to Edinburgh.[68] Friedl Gaertner was arrested by police for inebriated behavior and the Security Service had to intervene to protect her identity. The employment of Gelatine was officially terminated on June 16, 1945.

Roman Garby-Czerniawski

Roman Garby-Czerniawski was a Polish air force captain and commander of a Polish-French resistance group opposing the initial invasion of France and the subsequent occupation. This background did not insinuate from a surface perspective that he would be an appropriate candidate for OKW or military intelligence in conversion as an undercover spy. Garby-Czerniawski in 1940 had the astuteness and battlefield tactics to develop the Interallie, a resistance group in occupied France and an early example of later movements such as the Carte and Marquis organizations. Open dialogue was instigated with Allied governments and remnants of Polish intelligence now relocated to London, and Garby-Czerniawski began expanding his espionage network and recruit more agents. In November 1941 he was captured in Paris and transferred to a high-security Nazi prison along with his confederates. There they faced execution at the hands of the Gestapo.

At this point, Hamburg Ast station and other Abwehr posts were desperately researching to discover intelligence agents, as finding quality individuals since Operation Lena had proven challenging and time consuming. Colonel Joachim Rohleder, chief in Abwehr III (counterespionage), investigated the possibility of selecting candidates from POW or other prisoner lists. At Fresnes prison the name of Roman Garby-Czerniawski attracted his attention. Rohleder quickly determined that coercion could prove effective if members of Garby-Czerniawski's resistance movement or individuals otherwise under his command were threatened. Rohleder reasoned that an officer exhibiting camaraderie and commitment to the welfare of his troops, which the Polish air force captain certainly projected, would find this approach compelling. Garby-Czerniawski, seated opposite him in the Fresno interrogation room, listened to Rohleder's proposition. Accept a contract to become an undercover intelligence asset for German intelligence and the imprisoned personnel from Interallie would be spared execution or the excesses of incarceration. Garby-Czerniawski grudgingly agreed to the colonel's demands.

The Abwehr trained him in espionage skills and codes, furnishing him with spare elements for assembling a radio transmitter once on the ground. In December final preparations for the assignment advanced forwards to form duplicitous contact with the Polish legation and British intelligence. Garby-Czerniawski was presented with an intelligence questionnaire to orient information-gathering actions as well as espionage apparatus such as photographic equipment, enciphering information and a cyanide capsule. He departed for London in January 1943. The intentions of this prospective lucrative source were still unknown to British authorities; in fact, MI5 had received guidance from French resistance sources before his sudden appearance intimating that Garby-Czerniawski harbored an ulterior motive. He was questioned by a suspicious MI5 and Polish military and initially appeared reluctant or hesitant to divulge his genuine intentions, but he very quickly explained all about the Abwehr's secret agreement and adamantly insisted his involvement was categorically a counterintelligence operation. To Roman Garby-Czerniawski's credit he produced full disclosure on his intimate knowledge of Abwehr III and

Joachim Rohleder. His delivery conveyed a magnanimous quality and indicated his strong conviction that the foundation for his master plan had been imagined from the beginning. The Polish Air Force captain was inducted into the Double Cross program and code-named "Brutus."[69]

Garby-Czerniawski was assessed by MI5 caseworkers as dependable and a highly valuable asset, his prominence increasing in the Double Cross network in 1944. Brutus was destined to form a tactically vital dimension of Operation Fortitude while falsely claiming to the Abwehr controllers that he had infiltrated the Polish military establishment in exile. The first major operation on his espionage resume was leaking information to the Germans about Allied objectives in Norway in April 1944, under Operation Fortitude North.[70] Subject matter in the intelligence reports commented that Polish units were deployed in the Scottish Lowlands, the identified headquarters of the Fourth Army in Edinburgh, and placed locations of fictitious units, for instance the 58th Division outside Sterling. Garby-Czerniawski participated in other deceptions during Operation Fortitude. The Germans were informed by their former resistance member asset that British and Allied troops were concentrating in large quantities in Kent. Brutus continued transmitting the carefully proscribed content uninterrupted until the war's conclusion.[71]

Agent Kiss

Agent "Kiss" was a Persian citizen who had formerly decided on a semi-permanent relocation to Germany in 1936, for purposes of furthering educational studies in electrical engineering. Recruited by the Abwehr in 1941 he was first deployed to Turkey and then repatriated back to Persia (Iran). He instigated contact with a mysterious cloak and dagger British operative code-named "Blackguard." Kiss revealed to Blackguard his minimal conviction for activating his Abwehr mission to report on Allied activity in Persia. Blackguard persuaded him to continue with his preordained journey but explained in clarification that it was doubly important he redirect all Nazi codes and the shortwave transmitter to their control. Agent Blackguard's reports to commanding officers on recruitment and the subsequent encounters with the Persian double agent are retained in the Security Service case files and feature intelligence data that Kiss distributed to the British. It was intended by the Germans that Kiss should transmit information on the observed Allied intelligence community and military actions in Persia and neighboring territories of Iraq, Egypt and North Africa and the Middle East, with this program active from 1942 to 1944. This cultivating of nexuses in diplomatic and military circles of neutral nation states on Europe's frontiers, theoretically from an Abwehr perspective, circumvented defenses and opened a virtual backdoor into Allied objectives in the region. Cicero's assignment inside the British embassy in Ankara had indisputably showcased how effective this pathway could be.[72]

Kiss complied with Nazi instructions and in a Soviet-controlled district of Persia he obtained employment in an armaments factory. British intelligence commenced transmission utilizing the hijacked transmitter of the self-generated messages to Germany, acting completely outside of the awareness of German intelligence and thus retrieving intriguing facts concerning Abwehr interests in the region. In the Middle East region the Double Cross program was managed by a separate section entitled Special Section of Security Intelligence Middle East (SIME). German intelligence relayed requests about the internal political conditions inside Persia and especially the upcoming Tehran conference. Practicing covert action operations inside ostensibly Russian-controlled territory, which sections of Persia had become, produced some considerable impediments. In 1944 Blackguard, after securing confirmation from London headquarters, decided to reveal with full disclosure to the Russians the existence of Kiss. The Security Service case files depict an uncooperative ground-level interaction as the Soviet Union delegations initially proved deliberately obstructive. Towards the end of 1944 the Soviet Union's intelligence officers experienced a discernible moderation in their outlooks, and collaboration was conveniently more forthcoming. The Kiss case files contains MI5's analysis of the Russian-Persian connections and concludes that Soviet cooperative measures were probably in reality an information gathering program targeting British intelligence. An opportunity for obtaining an insider glimpse at British counterintelligence services and agent network structures was tempting for Soviet security services.[73]

The Double Cross System was one of the greatest intelligence coups of the Second World War. As the Allied preparations for the invasion of Normandy advanced inexorably towards fruition, the network moved into overdrive. Johnny, Garbo, Tricycle and others instituted feedback to their spymasters with meticulously scripted intelligence on military regiments and their assessed strengths and deployment status. Realistic purloined strategic plans produced by the British military establishment were dutifully furnished to mislead German military about the true intentions. An entirely imaginary First U.S. Army Group (FUSAG) based in southeast England was invented under the notional command of General George Patton. The Twenty Committee convinced Adolf Hitler and the German high command that the Second Front would be opening not through Normandy but through Pas de Calais. The Double Cross system provided an excellent conduit for strategic deception actions; a British intelligence report during 1944 estimated that 120 double agents were controlled by British intelligence at that time. Further effective diversions were achieved in U-boat and V-weapon deceptions, Operations "Torch" and "Husky."[74]

Changing Priorities Inside German Intelligence

Colonel Ritter's occupation in intelligence after early 1942 distinctly assumed a somewhat downward trajectory. The disappearance or underachievement of operatives under his command and insufficient penetration of Allied military did not constitute a satisfactory performance in the opinion of the Tirpitzufer superiors. Ritter was removed from his position as chief of British operations and transferred to a military post in Tripoli, Libya, in February. Not a prestigious assignment, this was a demotion and punishment for Ritter's alleged failures. The British and Commonwealth troops' resounding defeat of the Italians and interjection of a specially designated German military force, the Afrika Korps, opened up North Africa as an integral theater of operations. Ritter would instead be responsible for commanding a special detachment to deposit agents behind enemy lines on North Africa's frontiers. He was removed from the primary concern of MI5 and the Twenty Committee, no longer an adversary in Berlin. Colonel Ritter was arrested by the Allies in the aftermath of World War II and interrogated thoroughly by American and British intelligence officers. Cleared of war crime accusations he was released from custody in 1946 and published his memoirs in 1972.

By February 1944, Britain's other great intelligence adversary had also experienced removal from office, although in Canaris's situation summary demotion evolved into incarceration at a concentration camp. Questions after World War II persistently settle on his loyalty to the Hitler regime, and awareness has surfaced concerning clandestine diplomatic and intelligence actions engineered by Canaris opposing Hitler's objectives. Hitler summoned senior military officers to Berchtesgaden on August 22, 1939, to finalize preparations for the Wehrmacht invasion of Poland, sparing minimal details in explicitly depicting the violent and inhumane tactics planned for occupation. Communities expressly singled out for harsh treatment extended to communists, the intelligentsia, Jews, Gypsies and religious leaders. Canaris was on record as opposing wholesale disregard for traditional warfare, and his noncommittal attitude towards the ideological factions of national socialism was understood. It remains possible that Canaris's deficient appetite for warfare in western Europe translated into an internal campaign to impede German military advances. He certainly actively maintained dialogue with Lord Halifax and the British government for as long as it was feasibly possible in August 1939, having opposed the escalation of Anglo-German tensions back in 1937. Canaris distributed through various emissaries to British authorities in August 1939 the Nazi government's intentions in Poland. The trusted Abwehr liaison Kleist managed to orchestrate communications with British diplomats in Stockholm. While insufficient evidence exists of concrete associations with the anti–Nazi resistance there is speculation that Canaris implicitly displayed interest in dialogue on possibilities of a Third Reich without Hitler and orchestrated by military and intelligence figures. Indeed, Canaris's name was mentioned incriminatingly on several occasions during investigations in the aftermath of the July 20 assassination plot.

Nazi Intelligence from the Exterior

In August 1939 detouring through supposedly neutral destinations appeared to be an ideally camouflaged and less supervised entrance point into Britain, facilitated by an immense population of refugees flooding across Europe. Penetrating the British interior mainland preoccupied Hamburg Ast and Berlin. The enlistment of Scandinavian, disloyal British subjects and interested volunteers cultivated a productive community of assets beyond Britain's perimeter. By July 1941 clandestine landing missions were inspiring mounting controversy with the navy and air force in reference to the requests for diverting resources and logistics persistently causing dilemmas. The Abwehr decided to permanently call a hiatus to strategies for planting further operatives inside British territories. Abwehr and SD VI maintained alternative pathways for uncovering sensitive information. In interrogating captured POWs and resistance personnel the Nazis had obtained data on Britain's wartime domestic picture and military preparedness. Similar tactics were utilized by RSHA and Abwehr pertaining to utilizing POWs as intelligence sources.

A memorandum produced by the Double Cross agent Zigzag on the Berlin security service personnel after the war listed for U.S. investigators a database of former Nazi agents and also uncovered information gathered by the Nazis utilizing these sources. From the accounts military intelligence received reports of British training centers and specialized schools for espionage and commando operations which had existed in Northern England and Scotland. Scattered reports indicated similar establishments present in the Soviet Union. Information dating to November 1944 reported that Nazi intelligence was informed about some of the arrangement and infrastructure systems pertaining to the inner workings of training centers. The subject focused categories diffusing content spanned radio communications, parachuting, infantry weapons, transportation and naval demolitions.[75]

In other document cases German intelligence discovered that commanding officers in Britain were identifiable as Axis deserters or former POWs. General information was retrieved on the extent of Luftwaffe bombing damage and civilian morale as far as they were understood. Agent Zigzag's report for U.S. investigators incorporated fragmented translations on descriptions of agents implicated in anti–British operations across Europe. Circumventing the British security systems from the outside progressed systematically as a strategic objective in another Nazi counterintelligence action, the Abwehr's own double cross initiative. Holland, from September 1939 until the Low Countries' occupation, functioned as a convenient listening station and operations center for British intelligence to observe the conditions inside Germany.

An underpaid and disgruntled Allied employee inside the MI6 Hague Station, lamentably for the security contingency measures, supplied the Abwehr with reports on intelligence activities. A Secret Information Service (MI6) file released in 2012 demonstrates beyond reasonable doubt that despite his initial hesitation Van Koutrik was a German intelligence double agent from October 1938 until evacuation from Holland in May 1940. Employed by SIS in the Netherlands from 1937 to 1940, Van Koutrik was reemployed in 1941 and 1942 and stationed at a refugee reception center.[76] In 1946 it was discovered from an interrogation of German prisoners that the Dutch national was turned by the Abwehr in 1938, his code name being "Walbach." It appears that, after 1940, in practice Koutrik had minimal access to sensitive areas and it's doubtful that he maintained contact with his German-based handlers past that period.[77]

In supposedly neutral Spain, the Abwehr substation employed more than 600 informers and 750 full-time spies. The station chief, Wilhelm Leissner, maximized the resources at his disposal to their fullest, with a competent operations team ceaselessly conspiring to recruit viable informants. Contacts existed in North Africa stretching in networks of controlled informants to distant regions of Libya and Egypt. The Spanish government and other important national institutions were breached by Leissner's minions, politicians and civil servants reporting information to their case officers. Informants from the multiple international intelligence agencies inside Madrid and Lisbon trafficked information to controlling reception headquarters, as the peninsula developed into a valuable frontier for belligerent Allied and Axis intelligence communities. Lisbon acquired the reputation of an urban environment figuratively deluged by foreign government operatives. The German informants were instructed to monitor British and Allied shipping movements at the harbors, activities at enemy nations' consulates and investigate any business connections. The Lisbon and

Madrid substations were encouraged to unmask and survey other intelligence personnel stationed in the region if possible, primarily British and American organizations.

Information on section chiefs or designation of security services on the ground level could be profitable and a nondirect pathway for counterespionage or counterintelligence to interfere with Allied interests. The Spanish substation incorporated a department ordained for tracking Soviet Union agents and any Iberian Peninsula connections.[78] This collection of raw information and sensitive material was transported to the OKW's analytical specialists at Fremde Heere West. Commanded by General Ulrich Lis, this station prepared analysis and assessment reports from subject matter collected by the Abwehr across the Reich's sphere of interest.[79]

A German spy with pronounced productivity inside neutral territory actively opposing Allied forces was Elyesa Bazna, employed as the personal valet for the British ambassador to Turkey, Hugh Knatchbull-Hugessen. Working under the code name "Cicero," he was probably the single most effective German agent of World War II specializing in British affairs. From all accounts Bazna regarded supplying information to German military intelligence as merely a financial opportunity rather than an ideological or nationalist commitment. He experienced no formal training in espionage or counterintelligence and for the most part operated independently.

Elyesa Bazna was born in Albania and by his adult years was residing in the Turkish capital. Drifting through a sequence of temporary manual labor jobs and participating intermittently in minor criminal offenses, Bazna found himself, perhaps fortuitously and with insufficient background checks, being recruited as a valet for the British ambassador to Turkey. As a member of the ambassador's entourage Elyesa Bazna manipulated his path to attaining insider access to secretive documents and diplomatic communications. Cicero's most effective covert infiltration scheme was to photograph secret paperwork retrieved from the Ankara embassy. He then preceded to sell the negatives to German intelligence for substantial sums. The Albanian adopted a multitude of strategies to smuggle documents and continue to operate outside the awareness of embassy personnel, which extended to cutting keys and using hidden cameras. Bazna requested compensation for his efforts from the beginning, and payment for the first batch of documents amounted to £20,000, paid in English notes. Cicero's case handler was L.C. Moyzisch, the Nazi military attaché at the German embassy in Ankara.[80] Cicero traded to Moyzisch minutes recorded during the 1943 Casablanca conference, in which Allied demands for an unconditional German surrender were originally articulated. Ambassador Van Papen proffered substantial capital from information smuggled out of the embassy in negotiating with the Turkish government. Both Joachim Ribbentrop and OKW incorrectly concluded that the smuggled minute reports were unconvincing and refused to accept their validity. The Abwehr, it transpired after the war, paid Bazna in predominantly forged banknotes.

Cicero's operation was belatedly unmasked in 1944 after Nele, a German citizen employed by Moyzisch in Ankara, nervously approached American consulate staff with an intriguing offer. Nele relayed to the Americans how her principled sympathies were on the anti–Nazi side, that her father was indeed a socialist and counseled profusely against the Nazis to the family in private. She declared her willingness to traffic information outside of the embassy and in exchange requested chaperoned safe passage from Turkey to America. A foreign service officer referred her offer to the ambassador, Mr. Steinhardt. Information on a German delegation employee with supposedly impelling intelligence next landed on the departmental desk of an American military attaché. Wisely he recognized the potential coup developing in their hands and accepted Nele's deal. Delivering a comprehensive report on Moyzisch's activities, she informed the Americans about Nazi spies working throughout the Middle East, and the connection between the German Ankara embassy and a Turkish man codenamed Cicero was discovered for the first time. Nele described how on specific prearranged dates, an unusual ritual occurred when Cicero telephoned the embassy. Moyzisch responded to the call by hastily instructing all present non-relevant personnel to remove themselves and locking himself in the code room.[81] The connection of Cicero to the British embassy was established, Ambassador Steinhardt then informed the British about a suspected German informant code-named Cicero engaging in transmitting data to the German embassy of considerable importance approximately every two weeks. The British determined finally the true identity of Elyesa Bazna, but they were essentially powerless to apprehend the unmasked figure. Spying on Britain was not a criminal offense in Turkey. The German handlers in Berlin continually suspected the motives of Cicero's activity and on multiple occasions mistakenly or perhaps overcautiously delayed acting on the information he leaked.

Switzerland

Switzerland was a compelling resource of espionage intelligence and economic data precisely because it retained neutrality throughout the conflict, attracting a refugee and dissident population of wealth and international holdings. Intelligence agents descended on Geneva and Berne investigating contentious activities of their national citizens and opposite numbers in enemy security organizations. Transcripts released after the war reveal how Western finance and stolen Nazi capital were both laundered through Switzerland (and sometimes the Vatican bank) to South America and until the culmination of hostilities back to Germany. This money laundering program was instigated to covertly finance the armaments and munitions essential for Nazi Germany's military, and figures within the Swiss banking fraternity approved the initiatives to launder German gold and valuable possessions. The German Reichsbank incorporated into the national gold reserves looted treasures from governments of countries occupied by the Nazis. Quantities of black market gold trafficked through Switzerland were sufficiently substantial for neutral countries to effectively facilitate Nazi military ambitions. It was not solely Axis or neutral financial establishments that exhibited interest in working with Germany in this financial operation: Allied interests also took advantage of the system.[82]

Declassified U.S. Military Intelligence documents from 2001 that discuss Switzerland and the Nazi black market laundering operations construct a picture of how a Slovenian bishop, Gregory Rozman, was implicated in arranging the transfer of massive quantities of Nazi-controlled gold and currency discreetly secreted into Swiss banks.[83] Gregory Rozman smuggled the lucrative packages working surreptitiously on behalf of Nazi associates, with Argentina the end destination for trafficking. U.S. Military Intelligence (Department G-2) files contain the affidavits of airport personnel and other workers who allegedly handled sizable quantities of German gold bars transported from Switzerland to Spain and Portugal with the cooperation of Swiss authorities. Thus, Switzerland evolved progressively into a veritable financial haven, and virtually all German corporations with extensive operations abroad directed business affairs utilizing Swiss bank accounts. The Allied nations, with America the central player, attempted via placements of fiscal and trade embargoes to fundamentally deny, with mixed success, Nazi Germany the economic capacity to wage conflict. The Third Reich increasingly depended on money laundering operations for fueling its ambitions.[84] Large amounts of "Escape Capital" were precipitously deposited by Nazi state officials in "friendly" Swiss banking establishments, a contingency reserve to be activated in the circumstance of Germany's unfortunate defeat. Both Abwehr and SD VI professional operatives were implicated in the money laundering schemes and discreetly funneling Escape Capital from Europe; indeed, not all related transactions were authorized by OKW or the high command. Postwar efforts to recover assets looted by the Nazis during World War II in order to compensate occupied countries and individual victims have proven immensely complicated.

Based on evidence obtained by Britain's Ultra program in deciphering Swiss bank messages, the Third Reich developed a smuggling scheme that centered around deporting gold into Turkey via consulate diplomatic pouches. This program had generated some lucrative returns for their Turkish coconspirators, but more bountiful profits were produced after the secondary segment in laundering operations, with the gold being smuggled into Bulgaria, Romania, and Hungary. Beset by financial turbulence and a multitude of collapsing currencies, the domestic German monetary system was in chaos. Domestic populations in copious numbers deserted trading in paper currency. An alternative route focused on neutral Portugal and alliances were prudently developed with Lisbon financial institutions, which included the Bank of Portugal (Minero-Silvicola). RSHA dutifully guaranteed that consignments of gold were distributed to neutral Portugal. This location transpired to be particularly productive, as Portuguese currency was demonstrating resilience to the external pressures impacting on currency elsewhere in Europe and remained backed by gold.[85]

The banking laws practiced in Geneva permitted the use of numbered accounts, an invitation for interested parties to route clandestine transactions through Swiss banks. American and British intelligence investigation reports discovered the existence of thousands of Swiss holding corporations used for cloaking Nazi assets. In Nazi Germany restrictions on the removal of financial assets were introduced in 1934, motivated originally by the desire of Nazi finance ministers to secure the German mark's value. Instability had inevitably surrounded the Hitler regime's succession to power, encouraging many German citizens to convert money into harder currencies and transfer life savings to other countries. Eager to forestall a mass exodus of German bank holdings abroad, the Nazi government instituted new banking regulations: transferring funds abroad without permission or refusing to repatriate funds was an offense meriting the death penalty. Germans were expressly forbidden to hold foreign bank accounts, and constrictive disclosure requirements were rendered mandatory. In 1934 the Nazis prosecuted and executed three citizens for the criminal offense of having foreign bank accounts. The Swiss Bank Act of 1934, Article 47, represented the original comprehensive secrecy measures in the national banking industry, beginning in an attempt to protect their German customers from harassment. Complete anonymity and discretion were promised to all customers. The Gestapo was assigned jurisdiction for investigating and seizing possession of assets, and operatives were dispatched to numerous foreign countries with instructions to uncover German-owned bank accounts. Agents sometimes attempted to transfer deposits or withdrawals in a suspected account, and the Swiss banks announced that they would no longer accept withdrawal orders from German citizens unless the owner of the funds appeared in person.[86]

Intelligence assets from active belligerent countries formed operations and backdoor channels in Switzerland. The Swiss government was targeted for penetration by Heinrich Himmler and his RSHA cohorts, but Canaris proved again to be more effective. Abwehr operatives were interjected in placements inside the Swiss Foreign Ministry and Swiss Secret Service, code-named by handlers as Habakkuk and Jacob respectively. Dr. Bruggmann, a legitimate Swiss diplomat based in Washington, revealed information to the Swiss foreign ministry he duplicitously acquired from U.S. sources. An OSS dossier from April 1946 on Jacob Fuerst, who penetrated the American military attaché office in Bern, indicates a sizeable operation, with the documents being spirited from the attaché's personal files for over eighteen months.[87] The Fuerst case is the most important example of the penetration of Switzerland by the enemy during the war.

The British and Americans had prioritized building alliances in Switzerland and recognized opportunities for installing information-gathering systems in this neutral territory. Allen Dulles, a future CIA chief, was appointed head of OSS operations in Switzerland. Dulles had prodigiously developed a catalog of personal contacts with considerable influence inside the German and European banking industry, his long career in foreign office and intelligence communities forming a distinct asset. His background, in conjunction with his peacetime occupation at the law firm of Sullivan and Cromwell, opened up opportunities for his becoming acquainted with European business leaders. American intelligence was aware of the growing financial importance of Switzerland and its banking industry to the Third Reich. As Switzerland was the world's major international banking center, the OSS assessed this zone as viable for transitioning into a valuable base for producing intelligence on fiscal engagements. In 1945 sources in the U.S. Treasury Department accused Dulles of allegedly laundering the funds from the Nazi-controlled Bank of Hungary to Switzerland. Comparable charges were rendered against OSS agent Hans Gisevius, who reported to Allen Dulles.[88] Gisevius was an informative OSS-controlled asset who had penetrated the Nazi Reichsbank and undeniably delved into laundering operations. Other connections with U.S. companies that accessed Switzerland as a convenient conduit emerged in postwar investigations. The RSHA purchased significant quantities of shares in American companies. Consequently, it was possible for SS representatives to launder money through the Corn Exchange and Chase banks.[89]

U.S. intelligence chiefs cultivated a high-profile source in German intelligence. Fritz Kolbe, code-named "George Wood," was adjutant to Karl Ritter, who in the Nazi central command structure was an individual responsible for liaison between the German foreign ministry and the military. In July 1941 Karl Ritter, a dutiful foreign office servant since 1921, received promotion, certainly pertaining to a career peak, as senior liaison officer. In this capacity Karl Ritter reported directly and without interruption to General Alfred Jodl, operations chief of the German General Staff and subordinate only to Keitel in the German military structure. Kolbe therefore gained access to General Jodl's office and acquired confidants within the OKW senior command. Karl Ritter was disclosed in certain quarters as somewhat of an unpopular and perhaps surprising selection for this promotion, as he was renowned for his overpowering personality and being obstructive. Kolbe had occasion for attending regular diplomatic expeditions to Bern, Switzerland. Beginning in August 1943 he expropriated hundreds of sensitive and classified German diplomatic and military documents and handed them personally to Allen Dulles, the OSS station chief. Rapidly this purloined content was being reviewed back at OSS headquarters in Washington by technical analysts, entitled with the code name "Boston Series." Kolbe had ascended to a posting with responsibility for sensitive records in the German foreign office, where he worked assiduously without attracting suspicion and earned the misplaced trust of his superiors. He was, however, passionately anti–Nazi and resolved to assist the Allied cause. This perceived diligence garnered a window for U.S. intelligence inside the Third Reich's most important military and intelligence secrets.[90] Fritz Kolbe continued to disperse sensitive German information to the Office of Strategic Services. The subterfuge of diplomatic traveling appeared to hold up and he was never suspected.

Switzerland was fashioned, when circumstances permitted, into a suitable hidden back channel for discussions between the intelligence personnel on opposite sides. As the exhausting conflict's resolution was manifestly on the horizon Allied and American security officers in due course rotated perspectives and priorities to acquiring services of German personnel. Both technical, as observed in Operation Paperclip, and intelligence agents were discreetly presented with employment contracts. Operation Dusty, under the auspices of G-2 and the U.S. War Department, was premeditated to fully exploit the possible application of German army and intelligence assets experienced inside the Soviet theater. Allied perceptions on German intelligence as a military and political entity were progressively modified during the final three months of hostilities, as Operation Dusty and Paperclip superseded neutralizing the enemy as the primary concern. In the climactic weeks, Nazi spies and intelligence officials opposing hardcore factions for resisting Allied forces searched desperately for an escape route.[91]

General Gehlen directed the eponymous "Operation Gehlen," with the purpose essentially of recruiting Abwehr and RSHA intelligence officers and to discover the surviving information stores and hidden vaults escaping destruction. G-2 and MI6 both advanced urgent commands for capturing unaccounted-for German intelligence officers, with time frames rapidly diminishing. Undoubtedly these individuals represented golden opportunities to dissect and evaluate the structure of German espionage networks. Permitting an escape was not considered to be a conceivable option by Gehlen. Persuading German intelligence staff to transfer information on the Soviet Union temptingly opened access to exigent information on their covert operations and methodology.[92] In the emerging Cold War climate, insider details from Nazi security files collated during four years of military conflict provided a glimpse into the complex Russian intelligence psyche. Predicting the tactical and strategic intentions of this superpower evolved into the next fundamental intelligence requirements in the later CIA administrations. Operation Gehlen succeeding in discovering answers to hitherto ambiguous content and satisfied gaps in Allied knowledge. An important informant in this venture was SS officer Wilhelm Hoettl, who managed without drawing awareness from superiors to contact the OSS in Switzerland through an intermediary. Despite points of conjecture raised concerning misgivings that officials considered Hoettl dangerous they reservedly believed he contained useful information. First OSS and then G-2 started supervising a compliant Hoettl in ferreting out senior Nazi intelligence operatives now in hiding. Hoettl cooperated obligingly with Allied investigators for a considerable time. His imparted knowledge on Soviet operations was interpreted by OSS staffers as being indispensable, and he demonstrated sufficient fundamental utility for testifying at the Nuremberg trials.[93]

Guido Zimmer was an SS officer generally deployed to relatively minor security placements and implicated after the war in atrocities committed in Italy; his recovered notebooks confer a fascinating insight into the Nazi intelligence activities during the last months of the war. In November 1944 a meeting of RSHA foreign intelligence officials in Verona was orchestrated by Switzerland expert Klaus Huegel. Zimmer suggested at the conference a subtle strategy for contacting Allied intelligence in Switzerland, exploiting a prominent aristocratic Italian connection, Baron Luigi Parrilli. On March 3 Zimmer and Parrilli, accompanied by Eugen Dollmann, Himmler's official representative in Italy, engaged in clandestine negotiation with OSS official Paul Blum in Lugano. This secret meeting developed into a preliminary testing ground for the rendezvous between Karl Wolff and Dulles himself later in March. The critical subject discussed was the potential premature surrender of the German armed forces in Italy and a complete end of hostilities. Dulles and Wolff attempted to hammer out finer principles of an agreement and the negotiations had advanced near completion. The rapidly moving conditions in continental

Europe ensured that the Wolff-Dulles deal was confirmed too late, as the Italian conflict ended.[94]

In January 1945 a decidedly more serious defection than Zimmer or Parrilli's perfidious measures occurred from inside the Fatherland's security services. Hans Eggen, an SS officer attached to the SD chief, Walter Schellenberg, without disclosure in RSHA corridors save a handful of discerning associates, arranged a dialogue with the respected American diplomat Frederick R. Loofborough. Eggen rationalized German military intentions to Loofborough by elucidating that Germany had zero contingency options to the perpetuation of armed struggle; the alternate scenario would indisputably be a Bolshevik invasion of Europe. He advocated a second meeting in Switzerland, this time inviting Schellenberg himself and Dulles for further constructive discussions.[95] Schellenberg negotiated his surrender to the Allied Supreme Command and accepted an agreement to fully disclose his complete awareness of Nazi intelligence matters to the Allied investigators. He informed G-2 personnel about hidden depositories of unearthed SD archives. Later, similar to the circumstances of Hoettl, he testified as a prosecution witness at Nuremberg.

Ireland

Contact between the Abwehr and the IRA first surfaced when members of the German Academic Exchange Service, a Nazi promotional movement, instigated contact with IRA chief of staff Tom Barry in 1937. The IRA and other nationalist organizations that harbored distinctly anti–British sentiments were identified as an imperative objective for a partnership. In 1937 Barry had proceeded to Germany for consultations with senior Nazi foreign office personnel, accompanied on this summit by German agent Jupp Hoven. Later, while undercover as an unassuming student, Hoven commenced spying actions in Belfast, Dublin and Cork. He was associated with Helmut Clissmann, a manager of the German Academic Exchange Service in Dublin, another German government agent seconded for gathering information in Ireland.[96] Secret Information Service (SIS) files declassified in 2010 revealed attempts by German military intelligence, including Hoven and operatives connected with his circle, to contact the Irish communist journalist Frank Ryan and other potentially sympathetic public figures. Barry's expedition to the Continent was an intervention to confer German allegiances for IRA attacks on British military installations in Northern Ireland. But an IRA convention in April 1938 rejected Barry's plan, favoring instead grandiose pro–German proposals conceived by the new chief of staff, Seán Russell.[97]

Oscar Pfaus, a military intelligence agent with motivation inspired by the Abwehr strategy for forming alliances with dissident or subversive groups to circumvent national security barriers, decided to revitalize German-Irish communication. In July 1938 he began preparing the foundations for talks with Seán Russell, who dispatched representative James O'Donovan as negotiator in Germany on his behalf. The IRA was interested by all accounts in purchasing more advanced weapons, and refreshing the outdated apparatus presently stockpiled was obligatory in launching renewed incursions against the British in mainland territory.[98] Between 1938 and 1939 O'Donovan evolved into a repeat visitor to Berlin, Russell dispatching his compatriot on multiple delegations to Berlin with instructions for the senior Nazi state officials.

On April 24, 1939, Jim O'Donovan disembarked at Hamburg again. Contracts for munitions shipping were confirmed but never enacted. The German ammunition and explosives were ultimately not delivered as the Nazi's developed some hesitation and doubts mounted concerning the legitimacy of various promises. But financial obligations as confirmed were indeed forthcoming and circuitously transported to Dublin via various entrusted agents. Tensions had irrefutably escalated after the IRA launched a bombing campaign in early 1939.[99] Under a campaign entitled Sabotage, or S-Plan, the cities of London, Manchester, Birmingham and Coventry were targeted by IRA divisions. No immediate prospect of supplementary funding was assured by Nazi Germany to sustain the bombing campaign. During O'Donovan's third expedition he was introduced to facilitating agent Oscar Pfaus. The German officer later recollected the Abwehr's ambitions on their relationship with the IRA: "to seek out the IRA leadership; make contact; ask if they would be interested in cooperation with Germany; and to send a liaison man to Germany to discuss specific plans and future co-ordination." The 1930s attempts to formalize consensus accords with the IRA and Third Reich failed to be manipulated into concerted action.[100]

Germany enacted a similar stratagem of cultural exportation in Ireland as perpetrated in other international theaters, exploring the potential for manipulating German interests existing in Ireland. An inaugural branch of the Ausland Organization was founded inside Ireland immediately after Nazi assumption of political power in 1933 as the foreign office maneuvered into overdrive in cultivating a domestic presence in tactically important regions. The Blueshirts, a fascistic and outspokenly pro–Adolf Hitler movement formed in 1933, mounted demonstrations and parades in Dublin and Cork. Business linkages internally in the mid–1930s profoundly exhibited symptoms of a flourishing dual relationship, as German companies and engineering professionals had relocated to Ireland for employment on hydroelectric plants and industrial projects. German populations, predominantly industrial workers, inhabiting Ireland substantially increased. The growing clouds of European conflict mobilization heralded an observable reduction in those numbers as many German citizens returned home in 1938 and 1939. The Abwehr employed freelance recruiters to construct relationships with the Irish citizens marked as possessing qualities or backgrounds suitable for candidate assets.

In many instances the Abwehr officials assigned abroad discovered language barriers and regional dialects transpiring to persistently create problematic conditions for infiltration. The Abwehr instead concentrated resources on German citizens with residency or influential contacts in Ireland. Abwehr assessed the burgeoning business community links associated with Ireland as amplifying prospects for turning informants. Thirteen German operatives were interjected into Ireland between 1939 and 1943. By October 1939 radio transmission networks had been installed for communication between Hamburg and agents deposited in Ireland. Similar to Operation Lena, Nazi operatives during the ensuing darkened four years breached Irish territory using multiple transport solutions, from parachute to small boat or submarine. Eleven were captured by Irish authorities and incarcerated in the Athlone Internment Camp. A twelfth, John Lenihan, after landing by parachute in Ireland, had traveled to Northern Ireland, surrendered to British authorities and was later inducted into the Double Cross program.

In British security service circles the department responsible for investigating IRA-related threats was the Metropolitan Police Special Branch. MI5 retained an interested capacity if military and national security interests were implicitly threatened. Security Service files released in 2003 reveal strategies pursued by British intelligence related to countering any threat from IRA-German cooperation in Ireland. Investigation of security matters involving the IRA or other nationalist groups frequently required engagement in dialogue with MI5, the Home Office, the police force and several other agencies. Concerns were expressed about the hypothetical threats from the employment of IRA sympathizers in strategically important industrial sectors and sabotage against vulnerable spots, and correspondingly strong measures were recommended for improving the internal security systems. Further declassified papers depict the communication exchanges between Éamon De Valera and MI5 officers during wartime.[101] With a governing cabinet populated by former IRA members, the Irish president had requested London's cooperation in propagating a negative publicity campaign against the organization's chief of staff, Frank Ryan, whom De Valera asserted to the Security Service was a communist agent. In a secret memo communicated to MI5 officers De Valera commented: "10 or 12 years ago, he was in Soviet pay as an agitator; If there is any information which could be made available to show that this was the case, or that at the present time he is in receipt of pay from foreign sources, it would be of the greatest possible assistance to the Dublin authorities in dealing with him since it would practically eliminate the risk of him being treated as a patriotic martyr."

Hermann Görtz was an Abwehr agent focusing on the Ireland theater. He was assured a controversial reputation in Britain because of a disclosed and publicly understood affiliation with the German security community and espionage activities, a perception that was a caricature by the British media. Nicknamed the "Flying Spy," the German citizen had previously, on November 8, 1935, experienced detention on suspicion of espionage activities for a foreign government. He was then convicted and sentenced to prison in 1936 and endured two and a half years of incarceration before he was released. This notoriety did not prevent a recall to the Abwehr during conscription. Initially commissioned as reserve second lieutenant, Görtz served without achieving significant distinction in several offices before assignment to Abwehr Section II on January 19, 1940, under Ernst Weber-Drohl. This commander was another with an equally colorful past selected to advance interactions inside Ireland. In the mid–1930s, Weber-Drohl toured nationwide in Ireland as the featured performer in a strongman exhibition, suitably skilled from a background in wrestling and weight-lifting.[102]

Relationships were developed during his Ireland excursions that he attempted to renew after his posting to Ireland. Weber-Drohl fathered two children in Ireland and believed that the German military intelligence had conveniently afforded him an opportunity for a family reunion. His auxiliary mission was as support staff and liaison to Görtz. Life as an Abwehr agent in Ireland did not begin smoothly, as almost immediately he was arrested by the Irish police. Friends recognized the German agent in their midst and his undercover identity was blown within a matter of weeks. He failed to formalize contacts with IRA or anti–British elements. Weber-Drohl was touted by the Abwehr as an essential wheel in the planning to undermine British security and encourage incitement in nationalist circles. But he was transformed into another operative instead, turned and controlled by John Masterson and the Twenty Committee. Destitute and without sufficient financial remuneration, Ernst Weber-Drohl had minimal remaining options but to cooperate with British intelligence.

Görtz's connections to Ireland greatly interested the Abwehr, as previous methods for enticing infiltrators or informants had descended to attempting to recruit Irish citizens who were prisoners of war. Operatives were required with demonstrable capability in navigating outside of the public or authority awareness in Ireland, which translated to language skills or the correct integral relationships. Under the Nazi program, code-named "Operation Kathleen," the German military forces' calculations depended on occupying Ireland as a prelude to a British mainland assault. Despite negative publicity Görtz had generated for the Fatherland he somehow convinced superior officers that he would be qualified to spearhead this mission. Görtz's participation included infiltrating Ireland by parachute and establishing contact with IRA; he was advised to stimulate revolts north of the national borderline if possible. Communications with the IRA presented a cohort of domestic alliances with a senior member who agreed to assist German operatives with housing, transportation and information. Görtz was issued contact names and addresses to rendezvous with IRA supporters, and a safe house especially for the German agent had been arranged in County Wicklow.

If Operation Kathleen had ever obtained a green light for mobilization, 50,000 Nazi troops were destined for the invasion of Northern Ireland in collaboration with IRA brigades from the south. In the preliminary strategy German armed forces were orchestrated for rapid deployment in Ireland at the designated vantage points of Coleraine, Larne, Londonderry and Sligo. The German divisions would then rendezvous with IRA brigades moving in from Ballyshannon and Dundalk. Operation Kathleen's specific framework emerged in the Security Service files released for public viewing in 2003. Major Ritter, based at Hamburg Ast station, issued the preparation orders for Operation Kathleen. He insured that German agents posted to Ireland received compulsory training in radio communications. To improve internal operational security the Irish networks were distributed complicated recognition signals, to which Görtz was obligated to respond with a preordained answer. If any doubts persisted regarding transmitted information Hamburg, as an operational contingency, planned on instead contacting another German agent stationed in Britain, Arthur Owens. Görtz was assigned the address of Owens, still perceived as Nazi Germany's major British operative.[103]

German intelligence's knowledge about the political and cultural environment in Ireland was not particularly advanced. In preparation for his mission Görtz conducted a fact-finding investigation on Ireland, firstly at the office of Dr. Franz Fromme. He contacted Francis Stuart and Nora O'Mara, both expatriates residing in Germany, to review information on the conditions he should expect in Ireland. Anxious about operating under the authority radar, Görtz peppered them with questions about currency, police tactics and modern customs. With cooperation from handlers in Abwehr Section II contact was arranged with expatriates from Northern Ireland residing in Italy and referred to as the "Independent Group." In his final orders there appeared instructions to direct the sabotage activities of the IRA towards British military targets and specifically naval installations. Captain Kaupert, a reserve officer, was the resident adjutant at the Fritzlar airfield near Cassell. His primary function was as a photographic interpretation officer attached to the commander in chief's Reconnaissance Group, but he received the directives to organize Görtz's flight to Ireland.

Görtz was mistakenly dropped a considerable distance from the designated target zone, precisely 80 miles outside the rendezvous location. Instead, he landed without injury in Northern Ireland on the opposite side of the national border and, intensifying further a demanding situation, the radio transmitter failed to survive the parachute drop.[104] He marched the entire distance, requesting directions from local passersby including a Garda police station, but, fortunately for Ritter's objectives, he was not detained. He reached the safe house on May 9. That night Görtz was collected by senior contact Seamus O'Donovan, who transported the protected Nazi asset to a residence, "Florenceville," on the outskirts of Dublin. He had successfully made contact with the IRA. On May 11 he was moved on a second occasion by O'Donovan and IRA member Stephen Held. This was a precautionary security measure, Görtz was informed. During this first encounter he had handed over $165,000 in American currency to the IRA coordinators and retained $10,000 for himself. Held was a sympathizer of German descent who had attended delegations to Germany in 1940 as an emissary of the IRA. The circumstances appeared positive on the ground and Görtz reported back to Eduard Hempel, based at the German legation, regarding completion of the mission's preliminary stages. Görtz remained in concealment by the IRA until May 23, at which juncture he was relocated in preparation for his next scheduled contact, the senior IRA chief, Stephen Hayes.[105]

The safe house was raided immediately after the meeting with Hayes took place on the 23rd of May. The IRA developed an alternative commercial method of securing operating capital by selling foreign government agents to the Irish police, and unfortunately for Görtz, as it transpired, his mission had been undermined by this venture. Highly incriminating papers and effects belonging to Hermann Görtz, including a parachute, Luftwaffe identity documents and intelligence reports on harbors and defense installations, were confiscated.[106] Descriptions of Operation Kathleen's proposals were also recovered by police searching the property. Hermann Görtz coincidentally happened to be missing from the premises attending business and narrowly avoided detention. The safehouse raid amounted to a damaging predicament for the Nazi directives focusing on Ireland and the caches of illuminating documents on Ritter's Western ambitions were shortly being examined by MI5 officers. The surviving remnants of clandestine chains of German and Irish agents was disrupted and shut down in September 1941 as Irish police arrested most of principle members still unaccounted for. Electronic surveillance by the Irish police was consistently the most effective weapon in tracking down and determining the location of German spies.[107]

Görtz was to remain temporarily at liberty. The Abwehr were informed and apprised of the circumstances by German Legation chief Dr. Hempel, assessing this precursor to Operation Kathleen as unsuccessful. Görtz recollected in later published memoirs "I realized that an agreement between the Irish government and the IRA was completely inopportune. The action against Held ruled out all hopes of bringing the IRA into association with the government." He was captured finally in 1944, his exploits underground numbered and subsequently imprisoned until the war's conclusion. Görtz was released in 1946 and decided to remain a resident in Ireland.

At first the disappearance of their primary agent confused German intelligence. With zero mentions alluding to corresponding arrests in the media Görtz had simply disappeared without trace. The German legation heard about the uncovering of incriminating documents and substantial elements of Nazi clandestine operations in Ireland following the arrests at Hold's residence. Abwehr Hamburg Ast deliberated on the possibility of British intelligence mistakenly failing to recognize significance of documents in their possession. Postwar debriefing of German personnel and examination of records confirmed that no further attempts were instituted for landing saboteurs or agents. Appetite for further penetrations of Ireland dissipated as the mission's failure became observable, Ireland was transferred to Berlin's back-burner firmly as Wehrmacht campaign against Soviet Union forces was floundering. The momentum of World War II post–1943 would cancel out further intelligence operations as Ireland and Northern Ireland disappeared as a realistic target for invasions.[108] The Third Reich would soon diverted its remaining resources into defense of the national borders.

4

South American Theater

Operation "Bolivar" was an operational code name adopted by branches of the Nazi security service for its espionage missions targeting the South and Central American zones. This program was under the jurisdictional control of SD Department VI D4. German intelligence first commenced the installation of a secret radio-relay system from its control station center in Argentina in early 1940. The Naval command had diverted all applicable resources into the Battle of the Atlantic against the Allied navies. Britain in outflanking the German U-boats switched a significant proportion of its naval and merchant shipping away from European coastal waters, instead Africa and South America became crucial regional territories to influence. This expanded the relative importance of maritime trading and the commerce emanating between Europe and South America. Dönitz and Raeder implemented every application to disrupt Britain's shipping and maritime communications post 1940. For these activities to succeed it was irrefutably important for German intelligence to acquire accurate information from the Latin American zone.

NSDAP policy on international relations and exporting ideology had ignored South America during the 1920s formative phase, with ideologues registering little attention in this distant corner of the globe. Expectations of Latin America amounted to trading in raw materials and economic treaties. Not until beginning-1941 did the Abwehr or SD commanders instigate a recruitment program that was designed for South and Central America. The Nazi bureaucratic machine decided to accelerate the development of the overseas state and quasi-government offices in the 1935–1937 period, transformed during the next 2–3 years into well-functioning and efficient exponents of a national fascist ideology. High profile demonstrations and parades were organized in South American cities complete with full Nazi regalia and uniforms, the emergences of the Third Reich and Adolf Hitler served as a pervasive impetus combining dual concepts of unity and nationalism for German populations abroad. Finances poured into organizations touring or permanently located in South American promoting Nazism. The Mexican Ausland Organization, probably the most extensive Nazi movement in Latin America, first orchestrated public demonstrations in 1934. The opposing political factions, generally communist or left-wing, but criticism was indeed noticeable from nationalist circles, warned that Nazi subversion potentially may culminate in revolution. Propaganda depicting the growing insular fascist presence as threatening generated popular sentiment, the anti–Nazi campaigns gained momentum and domestic intolerance to this supposed outside foreign "menace" was manifested in Rio de Janeiro, Bogotá and Santiago. Nazi Party affiliates and supporters were afflicted by the hazardous prospect of the domestic climate turning against their propaganda campaign complicating the efforts by German intelligence and their collaborating domestic partners.[1]

The 1938–1940 period witnessed a determinable upsurge in interest from the Nazi intelligence agencies towards the Latin American sphere. Propaganda activity efforts were redoubled by RSHA, the tandem demands of military objectives in Europe and ensuring a Wehrmacht sufficiently stocked with tactical intelligence proved motivational. The strategy of SD commander Walter Schellenberg, in a non-standard and rare collaboration with Piekenbrock of Abwehr I, concentrated on appealing to the German immigrant populations inside South America. Media campaigns were invested in with profound intensity to influence public opinion and expand access for commercial interests in the first instance. As with the previous recruitment drives Axis nationals and émigrés transpired as fertile and productive recruiting grounds for converting informants, alliances and agents. A consistent effort was enacted by the SD VI and Walter Schellenberg to engineer footholds in communities with substantial populations of German citizens and ex-patriots engaged either in commerce or a fostering of military connections. Military establishment figures rendered achievable the cultivation of desirable high value domestic assets and agents of influence. Colonel Hans Piekenbrock, questionably as it later transpired, had ordered the recruitment to be redirected at selecting and training as many operatives as feasibly possible on the rationale basis of supposedly engendering higher volumes of information, in contrast to prioritizing the development of supremely skilled groups of dedicated core professionals.

Nazi Germany encouraged close contact with ex-patriots through diplomatic representatives, Ausland movements and other pro–Nazi cultural organizations. German commercial interests in Latin America depended to an extent on permission from Berlin central, and various business organizations entered the National Socialist project by appeals to mutually patriotism, cronyism and patronage. The German populations in Brazil, Argentinean, Colombia and Chile undoubtedly contained a prominent contingent who espoused an attraction ideologically to Nazism, encouraged by the Germany's military performances and in nationalistic fever at the prospects of a powerful German state. But Nazi Party groups in South and Central America had also incited outspoken widespread opposition from resident German populations.

In July 1938, a conference was arranged in Montevideo of Third Reich ambassadors in Latin America, the diplomatic missions represented included Argentina, Brazil, Uruguay and Chile. By the virtual unanimous contention of the committee the attendee Embassy chiefs insisted on clarification concerning matters classified as emanating from an insufficient transparency. German Foreign Office delegates from the Berlin headquarters were pressured into redefining various critical policy matters: should embassy staff limit themselves to the expansion of economic and cultural influence in Latin America; did Germany intend to mount a counterintelligence or colonial operation. Diplomatic chiefs were antagonistic about the prospects of South America's incorporation into a U.S. dominated Pan-American system. The isolation of American continents and disrupting of any pact agreements could, the Third Reich ambassadors were informed, stimulate much apprehension and mistrust towards their intervention in the Western Atlantic. Fostering ideological separation between the population of both continents and European allies could be accomplished through the promulgation, it was proposed, of Latino fascist rhetoric in contrast to a hemispheric unity. The ambassadors' conference in Montevideo also revealed concerns about preserving the environments conducive to pro–German sentiment and methods of expanding quantity of nationalist movements forming in South American. Avoiding overt demonstrations of a supposedly foreign ideology was recommended as a strategy in establishing more positive relations. The conference was informed that frustrations were especially vocal in criticizing Ausland Organization der NSDAP.[2]

In Argentina, Ernst Bohle implemented a timetable of instruments for the express purposes of separating German citizens from Volkdeutsche and pro-fascistic movements in January 1939, but this was ineffectual in forestalling the growing alacrity of anti–German sentiment. Buenos Aries Ausland was instructed profusely through Foreign Office channels to inform members and associates about the importance of restricting its activities, which translated to prohibition on Nazi uniform wearing and non–German citizens attending meetings. Leaders were advised on restricting a public demonstration of Nazi symbols and emblems and in fact overt campaigns of all description experienced temporary and immediate suspension. The Argentinean government was under pressure from the United States to enforce measures against Nazi dissident groups and in May 1939 initiated new domestic legislation concerning pro-fascist and indeed all foreign influenced movements. Private associations, clubs and associations were required to disengage absolutely from involvement in local politics and discontinue Nazi symbology or propaganda imagery. All of the public assemblies and conventions were forcibly to be conducted in Spanish under the new regulations. Despite setbacks Bohle refused to admit defeat and continued his efforts to persuade the German Foreign Office that information gathering actions could continue behind the facade of a front organization.[3]

Latin America: Strategy and Methodology

Abwehr chief Admiral Canaris's long-term intelligence ambitions had called for developing a network of active espionage rings in South and Central America. His earlier career history as a Naval Intelligence Officer in Chile, Argentina and South America during World War I became a significant personal advantage in understanding the regional politics, cultural differences and realities of counterintelligence operations. As an Intelligence Officer Lieutenant Canaris was posted to SMS Dresden, in undertaking a mission in Chile, Canaris experienced first-hand imprisonment and internment by the Chilean government authorities. He escaped daringly from the internment camp at Talcahuano Naval Base and with the assistance from contacts in Santiago was spirited into Argentina, after a few months reappearing in Germany. Developing both an espionage and surveillance capability in South America between 1941–1945 was primarily delegated to the SD, with the Abwehr collaborating in operations primarily in a support function.[4] German agents uncovered and surreptitiously trafficked to home base estimates on military production figures, military information, reports on traveling movements and compliments of ships from primarily Caribbean and north-eastern South America and economic data.

A further motivation for the growing strategic importance of South and Central America to Germany was the establishment of mutually beneficial economic alliances and trading agreements during the mid–1930s, and a necessity for the Germany's Navy to preserve those relationships. Brazil, Argentina, Chile and Mexico were singled out as suitable targets for the more intense development of commercial relations with German companies. Brazil became Germany's leading international trading partner after 1934, in 1937–1938 the Brazilian government cemented its economic linkages by signing substantial armament contracts. As a consequence of these circumstances Brazil post–1939 converted into an important theater of clandestine activity and was regarded by Berlin as a priority to penetrate. Spy agent networks appeared first in Rio de Janiero, the SD VI directed considerable resources and institutional energy into ensuring a presence existed within the German ex-pat communities in Brazil. Information was collected on British shipping and forwarded by clandestine radio to Nazi Germany. Similar information from River Plate territory collected by operatives in Argentina was conveniently relayed through the Brazil stations.

Johannes Siegfried Becker evolved into a primary command figure in the Operation Bolivar project, the person responsible at ground-level for most Nazi espionage operations in South America. Becker was first deposited in Buenos Aires by the SD in May 1940. Becker and his associate Lange were inconveniently identified immediately by authorities as foreign intelligence agents, in September 1940 they traversed the northern border and decamped to Brazil where Becker made contact with Albrecht Engels. Johannes Becker transformed the fledgling Brazilian organization he encountered on arrival into an effective intelligence gathering network and maintained an ongoing dialogue with their control stations in Hamburg. By mid–1941, Engels's radio-communications station located inside an unassuming home residence in suburban São Paulo was functioning in reliable communication with all agents located in the vast and challenging expanse of Brazilian territory. The Brazilian detachment it was ascertained during the later investigations was fundamental to the systemic infrastructure of the asset network, acting as a central communication relay station for intelligence uncovered in other Latin American nations and United States, forwarding intelligence reports and messages to Germany from such agents as Georg Nicolaus in Mexico, Walter Giese in Ecuador and Ludwig von Bohlen, chief operative in Chile. All individuals were German ex-patriots or nationals becoming commanders of their own spy networks in Latin America.

Information gathered on the Latin American theater by regional substations comprising this internal network were collated and collectively dispensed to Hamburg Ast. Other important Bolivar spies included the German naval attaché in Rio de Janeiro, Hermann Bohny, Eduard Arnold and the Naval Attaché in Buenos Aires, Captain Dietrich Niebuhr, who masterminded espionage in Argentina. During the period between European outbreak of war and attack on Pearl Harbor the SD VI had streamlined operations and invested capital in protracting information gathering networks in South America.[5] In order to maximize distribution of activities, as discussed previously, Hamburg Ast and other comparable Ast and Nebenstellen or nest stations formed separate subdivisions under their jurisdiction. The two Nebenstellen most involved with Latin America were the Nest Cologne and Nest Bremen. Another Nazi organization present in Latin America was the Amstgruppe Austland division which exercised control over military attachés posted to diplomatic missions. In 1933, the German Foreign Office consented to allowing the Wehrmacht and Kriegsmarine to station Attaché officers at German embassies. Originally the deal was agreed with an understanding that the Attachés should under no circumstances engage in clandestine activities, but this was quickly reneged.

By 1939, Latin American political figures were acknowledging the gravity of an ideological war now spreading outwards from Europe. Increasingly, as Bolivar advanced and more prolific assets were recruited, the emerging fundamental priorities of ensuring the German Navy retained a tactical advantage in Naval combat was reinforced and relayed constantly by Colonel Piekenbrock. German technicians devised and invented mechanisms of communication over long distances, secret inks and microdot were utilized to transport messages clandestinely. In addition to employing agents resident in Latin America, the Abwehr and SD recruited members of crews of Spanish and Portuguese vessels to observe shipping in the United States dockyards and to report on maritime convoys discovered on their journey. These seamen were also encouraged to purchase American magazines and publications which if adjudged relevant were studied in Lisbon or exported for assessment in Germany. From these sources German Propaganda Office and Gestapo specialists researched methodologies for exploiting any discovered loopholes within U.S. security. Open source intelligence represented the convenient opportunity for obtaining information of over-all intelligence value, but Piekenbrock understood that little of immediate operational significance in all probability would be discovered submerged in this documentation.

By using harbors geographically situated in suitable locations and connections with Europe via compromised Latin airlines these scattered but interrelated sections were sufficiently competent to escape immediate detection by the Allied censorship and maintain reasonably expedient contact with Abwehr in Berlin. German intelligence worked to develop other communications relay systems and remedy any deficiencies present in trafficking data, the obvious inefficiency of international mail and transportation required investment in the radio transmitters. Financial reserves and institutional efforts were redirected into the production and establishment of clandestine radios and SD VI dispatched technician experts to regions of interest. As ever in espionage operations, planting operatives behind enemy lines is one essential priority and another is retrieving the covert information that is uncovered. Telecommunications inexorably developed into an active and critical theater of the counterespionage actions in Latin America. As an indication by March 1942 six clandestine transmitters were present in Rio alone. Operators of radio transmitter stations turned out predominantly to be unskilled radiomen, outside of the relatively non-standard mission compliment of technical specialists, instead country mission engineers were in most circumstances agents specializing in intelligence work. Personnel were seconded to further training if considered necessary in radio communications and encryption strategies. The receiving section of the Hamburg-Wohldorf radio station consisted of forty-three sets installed on the second floor of the facility. Transmitters for communications were constructed a few kilometers away in a remote rural area with structural mechanics added for remote control.

This overseas radio station, the largest inside the Abwehr's telecommunications network, developed into an essential conduit for transmitting intelligence reports from South America back to home base. The station's building complex and compliment increased in proportion to the German intelligence services demands during conflict, subsidiary augmentation relay stations for the purpose of boosting signal strength were assembled in France and Spain. In collaboration with major German telephone company, Telefunken, a specialist radio-transmissions device was invented and adapted. The equipment was designed to be lightweight and portable, correspondingly scaled for transportation without detection in a medium-sized suitcase. This Agenten-Funk became standard field apparatus for battlefield actions, but originally it constituted a core element of Abwehr strategy for communicating with overseas agents.[6]

A German Foreign Office appraisal discussed the preeminence of commercial contracts in place between German firms and numerous divisions of Latin American government, and how this could be exploited for Nazi ambitions. The Kilgore Subcommittee, of the Military Affairs Committee, discovered compelling evidence that I.G. Farben, Thyssen-Lametal and other German commercial enterprises submitted assessment reports on political, military and economic developments to German intelligence. A declassified U.S. report from 2005 permitted access to a 1945 government evaluation on Latin American collaboration with the Nazis.[7] Documents indicate a similar picture of industrial sector cooperation and supported allegations that several Latin American nations afforded minimal resources in containing Axis companies trading or operationally located in the region. These business representatives were generally extremely well informed about the domestic conditions and manifestly evident chains of information delivery that were established. The German Labor Front and Chamber of Commerce in connection with members participated in pro–Nazi activities and adopted guidance in promoting the regime through propaganda. Intelligence was trafficked through these conduits to SD headquarters. By the culmination of World War II restrictions on Axis companies and infrastructure had been introduced, but regulating the agreed framework was problematic.[8]

The Allied blockade on a practical level restricted smuggling or distribution of resources. But intelligence could be trafficked with detection and obscured via business connections until the war's conclusion. U.S. pressure to implement measures to control or eliminate enemy interests succeeded in expanding forfeitures, asset freezing and financial monitoring post–Rio Conference of January 1942, but the concessions were largely ineffective until January-February 1944. There were allegations by Britain's MI5 in 1939 about Siemens branches in South America being infiltrated and manipulated as a "vast organization for Nazi espionage and propaganda." An MI5 memo to military intelligence in late 1939 commented that it had come to their attention from various sources that Germany was using as subterfuge for their espionage activities certain important local industrial and commercial concerns. Security services analysis on German industry and allegations of collusion in espionage were divulged in the files declassified in 2010. In particular the names of Siemens Schuckert, Bayer and Schering & Co were mentioned in connection.[9] General concerns were expressed about calculating the levels of sensitive industrial knowledge acquired by Germany before the war. Documents indicate presence of suspicions directed at Nazi front organizations and penetration of multinationals back in 1935.

An intelligence analysis from April 1935 stated "Siemens concern being definitely used as a cover for subversive activities ... this same firm is in all probability being used for similar activities in other parts of the world." The prominence afforded to German industry in Latin America motivated the production and distribution of substantial quantities of Axis propaganda to persuade the domestic populations about the economic and political advantages of alliances. German propaganda proclaimed that in the aftermath environment of international conflict the United States national economy could not possibly compete with supreme position of Nazi Germany. Commercial firms from Axis nations promised their customers a steady distribution of commodities and other economic incentives.[10] If government and public support for fascism did not sufficiently subside more serious interruptions that targeted American regional dominance emerged as distinct security risks.

U.S. Reaction to Nazi Presence in Latin America

At the end of 1937, the United States was aware of the extent of Nazi-totalitarian presence in Latin America. By 1939, the Nazi underground movement though still in a formative and small-scale state was assessed in some quarters, for example the Dies Committee hearings, to be a credible and immediate threat to national security. The Department of State was relegated to a back seat as the FBI and other agencies attained jurisdiction on the Western Atlantic counterintelligence fronts. A small collection of diplomats and Armed Services attachés stationed inside the Latin American nations had attempted to organize intelligence data gathering in their host countries. The most sophisticated of the improvised intelligence groups operated in Mexico under the guidance of Pierre de Lagarde Boal, the Mexico City Counsel. In late 1939, a second individual appointed to a diplomatic posting in Mexico somewhat controversially prompted other advancements in covert action operations, a Naval Attaché Lt. Cdr. William Dillon. Boal established a three-man intelligence coordinating committee composed of representatives from the U.S. Embassy, the Military Attachés office and the Naval Attachés office. A letter sent from Pierre de Lagarde Boal to John Messersmith, December 22, 1939, described this system and functionality in detail. The intelligence reports these pioneers disseminated back to their superiors in Washington, D.C., performed an exigent role in alerting policy-makers to the necessity for a foreign-intelligence capability in Latin America and the inadequacy of existing applied resources for undertaking such a task.[11] U.S. officials expressed guarded concern over the levels of both German and Italian state economic competition and propaganda inside the Americas. Estimates claimed that 6 million emigrants from Italy resided in Latin America and approximately 2 million Germans inhabited the region. Chair of the House of Un-American Activities Committee Martin Dies discussed the issue of German settlers in South America, he estimated that a million German settlers were now organized in companies and battalions to invade from South America. In a defense report submitted to the White House by the Joint Board of Army and Navy it was reported that the policies of cultural, economic and political penetration in Latin America by Germany, Japan and Italy could certainly be estimated as substantial. Germany was also active in maintaining business and financial transactions in South and Central America, including radio broadcasting for the purposes of propaganda.

Industrial investment from the United States diffused at accelerated rates into South America during the previous 50 years and historically the South and Central American territory had represented sectors of strategic defensive interest to various American administrations dating back to the Monroe Doctrine.[12] Prior to the German invasion of Poland and subsequent Anglo-French war declarations the U.S. intelligence community had generally maintained minimal service capabilities within Latin America.[13] The relevancy of powerful and decisive military presence in South and Central America was re-established in the contemporary climate of international hostility, securing military and naval supremacy in the Americas territory compelled more inter-regional cooperation.

Admiral Stark, Chief of Naval Operations, realized that the Brazilian cooperation was tactically expedient, considering its geographical position and decided higher volumes of patrolling in the corridor traversing from South America to Western Africa was necessary. It formed a convenient traveling point for the transferring of munitions and supplies and decreased the inherent difficulties in replenishing soldiers stationed in North Africa if that was necessary. North-Eastern territory was valuable additionally from a strategic defense perspective because it then rendered nearly impossible a German invasion from the Central Atlantic route.

President Roosevelt concurred with Admiral Stark, that U.S. naval policy should recognize a vertical line extending between Eastern Brazil to West Coast Africa. Navy warships were deployed to accompany Allied Atlantic shipping convoys, the upgraded proposals established reassessed security precedents, in later measures their European counterparts received advanced warnings on positioning of German submarines and other Navy ships. Stark imparted directives to his subordinates, under the direction of President Roosevelt, regarding a program to construct offshore bases in Latin America and Caribbean.[14] To guarantee enlisting Brazilian cooperation in defense matters trade agreements were negotiated which promised lucrative loans and military aid. Brazil had benefited from a Lend-Lease scheme with the U.S. agreed in 1942, but arguably of more importance was the removal of anti-competition mechanisms from Brazil's domestic manufacturing industry. A focal point for the U.S. discussions reviewing Nazi security policies and undercover operations in Brazil and South America became the Pan-American Conference. United States officials strongly pressured the other powers to remain vigilant against the potential for interference from Nazi operatives.

U.S. leaders feared that the Nazi German government intended to entice German immigrants to support their foreign policy objectives for the Americas zone, the dividends generated in theory appeared damaging. Assistant Secretary of State Adolf Berle had informed President Roosevelt in a memorandum that populations of Axis nation and fascist sympathizing populations were substantial. Followers of the Falange political party in Spain, classified as a corporatist fascist organization, had emigrated to Latin America in considerable numbers. The 1930s witnessed 20,000–30,000 Falangists emigrate to different nations in Latin America and a prominent faction emerged in Cuba, the Falangist movement was assessed by the State Department as a serious palpable threat to security and a menace. On October 8 1938, Hitler and Franco had confirmed a treaty empowering Nazi Germany to control Spain's international policy. Spanish fascists were trained and re-oriented by Gestapo to proficiently serve the Fatherland and Axis block in Latin America. Espionage schools for Spanish citizens were installed in Hamburg, Bremen, Hanover, and Vienna. Graduates were commissioned as officers in the Spanish Army's Intelligence Service (SIM). Alberto Flores, a veteran Spanish Falangist official, was reassigned to Mexico to command the SIM operations there.[15]

In fact allegiance for Nazi Germany or generic fascism within the Spanish diaspora was not standard, but reports of Latin American political factions with sympathies towards that ideological perspective and presence of Spanish fascists inspired contention in U.S. authorities. Colombia was a major producer of the metal platinum ranking within the top three nations by global annual yield, a substantial proportion of Nazi operatives in Colombia were delegated powers to coordinate programs to smuggle platinum back to Germany. FBI and Colombian security forces exchanged information and enacted joint taskforces to disrupt the smuggling rackets and identify black market corridors.[16] In January 1939, Nazi Germany dispatched its operatives to German communities within Central and South America to supervise surveillance and information collection activities in Colombia. Earlier, in October 1938, agent J. Mueller had arrived in Colombia with the orders to publish propaganda and promote national socialism in Central America.

State Department officials and military commanders recognized vulnerabilities across South and Central America. The Panama Canal territory since its construction was prudently considered a high priority target area. This ten mile arterial pathway route leased indefinitely by Panama to the U.S. government was fundamental to Naval and commercial shipping transportation from the Atlantic to Pacific, both Army and Navy commanders insisted on defending the Panama Canal Zone territory with militarized fortifications, artillery and Naval support. Foreign intelligence sabotage and covert penetration operations orchestrated by Nazi Germany or Japan prompted critical implications for the U.S. Armed Forces in sustaining the resource requirements for military action.[17] Dating back to 1930 Japanese agents undercover in the Panama Canal Zone area photographed shipping crossing the channel and military defense systems. Admiral Stark in a 1938 memorandum had commented on the Japanese-Nazi pact and the implications for a tactical assessment in securing the Panama Canal. The memo referenced inherent dangers now prescient in collaborative efforts of respective intelligence services of Nazi Germany and Japan targeting the Canal Zone.

U.S. federal agencies proactively researched the efforts of Axis businesses and consortia to purchase land in the Panama Canal and Central American regions for colonization. Elaborate theories surrounded the possibility of Nazi agents transforming this territory into military or air force bases, attaining striking distance of mainland United States. While alarmist rhetoric only served to confuse the subject, Nazi front organizations did acquire strip land in Colombia, Costa Rica and other South American areas. A definite realization emerged about prospects of Panama Canal Zone evolving into a center of espionage activity. Another Axis power, Italy, similarly demonstrated considerable interest in Central America had become active in cultivating the friendship of Central American republics.[18] The Italian government offered educational scholarships for Guatemalan, Panamanian and Nicaraguan citizens to study in Italy. On December 14, 1937, an Italian ship departed from Napoli destined for a transatlantic crossing to Managua in Nicaragua. The compartment holds contained machine guns and munitions, armored cars and military equipment, for developing convivial relations with Nicaragua.

U.S. Intelligence Service Response

Radio communications and Allied signals tracking persisted as crucial factors in undermining Nazi covert espionage within Latin America. U.S. and British decryption experts had unraveled the German security codes as early as 1940 and signals tracking agency services developed the capacity for listened into Nazi radio transmissions from August onwards. This codebreaking accomplishment played a significant role in advance warnings for Allied shipping on potential enemy attacks. From May to June Ecuadorian authorities intercepted a number of signal transmissions from an unidentified radio station passing encrypted traffic and containing discernible German plain text. Suspecting Axis clandestine operations, the Ecuadorian government elected to approach the United States for technical assistance in detecting the illegal radio transmitters. This request initially covered a basic intervention but Boaz Long, the U.S. Ambassador to Ecuador, recommended nine radio personnel be dispensed. At approximately the same time the Colombian government issued a comparable request in the aftermath of a conference early in 1940 encompassing the American minister at Bogota, U.S. Army mission in Colombia and representatives of the Colombian government. This inquiry was referred to the Navy Department as no other branch of the Government possessed sufficiently high frequency direction finding equipment. The Ecuadorian radio intercepts had become the first tangible evidence of the existence of a Nazi radio net in Latin America.[19]

Signals intelligence developed from a multifarious array of state and military organizations. Intercept and analysis of communications constituted a major part of the Coast Guard's contribution to intelligence actions during World War II, the Communications Division of U.S. Coast Guard maintained an independent cryptographic and separate radio signal monitoring units. Coast Guard had pioneered signals tracking and decryption in border defense during the 1930s, its principle reason for existence as a service department traditionally was detecting smugglers during prohibition, but the enforcement of perimeter control from 1939 to 1942 escalated general responsibility to deterring foreign intelligence. These decrypted solutions if militarily pertinent or implied national security issues were forwarded to ONI, G-2, State Department, and the FBI.

Coast Guard Intelligence Unit, FBI and Navy were tasked with cryptanalysis in the segmented and non-centralized institutional culture. Office of Naval Communications (ONC), the cryptographic and intercept division of the Navy, employed a combined compliment of 11 officers, 88 enlisted men and 15 civilians in 1936, the Navy codebreakers demonstrated effectiveness in the field and decoded numerous clandestine ciphers. From 1939 the volumes intercepted in signals communications data and operational intelligence surpassed a content level manageable by ONC operators. An Executive memorandum of 1939 ordered the centralization of signals intelligence (SIGNIT), the proclamation combined agencies of the Army, Navy, and FBI, the cabinet secretaries were instructed to ensure the activities in their departments were disseminated to the agencies in SIGNIT. Later in 1939, Roosevelt ordered that a specialist intelligence coordination commission, the C.I. Committee, be instituted with representatives from each organization as supplementary adjunct in an advisory capacity. The Director of Naval Communications expressed the compulsory nature of a centralized infrastructure and had campaigned for its introduction.

The Federal Communications Commission (FCC) recognized as civilian telecommunications specialists were commandeered into signals intelligence in 1941 and actively intercepted clandestine circuits with a focus on South America. By end of 1941, the Radio Intelligence Division (RID) section of the FCC was formerly constituted. This department perpetrated tracking of Axis signals spanning Lisbon to Portuguese Guinea and Lisbon to Mozambique, as well as transmitters operating in Rio de Janeiro and Valparaíso.[20] The RID with patient concerted investigations discovered 75 individual stations, four of emanating from inside the Brazilian interior by June 1942. The U.S. Navy performed admirably in intercepting and deciphering cipher transmissions, in July 1941 a notable upsurge in detection rates occurred and by mid–February 1942 five distinct groups were identified, two of them operating out of Brazil and one emanating from Chile.

The FBI with authorization from the Justice Department and President Roosevelt formed the Special Intelligence Service (SIS) in July 1940, an intelligence department oriented towards Latin America. The Specialist Information

Service's internal structure harnessed overseas-based resources and mandated that legal and civil attachés reinterpret their traditional expectations to become SIS agents in the Latin American nation of their posting.[21] Other departments of state security with a jurisdiction to defend against Nazi infiltration included the Office of Naval Intelligence (ONI) and the Military Intelligence Division (MID). Military intelligence were endowed with the extra obligation for collecting military, political and psychological information pertaining to the Western Atlantic. A supplementary assignment entailed reserving a branch for special intelligence, relating to dossiers on politically subversive suspects within Latin America. The Office of Naval Intelligence (ONI) fulfilled a similar capacity for the U.S. Navy. Records indicate that internal friction existed nearly perpetually as manifold security divisions engaged in jurisdictional fictionalization and departmental competition. Inevitably reaction times slowed and coordination problems emerged related to overlapping areas of influence.

Hoover and the FBI were dissatisfied with the SIS playing an inferior role to Naval or Army Intelligence, believing that domestic security policy on the Nazi Germany threat should correctly be the domain of the FBI. The Bureau's standing jurisdiction was limited to the dominion of the domestic police and intelligence functions, J. Edgar Hoover had lobbied strenuously for the FBI's prerogative to be expanded and arguments about departmental territoriality lingered until the war's conclusion. The FBI succeeded to an extent in obtaining its demand to control all espionage and counterespionage activities in the region, an accomplishment partially motivated by Hoover's leveraging of the recently deciphered transcripts indicating a secretive Nazi espionage network existed in Latin America. Post 1942, while MID and ONI personnel still participated in foreign operations, day to day investigations of Nazi subversion or espionage fell under the jurisdiction of SIS.[22]

Maintaining hemispheric solidarity was defined by the U.S. State Department as essential in combating Nazi infiltration and domination. In order to accomplish this Roosevelt created the Office of the Coordinator Inter-American Affairs (CIAA) in August 1940 and appointed Nelson Rockefeller to govern the organization. The CIAA was recognizably a propaganda vehicle exploited by the United States, this agency launched propaganda campaign initiatives in an enterprising foray into cultural diplomacy, to persuade Latin Americans about the positive attributes of a United States partnership, Roosevelt realized definite advantages of CIAA in influencing government agenda and perspectives. Significant emphasis was placed on the concepts of the Americas as a singular cultural and geographic entity. Inter-American cultural values were promoted in tandem with political solidarity.[23]

Another formative U.S. intelligence office opened for business in July

1941, its jurisdictional remit predominantly in practice motivated actions in the European and North African theaters. Post establishment of SIS, Hoover channeled his personal influence and resources into preventing other agencies from interfering within the FBI's sphere of influence. He motioned interjections informing the contending parties about his opposition to the embryonic stages of a new international department. President Roosevelt pressed forwards with instituting the Office of the Coordinator of Information and Office of Security Services and on July 11th of 1941 the department was legally constituted and William Donovan appointed to the OSS chief position. This centralization of armed forces and civilian intelligence provoked considerable controversy and opposition within sections of the military. Critics had accused Donovan of assuming an authoritative control over all international U.S. intelligence and described his selection as the product of a political agenda, rather than a national defense solution.[24] Donovan continued unabated in developing clandestine missions inside Europe and exhibited largely disinterest towards the Latin American domain.

Brazil

Senior foreign and diplomatic community chiefs retained confidence that neutrality and even positive alliances were cultivatable with Brazil. Hitler's command staff had appreciated since outbreak of naval warfare and the ensuing Western Atlantic offensive the implications of investing energy, time and resources in a comprehensive intelligence system inside the Brazilian interior. The development of commercial relations and construction of facilities and production plants in previous decades by German businesses opened Brazil as a strategically important frontier, controlling the nearby Oceanic pathways were essential in protecting the importation of goods desperately required in wartime. As a consequence of the above, Brazil became an important theater of clandestine activity.

The First Brazilian Republic (1889–1930) was governed by a succession of unrepresentative oligarchies heralding from historically the most powerful economies in the country, São Paulo and Minas Gerais. Brazil's domestic economy during 20th Century's first quarter was foremost dependent on international commodity exportation. The Rio Grande do Sul's state governor, a Getúlio Dornelles Vargas, was destined for performing an important function in the neutrality debate. The revolution of 1930 forcibly removed Washington Luís from the federal government and recognized instead Vargas as Brazil's legitimate president, he continued to sustain presidential office in South America's largest nation during World War II. Introducing a comprehensive reform program favoring nationalism, populism, industrialization and centralization, the Vargas era centered on the integration of migrant communities and constructing a Brazilian national identity. German immigrants first arrived in Brazil in 1824, settled initially in São Leopoldo in Rio Grande do Sul. By the 1930's, German citizens and descendants living in this state counted around 360,000 people. The economic collapse of Germany in aftermath of World War I had prompted waves of demoralized and impoverished people to emigrate in search of improved fortunes to South America. A diverse group of immigrants landed on the Western Atlantic coastline, characterized by a distinguishable proportion of young men alienated because of the perceived failures of government in the postwar Germany. The new arrivals included discharged military officers, former Freikorps and associates of right-wing political organizations. Travelogues and publications produced by this generation of migrants revealed racist tendencies in depictions of Latin American populations presented in contemporary literature. One German émigré writer, Werner Hopp had perpetuated stereotypes and cultural misinterpretations describing the Quechua and other native populations as exhibiting "low mental capacity," he and similar Nazi theorists insisted that the Native American populations were inherently inferior to "whites." Established sections of populations still contained ideologies of Pan-Germanism and nationalism, another characteristic persisting was loyalty to the Kaiser and traditional Imperial Germany. News reports from Europe about conditions in their former homeland cultivated despairing perceptions of democracy and supposedly destabilized political conditions. The German language press generally backed-up this dark portrayal of European affairs and confirmed expectations of a diminishing global prominence for the homeland. Books and leaflets authored by Oswald Spengler and other anti-democratic theorists were promulgated by the German-language newspapers in South and Central America.

Getúlio Vargas, was an immensely controversial statesman in Brazilian history, he intervened to manipulate negotiations to exploit as comprehensively as circumstances would allow the conflict engulfing the United States and Germany. Since orchestrating a successful revolution in 1930 Vargas had pursued the perspicacious strategy of cultivating his international reputation as a right-wing conservative.[25] His consistent anti–Communist rhetoric appealed to many multiple foreign powers, overtures towards cordial diplomatic relations and political alliances were received from Mussolini's Italy and Nazi Germany. Preceding Vargas, the Brazilian federal government constituted a federation of autonomous states dominated by the landowning classes. Land reforms implemented by the Vargas administration would transformed Brazil's industrial and agricultural landscape, state intervention and stimulus packages sparked renewed economic growth and urbanization disrupting traditional social structures. This emergent corporatist system received diverse comparisons from international quarters to Mussolini's fascism and Roosevelt's New Deal, to many fascist theorists this constituted a hybrid state capitalism system. Briefly converting to a democratic government, a new constitution in 1934 reorganized the political system by founding a legislature with state and social-sector representatives. Universal suffrage and other liberal reforms were introduced, the governing national assembly elected Vargas president for a four-year term. In 1932, He endured a tumultuous period and survived a civil war, his resilience and survival instincts were further demonstrated in 1935 by holding narrowly the presidency after a radical communist movement attempted revolution.

International unity in opposition to communism formed a central framework of the Brazilian government's foreign and diplomacy policy, progressing into a convenient bargaining chip. Inside the national socialist theorists' and Foreign Office departments' interpretation of Latin American culture Brazil was regarded as an interesting prospect for a mutually advantageous anti-communist alliance. Both Italy during its military engagements in Ethiopia and Franco's Nationalists in Spain had obtained financial and operational support from Vargas. The anti-communist policies struck a distinguishable chord in Nazi Germany, Foreign Office and military intelligence experts developed high expectations of a coalition agreement with the Vargas administration. In 1937, domestically Brazil maneuvered decisively in the opposite political trajectory, a realignment towards autocracy was orchestrated with abandonment of 1934's liberal constitution and unsanctioned closure of Brazilian legislature.[26]

In 1938 the Integralists, commanded by Plinio Salgado launched an attempted overthrow of the Vargas administration. U.S. officials speculated that Nazi operatives had financed or orchestrated the coup, but the nationalist program of Integralists on inspection favored a forced assimilation of all minority groups and an anti-foreign influence message. While conceptually extreme-right the primary instigators were insular. Karl Ritter, the Brazilian Ambassador proposed that U.S. intelligence forces in fact interfered within the Integralists endeavors to engineer a change of government. With Europe and Asia descending into industrial-scale armed conflict the Brazilian position of splendid isolation appeared in considerable jeopardy and plausibly untenable, the Brazilian government reassessed this foreign policy so successfully pursued in the 1930s. The "pragmatic equilibrium" policy consisting of neutral relationships maintenance between the three contending world powers of the United States, Britain and Germany had served Brazil effectively. The nations in question incontestably depended on major strategic and economic interests that were constructed in Brazil during the 1930s. Comparably with Latin America in general Brazil was placed in a compromised position and policies of neutrality were tested to their limits.[27]

Expanding NSDAP and National Socialism in Brazil

Abwehr Section I and SD VI D4 dependent on the unfolding circumstances either separately or in conjunction were in command and accountable for German espionage operations in Brazil. The Brazilian government and military agreed to armaments deals with the Third Reich, forming a closer relationship with the German Military Supreme High Command (OKW). A sanctioned alliance for the purposes of coordinating their opposition to communism was founded between the domestic Brazilian intelligence services and the Gestapo. This commitment to expand the NSDAP into a global network with branches in all prominent nations was symptomatic to the Party leadership's commitment to congregating German citizens living abroad under the banner of National Socialism. Originally small-organized groups were formed overseas semi-independently by enthusiasts in the 1920s, from these underfunded offices rose structured cells comparable to models installed in Germany and subordinate to the Ausland (official title in English: Foreign Organization of NSDAP), abbreviated to A.O. in discourse. First established in Hamburg in April 1931, the A.O. by 1939 with meticulous attention to localized policies supervised representative organizations in eighty-three countries and territories, as the NSDAP focused its structural efforts on uniting German citizens abroad under Nazi doctrine.

Convincing this population was the central occupation of the Ausland group established in the state capital city of Porto Alegre. General campaigning objectives ratified by the branch organization aimed at expansion through forming additional groups that promoted national socialism and autocratic principles. Other key national socialist themes were systematically promulgated to memberships: a citizenship concept based on ethnicity; the boycott of Jewish business; and volunteer recruitment for military action. Long-term, the political commitment was to explore and investigate methodologies of reproducing in Brazilian society the concepts of a national socialist ideology. The Porto Alegre branch was ordered to report on the possibility of commercial transactions with local enterprises before and during World War II, as Latin America emerged as a Foreign Office major theater of operations. The Ausland branches would become objects of considerable scrutiny by Allied intelligence agencies.

Brazilian Interior Minister Francisco Campos expressed his frustration and security concerns in observing the growing strength of communism to a notable representative attached to the German diplomatic delegation in Rio de Janeiro. Conversations occurred between Interior Ministry personnel and the German embassy about the possibility of collusion with Nazi Germany in an anti-communist pact. A German consular employee, Cossell, informed the Ausland chief Ernst Bohle that Campos was prepared to dispatch his most trusted security operatives to Nazi Germany for specialist training in the crucial struggle against communism. Cossell described Interior Minister Campos to his superiors as the second most important political figure in Brazil after Getúlio Vargas, but the German Foreign Office and the ambassador to Brazil Curt Prufer exhibited more caution. The Vargas administration's campaign against movements indicating foreign allegiances and dangerous external influences incited renewed disquiet about prospects of the deteriorating diplomatic relationship. A number of German citizens were arrested for violating the recent government restrictions and publicly desecrating the Brazilian flag, the state police uncovered the connections between some of those arrested and Nazi Party organizations including the Ausland.[28]

The Nazi-Brazilian relationship did not flourish for long as conflicts developed and prominent anti–Nazi campaigns expanded. A faction with proclivities oriented towards physical violence and street oriented campaigning within Ausland organization movement of Latin America developed a reputation for frequently engaging in parades and demonstration with overtly Nazi rhetoric. This open display of foreign political and cultural identity apparently motivated a transition in the domestic attitude and offended the host community, a distinct possibility emerged of jeopardizing long standing connections of solidarity. This backlash beginning in late 1939 and gaining momentum during early 1940 held potential to deteriorate the perceptions of German community members they proclaimed to represent. Recruiters for Nazi Party in this highly visible movement in the exertions at mobilization ended up alienating their host community and provoking anti–German campaigning nationwide. The culmination of this process witnessed Vargas and other Latin American administrations resorting to mass deportation of suspicious German and Axis residents in autumn 1940.[29]

During the abortive communist revolution and later draconian crackdowns on subversive groups, pro–Nazi groups received remarkable protection and were largely ignored. The Integralists, Communists and other opposition political parties were not as fortunate. In 1937, all political groups and the assembly dissolved as the repressive nature of Vargas's government expanded to perceived internal security threats from every source. This elimination of international corrupting influences was announced as a fundamental objective of the government and the administration released propaganda advocating the destruction of cultural differentiation inside Brazil. A vigorous campaign was launched by Vargas against pro–Nazi movements and part members in combination with mass deportations in September 1940. A policy of forced assimilation and nationalization was imposed by Vargas and the military concentrated on immigrant populations including German and other Axis nations. Measures explicitly prohibited political activities that were not directly endorsed by the government. U.S. State Department pressure being another influence behind the scenes. A reconciliation period conversely occurred between Brazil and Germany in between late 1940 and 1941.[30]

Bohle ordered German citizens in Brazil and Latin America to withdraw from movements and organizations with non–German citizens members and to discontinue parades. Curt Prufer, who served as German ambassador to Brazil dating from the beginning of 1939 and until mid–1942, claimed in a statement he released after the cessation of hostilities that the Nazi Party functionaries in Brazil had avoided illegal activities as directed by Bohle. From 1942 and 1943 onwards Vargas protractingly in radio and media broadcasts and speeches proclaimed his commitment to Pan-American cooperation. Still, while Vargas apparently recognized America as a principle ally, German business was engaged in commercial transactions in Brazil.[31]

U.S. Reaction to Nazi Presence in Brazil

Neutrality practiced by Brazil and majority of South-Central American nations from 1940 to 1942 was severely tested with the upsurge in rivalry between the Third Reich and United States. Military strategists in the United States agreed on importance of North-Eastern South America in the nation's defensive sphere, Navy policy advocated the establishment of naval bases dominating the region and Caribbean. Roosevelt and State Department adopted a strategy of proffering economic inducement packages to the Brazilian government in encouraging a pro–American stance, the enticing contracts ranged from military aid, to the construction of steel plants at Volta Redonda. Preferential purchasing programs and negotiating a price-support agreement for coffee opened up the discussions regarding the building of maritime bases. In a supplementary persuasion device utilized by the United States, its negotiators referenced the decidedly ominous behavior, real and imagined, to both North and South America emanating from Nazi Germany and menace of global conquest associated with Axis military objectives. U.S. diplomats in discussions with their counterparts reinforced the notions of continental solidarity as the best methods of defense.

U.S. Embassy officials by November 1941 had resourcefully created an intricate network of observers and informants who were entrusted with the specialist task of observing Nazi suspects. In Brazil, utilizing undisclosed funding, Jefferson Caffery, U.S. Ambassador, and James O'Shaughnessy, an Embassy staffer, headed up the State Department's counterintelligence operations. Mandated an operational budget of $6,000, the two operatives purchased loyalty from individuals in convenient positions to instigate surveillance details on suspected travelers and German embassy personnel. The Ambassador agreed in reimbursing a commensurate salary and expense payment to individuals who furnished the Embassy with a regular intelligence report. A comparable amount was distributed to informants supplying lists of foreign customers registering at local hotels and passengers on German airlines established in Brazil, Condon and Vasp.[32]

United States was in January 1941 refraining in compliance with the neutrality policy from entering into violations of non-aggression commitments, despite the naval agreements and armaments supplies. Contingents of the domestic political class and population still exhibited outward disinterest in military intervention against Germany. The British discovered a hidden map in October 1941 while searching an irreparably stricken German trawler that held the potential to change alliances in Latin America. The geographical map was a hypothetical atlas of South America divided into enormous states to be administered by Nazi Germany: Brasilien, Argentinean, Neuspanien. It was invaluable evidence of Nazi aggression directed consciously across the Atlantic, touching its closest neighbors. The later hypothetical state included the Panama Canal Zone to be totally annexed. Other information was discovered in the secret document detailing Lufthansa routes from Europe to South America, extending into Panama and Mexico.[33]

To President Franklin Roosevelt, resolutely determined to end U.S. isolationism, this was a sensational propaganda coup. Nazi Germany's imperial were ambitions exposed to public opinion, an important achievement for the pro-intervention campaigners who anticipated that American decisive intervention was now imminent. The origins of this treasure of Nazi strategic plans for South America remain obscure and the authenticity has raised questions.

Albrecht Gustav Engels

Albrecht Engels as a teenager had experienced military service in World War I, scarred by a wartime spent in the trenches. He had demonstrated important technical knowledge and administrative prowess while employed at

German company Siemens. Code named "Alfredo," he developed into the central hub of RSHA controlled espionage movements, with arms extended throughout the American sphere of influence. His transmitter formed a conduit to Germany for political, economic and military information. A wartime secret assessment produced by the FBI, described Alfredo as an "integral wheel" within Latin Americas for transmitting information from the Eastern seaboard U.S. cities of New York and Baltimore, but also West coast Los Angeles. Alfredo's coverage expanded internally throughout the South American terrain from Ecuador and Brazil to Argentina. Engels was subordinate technically in the Nazi command structure to Captain Hermann Bohny, assistant Naval Attaché of German Embassy in Rio de Janeiro. The main operational objectives as ordered by SD VI handlers in Hamburg were offensive penetration and information gathering operations to obtain intelligence about the movement of British and American shipping at Brazilian ports, which could be analyzed at headquarters or transmitted to German submarines patrolling the Atlantic Ocean. Engels also received letters and paper documents from the U.S., Mexico and Panama with confidential information, re-routing them to Berlin.[34]

In 1923, Engels originally emigrated to Brazil as an employee of Siemens firm attracted by the nation's advertised good economic prospects. Occupational reputation and technical qualifications convinced other locally-based employers and transfers followed to major industrial and commercial centers in the South-Central regions of Brazil. He productively built-up and cultivated contacts in the region's business and political circles during the 1920s and early 1930s. Other assorted employment roles soon materialized, he was head hunted as chief engineer for AEG in South American operations and acquired an impressive career portfolio at other prestigious German companies. Albrecht Engels commented on media reporting of the resurgence associated with his native country in 1935–38 with considerable pride. In South America a biproduct of the cultural separation and limited possibilities for contact with the homeland ensured that German immigrant populations commonly were unaware of the whole picture of European conflict. Engels was recruited without complications arising by the Abwehr in 1939, during a family expedition taken in Germany and Switzerland.

An old acquaintance, Jobst Raven, at this present occurrence a commissioned Abwehr officer, unexpectedly contacted Engels. Raven, a comrade World War I veteran, had recognized a surreptitious opportunity for conveniently visiting his old friend in Genoa and proposed involvement in the sacred service of the Fatherland, by the time Alfredo returned to South America in October 1939 he was a German intelligence asset. The first reports distributed to Raven concerned relatively harmless open source intelligence and production data regarding South America and United States industry. Business contacts cultivated during his 20 year association with Brazil and in Latin America proved valuable intelligence sources for an individual converted progressively into their prize asset. The SD needed a communications point for collating and transmitting intelligence from inside the Americas back to Germany.[35]

In order to achieve this objective "Alfredo" had invested considerable time consuming efforts in assembling a shortwave radio station in a suburban district of São Paulo, the transmitter's actual purpose was masked by technically being the registered property of his electric company, Allgemeine Elektrizitäts Gesellschaft. He was now capable of secretly dispatching the intelligence documents supplied by their operatives to the Hamburg listening station. Raven figured out another efficacious method of exporting information back to handlers in Berlin and avoiding unwanted attentions of ONC or FBI detection systems, the planes of Italian Transcontinental Airlines were seconded to smuggle documents into Europe. As espionage operations developed in sophistication and quantity, in addition to collecting economic information, agents were instructed to contrive the acquisition of information on industrial affairs, war production and military movements in Brazil and the United States.[36] Albrecht Engels initiated contact with German intelligence operations inside Mexico, headed by Karl von Schleebrugge and Georg Nikolaus, and recruited new radio technical experts in Beno Sobisch and Ernst Ramuz. Hermann Bohny dispensed mission funds and handled the diplomatic cables and pouch. By mid–1941, Engels's radio station disguised in a discreet, unremarkable suburban residence inside São Paulo was functioning smoothly in trafficking relatively unfettered the information recovered by operatives. Collaboration between the Abwehr and its traditional enemy the RSHA's SD temporarily halted the standard picture of rivalry and hostility. A senior operative from the SD found himself deployed to South America in November 1940, Johannes Becker by this period was a ten year veteran of the SS, he transpired to be an important asset for intelligence missions based on his experiences of inhabiting and formerly conducting business relations in South America and Argentina in particular. Cooperation was briefly formulated between the two intelligence services by mission requirements as both agencies were mandated for supplying personnel to covert operations on the continent. When Johannes Becker arrived in São Paulo he transformed Engels's spy network into an organization that reported on all subjects of interest to German intelligence. Becker before embarking to São Paulo was briefed on the expectations and ambitions by the SD VI chief, defining the magnitude of importance attached by Nazi Germany officials in strengthening its foothold internally.

After making contact with Engels in Rio de Janeiro, Becker established a permanent base of operations in Brazil and endorsed an assessment of the present standards and practices. He informed superior officers in Berlin on his proposals for installing and reforming covert action and contingency response programs, Becker advocated setting up a region-wide integrated espionage network, he introduced advanced methods for trafficking information and sanctioning new encryption procedures to improve security measures.[37] Becker's intelligence reports from January to June 1941 covered neutral and Allied merchant ship movements in North America and Caribbean, activity in port areas, the industrial production of naval vessels, airplane technology and weapons systems. Submissions on shipping routes comprised if possible consignments, their names and designations, crew compliments and movement analysis reports. Captain Bohny in the capacity of assistant Naval Attaché and his immediate commanding officer, Captain Niebuhr, both evolved into prolific sources of information on military production and policies. To ensure secrecy and avoid attracting unnecessary attention Bohny arranged for an assistant named Gustav Glock to act as conduit.[38]

The Engels network was not the only German intelligence cell engaged in espionage or covert penetration operations in Brazil, three other underground and equally industrious spy networks with separately controlled clandestine radio stations existed, all beginning operation in 1941. In May, Rio de Janeiro's separate shortwave station advanced a major step forwards by commencing contact and consequently ongoing two-way dialogue with the designated radio-communications post in Germany, the group expanded to supervise informants and sources nationwide in Brazil. This espionage network was centered around a commercial service, the "Informadora Rapida Limitada," managed by Herbert O.J. Muller. The radio station itself and most of the cellular undercover projects were coordinated by Friedrich Kemper and Herbert von Heyer, the second individual a productive member of this spy network submitted recurrent encoded communiqué documents to the Engels group.

The geographical isolation and insufficient centralized support mechanisms resulted in Latin American agents constructing a semi-independent and insular culture. Von Heyer's cover persona, was concealed as a security measure within his respectable employment status inside the Theodore Wille Company, in fact several company employees were actively engaged in another spy network centered on a station located in Recife. The Chilean net's connection with Operation Bolivar was revealed through intercepted documents pertaining to the Rio underground actions. A particularly unguarded exchange delivered transparent insider content to the U.S. authorities in July 1941, Chilean German Embassy official, von Bohlen, first opened communication with von Heyer in Rio de Janeiro to obtain secret espionage equipment which von

Bohlen had ordered from Germany. Herbert von Heyer was a business community leader with an occupational background of employment contracts in high profile German-Latin American interests, he was summoned by the expanding Brazilian espionage network in March 1940 and exhibited minimal hesitation. Heyer was born in Brazil, spending his childhood period in Santoa. His first experiences of Germany were a product of schooling and military service during World War I.[39]

Within the Becker-Engels network agent Hans Muth confirmed himself to be an instrumental technical expert and specialist support personnel.[40] A former Brazilian Navy employee and long-term German immigrant in Brazil, previously Muth had showcased his considerable and proficuous talents by improvising shortwave radio devices for German merchant ships languishing afflicted by the restricted movements and blockades in Brazil's harbors. The British and Commonwealth navies in enforcement of their Atlantic blockade stipulated a policy of vetting every passing vessel, an obvious suppressive dilemma for the German and other Axis merchant fleets. In preparation a secret laboratory specializing in shortwave radio technology had been temporarily installed in the basement of Muth's home residence, to present a limited solution to communications blackouts. Radio transmissions from the Brazilian espionage networks back to headquarters in Berlin, in this emergent climate of advanced technical apparatus, steadily increased post–July 1941. The consistent relay schedules for transmitting routine communications and the code encryption systems were established by Muth with the Abwehr's signaling and cryptography experts in Hamburg.

A third espionage cell associated with the Becker-Engels network was activated in the major urban conglomerate of São Paulo, further south. Commanded by Eduard Arnold, the cellular members were trained to concentrate combined efforts on fulfilling intelligence requests about the production of armaments, labor conditions pertaining to domestic civilian and employee morale and possibilities of sabotage. In Brazil, Eduard Arnold had been converted into an energetic and somewhat impetuous dilettante of national socialism. Analogously to "Alfredo" he was originally head hunted by the SD operative Jobst Raven, prominent connections in Brazil Ausland group impressed by Eduard Arnold's commitment had recommended his recruitment to senior intelligence officials. In April 1940 Arnold established his infiltration vehicle in São Paulo, intelligently converting a nondescript commercial sales office into a front organization to camouflage actions and prevent observation. Disguising an agent's genuine underground activities was a compulsory requirement for a SD VI field mission. The São Paulo espionage ring was ordered to initiate a mutual assistance system with Engels in Rio de Janeiro, subsequently secretive documents recovered by the Arnold cell were transported via the front organization office to Hamburg.[41] In the summer of 1940, Arnold obtained a new collaborator and accomplice as the Abwehr introduced another agent to its São Paulo operation, Erich Immers.

The ambitious Immers conspired in hatching an elaborate scheme to penetrate interior United States by couriering an underground agent into U.S. territory under their control, a Nazi Party member who was personal associate passed selection. Unfortunately, the plans were irrevocably derailed after the individual in question was refused an American travel visa application. Instead Arnold resolved to transfer his protégé to Porto Alegre, a city in the Southern region of Brazil. In September of 1940, he departed with explicit instructions to observe ship designations and movements at harbors, once on the ground in Porto Alegre the informant enterprisingly found rental accommodation in a boarding house and cover employment at a local furniture store. As it transpired Immers developed powerful enemies within the Nazi underground operations of Latin America. He displayed minimal interest in observing instructions or following the chains of commands, traveling to neighboring South American nations without permission. Immers was accused of displaying a scant regard for security measures. Bohny and Prufer registered unambiguous personal animosity towards Immers and actively worked against him, pressing demands that Berlin admonish and replace the new recruit. Immers was destined to lose the internal power-struggle and a waiting transport vessel shipped him back to Germany. Close collaboration of the Arnold and Engels-Becker networks was practiced well into 1943.[42]

Operations of Brazilian Spy Rings

Nazi Germany's presence in Brazil was at least tolerated if not encouraged during the Vargas regime until mid–1941. The fear of communism and the importance of trade and financial agreements with Germany were principle factors for Brazilian state security organizations exhibiting apparent disinterest concerning the expansion of political ideology or departmental offices in the nation at first and then re-initiating contact in the early wartime years. Pro-Axis and pro-fascist sympathies certainly remained present in many sections of the Brazil's ruling elite most notably in the military. Information from inside the Vargas administration was uncovered by the informant's network, with Schellenberg demanding conclusive evidence of Brazil's resistance to mounting pressure from Washington and the government's evolving interpretation of the Atlantic security threats. Engels transmitted by radio to Hamburg receiving station, between August and October 1941, that President Vargas planned to enlist 100,000 reservists and had conveyed the orders for augmenting resources relating to national security measures. An additional 35,000 soldiers were redeployed and converged in Pernambuco and other Northern states.

The network reported in December 1941 information containing insider details of President Vargas denying permission for U.S. armed forces to be stationed full-time at various defensive points in Brazil's North-Eastern territories. On the maritime front in the immediate aftermath of Pearl Harbor January witnessed reports multiply in frequency on the movement of shipping traversing Brazilian coastal zones and patrolling missions of both Brazilian and American Naval forces in the Northwest Atlantic. Schellenberg and the SD VI command staff developed an awareness from the Becker-Engel's informants of a mounting propensity towards anti–Nazism and the scale of demonstrations in several regions. In February, technical information was transmitted to the Hamburg listening complex covering blueprints of a Curtiss manufacturing facility in Ohio, a location selected by the U.S. Navy for construction of an advanced single-seat dive bomber. In communications Herbert von Heyer had discussed obtaining this information after inducing a reliable informant employed in Brazilian State Department. Microdot intelligence surfaced in SD's Berlin headquarters reporting on the production difficulties and hold-ups in U.S. aircraft industry.

Recife, in North-Eastern Brazil, emerged as a prominent staging ground for covert infiltration, as multiple informants inhabited the strategically critical harbor and dockyard districts. Intelligence reports at the time suggest cooperation occurred between the Rio and Recife groups on a routine basis. Recife, a territory traditionally associated with naval engineering and industrialization was researched and selected as a viable option by von Heyer. Directorate of Naval Intelligence intercepts dating from February to August 1941 uncovered that von Heyer had distributed reports to Alfredo regarding the construction of Airbases by American commercial airline companies. Other documents discussed how surveillance teams in Recife reported on the neighboring coastal zone for four months being used as a traveling passage for U.S. Air force and South Atlantic Naval force. Functionally, the Recife network at ground-level acted semi-independently, checking in with Engels monthly to be informed on updates or supply information. In January 1941, von Heyer had launched and invested resources in a Recife oriented recruitment campaign, purchasing illegal services of sailors, harbor officials and restaurant workers.[43] The 1941–42 reports indicate inclinations for considerable antagonism and individuals friction developed from this semi-independence, usually a product of "turf warfare." A recurring cause for dissension appeared to surround which agents held higher positions in the chains of command.

American airline routes were customarily monitored by espionage teams in Recife, with the incoming and outgoing flights documented and analyzed by observers. Once again employees from German companies were approached and seduced, with 3 employees of the Stolz businesses recruited. This included a technician who relayed information on a Pan Am facility. Other airports and airbases came under scrutiny, European and American civilian airlines operating in Latin America fell into the categories designated for the special surveillance measures. SD VI transmitted intelligence requests throughout September to December 1941, for example information on U.S. transporting cargo planes in collusion with British armed force in Africa. A translated cable dispatched by Alfredo in November conveyed the message of "cruiser is supposed to go from there to U.S. or Capetown to dock," "Robin Gray ready for departure laden under decks with tanks, automatic weapons, munitions and will go to Africa." The primary geographical regions categorized in intelligence reports shifted as Porto Allegre and Rio Grande do Sul developed into hotbeds of Nazi clandestine action.[44]

Admiration was observable towards the NSDAP and various deviations of national socialism present within the resident populations of operational centers in Rio Grande do Sul, Recife and Porto Alegre. The proportion who consciously asserted allegiance was still relatively minor compared to population of German citizens who actually inhabited the territories according to population statistics. Interactions that were uncovered between residents and the Porto Alegre German Consulate attracted attention, investigation and surveillance of suspected individuals by domestic law enforcement and security services. Brazilian Police surveillance teams observed anomalistic individuals and unknown representatives of the German Embassy staff who were circulating incriminatingly, confirmation that German intelligence agents were present in Recife and Porto Alegre transformed residually into an open and unconcealed secret. The detection of an illegal radio transmitter stationed permanently in the Porto Alegre locality motivated further alarmed warning flags and premature speculation within the Brazil's security community, the formerly ambivalent attitude of police the and Interior Ministry was altering.

Exposure of Nazi Spy Rings and Detention

Brazil and other Latin American cells suffered a setback in July 1941. The Mexican operation was exposed first and activities had drawn unwanted public attention to Nazi undercover espionage networks much wider in scope. A number of Latin America networks had linked up with a counterpart situated in

New York. A radio transmitter station in Long Island managed by an agent code named "Tramp" performed a focal point service for communications within the Americas Nazi operations. Agent Tramp's real name was William Sebold, his story was discussed in chapter 3. The radio relay system was compromised following a revelation that Sebold was an FBI double agent, from July to August arrests of 33 suspected Nazi clandestine agents in America was initiated by the FBI. The fallout reached Mexico and Latin American nations as further radio stations were exposed. But Brazil for the next 3–4 months was largely uncompromised by discovery of this network extending through the Americas, Engels's operation developed into a semi-official secondary communications point for deserting operatives.

The remaining security service and otherwise underground operatives in Mexico and Central America, including Georg Nikolaus and his informants circle, transported surviving documents to Brazil's headquarters. Reports originating in Ecuador and Colombia were now routed through Engels, other communications from the Andean region were trafficked to Brazil. The Chilean network headed by von Bohlen and Reiners, embedded inside the diplomatic and business sectors in Chilean capital of Santiago, formed integrated links with Becker-Engels in Rio de Janeiro zone to distribute documents back to Germany. By February 1942, the communications intercepts from SIGNIT were accumulating faster than FBI specialist analysts could form an assessment of the data. The FBI slowly unraveled the multiple threads presented to them. Ambassador Jefferson Caffery's U.S. Embassy labors transpired invaluable, meticulously records were examined to identify foreign intelligence suspects.[45] Hoover announced the FBI's contentions regarding Nazi espionage networks in a document distributed to the State Department in March 1942. The analysis confirmed that radio transmitter contact code named "Alfredo" in Rio de Janeiro was an identical person to Albrecht Engels. Alfredo's position within the Brazilian network was clarified, the electronics expert was a senior commander in a German security service espionage cell and served as organizer for other territories in Brazil, primarily Northern.[46]

An FBI informant identified without hesitation Albrecht Engels as the exact individual he had observed surreptitiously traveling to Esplanda Hotel, São Paulo and engaging in private encounters with prominent Nazi Party officials, consulate personnel and operatives. The FBI report identified 25–30 figures recognized to be participating or suspiciously consorting with individuals connected to the exposed Engels espionage ring, who were assigned 24 hour surveillance details. Hoover informed his colleagues that Antonio Pinto was a German SD VI operative feeding intelligence through Engels, Pinto exploited distinguished connections inside the Rio de Janeiro police department and obtained information from docked shipping crew members. The SIS in Brazil commanded by Jack West and later William J. Bradley conducted intensive hours of surveillance field work in combined operations with Brazilian Police. SIS teams operated by necessity in undeniably ambiguous conditions during the department's inaugural chapter of counterintelligence, but eventually the genuine identities of the code named German agents were discovered.

Kempter, Arnold and numerous figures within Brazilian network were identified. Brazilian police organized a round-up of enemy agents in Rio de Janeiro on March 18. Engels, von Heyer and a scattering of other prominent operatives were exfiltrated or slipped through police nets and managed to temporarily evade capture. A depletion of experienced personnel definitely restricted the Brazilian covert penetrations for remainder of World War II, but nevertheless underground activities continued elsewhere in Latin America despite inconvenient interruptions. U.S. State Department officials or the FBI had not authorized or collaborated directly in Brazilian police raids, and both complained bitterly about the premature timing of the police intervention and escapees. The timescale later divulged some premeditated involvement of the U.S. government, Brazilian police received advice and operational support from U.S. Embassy officials outside of SIS, who had promised to consult police and federal security services and forward the decrypted messages as evidence. A U.S. Naval Attaché in Rio de Janeiro requested reproductions of all intercepted and decrypted messages handing them to Brazilian colleagues.[47]

On April 2, 1942, a conference was organized at the State Department, chaired by Assistant Secretary of State, Adolf A. Berle, and attended by representatives of Military, State Department, FBI and FCC. Hoover and Berle repeated demands at April's conference concerning formally establishing a workable and secure methodology for future disclosures. Undoubtedly, distributing any intelligence to security agencies outside of American or insular Allied command chains presented significant risks. In Brazil's instance the deficiency in safeguarding protocols mitigating this unilateral action resulting in obvious inconsistencies, an unacceptable outcome. Berle stated his personal contention that State Department should be the determining authority on disseminating covert intelligence information. The committee agreed and further concurred that major offensives against espionage nets in Latin America could not be sanctioned without joint approval of the Chief of Army and Naval staff's.

At the end of November 1941 Johannes Becker had fortunately returned to Germany for a meeting with superiors and was therefore conveniently out of danger's way for the disastrous events befalling Brazil's network, as police rounded up and detained their agents on March 18. During this conference, as Schellenberg later described during interrogation by the Allied investigators postwar, a comprehensive alteration affecting organizational structure and focus was summarily agreed upon. Becker, the conference ordered, would become the recipient of a prestigious honor recognizing his efforts, a promotion to commander of combined South American operations. Buenos Aires obtained designation officially in this reformed command structure as the control station and reported directly to Berlin. Herman Lange was transferred and appointed to coordinate an espionage network in Chile and Johnny Hartmuth (GUAPO), a Department VI 02 agent who had elected on individual volition to remain in South America, was assigned to manage a network in Paraguay.

An agent named Franczok was appointed to supervise the latest radio-relay network and trafficking information. Since, Engels, Becker and most of the remaining Brazilian agents possessed compromised decrypts transmitting messages was temporarily halted until finalization of analysis into reliability. An operational security check was to be instigated for determining thoroughly if police had uncovered any cryptographic information. To circumnavigate this problem Abwehr encryption experts distributed new and upgraded mission ciphers on 12th August 1942. Clandestine Nazi covert actions throughout Brazil ceased in genuine productivity or penetration after the March round-ups, but instead Argentina, Chile and other Latin American nations emerged as the replacement epicenters of Nazi intelligence.[48]

In the aftermath of the principle affiliates being ruthlessly exposed, with formerly valuable members either languishing in Brazilian detention centers or threatened with deportation, alternative options were explored for accomplishing their objectives. In 1943, the SD advanced preparations for forming contacts with Integralists traditionally no admirers of Nazi Party or fascist elements in Brazil. Operatives in Buenos Aries orchestrated a promising sounding dialogue with two leading Integralist commanders residing in enforced exile. Direct interaction was established with Jair Tavares and Dr. Caruso. Becker, now securely based in Buenos Aires, maneuvered the proceedings a stage further and attended a meeting between future president Perón and other Argentinean government officials, who allegedly exhibited pronounced sympathetic tendencies towards a Nazi collaboration, and Integralist delegates. Negotiations progressed and both factions were prepared to consider a formal exchange, the Nazi delegation outlined a commitment to furnish the Integralists with weapons systems. Raimundo Padilha, the Integralist leader entered into discussions.

Despite the original hesitation by Getúlio Vargas there was minimal realistic option of Brazil refuting both the political and economic considerations to abandon diplomatic relations with Nazi Germany and form an alliance with the United States. The declaration of war against Nazi Germany and Japan in

May of 1942 and U-boat targeting of Brazilian shipping ensured a hazardous time for espionage networks no longer tolerated or protected. As early as January 1941 Vargas had secretly authorized the construction of U.S. Air Force base facilities. Brazil accepted the U.S.'s contentions regarding hemispheric solidarity principles and Integralist or other domestic political collusion failed to substantively materialize. In Argentina and to an extent Chile subversion attempts achieved more tangible results.[49]

Another factor had compromised German penetration of Latin America and cultivating agents of influence completely unbeknownst until postwar period. In expanding territorial coverage Berlin SD headquarters cooperated with the Abwehr in redeploying an agent posted originally in the United States temporarily to South America. A concept had gradually achieved momentum in RSHA high command to establish a more sophisticated transmitter station inside North America. The identity of this transferred operative code named "Ivan" was Dusko Popov, a Yugoslavian citizen. The agent in October 1941, as instructed, completed his expedition from the United States to Brazil and pursuant to mission objectives contacted a prearranged Nazi intelligence operative, Albrecht Gustav Engels. A journey requiring considerably delicacy transported "Ivan" to Rio de Janeiro on several occasions. Northern Brazil was being surveyed in preparation for adaptation into an enhanced focal point for trafficking information from the United States. He was introduced to the technology of the microdot. Employing this new development the Germans could reduce a full page of information requiring concealment to the approximate scale of a period.[50]

The technology Engels advised him held the potential to transform the trafficking of secretive information. Popov in reality was a British double agent, a master spy inside the Twenty Committee's Double Cross program. All information recorded found itself relayed to Allied intelligence. He was supplied by Nazi Brazilian detachments with intelligence analysis questionnaires, and an examination of these highly sensitive documents has revealed categories of data pertaining to Naval information and shipping, convoys, ship designations. One U.S. Naval base featuring extensively in questionnaires was Pearl Harbor, this latest visit occurring weeks before the Japanese attack on December 7. The questionnaire demanded specifics about naval ammunition dumps and defenses, if possible sketches were to be produced. The Abwehr advised that Engels should encourage Popov to obtain information on specific U.S. companies with expertise in fields of nuclear energy. The purpose of the mission handed to Alfredo implicated personnel in ventures to penetrate the top secret U.S. nuclear weapon research program, the Manhattan Project.

Chile

Contemporary FBI reports depicted the German diplomatic company in Chile as the principle intelligence gathering outlet in the Western territory of South America for Nazi foreign intelligence services. The German Embassy in Santiago served as mission control for everything from propaganda and media manipulation efforts to covert espionage. An indication of German intelligence's infiltration of the Santiago Embassy is the plethora of diplomatic and consular staff in Chile, disproportionate to actual demographic statistics. SD VI established several remarkably active spy rings, the operators on the ground determined that southern province in Chile should be classified as strongholds because of ideological proclivities present in a more fascist oriented population. The historically close economic connections between Germany and Chile motivated the latter to practice neutrality until 1943, despite internal disputes and pressure from the United States to cooperate with their agenda.

The Ausland Organization der NSDAP in Chile was instituted before Nazi assumption of power in 1930, membership lists registered five affiliated individuals. By the period of Adolf Hitler becoming Chancellor the numbers had progressively elevated up to 155. Ernst Bohle's appointment as director of NSDAP foreign office following Nazi consolidation of power in 1933 and reconstruction of traditional political structures motivated some substantial adjustments. He had introduced trenchant policies to bolster the influence of the Ausland regional offices over the German populations abroad. Overseas departments were ordered to encourage sympathy for national socialism through propaganda and administer greater exertion of hegemony over the resident German organizations and businesses operating in-country. In Chile, despite offended protests circulating and resignations of membership by 1935 the German associations and groups were adamantly under the Nazi Party and Foreign Office control. Many organizations for example Deutsch Chilenischer Bund (DCB), a leading German trade union, started avidly promoting national socialism in all its publications.

Ernst Bohle garnered substantial political protection from his mentor Nazi Party Deputy, Rudolf Hess, a factor undoubtedly influencing the accomplishments of his career. He was born in Bradford, England, paradoxically the homeland of his future adversary. Occupation in international diplomacy was a traditional family convention, Bohle gained his first experiences of Ausland as a NSDAP activist and then Chief in South Africa. Local Nazi groups between 1936–1939 across South and Central America with Bohle's stewardship orchestrated regular festivals and demonstrations.[51] Segments of the NSDAP in Latin America defended their obligation publicly to extol the virtues of German culture and promote national socialist rhetoric on biological nationalism. Disseminating this overtly international sounding ideology attested misguided as relations with resident populations and governments were crucial in guaranteeing an influential presence in Latin America. Powerful enemies within the Brazilian and Venezuelan interior were imprudently generated because of public vitriolic attacks on politicians and community leaders.

In Chile, after a program of centralization spearheaded by Ernst Bohle, the Ausland branch moderated its official tone and avoided controversial statements, a departure from Brazil. A general policy developed of engineering positive alliances with the existing Chilean political structures and associations, rather than promoting either antagonistic or hegemonic rhetoric. The Nazi Party received a comparatively improved persona and flourished in Chile, friction however undoubtedly developed between Bohle and local spy chiefs early into the introduction of Abwehr operatives to Chile. In 1938, the Movimiento Nacional Socialista de Chile had orchestrated an attempted political revolution. The fascist organization adhered to tenants of extreme-right politics and racism. While not connected with the NSDAP or any other German organization, ideologically a prescient synergy clearly existed. The intellectual inspirations of the domestic fascism derived self-proclaimed from Chilean nationalistic writers and philosophers, comparable to the Brazilian Integralists they championed Chile's authentic insular brand of extreme-right politics. While decidedly unsuccessful in accomplishing objectives, the prospective revolution culminating disastrously with a violent massacre killing 60 members of the group, the Movimiento Nacional Socialista indicated a malleable cultural landscape and potentially a conducive environment from the Ausland's perspective.[52]

Right-wing and nationalistic politics remained unmistakably popular in Chile and NSDAP local officials optimistically declared that significant pro–German fascist sentiment was cultivatable. In 1942, the political landscape experience considerable alteration as a previous more sympathetic governing administration was elected out of presidential office and no longer controlled the Chilean legislature. Radical Party's Juan Antonio Ríos defeated the incumbent Conservative leader, Carlos Ibáñez. During the election campaign Carlos Ibáñez had stockpiled generous financial donations and enticements from the Japanese government and German military intelligence, on January 2, 1942, an Abwehr operative in Santiago solicited authorization from his handlers to dispense $150,000 to the Carlos Ibáñez re-election campaign. But the Abwehr's machination efforts transpired to be futile, as Juan Antonio Ríos assembled a new government. Despite Nazi provocation and diplomatic blunders offering justification for rupturing of cordial relations Juan Antonio Ríos publicly asserted his policy on persevering with the outgoing administration's neutrality agreements. Indeed, with Japanese and German powerful Naval capabilities and comprehensive national security risks to Chile's coastline, opinion was divided within the government about which contending alliance to back. Nationalist factions, including Foreign Minister Barros, furiously insisted on a refusal to capitulate to American pressure and championed both Chile's national interest and the right to neutrality.[53]

In Chile, Heinrich Reiners, unofficially commanded the Nazi intelligence network. Reiners was a German-born businessman residing in Valparaíso. From all accounts a familiar figure in local commercial sectors and conveniently for Operation Bolivar coordinators the manager of a profitable shipping concern. For several years Reiners had attended meetings and demonstrations of the Chilean Nazi Party, developing the personal reputation of a devoted and committed adherent of the movement. Closely connected Nazi espionage groups in Argentina, the spy network organization was bolstered by attachment of Air Attaché Ludwig von Bohlen. The Embassy official in Santiago, code named "Bach," was sufficiently cunning to conscript willing accomplice informants in this conspiracy, an assortment of individuals and companies from the German population in Southern Chile. Operations in 1940–42 were reconvened in SD's command structure under the jurisdiction of Johannes Becker. In mid-1940, Becker was an aspiring activist in Argentina and he solidified the Chilean nets as a oriented of the Buenos Aries detail. Similarly to operatives in neighboring territories primary hunting ground in recruiting informants were dockyard and harbor areas.[54]

The principal source transmitting data from Chile back to headquarters in Germany was a clandestine radio transmitter located at Quilpué, Valparaíso. The wider communications network was connected to Albrecht Engels in Brazil and registered contacts across Western coast South America. In Chile, radio transmitters were recognized by the ground-level operatives from the beginning to be supremely practical and irreplaceable trafficking systems because of the geographical barriers and restrictions on international mailing. Technical engineers were smuggled internally to coordinate radio transmissions and unexpectedly for undercover foreign government spies tuition lessons purchased. The Valparaíso station was directed by Albert von Appen, a Nazi Party member dating back to 1933. According to Chilean Police surveillance von Appen was witnessed recurrently accompanied at the installation by another principle spy network collaborator in Ludwig von Bohlen. Once the Valparaíso station had been established in April 1941 simultaneously with Brazilian counterpart the trafficking streams of information exported from Chile were accelerated. The Chilean organization managed to function productively in somewhat relative obscurity for 15 months because it was disguised within a private business, the

Compania Transportes Maritimos, itself a sub-branch of Norddeutscher Lloyd which was later unmasked as a front company for German intelligence.[55]

In 1940, Friedrich von Schulz Hausman a trusted manager employed at Norddeutscher Lloyd Shipping Agency opened the company enterprises to his beloved Fatherland's agent provocateurs and spies. Other RSHA and Abwehr staff personnel intrinsically associated with the private concern of Norddeutscher Lloyd were Hans Blume, the Valparaíso radio technician, and spy ring commander himself Heinrich Reiner records authenticate was indeed previously a salaried employee in Central America. Reiners's sister to complicate further the network's interconnected relationships a habitual resident of Valparaíso was married to Hans Blume. Family connections reappeared as a standard and unavoidable motif within the Chilean espionage network, Reiners's wife volunteered for performing a crucial individual function in drops, couriering secretive information within the secret network and exporting the documents overseas. Hamburg Ast and Johannes Becker's original intention was for the espionage nets once operational to assume burden of identifying prospective converts and intercept strategically informative data semi-independently. In practice, because of workload volumes and a challenging communications environment the German-Chilean Embassy and Ausland organizations were already fulfilling this requirement.

The Chilean group particularly concentrated on reporting the movements of United States maritime vessels on the West Coast and collected intelligence data on anti-submarine equipment and armaments of both merchant and naval vessels. Late in 1943 a report was distributed back to Germany from Chile, via Argentina, containing details of United States naval gunnery practice and intel on torpedoes. This information was obtained from Chileans who had visited U.S. and from observations of gunnery exercises held aboard a United States cruiser off Callao in the summer of 1943 for the benefit of the President of Peru and a large party of Peruvian officials. In December 1943, a German agent in Chile discovered from a Chilean Air Force officer who had expended 9 months training at the Naval Air Station, Corpus Christi, technical details of U.S. aircraft construction and performance stats reports on naval flight instruction and training accidents. Reiners managed to intrusively uncover information in both Chile and Ecuador utilizing political contacts. One valuable internal document produced for the Ecuadorian President revealed details of $17 million lend lease agreements with the Ecuadorian government and United States, provision of military hardware was also mentioned which included consignments of rifles and machine guns.[56]

In immediate aftermath of Pearl Harbor and mutual declarations of war Japanese espionage agencies diverted resources into cultivating military and political contacts inside South and Central America. Haruo Tesima, Japanese Military Attaché, organized weekly conferences with von Bohlen. According to U.S. led Inter-American Emergency Advisory Committee he attempted to bribe Chilean government officials to obtain secretive intelligence on the Panama Canal. Hamburg Ast Station had submitted strategic proposals that circulated in German-Latin intelligence community for converting Chile into a permanent base of operations to monitor regional air force movements, and transporting resources to the Caribbean stretching from Barbados to Dutch Antilles. This development was in response to notable progress of the Reiners-von Bohlen espionage network.

Handlers energetically labored under consummate direction of Military Attaché von Bohlen, he described in postwar statement motivating allegiances of informants, postulating that maintaining commitment for at least several months to a year was crucial to SD VI's ambitions in Latin America. Ambiguity inevitably persisted concerning some cultivated relationships as the reported intelligence transpired to be worthless or sources turned cold. Becker repeatedly cautioned von Bohlen and his spy ring colleagues on avoiding any public revelation of their insidious connection to the Nazi German government. A relatively tolerant environment could transform overnight if scandals were exposed. Network members were ordered to stringently observe at all times operational security protocols and maintain cover identities, productivity was considered secondary in importance to safeguarding covert presence.[57] The Latin American underground communications system was firmly established by August 1942, reports were being transmitted from the operations teams embedded within Chile, Peru, Colombia, Ecuador, Guatemala and Mexico. Becker decided on dilating operations by deploying one Herman Lange to Santiago. On January 15, he organized an assembly in Río Cuarto for the purposes of exchanging concepts on present conditions of underground movements and transportation routes with Lange. He bestowed comprehensive instructions at January's Río Cuarto conference about the penetration actions the redeployed SD operative should expect to command in Chile, promising to forward sufficient financial reserves through another agent. Lange responded by stating his intention was to smuggle himself in disguise over the land border utilizing counterfeit Paraguayan documents, which he had prudently purchased during a stay-over in Asuncion. When Lange finally ventured to Chile he encountered an organization and radio station already in operation, and Lange fused himself into proceedings as a quasi- independent operator with his own sources.

The Inter-American Emergency Advisory Committee was founded by U.S. State Department in March 1942, comprising government and foreign office representatives from the South and North American nations. Parameters as an intergovernmental agency related to preparing for defense of the hemisphere by developing and recommending the measures required for its execution. The IAEAC agency published a memorandum revealing key details on the Nazi covert operations in Chile in July 1942, the file contained intercepted messages transmitted between Chile and Germany captured by the FCC. A German agent's Chilean wife acquired pages of an American aircraft design from the 1941 Aircraft Yearbook with maps of American air routes and bases. A Santiago based theology student trafficked data originating from a pronational socialist priest residing in Ecuador. The memorandum listed 72 cases of documented espionage. Ludwig von Bohlen was branded a senior controller in the clandestine network, personally supervising the transmission of secret radio messages on shipping movements, U.S. military aid to Latin American, hemispheric defense and political information.

A private residence of Seidlitz in Calle Ugartesche was established as the mission safe house for hosting concealed rendezvous and securely transferring correspondence. Later, communication points shifted to commercial locations purchased for Latin American operations, the Cangallo office and Oro residence. Despite explicit instructions not to contact the German Embassy in Santiago, upon discovering that von Bohlen lamentably was deprived of methods for communication with Argentina, Lange resolved on personal initiative to contact von Bohlen and proffer his services in forestalling difficulties. Security measures demanded strict boundary demarcations clearly separating the different espionage networks, enemy surveillance could otherwise disastrously unmask a significant proportion of Latin American operatives. Lange suggested installing a second radio transmitter in Argentina to improve the cumbersome information trafficking systems and awkwardness of cooperating with the German Embassy. He dispatched an agent, Gertrudis de Schlosser, to a Buenos Aires private school specializing in radio telegraphy. Where a member of the technical organization trained him for the purposes of receiving and transmitting radio signals.[58] The strategic importance of Chile and its Western coastline to both Nazi Germany and Allied nations could not be underestimated, disruption of Pacific transportation or transatlantic and Western hemisphere transportation via penetration of the Chilean government was a distinct possibility. Geographical proximity to important oceanic passage routes, in the Panama Canal and Cape Horn, aggravated implications of espionage for attainment of a naval advantage. An abundance of natural resources equally intrigued the central protagonists.

Friedrich von Hausman was appointed chief of the Chilean operations in late 1942 replacing Reiners. Sources from the Chilean government however were beginning to diminish in the ensuing environment of Rio Conference and

IAEAC, the Lange controlled espionage network disintegrated shortly after this time. Lange, Schlosser's partner and other agents abandoned Chile in the middle of October 1943, claiming that Chilean authority action was becoming too intense and risks of exposure were insurmountable. Becker unconvinced about the legitimacy of Lange's behavior and his sudden and insufficiently justified departure from Santiago resolved to avoid his company completely. Becker supplied 10,000 pesos to Lange and explained it was in his undoubted interest to extradite himself from Buenos Aires and not return again.[59]

A secondary strategy of Nazi penetration machinations inside Latin America progressed to investment in encouraging subversion against pro–Allied governments. By destabilizing and fostering dissent in opposition and dissident groups the governments classified as "unfriendly" towards Nazi Germany could notionally be removed and the policies reversed policies forming an Axis bloc. Nazi representatives in Chile constantly investigated opportunities for disrupting solidarity with the United States and its "Good Neighbors" strategy. Relationships with the resident government officials were reaffirmed as foundational prerequisites for achieving execution of these objectives. Collaboration with pro–Nazi organizations domestically was pressed forwards, intelligence assets were appointed special powers to negotiate in April 1942.

SD headquarters expressed its confidence interpreting the prospects of revolution removing President Ríos and installing an alternative pro–Nazi government. Chilean agents were as instructed to incite widespread agitation among Chileans, pro–Nazi nationalists and military sympathizers. Juan Perón a prominent Nazi Party sympathizer in Argentina was a fundamental instigator in pressurizing political dissidents in Chile to express opposition towards the Ríos government. A U.S. intelligence report divulged that Juan Perón had donated $1 million for financially subsidizing pro–Nazi Chilean revolutionary movements by end of 1944. This integrated plan encompassed Chile, Brazil, Argentina, Paraguay, Bolivia and Uruguay.[60] The existence of Chilean agents originally became conclusively demonstrated through Allied censorship, largely because police forces in conjunction with the U.S. investigators discovered compromised cover addresses. FBI and SIS analysis of intercepts required a meticulous and painstaking research and the comparisons of thousands of handwriting samples to identify them and their confederates.

In Chile the SIS, headed by legate Robert W. Wall since August 1941 and Dwight J. Dalbey operating undercover, patiently investigated the discovery of a suspect unlicensed radio transmitter. After prolonged examination the signal was traced to an unremarkable farm outside Valparaíso. By the time Chile severed diplomatic relations with Nazi Germany and Axis nations without exception in 1943 the radio transmissions had been silenced. As with the other operations inside South America transferring secret information back to their German headquarters using radio technology resulted in barriers. The singular columnar transposition was the standard method for encryption employed in Latin America. This identical system was adopted by the Mexican network and segments of Brazilian conspirators.[61] In fact this cipher method had been extensively practiced during World War I and persisted in dominating German secret communications despite being long uncovered by British and U.S. cryptographers. After the intelligence division of Federal Communications Commission (FCC) began intercepting encrypted messages in 1941, the Treasury Department and later a FBI Technical Laboratory deciphered the German codes without difficulty. Other Nazi networks employed alternate ciphers but the success ratio only marginally improved. The FCC radio technicians and SIS staff had complained about technical limitations in tracking radio signals within a mountainous nation and insufficient cooperation from Chile's government, but persistence paid dividends. The Allies correctly extrapolated from analysis of intercepted clandestine traffic the insular planning specifics for a 20th December 1943 revolution in Chile which was subsequently prevented. Chilean authorities raided the implicated properties and estates on three separate occasions, but the Nazi operatives managed to narrowly escape the police dragnet each time. For several months the Nazi spying proved ominously elusive and for three months total radio silence was observed. In February 1942, the placement of the radio transmitter was confirmed once again, the Navy intercepted cipher transmissions from Chile to Hamburg.

On this occasion the Chilean authorities and police made no mistakes, launching a surprise raid targeting a residential property owned by Hans Hofbauer situated outside Valparasío and arresting the majority of the spy ring associates. As a result of information collected by the American counterintelligence agencies, and conferred to Chilean government by the State Department, other prominent operatives of the Chilean ring were detained from September to November of 1942. The Chilean cell network's core members were at this juncture either arrested by authorities or scattered and forcibly living in hiding. Air Attaché von Bohlen, protected by diplomatic immunity was arrested in 1943 and then repatriated back to Germany ending his involvement.[62]

The local Santiago branch of Norddeutscher Lloyd was identified as indisputably the central nucleus sustaining multifarious underground segments. Seven company employees were specifically charged with espionage. Ríos and the Chilean government had begrudgingly conceded to enforcing measures against the enemy agents, 12 individuals were summarily deported because of unregistered associations with a foreign government intelligence service.[63] U.S.

Secretary of State Cordell Hull pronounced his satisfaction and gratitude on the Chilean government's actions. After this expulsion, a residual presence was dutifully preserved by surviving remnants, but any formidable capabilities were long since extinguished. In September 1943, finance and apparatus arrived for constructing renewed networks under the auspices of Bernardo Timmerman, who managed Chilean information gathering until his arrest in February 1944. With Timmerman's confinement the espionage rings in Chile were finally inoperable and clandestine missions ceased completely.[64]

U.S. security operations were constantly undermined by a political environment conducive to protecting the Nazi operatives. The Chilean authorities and police departments until mid–1942 posed only minimal interference to Ausland or other Third Reich business. FCC and SIS personnel reported on the necessity of security countermeasures to prevent domestic police surveillance of their own investigations. The Chilean authorities were determined to be unprepared for coping structurally with espionage and sabotage reality. Prosecutions of spy ring organizations transpired to be problematic, the only existing statute under which subversive activities could be lawfully prosecuted was the Electrical Services Law, preventing the clandestine installation of a radio transmitter.[65] In February 1943, the Chilean President announced a severing of diplomatic relations pertaining to Germany and Japan. The momentum turned fundamentally against German intelligence and suspect political groups were now subjected to greater interference. U.S. administration officials had continued with efforts to pressurize the Chilean government and announced a series of inducements, agreeing to supply military hardware and industrial support in exchange for reversing neutrality accords. Argentina at this time remained the singular South American country to maintain diplomatic relations with the Nazis.

Argentina

Argentinean administrations ignored U.S. and Allied recommendations and any declarations to desist all financial interaction with Nazi Germany up until January 1944. The extreme right factions had advocated continuing in transparent defiance of United States pressure for alignment with the Allied Nation's cause. Governments from 1942 to January 1944 stuck resiliently to non-intervention and factions led by Juan Perón perceived considerable advantages in inducing Chile, Paraguay and Peru to form a pro–Nazi block. U.S. authorities expressed circumspect attitudes about the activities of Argentinean based subsidiaries of Germany's foremost multinationals including IG Farben,

Staudt and Co. and Siemens Schucket. These private institutions were accused of maintaining active connections to intelligence communities within Germany throughout wartime era and supported major espionage operations in Latin America. Nazi Germany's financial operations in Argentina centered around two massive banking institutions the Banco Alemán Transatlántico and Banco Germánico de la América del Sud. For black market transactions holding companies were first structured in 1939 by Johann Wehrli & Company of Zürich, Switzerland.[66]

The representative front or "dummy" companies maintained secret numbered accounts owned by senior ranking Nazi officials. Comprehensive salvaged U.S. Embassy of Buenos Aires documents authenticate that prominent German financial and insurance firms reserved offices in Buenos Aires and a plethora of industries operated in Argentina with commercial partnerships in metallurgy, arms and munitions. Allied wartime blockades rendered conditions impossible for substantial transportation of exports from Argentina to Germany, testing conditions indeed. From 1936 to 1939 the expanding volumes of investment and industrial development guaranteed that Germany emerged as a principal and lucrative commercial trading partner, preserving economic partnership was an exigent strategy. Buenos Aires by 1942 was the most prolific Latin American port implicated in smuggling valuable goods and commodities such as platinum, palladium, drugs and other chemicals. While Argentina undoubtedly prospered immensely from the economic and financial dealings with Nazi Germany, the industrial production and foreign export markets equally certified essential connections to the Allied Nations.[67] Economic sanctions and diplomatic pressures culminated in the Argentine Government in October 1944 establishing an administrative council to control Axis firms. In November, Third Reich connected banks and financial companies were subjected to obstructive supervision. In reality the controls were implemented rather superficially and minimal damage was inflicted arguably up until early 1945.[68]

Subdivisions of Third Reich ministries were inaugurated and endowed in South America and Argentina in the 1930s which included Ernst Bohle's NSDAP Foreign Office (A.O.) branches, Robert Ley's German Labor Front and Hitler Youth squadrons. Quasi-government bureaus were represented in the Office of German Railroads, Office of Trade Promotion and German Artisans Cooperative, all influential organizations. Johannes Becker had first emigrated to Latin America under the auspices of the membership of a German-Argentinean committee. In the German-Argentinean community 60,000 individuals belonged to the Argentinean Ausland movement, originally instituted in Buenos Aires by influential German business community members. By 1939, this division controlled shipping lines, a special news service and other entities in Argentina. The German business community outside of Nazi sphere of influence in general held economic influence in Argentina and intrinsically were associated with a considerable degree of the nation's industrial, chemical, pharmaceutical and electrical goods production, and significant players existed in military and civilian construction.[69]

The tumultuous conditions during the previous decade produced in Argentina a landscape not conducive to the political or social progress demanded by pro-democracy factions. In September 1930 a revolution commanded by General Jose Felix Uriburu restored conservative oligarch structures to power. Classified a parliamentary democracy in artifice only, the traditional democratic structures and political chambers technically still existed but were diminished in actual authority. The government demonstrated increased proclivities towards the suppression of internal dissenting influences and any opposing political movements. Economic reforms dominated 1930s interior policy, President Uriburu and successors advocated stimulating accelerated industrialization. Agricultural exports trading had traditionally sustained modest economic performance and represented the nation's primary employer. In the early Twentieth Century a triangular system of international trade emerged with Argentina's most prolific trading partners, the United States was by volume the foremost exporter of products to Argentina and secondarily Britain.[70] In national socialist ideology the unyielding living space of Argentina promised lucrative material rewards for Germany's endeavor and vision. With a continuing tutelage and an infusion of more European settlers this undeveloped nation could be re-engineered to achieve its full promise. A 1936 Ausland Argentina report on the domestic culture endorsed highly the recommendations of converting the territory into a technologically advanced mixed industrial and agricultural economy. Unlike tropical regions of Latin America, in the national socialist interpretation, Argentina had in geographical and cultural isolation been spared the debilitating effects of integration with other ethnic groups. Bohle advised Ausland Buenos Aires members to promote the Nazi Party's ideological sentiment within right-wing movements and quasi-fascist political organizations.[71]

The Beginnings of a Nazi Espionage Program

German commercial enterprises first obligingly opened the necessary pathways for the Nazi Party, their representatives and agents descending into Buenos Aires and other metropolitan centers. A major German shipping company with business concerns in Argentina was exploited as a semi-covert conduit for its managing executive, Thilo Marten, to engineer the transferring of any sensitive subject matter to his German Naval contacts. A secret mission entrusted to Thilo Marten required research and groundwork in preparing the logistics and maritime bases on South America's Atlantic coastline for provisioning and resupplying German Naval vessels. This underlying expectation was for sustaining a concerted German military presence in Western Atlantic and Caribbean. Karl Arnold on the surface was a respectable industrial sector employee at Norddeutscher Lloyd in reality he supplemented his personal income as a Gestapo asset, performing assorted intelligence and informant functions for the Fatherland in Argentina and in the Brazilian network. Arnold was assiduously connected to influential figures inside the Third Reich's government departments. German businesses and subsidiaries outside of Norddeutscher Lloyd gathered intelligence and approved cover subterfuge for transfers of finance and agents moving between Europe and America.

In May 1939, Joachim Rudloff, a known senior Abwehr operative, traveled to Buenos Aries and participated in a secretive meeting with the Naval Attaché Dietrich Niebuhr. Rudloff arrived with instructions from Colonel Lahousen, commander of Abwehr II, to pioneer the construction of a secret espionage unit separate from other intelligence groups. Lahousen assumed that while Latin American governments may profess neutrality and indifference to German intelligence operations, pressure from the United States in the escalating conflict represented the potential for altering this perspective. For implementing contingency measures to control this identified risk Lahousen, with Admiral Canaris in agreement, announced intention for forming a select group of saboteurs, completely unknown to other Abwehr networks and secure from any enemy penetration. Rudloff, garnished with a comprehensive catalog of Argentinean located candidates, selected Karl Otto Grohl a German engineer employed by the Brazilian government and Albert von Appen, then a shipping inspector residing in Valparaíso. The latter re-appearing in Santiago and the Reiners operation.[72]

Grohl and Appen briefly attended training at Charlottenburg espionage school in Berlin. The identical training school housed Spanish pro–Franco fascists in preparation for disembarking to Latin America later in World War II. Georg Blass was appointed commander of sabotage in South America, he organized a meeting of the assigned covert operative teams in Rio de Janeiro, Brazil and explained the destructive missions against the enemy shipping would begin shortly. The execute message from Berlin was however never received, Abwehr high command remained unconvinced with the missions success. The Naval Attaché Niebuhr advised the Abwehr commanders and Lahousen cautiously that a militaristic or terrorist actions against Allied targets in this manner could prompt an uncomfortable adverse reaction from local governments. He predicted that the mission's aftermath may produce an environment nursing an unrecoverable reduction in colluding intelligence sources. Historical records demonstrate that sabotage acts were attempted, Grohl orchestrated a mission for planting a delayed action explosive device aboard two British freighters which were unsuccessful. Blass and Grohl later conceived of a scheme to attack a hydroelectric plant in Cubatão, Brazil. The operation advanced to the actual delivery phase with explosives prepped for installation at a suitably vulnerable location, but Grohl abandoned the mission at the last moment.[73]

Johannes Becker had enlisted in Himmler's SS back in 1933, the Fatherland was channeling resources into its first massive propaganda campaign to encourage young loyal Germans to serve the Third Reich. By 1937, Becker had accomplished promotion to 2nd Lieutenant and was acknowledged by superiors to be a promising rising star in the organization. He advanced to Sicherheitsdienst Chief with the rank of Hauptsturmführer in the SS in 1942. A converging of multiple commitments during 1939–1940 called on Becker to chart regular passage to Argentina, his professional career fluctuating between numerous business and diplomatic postings. The comprehensive South American background later resulted in being head hunted and selected for the task of reorganizing and commanding counterespionage services in Argentina. The mission was conferred on him by RSHA agent Major Rossner, in April 1940, who convinced him that his services in South America would demonstrate superior utility than entering active Wehrmacht duty.[74]

Becker in the Security Service jurisdictional structure was destined to initially operate under the immediate supervision of Rossner, his handler Becker later discovered was the chief of American division Amt VI of RSHA. In May 1940, Schellenberg decided that Becker would inherit command operations and replace Lange in Argentina, the previous senior agent. He was instructed to supervise an expansion of the organizations set up by Lange according to his judgment and in conformity with possibility for communications. The first priority as announced by Rossner prior to departure was the procurement of collaborators. Under American pressure a blacklist of German private companies had been reluctantly agreed by the traditionally noncommittal Argentinean government. Discovering the consequences for the German commercial interests was another instruction relayed to Becker. Before leaving, Major Rossner handed over $20,000 in bills of different denominations, all were under $500. Rossner promised that once in Argentina he should await the allocation of more finance, Becker was informed that a further authorized 284,000 pesos had been designated to Argentinean operations and would be available through contacting the Ministry of Foreign Affairs. Generally mission subsistence funding was earmarked for covering the expenditure associated with technical apparatus, purchasing informants and espionage expenses. Once operational in Buenos Aires he was instructed to construct mailing services adequate to efficiently transmitting and receiving communication between Europe and Latin America, taking advantage of any neutral ships and existent airline routes via Spain, Italy, Japan, China and Manchuria was recommended.[75] Further imparted instructions elucidated on some operational security measures, avoiding contact with any local diplomatic representatives and in no circumstances should he disclose to the legation the missions conferred on him. Becker returned to Argentina in 1943 as the South America espionage network commander.

During 1941–1942 a more dominant position was assumed by Capt. Dietrich Niebuhr and his two assistants Hans Napp and Ottomar Mueller. The former individual would later enlist the services of spy ring personnel escaping from Brazil post intervention of police crackdowns. His assistant Napp controlled an eclectic congregation of informants within Buenos Aries and the surrounding area who covered multiple social strata, occupations and personal experiences. The directory featured a Spanish waiter, a German-Paraguayan and a veteran pro–Nazi Swiss businessman.[76] Napp transferred his headquarters to a rather expensive villa at Calle Pedro Goyena. At this point the covert exercises were discreetly hidden within a front business concocted by Hans Napp. A central thrust of the undercover movement was engrossed with maritime and shipping information gathering, FCC intercepts from April 1942 disclosed how Becker relayed directives from Nazi military command to Hans Napp for expanding the awareness and coverage of shipping movements in the Caribbean and Latin American sphere. Napp responded in May 1942 with messages containing information on Allied naval standings and surveillance reports of merchant convoys surrounding Buenos Aires. Hans Harnisch, in a previous legitimate life, was general manager of a German steel company in Argentina. His targeted infiltration of the political and military communities and establishment circles produced dividends. By February 1943, Harnisch had confirmed agreements for exchanging information with senior serving members of the government including Admiral Fincati and Captain Aumann, Naval Aide-de-Camp to President Castillo. Another key associate was Osmar Hellmuth. With Niebuhr's complicity Hans Harnisch had constructed phantom operatives and information couriers to maintain the illusion that the two sections operational at that time remained totally independent. Niebuhr's spy ring in secret collusion with other domestic connections continued this unsanctioned mutual assistance until Becker discovered it.[77]

In the majority of circumstances informants controlled on the ground at dockyards, airports and restaurants were issued subsistence via their handler and a paymaster at regional headquarters. In clandestine field operations tracking the financial outlays customarily proved inherently problematic, stemming from a security rationale of preventing exposure. This relatively uncontrolled distribution of cash payments opened the passageway for many indiscretions. Within Argentina the standard financial reimbursement ranged from different levels dependent on expertise and value. Hans Napp received £1,250 for his services, while the head of SD Johannes Becker was paid $50,000 in advance.[78] The communication infrastructure embedded in Argentina by December 1941 consisted of several semi-independent radio terminals transmitting on a multitude of different frequencies, the useful adaptation instigating a sufficiently versatile system to alternate between frequencies comfortably and rapidly, radio transmitters were concealed inside suburban areas and residences of pro-Nazi German citizens, if feasible and contingency plans permitted. SD VI and military intelligence in Venezuela and Chile had experienced police raids searching for forbidden radio transmitters and other espionage nets in Latin America had subsequently been closed down. Avoiding detection by U.S. and local government investigation remained a constant dilemma.[79] In late 1942 Dietrich Niebuhr was uncovered by the Argentinean security police and forced to return to Germany.

Schellenberg later recollected, in postwar Allied interrogation, the motivation behind SD VI department launching covert penetration operations inside the Argentinean theater. In sections of his statement not publicly available until 2005 he had commented that the senior commanders recognized necessity for strategies centered on South America in containing the United States and Allied armed forces present in the regional and military mobilization.[80] The Argentinean espionage cell network received orders from Amt VI in April 1941 that guidance was desired on the departure locations of Atlantic convoys in Latin America and attention should be directed at any shipping destined for North Africa. Amt VI station transmitted follow-up requests as the German offensive inside Africa continued into 1942. Informants recruited by the spies discovered temporarily several Atlantic transit corridors from October 1940 to February 1941, German intelligence reports document, utilized by Allied and neutral shipping.

A New Underground Regime 1943–1945

In most Latin American nations pressure from the United States succeeded in eliminating the most dangerous and productive German agents by mid–1942. This success was tempered by continued toleration of proficient German espionage elements by Argentinean and Chilean governments. In both countries Axis agents garnished their support from German colonies with strong local connections, the perseverance with diplomatic relationships until relatively late and compliance of the local officials prompted significant apprehension in United States. After the break-up of the Engels-Brazilian groups the organization in Argentina was transformed into the most important in South America. Between January 1942 and spring 1944 the German espionage networks inside Argentina implemented some insular modifications in structure, invariably in response to arrests or exposure, but a core nucleus was still maintained.

In February 1943 after considerable exertion Johannes Becker had managed on circuitously returning to Buenos Aires concealed aboard a vessel traveling from Spain to Argentina. The scattered survivors of Engels's cellular divisions had formed a temporary headquarters outside Asuncion and instigated contact with Amt IV Berlin. As Becker instructed this improvised station was transferred to Buenos Aires in May, Osmar Hartmuth was selected to remain behind and administer covert actions in Paraguay. Once the various contrivances necessary for transferring their tactical covert operations headquarters to Buenos Aires had achieved completion Becker and Franczok then established the new planned radio transmitter. Becker had adamantly wanted to re-position a transmitter in every South American republic, but this was not accomplished. As the reorganization became mandatory General Friedrich Wolf, the new Military Attaché replacing Niebuhr, was appointed to assist Johannes Becker in coordinating the ground-level operations. These two commanders had transferred to their disposal renewed financial allocations, the not unsubstantial facilities of the collaborating German Embassy, possibly still loyal segments of insular pro-fascist movements and other pro–Axis local organizations and colonialists. From these diverse elements Becker had intended on weaving a second front in Nazi-Latin American underground espionage. By July, communication channels and information sharing schemes were running in Uruguay, Paraguay, Chile and Mexico.

Three groups of accomplice network cells were divided into separate and semi-independent units. All networks reported back to Berlin through Havel Institute and human couriers orchestrated by Becker.[81] By August 1943, the new Argentinean front comprised agents primarily controlled in three different command structure segments. Friedrich Wolf, the Military Attaché, was code named Blue, which trafficked diplomatic and military data to Ast Hamburg. He was also Johannes Becker's primary information source in the vicinity of Buenos Aries. Intelligence analysis reports relating to the common tactical pictures were further disseminated to Counter Intelligence 1, the Navy and OKW's Attaché Division. Becker himself commanded the Red contingent responsible for political intelligence and governmental sources, under jurisdiction of SD headquarters in Berlin. His individual squadron included a pharmaceutical expert working for the German company Bayer in Argentina and Seidlitz. Hans Harnisch's group code named Green reported on economic intelligence to the Ast substation in Cologne. He commanded a more diminutive team compliment, a departure from his other colleagues. Psychological impressions of intelligence missions altered drastically during the second generation, remote from Nazi Germany and often subject to an erratic direction, the indigenous espionage systems become nearly autonomous.[82]

German Intelligence in Argentina and U.S. Awareness

U.S. State Department sources reported to Roosevelt in May 1942 that the acting President Castillo had apprised prominent Third Reich government officials using authorized channels that he expectantly supported an Axis victory against Allied forces. Argentina requested from Nazi Germany the military and practical support for preserving Argentina's isolation policy. Nazi intelligence staff in Argentina an obtained assurance that the authorities would refrain from materially interfering in their operations.

A declassified Operation Bluebook report from 2005, originally produced in 1945, identified Becker and Harnisch as attending meetings with senior Argentinean military official, Major Bernard, and presidential aides from December 1941 to August 1942. Their confidential assessments forwarded to Schellenberg indicated that Castillo's government was still actively contemplating the outbreak of conflict if Argentina did not comply with commitments as enshrined in the Rio de Janeiro conference. Major Bernard had again promoted a military accord in his conversation with Harnisch and Becker, claiming concerted armed hostilities against Brazil and the other South American nations would be definitely unobtainable without the assistance from Germany and the Axis forces. The Argentinean officer appealed for German naval and submarine protection for their coastline and the distribution of other defensive weapon systems and anti-aircraft guns. In April, the Castillo administration negotiated with Third Reich delegates on formalizing a trade agreement on munitions shipments. The navigation of manifold political alliances proceeded without encountering impediments during months of July to September 1942, the exchanged content matter disclosed requests for submarines, airplanes, anti-tank guns and other armaments.[83]

In July 1942, General Martinez, the Buenos Aires Police chief and temporarily a government minister, arranged a secret conference as special representative of President Castillo with the German Chargé d'affaires, Erich Otto Meynen. Discussions emerged that were promising for both delegations, movement was prospectively secured on Nazi Germany's willingness to distribute munitions. Meynen was granted verbal guarantees that Castillo intended an active and unequivocal resistance to pressure from America, he assured the German government representative that President Castillo would under no conceivable circumstances assent to an alliance with the U.S. Government. Meynen had previously received edifying correspondence from the Argentinean Foreign Minister which had convinced him that President Castillo would soon openly declare allegiance to the Tripartite powers.[84] The Castillo administration was unexpectedly replaced by a government headed by Pedro Ramírez in the aftermath of a successful revolution in June 1943. He immediately declared a resumption in negotiations and a renewed emphasis on positive relations, Ramírez insisted that munitions contracts remain a foremost objective.

The activities of Niebuhr and his assistants were exposed in a memorandum handed to the Argentine Government by U.S. Ambassador Secretary of State, Cordell Hull, late in November 1942. The document declared their awareness of two senior government figures Paz Estenssoro and Foanini with deep involvement in Nazi intelligence. Declassified SIS documents released in 2004 explained that Hull revealed his Government's contention that the recently occurring transference of governance and selection of the new President were both influenced by pro-fascist factions. The State Department turned up the pressure incrementally as Hull elaborated on the accusations, professing awareness of the Argentinean administration's collusion with the Nazis. Investigations unmasked Paz Estenssoro as a validated German secret service operative. Gualberto Villarroel the Bolivian President implicated in a conjoined pro–Nazi relationship responded by summarily removing two cabinet ministers, Augusto Céspedes and Carlos Montenegro, in the expectation of achieving an improved environment.[85]

The Special Intelligence Service (SIS) counterintelligence program, administered by J. Edgar Hoover and the FBI, were by now stimulating increasing detentions in Brazil and Mexico. However, in Argentina the FBI's cryptanalysis team and the FCC experts transpired to be decisive agencies in tracking enemy positions. Locating and neutralizing the concealed German secret service controlled radio communications systems and activities in Argentina became a preferential objective outlined by Adolf Berle in March of 1942, following the initial discoveries of clandestine and unlicensed signals corresponding to Nazi activity.

FCC case reports corroborate that originally message detection and decryption commenced targeting Argentina in February 1942, a network of secret and unlicensed radio stations in Argentina were immediately discovered. Examining the inaugural consignment of radio intercepts received from February to May 1942 propelled American authorities into an awareness for the first time about the prominent intelligence role of Johannes Becker. Codebreaking systems advanced discernibly after the Army and Navy signals teams had adopted improved technology, which included the Ultra and Magic programs. Improving interception demonstrated some immediate and highly productive results in the investigation of the enemy movements, this damaging exposure of Nazi assets and double agents had proposed critical implications for sustaining Nazi intelligence's underground operations. The State Department coordinated with the Argentinean authorities on raiding the suspect addresses discovered. Cooperation with the Argentinean federal police had failed previously to develop into a cogent dual enforcement partnership. In fact the State Department was understandably doubtful about efficiency of Argentinean secret service or police authorities.[86]

In Argentina's northern neighbor, Uruguay, the underground SD informant networks and infiltration taskforces were uncovered at approximately the same instance, but minimal collaboration with the U.S. had occurred in ground-level detection and surveillance. The principal communication link-ups had required the Uruguayan-Nazi operations to manage their affairs in synchronization with Argentina. Back in 1940, the NSDAP Foreign Office party in Montevideo instigated an ideological struggle against the United States by conspiring with the Uruguayan National Party (Herrerista) to discharge intensified political campaigns against pro–American leaning President Baldomir. A pretext of national sovereignty and protecting Uruguay's interests from a zealous American imperialism were the prevailing themes of this propaganda effort, the contents were scripted by the German operatives based in Montevideo.

Herrerista, ideologically extreme right, had long presented a profitable mechanism for the Nazi Party to exert its influences inside Uruguay, several newspapers published by Herrerista placed articles attacking the government's policies of cooperation. The National Party leader, Luis Alberto de Herrera, in public speeches extolled an approval of the national socialist regime, he visited German officials in Spain during European expeditions. A semi-independent SD VI supervised cell appeared in Uruguay, an unknown informant, but evidently a businessman residing near to Montevideo initiated contact with the Argentinean and Brazilian spy networks. Code named "Union," he distributing reports on maritime information and Uruguayan and U.S. Naval movements in Southern Atlantic. Recruited originally in March 1941, the secondary twelve months of this operation transpired to an especially industrious period, with over 40 intelligence reports disseminated back to Germany.[87]

In June 1941, dialogues opened between the contending governments of the United States and Uruguay regarding hemispheric solidarity and the installation of common defense systems. The police authority response towards combating the suspected foreign government agents thus far had graded as distinctly lackluster and non-committal. But political pressure and cautionary warnings of economic sanctions from the State Department and realization of threats posed by German intelligence agents domestically convinced the Uruguayan President and Cabinet on decisive action. State Department representatives communicated to the Uruguayan government during Rio Conference of January 1942 their desire for a realistic understanding of Uruguay's capability in regards to defense security measures and practical combat functions the nation's military could conceivably perform. Government officials in discussions with the Americans revealed that regular armed forces were insufficient to defend the nation's boundaries. The importance of collective security over the River Plate area and consolidating Southern Atlantic defense weighed heavily on the minds of the U.S. officials charged with negotiating at the conference.

Julius Daldorf, a NSDAP member and propagandist for the Nazis, was exposed as employed by a foreign intelligence agency in September 1940. He was protected by diplomatic immunity as a legitimately registered Embassy official and the Uruguayan Prosecution Office refused to authorize detention. Eight confederates in Daldorf's network without the ringleader's personal appearance were prosecuted on espionage and subversion charges. Documents were retrieved in searching suspected residences and property during the ensuing police investigation implicating the agents in concerted action against the Uruguayan government. The evidence had included military planning and analysis scenarios for seizing control of Uruguay and the prospects of converting territory into an agricultural basin for the Fatherland. Techniques for eliminating any threats within the population were discussed. By authorizing measures for launching prosecution proceedings against the German interests in the nation, the Uruguayan government had signaled its willingness to back the United States in defense matters.[88]

Conclusion to the Argentina Operations

Argentine naval officer, Hellmuth, unbeknownst to his military superiors or government was a German collaborator. His control, Hans Harnisch, had presented himself as personal representative of RSHA senior command and boasted of exclusive contacts in governmental and commercial circles. Harnisch in conjunction with behind the scenes internal machinations of the President Pedro Ramírez assured that Osmar Hellmuth was appointed as consul in Barcelona, Spain. The exterior perception of a standard diplomatic reshuffling was camouflage for this underlying mission of pursing negotiations with Berlin. In November, Hellmuth departed with a heading of Trinidad before intending to board a chartered vessel for the journey to Barcelona and his entrance into dialogue with the SD officials and Schellenberg. He was preparing to obediently convey his own government's stated inclinations for perpetuating a political alliance and cultivating interested linkages in suitable Latin American nations. Hellmuth was hand-picked for this ill-fated expedition by Schellenberg's intelligence commanders. According to U.S. intelligence reports produced after the culmination of World War II and declassified in 2004 Hellmuth was selected as the representative to handle negotiations on multiple broad ranging subjects encompassing munitions shipments, mutual assistance programs and combined efforts in the subversive missions targeting neighboring nations in South America.[89]

Breaking the Allied blockade of the Iberian Peninsula and Europe would be a challenging test, Schellenberg, adopting the position of Hellmuth's handler once he reconvened in Europe, was aware of numerous potential pitfalls. However, Osmar Hellmuth unfortunately for Schellenberg's ambitions failed to penetrate the Atlantic defensive grid, his chartered vessel Cabo de Homos was detained at Trinidad by British authorities. U.S. radio intercepts decryptions were sufficient to enable the mission objectives to become transparent to the British Commonwealth authorities located at Trinidad, who forcibly detained the Barcelona Consul. President Ramírez's re-interpreted foreign policy assessment remained to be observed.[90] Detection and capture of Hellmuth while traversing the Caribbean in November 1943 revealed information on a conspiracy emanating from this renegade domestic faction and Nazi intelligence agents to the other Argentinean cabinet ministers. This disclosure precipitated a disruptive rupture of diplomatic relations and President Ramírez ordered the round-up and detention of foreign agents in Argentina.

Complications existed in reaching the American continent pertaining to the Allied blockade and this was magnified after the November to December detention of Hellmuth and other operatives. The RSHA proposed in September 1943 utilizing a submarine for distributing replacement provisions and mission paraphernalia, and inquired if the organization in Argentina still maintained the capability to rendezvous with a submarine under the complex conditions necessary for just such a maneuver. An individual with maritime connections was selected, Becker arranged the renting of a mercantile ship at

$28,000. Within three months a consignment had arrived pursuant to endeavors at recovering from the depletion in finance. In June he received further reinforcements from Germany with the deployment of two additional agents. Schedules were debated for further clandestine landings and replenishment missions on Argentine coastlines including a trawler crossing the Atlantic from the French coast. The network suffered losses and arrests in August 1944, but was able to continue some activities until the very end of the war.[91]

Collusion of Argentinean Government and Nazi Germany

The State Department on October 3, 1945, initiated an assessment concerning the wartime collaboration of the Argentinean government with Axis espionage. The results of investigations were published in a memorandum entitled "Consultation among the American Republics with respect to the Argentine situation," commonly known as the Argentinean Blue Book. Substantial records associated with the Blue Book report were declassified in 2005. In disclosed cases the Argentinean government's collaboration extended to obligingly passing intelligence to the German secret service personnel on American and British military. Other subjects of cooperation culminated in an exchanging of sensitive information on the domestic picture inside neighboring states relating to political developments and unfolding crises. The Argentinean government allegedly engaged in complicity with Nazi Germany from the time of American entrance into World War II until its finality.

The driving force behind the political subversion schemes was portrayed in the Blue Book investigations as a collection of Argentinean senior military officers including Juan Perón, General Giovannoni, General Sanguinetti and Colonel Saavedra.[92] A strategy developed in this secretive faction of undermining the pro–Allied governments in Latin America and deliberately fostering an environment conducive to division and revolution. There is abundant evidence that Axis interests in Argentina were engaged in conspiracies with Colonel Juan Domingo Perón and members of military government to expand beyond just rearmament and institute a program to extend pro–Nazi hegemony over River Plate basin. Until Buenos Aires terminated diplomatic relations with Germany and Japan on January 26, 1944, the Axis penetrations into South America were channeled through the German Embassy and Consulates. The coconspirators actions in funneling of intelligence according to a 1943 assessment report propagated by the U.S. Emergency Advisory Committee for Political Defense of the Continent were responsible for estimated losses of millions of dollars worth of United States ships and supplies.[93]

After the cancellation of diplomatic accords some German enterprises in Argentina persisted in the financing of the Nazi movements as evidenced in the Blue Book investigation. The proportion of German investments in Argentina were substantial and extremely diversified in character, minimal appreciable alteration occurred initially stemming from the January 26 abandonment of diplomatic recognition. Germany's combined investments in electrical, metallurgical, chemical, construction and other lucrative commodities markets such as sugar, cattle and rural enterprises have been estimated to total 2,500 million pesos or $600 million. This estimation ignores the clandestine accumulations of Nazi fugitive capital. When it became obvious that a Nazi defeat was irreversible the "Ratlines" were enacted for secreting of German economic assets in neutral countries where control could be retained through "dummy" organizations. In this fashion, German escape capital and looted commodities from occupied countries were transferred across to secure territory in Argentina and Latin America. Nazi personnel escaping activating the Ratlines rapidly followed generally under an assumed Spanish or Argentinean identity.[94]

The Argentinean government on April 3, 1945, announced self-vindication upon confiscation or reclamation of 150 German subsidiaries pursuant to interior policies, estimating an aggregate value of $40 million. The decree purported that government inspectors were placing control mechanisms on the identified companies pending a transfer to Argentine hands. Assistant Secretary of State Clayton declared before a subcommittee of the Senate Military Affairs Committee on June 25, conflictingly, that precisely no major commercial enterprises from their assembled catalog of 108 now suspected of Nazi economic penetration had been eliminated to his knowledge. It was the coherent and unflinching contention of the Secretary of State and United States that nothing except complete liquidation of Axis interests appearing on U.S. "blacklists" was adequate. By the interlude of Clayton's testimony at the Military Affairs Committee the Argentinean government had officially engaged in conflict opposing the Axis powers for over three months. July passed with four alleged pro–Nazi corporations forcibly entering into liquidation.

Speculation on allegations of complicity surfaced from independent sources as recriminations commenced in the conflict's aftermath. Domestic newspapers reported on suspect relationships jointly accusing the police and Ministry of War of connections with the Nazi espionage. In an article entitled "Nazi Germans are Well Protected" the Socialist Weekly newspaper *La Vanguardia* had published the identities of the prominent Argentine-German commercial directors, Ludwig Freude and Fritz Mandl, who possessed an interest in the IMPA arms corporation. Ricardo Staudt was identified as lamentably associated with the Foreign Minister. Insinuations covered apparent protection from deportation and under the table preferential treatment in the securing of government contracts. These individuals were reputedly influential figures in contributing substantial financial investments to Perón's Presidential campaign.[95]

Mexico

German intelligence first deposited a covert division in Mexico in 1931, selecting a home base of Monterrey. A primitive forerunner of later infiltrations targeting Latin America it turned out. Before the Nazi revolution the Nazi German government interpreted Mexico as a convenient vantage point for determining the military capabilities of U.S. Armed Forces, an opinion perpetuated by the intelligence community throughout the Nazi administration. Later in 1940 Mexico was selected as an important operations center because it supplied petroleum to Hamburg for refining into aviation fuel. Hitler recognized controlling Germany's oil supply as fundamental to the prosperity of Nazi military ambitions. Originally, SD VI's strategy concerning the Mexican frontier had called for landing SS explosives specialists from German submarines and for the nation to be converted into a platform for sabotage specialist to enter the United States.[96]

In January 1941 the emphasis rotated towards counterintelligence as the revolving demands of warfare drastically altered the requirements. Abwehr agents embedded into Mexican docklands and harbors were ordered to survey the movements of Navy ships, industrial sector pro–Nazi informants received monthly intelligence requests on American steel, materials and commodities capacity and technological advances. Schellenberg, during postwar interrogations divulged his pronouncements to the senior agents about the necessity of discovering information on Mexican authority awareness of the economic and military aid that the United States was offering to Latin American nations.[97] The vitriolic anti-communism inherent in German national socialism and the Mexican equivalent inspired noticeable positive affirmations with sections of business community and landowners. A decade long simmering social and rural environment with a propensity for worker agitation resulted in expensive destruction to property and acquiescent government sponsored land reforms. An agrarian uprising in Ecuador, La Matanza, propelled the more draconian Ecuador authorities to respond with a violent suppression, the ensuing massacre claimed over 10,000 lives. In this volatile and antagonistic climate the Mexican government launched a nationalization program to forestall an uprising in Mexico. The anti-communist rhetoric pervading the fascist propaganda attracted adherents to an extent within the Protestant churches, who assisted in fostering a positive atmosphere towards Nazism. A significant number of Lutheran pastors had joined pro–Nazi organizations and championed a restoration of Pan-Germanism.

Axis businesses prominent in the Mexican commercial sectors and employees assessed as harboring sympathies were approached and invited to jointly collaborate with the military intelligence operatives. Evidence intimates that Germany's agents, businessmen and politicians navigated outside of any government obstruction, with financial connections proving influential. Government Secretary Miguel Alemán was uncovered as maintaining a relationship with Hilde Kruger, an operative working directly for the Nazi propaganda chief Joseph Goebbels. A plethora of individuals in the commercial enterprises and financial institutions conspired in acquiring the information. The compliant businesses encompassed Lahusen y Cía Ltda. and AM Delfino y Cía, two of the oldest German companies with installations within Latin America, and the Banco Germánico and Banco Alemán Transatlántico. Extra resources became readily obtainable thanks to the collusion from German corporations with business holdings and facilities in Mexico including Siemens and AEG. The 1946 U.S. assessment of the Nazi-Latin American collaboration, many pertinent volumes of which remained classified until recently, produced a summary detailing the companies retaining underground affiliations with Nazi figures in wartime. The Mexican nation from 1940 to 1942 developed into a discernible frontier for the competing European and American spheres of influence, with rivalries surrounding the different commercial interests.[98]

Domestic Support and Political Influence in Mexico

German business communities in the Northern territory of Monterrey, perhaps an inherited legacy from 1931's incursion, performed exigent functions as a fifth column collaborating with Nazi espionage targeting the Americas. The Nazi spy ring's commander in Monterrey was Otto Moebius, a powerful local Monterrey businessman who controlled an industrial empire, personal contacts covered convenient alliances with the foremost corporations within the nation's northern states. His prestigious family connections opened numerous doors and profoundly resonated inside industrial and financial sectors. Employing a large radio antenna inside a secluded and controllable industrial facility Otto Moebius routinely communicated with Berlin from January until May 1942. The business leader had assiduously attempted to confer his assistance to Operation Pastorius and other sabotage programs in the preliminary or conceptual stages targeting the northern locations. Moebius and associated Abwehr operatives were detained before instigating any major damage by the Mexican Federal Police under pressure from the United States. But this incarceration was short-lived and the Mexican government protested claiming insufficient reasons for criminal prosecution proceedings.

In addition to Embassy personnel the Nazis supervised sixteen movements and associations for German citizen ranging from Mexican branch of the Nazi Party to the Ibero-American Institute and German sports clubs. German Workers Front (Deutsche Arbeitsfront) collected information and statistics on the racial constitution of populations in Mexico, this organization furthermore researched the prospects of colonization and relocating large quantities of German citizens to Mexico.[99] Arthur Dietrich, press attaché, was appointed by A.O. to manage propaganda output and media manipulation, he answered directly to Ernst Bohle. He amalgamated this function with a second duty in coordinating the local NSDAP branch. A selection of national socialist themed newspapers and pamphlets were published for both interested Mexican and German audiences, one notable periodical the *Deutsche Zeitung von Mexico*, retailed impressive numbers in the German population. Before the outbreak of war Dietrich had sponsored influential current affairs oriented Mexican newspapers, the propaganda operation was first launched to improve Nazi Germany's image abroad and evolved inexorably into financing pro-neutrality movements and the concerted endeavors to stimulate internal dissent. The German legation subsidized *Timon*, a renowned right-wing newspaper published by former Education Minister Vasconcelas, this periodical consistently published pro–Nazi articles and editorials. Dietrich and others inside Ausland movements were cognizant of the potential rewards from influencing pro-neutrality and independence political groups. A.O. funded, in relatively modest amounts, sympathetic local and national politicians.[100]

Prominent segments of the Mexican popular conjecture and media debate throughout 1941 opposed intervening in European and Pacific conflicts, plunging the nation into conflict against two industrialized factions was not endorsed in all quarters. Major opposition disseminated from the right-wing Sinarquista movement, an influential Catholic cultural organization with standing connections to the Spanish Falange. Sinarquista membership in Mexico had reportedly exceeded 500,000 in 1940, which included the divisions of trained paramilitaries within the movement's subsidiary Gold Shirt branch. Opposition had circulated from other extra-parliamentary and political sources, for instance Mexico's Italian expatriate pro–Mussolini community. The seasoned Sinarquista commander Salvador Abascal acquired a public reputation of unmistakable notoriety in the United States after he pursued a project conceptualized of as a "Garden of Eden," purchasing land and establishing a colony in Baja, California. While the imaginary colony failed to be converted into a reality, U.S. State Department intervention removed that possibility, smuggling operations were developed trafficking weapons and commodities across the border. Relations are documented between the Sinarquista and other dissident anti–Mexican government factions including Augusto Ibanez Serrano, and elements of the Nicolaus espionage network.

The Falange de la JONS Mexico had an estimated 50,000 uniformed members by 1939, reaching Mexico under Nazi supervision within weeks of the Spanish War's outbreak. This fascist party emerging victorious after alliances with General Franco's Nationalists in Spain's 1936–39 civil war embarked on a non-disclosed campaign of foreign policy investment. By the period German, Italian and Japanese legations were expelled by the Mexican Government in December 1941 the Axis had assembled in the Mexican Falange an instrument for advancing anti–American policies from this strategically valuable base. Serrano directed all Falange activities in Mexico forming a direct linkage with Nazis in Europe and the pro-fascist organizations on the American border.[101] Through special couriers Augusto Serrano remained in constant touch with Colonel Sanz Agero, the chief of Falange activities in Central America and the Spanish Embassy in Washington.

Spanish fascists under the standing jurisdiction of the Nationalist controlled Spanish Army intelligence, with some collaboration from the Gestapo, invested its resources into orchestrating their own intelligence gathering network and infiltration operations. In April 1939, the War Ministry senior command accepted Gestapo officer Faupel's recommendation was that the Spanish fascists should be trained by the Gestapo to embed clandestine cells in Spanish speaking communities in Latin America. A foothold in regions distant from the present undercover actions in German oriented districts would ensure a continuity of operations. Specialist schools for Spanish speaking agents were authorized by Himmler to begin construction in Hamburg, Bremen, Hanover and Vienna, the recruits experienced intensive training by specialist SS instructors in sabotage, enciphering, advanced map-making and microphotography. The candidates for Gestapo spy colleges were identified from the ranks of fascist dilettantes, the majority transpired to be either Falangists or had backgrounds associated with other pro–Franco movements. Graduates from the spy training schools automatically gained promotion as commissioned officers within the Spanish Army's Intelligence Service (SIM), under Gestapo control. A small number were detailed to obligations under the supervision of Gestapo officers in Spain.[102]

The remainder departed to Latin America operating under the supervision of Gestapo and SIM officers abroad. In December 1940 Faupel had issued directives authorizing Alberto Mercado Flores, the veteran Spanish Falangist, be placed in senior command of SIM operations for Mexico. Ground-level agents concentrated on two divergent categories of surreptitious activity: military and economic espionage, and suppression of the Spanish-Mexican population. The espionage arm of SIM operated in cooperation with the German and Japanese informants still actively working in Mexico. Information was acquired allegedly through the utilization of thousands of Falangist members and the Falange controlled organizations.

In January 1941 further coordination between Nazi and domestic fascist propaganda was revealed when an Allied cruiser boarded an Axis vessel in mid–Atlantic and confiscated caches of propaganda printed in Spanish. Hitler was presented in superlative language as a savior and semi-heroic figure, the propaganda material's sentiments informed readers about the Nazi commitments to restore Catholicism, and proclaimed that Franco's Spanish Civil War victory was a conspicuous example of Nazi Germany's aspirations for the Spanish speaking peoples. The discovered documents contained pictures of Adolf Hitler shaking hands and in close personalized association with Spanish Catholic priests. Conversely, rhetoric portrayed the Allied nations as being controlled by international Zionism and enemies of Mexico. Other publications had offered justification for the Nazi policies referencing parallels to traditional catholic theology.

With surmounting political opposition manifesting and a downturn in the national economic performance President Cárdenas's position in February 1940 appeared increasingly difficult. A 1938 oil nationalization program resulted in the expropriated oil companies declaring a trading embargo, Cárdenas's maneuver to counteract these precarious and insecure conditions was to initiate bartering trade arrangements with Nazi Germany and fascist Italy.[103] The center-ground and liberal political factions, newspapers and intellectuals generally endorsed Allied Nations, but Vice-President Ramón Castillo advocated neutrality. Argentinean nationalists, with some considerable weight inside Mexico, motivated the domestic Mexican extreme right factions who persisted in campaigning outspokenly for continuing neutrality. Other postulated interjections understood the prevailing international climate as an opportunity for removing imperialistic meddling with the economy. President Cárdenas continued in perseverance with his ideological stance against fusing bilateral U.S.–Mexican defense security cooperation.[104]

The Fatherland conspired to subvert presidential elections in 1942, funneling $100,000s into campaign finance for opposition candidate Juan Almazan. Documents released to Mexican national archives indicate that Berlin officials organized secretive dialogues with Almazan's representatives and expressed privately a definite willingness to formalize agreements with the presidential candidate in exchange for collaboration with presiding political and military objectives. Support in Mexico during previous eighteen months was substantially growing for Almazan, who promised resolutions to end the economic crisis and a reversal of nationalization policies. In several districts civilian unrest sporadically erupted and Cárdenas attracted rancorous opposition, an Almazan presidential succession persisted as a distinct possibility. The Roosevelt administration was fully cognizant that Nazi interests may indeed propagate resources and deploy agent provocateurs to Mexico City for exploiting this instability. As the months progressed towards the imminent election Cárdenas and his self-appointed successor Manuel Avila Camacho were disposed to finally cooperate with the United States. Cárdenas privately expressed mounting anxiety to his friends and associates regarding the prospect of Almazan outflanking his position and forming a political alliance with the Americans. Under Secretary Sumner Welles discussed the upcoming elections with Mexico's ambassador and a veritable catalog of subject matters from preferential trade agreements, Import-Export Bank aid and hemispheric defense. Sumner Welles outlined his understanding of the Camacho faction's position to Adolf Berle and the broad agreements in principle on pursuing friendlier relationship were subsequently confirmed. But Manuel Camacho was still determinedly presenting other condition terms expected by the Mexican people in return.

The SS financed candidate was ultimately defeated by Manuel Avila Camacho, but that did not entirely impede the German government's ambitions in Mexico or resolve the neutrality debate. Cárdenas, a longtime advocate of Mexican neutrality, retained his traditional stance and outspoken opposition to abrogating cordial relationships with Axis powers or declarations of war. He barracked pro–American speakers in Mexico's legislature and the former president was starting to develop into a prominent obstacle to U.S.–Mexican military relations. The Roosevelt administration's perseverance in engaging with Mexican negotiations was slowly beginning to produce worthwhile results.[105] Berle and Roosevelt in January 1942 advocated to Camacho a platform of articles on regional security and progress in negotiating solidarity pacts with Central and South American neighbors. In aggressively pursuing a strategy of hemispheric defense the U.S. committed itself to intervention with military and economic support if necessary to ensure regional defense from hostile external threats. The June 1942 landings by Japanese troops on Attu and Kiska in Alaska's Aleutian Island chain demonstrated that Japan was prepared to attack America's outer defensive perimeter.[106]

Georg Nicolaus and the Nazi Underground

Georg Nicolaus's nefarious underground presence in Mexico distended from employment in the banking industry which had comprised prominent roles at Deutsche Überseebank and the Banco Alemán Antioqueño. In 1937, he was reassigned by the second institution to Medellín, Colombia, and inhabited that nation for eighteen months before returning to Germany with a bolstered occupational pedigree in November 1938. By January 1939 he was a commissioned officer in the Wehrmacht and immediately appointed to Ast Hanover of the Abwehr. Nicolaus would eventually command all Nazi underground operations in Mexico. Under his jurisdiction Mexico served as a critical junction point for communicating with operatives located throughout the South American continent. Nicolaus was originally handled by Abwehr Group I (economic espionage), but in June 1940 the Abwehr demanded in a shortwave radio transmission a refocusing on maritime intelligence. Maria Teresa, confident of Nicolaus, provided a statement to the FBI released for public consumption from the U.S. Justice Department files in February 2007. The principle individuals in Nicolaus's operations were identified as Baron von Schleebrugge, Fritz Bieler, Werner Bare, a naturalized Mexican, and H.F. Klein. Fritz Bieler was conscripted into acting as pilot for the espionage group, Bare was a principle associate of George Nicolaus and rated as instrumental to collecting information on international ship movements and cargoes in Mexican ports. Somewhere in the region of twenty thousand Germans all over Mexico paid their monthly subsistence payments to Nazi collectors and theoretically followed the orders of their local leaders. The Abwehr managed a smoothly-running center in Mexico City headed by Georg Nicolaus.[107]

Abwehr Group I had declared, in intercepted communiqué orders in November 1940, that Nicolaus was endowed with three objectives to be accomplished in post: to ensure that Mexico is transformed into a center for organized acts of sabotage against United States; disrupting the export trade for preventing the U.S. from sending any supplies to nations militarily opposing the Axis; and establishing a center for Fascist provocation against the United States, thus distracting that country's attention from European and other theaters of war. Intercepts of microfiche and other correspondence in December 1944 had indicated some major examples of Nazi intelligence successes. Mexican based operatives uncovered information on a connection between United States security organizations and officers of the German army. This source confirmed that Abwehr Hamburg had received information about U.S. awareness of Germany's advancements in airplane technology including jet propulsion. Nicolaus obtained content implying that Remington Rand Corporation had confirmed acceptance of an order for the construction of a munitions factory in Missouri in fulfilling a government contract amounting to $15,000,000. He later relayed supplementary suspicions that this factory was designated to manufacture airplane cannons.[108]

Abwehr Hamburg submitted monthly intelligence requests from February to June 1941 in a further intimation of the evolving Nazi intelligence requirements on schedules of U.S. manufacturing, capacity information and design specifications for aircraft construction models. A virtual database of independent streams was developed to capture sensitive and sometimes unclassified content. Nicolaus discovered valuable information through open source intelligence from newspapers and magazines, technical data found in United States publications was extracted or photographed and comparable general information recovered from contacts in United States. The Nicolaus spy ring was encouraged by Abwehr I to redirect resources for disbursing capital into fostering collusion in senior government and military environments. Georg Nicolaus had presumed that elite socio-economic classes opened up pathways into Mexico otherwise inaccessible to the outsiders. The spy kingpin advocated a concerted effort on recruiting a committed band of agents voluntarily serving the Fatherland motivated by loyal adherence, he cautioned his subordinates on the apparent wisdom of refusing solicitations for bribery or cash payments if not strictly necessary. His own personal reputation suffered some maligning as he increasingly projected a paranoid attitude, Nicolaus invested where possible in advanced technology in concealed microphone and spy apparatus to prevent surveillance.[109]

Informants approached Nicolaus on occasions without provocation or prior contact, desperate for opportunities to establish important social connections and relationships with prestigious members of the German community in Mexico. Many dilettantes still persisted in holding grand illusion about the apparent golden dawn in Nazi Germany and consciously practiced ill-disguised loyalty to their former homeland. The informants recruited generally emerged as individuals selected from proactive recruiting campaigns, Nicolaus endured numerous hours assessing the analysis reports on potential candidates to contact, those with links to the Nazi Party or media publications were prioritized as a standard policy. The SD VI office that coordinated relations with foreign countries delivered listings of business and industrial employees with any Nazi Party associations and German citizens residing in Mexico with credible records. He attended and maintained a close watch on associations and clubs of present and former German citizens, or reunions of specific professions. During which he insinuated that there were methods to assist the Fatherland's important interests in Latin America and espoused nationalistic and patriotic calling card sentiments to attract devotees.

Another individual exposed as an accomplice and fundamental connection point inside the Nicolaus espionage cellular divisions was Ernst Max Vogel. He performed an indispensable structural link with embedded Nazi movements, centering on an internal communication system in Central and South America. This long-term associate of Georg Nicolaus also gathered information in his semi-independent and remotely operated network. Ernst Max Vogel was inducted into Abwehr service after occupational relocation resulted in employment at Breuer Moller Company in Bogotá commercially retailing hardware. He experimented in small-scale trading as a stock broker, purchasing and selling shares on behalf of clients, opening an account at Bank of Manhattan Company in 1939. One of the inaugural deposits was an amount of $4,500 by one Georg Nicolaus. Vogel and Nicolaus were already familiar after their trajectories had coincidentally crossed inside the Americas multiple times during Nicolaus's residence in Bogota. In the British Secret Information Service "Georg Nicolaus" case file, not declassified until over 50 years later, the "Statement of Ernst Gustav Max Vogel" corroborated this association with Georg Nicolaus. The documents describe how Colombian police raided Vogel's home residence.[110] The resultant confiscation of hidden depositories of Nicolaus's personal belongings and correspondence proved highly compromising.

U.S. authorities ascertained from examination of the documents that Ernst Vogel acted as an intermediary channel for Nicolaus's Mexican operation in forwarding data on the United States and Latin America back to Germany. As the standard protocols dictated he distributed communications to Vogel's post office box with instructions for sending the documents to other selected drop boxes in Peru, Chile and Argentina, the couriering routes installed for contingency measures in protection from the Allied censorship. From February 1940 to October 1942 Vogel was enlisted by Nicolaus to gather information on the oil industry in Colombia and Venezuela. He imparted correspondence to Bogota station inquiring on subject matter that encompassing the Colombian Air Force and "under the table" associations with U.S. forces. A munitions company in Denver, industrial production in other major cities and commercial agreements between Germany and Colombia all featured in reports distributed from Colombia to Mexico City. Long-term links documenting Nicolaus's relationship with Vogel are substantial.[111]

Vogel was detained by Colombian federal authorities in January 1943, who originally expected to deport him. Unfortunately, immigration complications emerged and he was unsuccessful in securing the necessary transit visas and subsequently rearrested and then held in custody pending sentence to a penal colony. In Trinidad after considerable diplomatic wrangling the German national was taken into custody by Britain and transported to Ellis Island, New

York. In Colombia, Vogel during interrogation claimed he was not a Nazi sympathizer and in fact practiced separation from any Nazi Party members he became acquainted with. Insisting that credible evidence of his innocence was attainable in that no records existed of an application from Ernst Vogel for official membership of the NSDAP. Nicolaus had been increasingly frustrated by the Allied forces supposed constant harassment and surveillance, complaining to comrades and trusted confidants that the Allied censorship was irrefutably a principal culprit in disrupting their correspondence lines. He displayed anxiety concerning whether or not the correspondence reached the designated locations undetected. The realistic prospect of losing Mexican residency permits and deportation also raised problems. An intelligence assessment from 1943, based predominantly on scrutinizing radio transmission intercepts, commented that in the period of January 1940 to May 1941 the Mexican spy networks must be credited with accomplishments indisputably of considerable value to Germany. For example the repeated forwarding of both proficient quantities of economic statistical data for the Nazi analysis and shipping information. Evidence on precisely how influential military or economic secrets emerged to become and the implications for national defense policies is still difficult to determine. He was effective in forming the nucleus of an organization with contiguous potent operations until 1943.[112]

Nicolaus was observed in multiple secluded and non-sanctioned conferences with Mexican government officials, in May 1941 three Mexican immigration service agents in Guadalajara city had attended confidential talks with the espionage chief. The central secret police bureaucracy in Mexico was the Direccion General de Investigaciones Politicas y Sociales (DGIPS), located in Gobernacion city. The manifold intelligence agencies with a presence in Gobernacion guaranteed that this city was converted into the unofficial center for spy agencies. A culture of intelligence community infiltration emerged, as the DGIPS represented a potential breeding ground for enterprising Nazi agents and an invaluable resource for U.S. officials hungry for intelligence breakthroughs. Alfonso González García, a senior DGIPS officer, offered to unlawfully supply the Mexican espionage network with permanent resident cards and citizenship papers in exchange for cash payments. In October of 1941 a U.S. naval attaché reported that Nazi agents controlled a radio transmitter station somewhere in the surrounding vicinity of Veracruz, the collusion of Mexican security officers in camouflaging the operation of this station was alleged. Just as an investigation was initiated the station mysteriously and without prior explanation concluded transmission and promptly disappeared. FBI sources, including the director in a 1943 memorandum, had criticized DGIPS senior personal and accused the department of practicing institutional tolerance towards Nazi operatives and indicated that the insufficient controls presented impediments. The DGIPS chief Alemán was especially singled out for criticism.[113]

The Mexican intelligence bureaucracy was deeply conflicted during the period of 1939–1942. An awareness existed in the Mexican secret service of a nationwide political espionage network and informants within political and establishment circles and several German-Mexican business. Officials at Eriksson, including the Technical Director, actively engaged in intercepting calls for intelligence related purposes. The Mexican telephone system was dominated in this era by Eriksson and ITT.[114] Alternatively, evidence is also indicative of desirability for mutual cooperation from senior Mexican security service officials with the U.S. counterparts. A distinct conformity was signaled to both Welles and Berle of the State Department on the future complicity in Mexican-U.S. alliances, focusing on surveillance, observation and if necessary deportation of any German undercover personnel. Certain extreme right sections of the national legislature had stubbornly exhibited sympathy towards the Axis powers, but parliamentary support gradually favored the Americans. In the aftermath of Pearl Harbor the government transitioned more decisively into an open collaboration with the U.S. and a counterespionage union. Mexican intelligence officials instituted a 24 hour surveillance in January 1942 on suspected fascist sympathizers and instructed the DGIPS to retain files on politicians and military commanders for investigating ideological interests.[115]

U.S. Response to Nazi Activities in Mexico

Meanwhile, radio transmission signals recorded emanating from Mexico were still causing considerable consternation north of the border. In early 1942, U.S. Naval SIGNIT stations intercepted communications from Chapultepec radio, which appeared to justify the conclusion that a German spy was sending out intelligence reports in a private code, the identical transmitter it later transpired was employed for the clandestine communication with Berlin during World War I. In the aftermath of the Pearl Harbor era private code utilization on commercial radio was prohibited in Mexico and certainly traceable. This unknown individual resorted to installing a replacement clandestine radio transmitter. Naval listening stations intercepted traffic from Mexico spanning January to June 1942 concerned with the local economy, foreign intelligence messages, Argentinean politics and assembling a secretive courier system to avoid censorship restrictions. Once the SIGNIT tracking maneuvered into full operation the traffic volume increased to 10 intercepted messages per day. During the summer of 1939 the Naval Attaché to Mexico, Lieutenant Commander William Dillon, was ordered by the State Department to commence monitoring of Axis intelligence activity. In an environment before SIS the Naval Attaché diligently pursued objectives with volunteer embassy personnel. Gradually, Dillon developed the first comprehensive U.S. counterintelligence program inside Mexico, he cultivated contacts and formed a network of agents answerable to himself.[116]

Initially the results obtained were minimal, but in December 1939 Lieutenant Commander Dillon accomplished a major discovery. An informant expropriated a German diplomatic telegram and tellingly the accompanying cipher allowing the document to be understood in full detail. The Naval Attaché later recalled his professional elation, however his breakthrough triumph proved short-lived. His penetration actions had provoked an unintended repercussion and alarmed the upper echelon of local embassy officialdom. As Germany and the United States officially practiced neutrality Dillon's activities, the U.S. Mexican Embassy indignantly proclaimed, could damage fundamentally Mexican diplomatic relationships long-term. A substantial proportion of the senior diplomatic core continued in promoting a non-interventionist foreign policy and noted anxiety reverberated about obstructing the cordial business of international diplomacy. U.S.–Mexican relations had experienced other damaging incidents since President Cárdenas launched a drive against American-owned petroleum properties in March 1938. A departmental rupture within intelligence community circles appeared possible in the pervading antagonistic environment as other State Department officials interjected comments into the dispute.[117]

Dillon unabashed had requested funding from the Office of Naval Intelligence, in conjunction with permission to expand the operations and authority. Pierre de Boal, Embassy delegate, declared his office's opposition to Commander Dillon's premature strategy for an unmitigated entrance of U.S. intelligence full-time into Mexico. On January 11th of 1940, Pierre de Lagarde Boal in a confidential discussion with George Messersmith, the Assistant Secretary of State for Latin America, complained unreservedly about the Naval Attaché's programs in the intelligence underworld. In addition, de Boal characterized Dillon as impulsive. He repeated the alleged concerns of key diplomatic officials and cautioned that if uncovered or publicly revealed these unsanctioned infiltrations could reprehensibly generate serious blowback for U.S. standings, the Embassy especially disagreed with the assertions that Naval Intelligence intended to coordinate ground operations independent of embassy control. The potential for a public relations disaster stemming from this investigation of any Nazi subversion and Gestapo presence were considered more deleterious than any advantages gained from secret materials potentially elicited.[118]

Adolf Berle, since February 1940 an Assistant Secretary of State, had executed policies as the primary diplomat coordinating Latin American intelligence matters, this preceded the formation of a dedicated intelligence service concentrating exclusively on Latin America. Overcoming his previous stated objections in May 1940 de Boal expressed interest in circulating briefing papers debating the establishment of a distinct intelligence agency in Mexico. This new theoretical organization required Assistant Secretary Berle to convince Secretary Cordell Hull and Under-secretary Sumner Welles to confer at least moderate vocal support. With the formal inauguration of the FBI's Special Information Service (SIS) in June 1940 covert infiltration of Mexico accelerated. A secret bi-lateral surveillance agreement was hastily confirmed with Mexican security forces. To counter Nazi espionage networks and Fifth Column in Mexico the United States selected veteran FBI agent, Gus Jones, for the office of U.S. intelligence chief. The new pointman was disguised under diplomat cover within the Embassy as a nominal civil attaché. He observed enemy activity in conjunction with his Mexican federal agency counterparts, principally Secretary of Interior Miguel Alemán and Colonel Alvaro Basail of the Secret Service.[119]

Gus Jones advised his Mexican colleagues on installing surveillance details on suspected Nazi operatives and informants secreted in Northern states a first order objective. The FBI's Cryptographic section and Radio Intelligence Division of the Federal Communication Commission's joint program for interception and decoding of enemy signals attested crucial. Mexico was the first Latin American nation to approve the Radio Intelligence Division agent's permanent deployment of their mobile radio detectors inside its territorial boundaries. The investigation had also depended on paid informants, the ONI reiterated an ongoing policy of procuring intelligence matter by utilizing cash payments. An ONI representative stated on the record that "judicious bribery obtains more cooperation and information than anything else." Naval intelligence enlisted the publishing industry employees inhabiting Mexico including Holland McCombs, Foreign Editor of *National Geographic*, and Owen Williams of *Time* and *Life* magazine, in funneling the payments to informants. A standard market rate varied somewhere between $20 and $30 dollars.[120]

An exigent human source of information for Washington, D.C., disclosed postwar was world renowned muralist Diego Rivera, consorting with a team of thirty confederates he had uncovered abundant records on the fascist underworld for intelligence officials. In May 1942 Nicolaus and the principal members of this espionage division were arrested. Mexican police and the SIS surveillance teams had cataloged sufficiently their movements and interconnected nature of spy ring personnel to assemble incriminating evidence, tracking shortwave radio emissions allowed the radio stations to be pinpointed and then seized. The momentum of intel traffic flowing from Mexico to Latin America had exponentially reduced beginning in December 1941. Becker had relayed misgivings in March 1942 concerning Mexican operations, the content quality and regularity of information was proving highly uneconomical. The Nazi underground movements were restricted massively post–Nicolaus's detention and while informants still continued to feedback intelligence it was now largely discontinued.

The Nazi covert infiltration assessed as both simultaneously high risk and absolutely integral to combating the U.S. industrial power backfired and shifted the balance of power in Central America firmly towards American and Allied interests. Axis power attempts, namely by Germany and Franco's Spain, to conduct intelligence operations in Mexico were hampered by the growing hostile political climate beyond repair. Mexico severed diplomatic relations with Germany, Italy and Japan following Pearl Harbor. The German government in a misguided coercion strategy ordered Doenitz's submarines to target Mexican shipping as a battlefield component of Operation Paukenschlag, a Western Atlantic submarine offensive. The U-boats attacked two Mexican vessels during January and February 1942, including an oil tanker a short distance from the Florida coastline. Mexican President Avilo Camacho demanded an explanation from Germany utilizing the Mexican ambassador to Sweden. The federal police agencies expanded definitive security measures and its surveillance of fascist movements and organizations. Mexico declared war against the Axis powers on May 28, 1942.[121]

Right-wing and nationalist reaction hostile since 1939 to discontinuing neutrality opposed the declaration of war persisted with a sufficient vehemence that Mexican President Avila Camacho was forced to parade on the National Palace balcony accompanied by all living Mexican ex–Presidents. This extraordinary show of national solidarity was a strategy employed by Camacho to persuade the nation's population that his decision was correct.[122] During the ensuing three years of European and Pacific theater conflict the U.S.–Mexican economic and political links were fortified and future mutual cooperation agreements were in their infancy. In exchange for joining forces with Allied Nations and solidarity in hemispheric defense the United States reciprocally sanctioned agreement to concessions on immigrant labor, commercial contracts and the construction of industrial plants, bi-lateral trade and defense cooperation. The United States gained substantially from arrangements in this new climate in securing oil and other mineral resources crucial in military rearmament. This revaluation of national defense policies had stimulated heavy U.S. investment in training and supplying of Mexican forces, in order to guarantee their cooperation in protecting the shared borders. The Lend-Lease Act funneled millions of dollars into the Mexican military development, advanced modernized aircraft for the Air Force and a mechanized ground division for the Army were financed by the Lend-Lease payments. A Mexican Air Force squadron with a compliment of 300 men was transferred to Pacific theater in 1944 and Mexico's 201st Squadron experienced action in the Philippines.[123]

Cuba

In the Caribbean and Central American regions the SIS divisions established a presence in terms of operations and personnel to a greater extent inside Cuba than any other nation. Collaboration with President Batista's governing regime and the Cuban Security Service was instrumental. Batista projected the persona of a national statesman committing to hemispheric defense alignment with U.S. power, Cuba declared war against Japan on December 8 the day after the Pearl Harbor attacks. This strategy of constructive relationship building fragmented any potential for an establishment seduction to Axis economic power or counterintelligence networks. At the beginning of the turbulent chapters of World War II Heinz Lüning, disguising his identity as a Jewish refugee escaping from Europe, was surreptitiously smuggled into Cuba with the authorization to engineer conducive partnerships for the Fatherland. Lüning was the espionage chief for Abwehr II in Cuba. He was nicknamed locally "the Bird Man of Morro Castle," relating to his peculiar penchant for canaries, insisting on accommodating the canaries even inside the radio transmission station.

His assignment was to monitor activity on United States and Allies and report back to German military intelligence. A lifeline of indispensable raw materials and commodities were transported from South America to supplement European armed forces and domestic needs.[124] The Caribbean waters Lüning monitored were important to the Allied maritime strategy both for transatlantic trade and for deploying ships between the various front lines. The period of September 1941 to June 1942 propelled Naval warfare in the Caribbean theater into the international spotlight as Admiral Dönitz identified the region as essential in re-stocking and augmenting U.S. and Allied forces. In mid–1943 and 1944 seven Cuban vessels was destroyed by U-boats in action which killed more than eighty Cubans and three Americans. In the Caribbean region the Allies experienced among the highest prevalence of enemy submarine activity and shipping attacks of the Atlantic conflict. Lüning as the spy ring's master was instructed to transmit the coordinates and destinations to awaiting German naval ships and U-boats.

Despite setbacks Lüning accomplished a modicum of success in obtaining information on the naval activities for Dönitz, a subject of contention is the extent that Lüning's penetration actions were culpable for the destruction of Allied shipping. A secondary strategy was acknowledged by German intelligence in Caribbean operations in perusing an agenda of disrupting and debilitating U.S. efforts to manufacture war materials. Studying the Nazi underground network and determined attempts by SIS to dismantle the net revealed Lüning as an individual with a comparable proportion of mistakes and successes. He departed to Cuba in September 1941, by the time of the operation's closure he had distributed a total of 48 letters back to Germany packed with intelligence data.[125]

From January to June 1942 content in Lüning's message reports to Nazi Germany observed that a combined seventeen U.S. and two British vessels were presently docked at the Havana port. He reported on trajectory of British merchant shipping in chartering courses to central Caribbean islands, containing sugar, food supplies and raw materials. Lüning issued data describing the consignments of merchant vessels and if possible destination and schedules, he divulged that the U.S. was purchasing scrap metal from sources in Cuba. The Cuban network discovered intelligence concerning the Atlantic convoys. Lüning was not averse to informing his superiors about rumors and innuendo he heard or acquired by chance. Speculation on the Batista regime falling from power and an American airline company purchasing land in Cuba for military bases are instances of unguarded innuendo replacing hard intelligence.[126] In December 1940, an examiner employed at a British censorship offices in Bermuda analyzed a letter intercepted in transit to New York from Berlin. The suspicious censorship team, residing at the Prince Hotel, prudently settled temporarily their apprehensive reservations by placing sender and destination route on a watchlist. Indication of the presence of invisible ink was detected and a viable chemical solution pioneered by the Caribbean division of applying iodine vapor was available for further analysis. The identical department intercepted a Spanish language letter from Havana to Lisbon a few weeks later. The first intuition of the investigators was confirmed after the exposure of the invisible ink revealed a document listing designations of vessels loading in Havana harbor and an airfield under construction. Further letters intercepted from this compromised source discussed with apparent precise knowledge the merchant shipping within Cuban coastal waters and information on the U.S. Naval base at Guantanamo, including specifications on its proportions and complement.

The foreign ministers of the Americas held a conference in Havana on 21 July 1940, in reaction to state security and the growing alarm, the delegation included the Secretary of State Cordell Hull and Under Secretary Sumner

Welles. An agreement was brokered which transitioned the Monroe Doctrine into a new political treaty, a collective shield was to be constructed across the Americas. The Havana and Rio conferences insinuated that U.S. administration strategy for the foreseeable future gravitated around extending the Good Neighbor policy with Latin America.[127] Relations between U.S. and Cuba tightened following first half of 1942. The Batista government of 1940–44 collaborated with the United States and garnered in response increased economic aid for agricultural and public works program and developmental loans for increasing its annual sugar crop production. In 1941, the Roosevelt administration purchased Cuba's entire sugar harvest. The outcome of cooperation would be nine separate military agreements and U.S. forces stationed at Cuban military bases.[128]

In November 1942, the FBI and joint chiefs of the Navy and Army reached agreements on the operation of a radio tracking network in the Caribbean and Latin America. From this period onwards the FBI and War Department's MID division were responsible for implementation and manpower in installing communications technology and furnishing the technical assistance in cooperative friendly nations. State Department and FBI were to coordinate action on clandestine stations after conferring with other agencies, technical capabilities remained fundamental in the challenging environment and the FCC experts were stationed in reserve if they transpired to be necessary. Charles Hogg of the FCC had been designated for assignment to Cuba and agents on the ground demanded that he be deployed as soon as possible. Hogg arrived in Havana with the equipment on April 10th, Sumner Welles had previously in 1940 transmitted a memorandum to the FCC on the options for collaboration emanating from Cuban Government, with agreements in principle for U.S. monitoring stations to be assembled. The Cuban Secret Service were bargaining in return, according to the American sources, for advanced technical apparatus assisting in the detection and suppression of domestic political groups. Military Attaché, Major Charles Youmans, contributed his office's resources to the U.S.–Cuban policy. In May 1943, this project was converted into a 24-hour operation and became a crucial segment of the Latin American direction-finding network.[129]

Mailing routes and the destinations associated with the marked correspondence were placed under constant surveillance. FBI investigators and Cuban police in time uncovered sufficient evidence to unmask Heinz Lüning, operating under the assumed identity of R. Castillo, as the Nazi espionage chief in Cuba. Despite initial hesitation from the U.S. front Cuban police commanded by a zealous police captain launched a raid on the Lüning home residence in August of 1942 shortly after his full culpability was understood. An alternative tactic proposed resisting the premature temptation to arrest immediately and instead identify other spy operations using surveillance of Lüning.

Batista launched a program of detentions and criminal prosecutions against the Falangists and rendered illegal the Cuban Nazi Party, in 1940 a preemptive intervention had witnessed the internment of 700 German and 1,370 Italian citizens. In September of 1942 a further intensification of the U.S.–Cuban relationship occurred with the general agreement on military and naval defense strategies. The United States had leased several naval bases from the Cuban government and substantial Lend-lease contracts were signed with the Cuban military. This prominent Cuban role in consistently opposing European fascism was an obvious asset to the defensive policies in Caribbean region. The stringent impediments to foreign political parties and Nazi affiliated movements restricted options internally in Cuba for Axis intelligence or a possible Fifth Column presence.[130] On November 9, 1942, Lüning, after a guilty verdict and the rejection of defense arguments, was executed by firing squad at Príncipe Fortress, becoming the singular Nazi spy to be executed in Latin America during World War II.

Final Years

On January 12, 1944, President Ramírez authorized an offensive against suspected German and Spanish agents. On the 26 January Argentina officially renounced diplomatic recognition of the Axis nations, a decision upheld by his successor Edelmiro Farrell. The detentions landed a detrimental and probably fatal compliment of the Buenos Aires underground network in prison cells, Becker was temporarily forced into hiding, as authority heat definitively closed in on remaining Bolivar agents. Communication with Department Amt VI D4 and Chief Kurt Gross suffered interruption and failed to resume a comparable volume to pre–January statistics. In February, Becker had managed finally after considerable time consuming efforts to contact Security Service headquarters, depleted of financial resources and any dependable ground-level assets Becker urgently implored Kurt Gross to requisition reinforcements and cash funding. The divisions now radiating back from South America threatened to jeopardize the future subversive operations. These uncertain conditions motivated an instigation of a contingency response measure code named "Operation Jolle." By spring of 1944 the declining fortunes of Admiral Raeder's U-boat offensive and the undisputed control of Allied Naval forces in the Atlantic presented obstacles in replacements for Abwehr or SD VI in overseas actions.[131]

A primary methodology by Nazi agents in financing covert operations abroad and avoiding exposure in neutral countries was the smuggling of precious gems and expensive commodities, and finding suitable buyers without any interference in various Latin American black markets. Smuggling expensive pharmaceuticals turned into a lucrative alternative enterprise. The model utilized to deploy the agents into hostile territory, if the transportation systems were either insecure or non-existent, had previously been submarine landings. Becker was not convinced about transporting heavy equipment with mounting Allied dominance of the Atlantic Ocean. Similarly, the smuggling arrangements were in a precarious position because of the prospect of a termination in Spanish support. Operations Jolle amounted to the Security Service's latest solution to counteract this dilemma of a dismantling of the Oceanic pathways vital for sustaining the covert penetrations.

Chief Kurt Gross selected a lightweight ketch vessel for the expedition capable of achieving high speeds and renowned for performing stealthy crossings. Code named Mercator I, the mission's crew departed from Brest heading to South-West Africa on 27 April 1944, the vessel supplied with an assorted consignment of precious commodities for reselling. German companies in Argentina who included Siemens, Telefunken and Merck Chemical had disseminated orders for radio and electrical equipment, chemical and medical supplies. This infusion of products should theoretically resolve any financial shortfalls encountered by the spy rings. Gross informed the agents about the precise details of their mission and supervised the training and briefing session, the two SD agents selected were Hansen and Schroell. Gross would command the Jolle operation on the Berlin side. The Mercator I team were informed about the project specifications when it was determined absolutely necessary and understood minimal facts regarding the Becker-Argentina operations, prior to landing in Argentina.

The mission required both Hansen and Schroell to separate from Becker's supervision and travel further northward. As a supplementary method of transmitting new information the agents were instructed to develop a new courier trafficking system for communication with Gross in Berlin post-landing. Hansen was earmarked in the planning and training stages for isolating discreet shelter in Mexico, while Schroell maneuvered inside the United States, both were briefed on the techniques for securing employment positions in local factories and industrial centers. The former was instructed to set-up a radio transmitter inside Mexico and communicate reports of information discovered. Gross emphasized that the future secondary operative teams, if possible, were anticipated by Amt VI D4 to follow in their footsteps. All embedded personnel were expected to exercise initiative to a significant extent and capitalize on any opportunity which presented itself.

Shortly after Mercator's field operatives, Hansen and Schroell, arrived in Argentina most of the Operation Bolivar personnel still in action or unaccounted for were arrested, dismantling the remnants of the espionage ring. Hansen and Schroell's mission was short lived with both captured immediately upon landing, U.S. dollars and foreign currency worth a combined value of $100,000 and diamond caches were confiscated. Another Nazi intelligence plot had failed because of Allied counterespionage intrusion into Nazi radio transmissions and efficiency of decryption programs. Espionage activity by the SD VI inside the Americas territory was brought abruptly to a conclusion. The Farrell administration sponsored a new governmental body entitled the Investigation Commission on Anti-Argentinean Activities, a U.S. placation succeeding the Axis diplomatic accords, rooting out to an effective degree clandestine spying operations.

Many senior operatives of Nazi espionage in Argentina in the wartime period including Napp and Muller were languishing in detention facilities, Seidlitz and Harnisch similarly resided securely in police custody. After disguising his movements and hiding in hotels and rented accommodation in the Buenos Aries area Johannes Becker was finally captured.[132] He endured 14 months evading capture and incarceration by security services. The Argentinean police caught up with Becker in April 1945 two months before the war concluded. At the Rio Conference in February of 1943 the delegate Latin American nations agreed on suppressing clandestine radio and substantial motions towards a common defensive block were proposed. The joint Directorate of Naval Intelligence, Military Intelligence and the Federal Communication Commission services could feasibly conduct a portion of radio tracking directly from the United States, but the coordinates pinpointed were rarely sufficiently accurate. Radio transmissions in Argentina and Uruguay presented more problematic technical barriers in both signals detection and intercept. Lengthy and invariably mutually distrustful negotiation emerged concerning pace of negotiations and agreements, but cooperation with the security services ultimately produced dividends.[133] The uncovering of clandestine radio locations evolved into a fundamentally critical investigative technique in exposing espionage assets. The FBI's Special Intelligence Service (SIS) in partnership with military and federal offices maximized resources with great effect in disrupting Axis intelligence operations in both Central and South America. Between July 1, 1940, and December 31, 1945, the SIS identified 832 Axis espionage agents, apprehended 336 of these and ultimately gained convictions against 105 individuals. The SIS further identified 222 smugglers of strategic materials in the Western Hemisphere, capturing 75. Agents conducted 641 separate investigations at the request of U.S. government agencies and completely shut down 24 clandestine radio stations used by Axis agents to communicate with their handlers and inter-network.[134]

The outbreak of conflict between the United States and Germany fundamentally altered the fortunes of the Nazi spy rings in Latin America. Two months after Brazil reached security and defense agreements with the U.S. and severed German diplomatic relations the police authorities had arrested members of three different Nazi espionage networks. Military action progressed to engulf formerly neutral terrain, the torpedoing of Brazilian merchant shipping by U-boats in February–May 1942 had precipitated the Vargas administration more decisively combating the Axis powers. Brazilian armed forces, navy and air forces later served in the European theater. NSDAP faced the consequences of a fundamental modification in the Latin American political orientation after a decade of activities with minimal restrictions. The nationalist character of domestic political culture refused to coexist with an ideology professing theories about race and cultural imperialism that the contemporary trends did not recognize. Geographical and economic proximity of Brazil to United States must be considered as principal factors that contributed to banning the Nazi Party and the harassment actions leveled against its members. The final argument for banning the NSDAP and decisive action against Axis intelligence nets was a desirability for insular administrations to reinforce its grip on power and outflank dissident factions. Vargas was able to manipulate both sides against the other for several years, until declaring war on the Axis.[135]

U.S. pressure on hemispheric solidarity motivated concessions across a majority of South and Central America. Under the Rio Conference and later January 1944 resolutions the nations agreed on consultation before recognizing any governments established through revolution, with enforcement by collective action against any perpetrators a possibility. For a majority of 1940–1943 the Argentinean politicians observed minimal foreseeable advantages in accepting the diplomatic overtures from the United States. Argentina eventually also entered into an identical collective framework to its South American neighbors.[136]

5

Southern African Theater

Cross cultural federations had proliferated uniting both the German Nazi Party in Europe and the nationalist factions of Afrikaner republican movement from the beginning of mutual recognition in 1933. The Ausland Organization in Berlin diverted interest to Southern Africa before and during the Second World War. South African intelligence sources articulate how Bruno Stiller, the Nazi Party leader in South Africa, propagandized fascist rhetoric to potentially sympathetic grassroots audiences and engineered standing relationships with mainstream parliamentary nationalists and radical fringe elements. The Ausland Organization drafted an assessment summary on South Africa's potential for their auspices, political affiliation to the Nazi doctrine and Aryan ancestry were dually described, and possible alliances on multiple themes appearing to share common ground. The complexity of South Africa and the Cape of Good Hope region were axiomatically determinant factors in guaranteeing a German interest. When Japanese hostilities began and declarations of war proclaimed against Britain and other regional allies Southern Africa was then consequently transformed into a major resupplying territory for the Pacific and Asian theaters. The Japanese territorial advancement had rendered land masses in mainland South East Asia and prominent economic and military sites in Hong Kong and Singapore unreachable. Other destinations fundamental for commodities supply channels and arterial transportation were being either compromised or directly threatened.

The Axis flotillas controlled the Mediterranean presenting a formidable defensive barrier to Allied shipping, propelling the Cape of Good Hope into a sustaining pathway for provisioning Allied armed forces. Atlantic submarine warfare was another factor that had impacted import substitutions of commodities, in South Africa's instance the War Cabinet was contented to witness Britain replenished by production beyond Luftwaffe reach. The terrain of Southern

Africa was a reservoir of the strategic minerals that the British military demanded, the resources exported included gold, uranium, clothing, munitions and iron. Cape Town and Durban regions were converted into integral distribution zones for loading cargo onto the immense quantities of transport vessels and shipping destined for North Africa. Domestic industry experienced a structural expansion and new factories were constructed in buckling to manage intensified demand, promoting a renewed impetus to the South African economy. Even local food produce and animal livestock were exported northwards to Britain. The Second World War stimulated internal industrial growth in an economy which was already diversifying rapidly.[1]

As replenishment from Asia and Indian Ocean regions diminished and South African land and oceanic pathways inflated in importance increasingly Nazi Germany and Japan focused on tactics for removing this crucial junction point from the British and Allied control. Admiral Canaris authorized military intelligence agents to initiate communication with rebellious factions demonstrating strident opposition to the pro–British oriented government and Abwehr II covert operations teams embedded in consulate and diplomatic circles of South Africa, Portuguese East Africa (Mozambique) and other nations in the regions swelled. Madagascar, post 1940, would be governed by the fascist Vichy France and Germany's military ambitions could be prospered from this location. With outbreak of World War II the South African population was polarized and discordant social divisions were exposed on the national policy. Prime Minister J.B.M. Hertzog was vehemently opposed to any military agreement with Britain or Commonwealth nation, representatives of nationalist Afrikaner population, Hertzog's political faction espoused anti–British sentiments and advocated against the participation in another Commonwealth war. Afrikaner society was engulfed by the factionalization and disagreements about a militant approach, the mainstream exuding contentedness with retaining a parliamentary instrument in opposing coalitions with Allied Nations, but movements materialized which preferred confrontation and overt allegiance to Nazi Germany. Hertzog had consistently maintained that South Africa should follow the example of Ireland and remain neutral.

General Smuts, connected to the pro–British and Commonwealth government sections since the First World War, responded to the mounting dissension by postulating that the combined destiny of South Africa manifestly depended on the outcome of conflict. South Africa's national interests he declared were jeopardized by the German and Japanese aggression. Furthermore, South Africa was a Commonwealth nation and regretful circumstances of Australia, Canada and other aligned territories precariously performing a balancing act, without urgent intervention, could expose the civilized world to catastrophe. The parliamentary opposition headed by Jan Christian Smuts managed to topple the Hertzog government as the vacillation forces subsided. Smuts's amendment to the Nationalist Party's original parliamentary motion was approved by eighty votes to sixty-seven on September 4, 1939, and J.B.M Hertzog resigned as Prime Minister immediately. A hastily assembled replacement Cabinet encompassed remnants of divided mainstream factions, Labor and Dominion Parties. The opposition movements now reformed deeply embittered with the subdivisions proliferating and divergent sub-cultures on the periphery of South African politics, the Re-United National Party or People's Party developed into a prominent and unmistakably audible anti–Smuts faction. Departing Nationalist Party members, Hertzog counting among defectors, founded this new non-conformist organization. Other opposition political movements included the Afrikaner Party and Oswald Pirow's New Order Party.

South Africa declared war against Nazi Germany on the 5th of September 1939. The incoming government decided to foster a decline in the prevailing environment of vitriolic opposition exhibited in Afrikaners movements by refraining from implementing conscription, all military personnel serving in the South African armed forces would be volunteers. Many Afrikaners had enlisted alongside pro–British communities and non-whites, approximately 300,000 personnel were mobilized for the armed forces. Naval personnel were distributed in the Commonwealth vessels and indeed ship compliments were entirely staffed by South African personnel, Air Force pilots were enlisted immediately after war declaration and participated in the later Battle of Britain. The opposition dissenters including senior establishment figures in Dr. Malan and Oswald Pirow to the paramilitary pro-fascist movements of the Ossewa Brandwag and Stormjaers demonstrated a motivation for colluding in secret discussions with Nazi Germany and a propensity for collaborating in pro–Nazi actions. This underground movement commenced installing pathways for a removal of the governing administration and switching national allegiance to Nazi Germany. Canaris and Abwehr resorted to conspiring with the domestic extremist factions to assassinate Smuts and provoke revolution, with Jan Van Rensburg, the Ossewa Brandwag commander, recruited by German military intelligence to mastermind the operation.[2]

The post–September 4 governing administration was classified as more English speaking than Afrikaans. Prominent figures within Smuts's government had displayed in parliamentary offices an interest in liberal reform policies and a more conducive atmosphere for centrist politics emerged. The Social and Economic Planning Council associated with the liberal politicians dutifully explored aspects of deprivation in the African population and resolutions to poverty, social problems and the complex conditions of internal migrant labor.

Smuts's deputy, Hofmeyr, demonstrated a commitment to manifold liberal causes of the early 1940s period.[3] Alarm circulated in the South African police on prospects of disruption and possible repetition of 1914–1915 uprisings, this apprehension inside an administration cognizant of unfolding national controversy prompted the War Cabinet to issue several preemptive control measures. Smuts immediately set about fortifying South Africa against theoretical German or Japanese invasion, Naval commanders recommended the implementation of new defensive and security mechanisms on the major transportation routes surrounding the Cape of Good Hope. The government removed or restricted the methods by which the anti–Allied movements could organize in opposition by passing Proclamation 201 of 1939 and the War Measures Act of 1940 (Act 13 of 1940). To suppress dissenting individuals these proclamations granted Smuts administration new arbitrary powers, the suspects and enemy aliens risked internment, privately licensed firearms and ammunition were confiscated. Under Proclamation 139 of 1940 trade union activities endured a suspension to prevent industrial unrest.[4]

The National Party was founded by J.B.M. Hertzog in 1914, its membership following had incorporated Dutch-descended Afrikaners and English speaking whites. Dedicated to the policies of apartheid and white supremacy, Afrikaner exclusionist rhetoric concerning the equation of ethnicity and nationhood gradually transitioned into encompassing a broadly-based "white" term. A secondary purpose embedded in National Party rhetoric in 1914 was protesting against what were considered the Anglicizing policies of the government of Louis Botha and Jan Smuts. In 1924, in the turmoil and unpredictable aftermath of moderate attempts at relaxing the ethnically discriminatory legislation, the government was defeated by a Nationalist-Labor coalition faction headed by Hertzog. The incoming administration advocated programs for a further emancipating of South Africa from British imperial control and to institute improved protection for the "whites" from black Africans. Hertzog's "Pact" government promulgated rhetoric on the contentious subject of language equality with English and Afrikaans speaking South Africans, elevating Afrikaans to official language status alongside Dutch and English. A bi-lateral fusion of the National Party and Smuts's South African Party in 1934 had disillusioned many Nationalist Afrikaners.

From 1934 to 1939 Hertzog and Smuts despite manifest ideological differences presided over a coalition government and amalgamated respective grassroots bases. Post declaration of war against Axis power belligerents in September 1939 the insular political environment altered dramatically, the Purified National Party governed by Dr. Malan merged with Hertzog's faction and confirmed him as director, reorganized as an opposition party. The new political movements were confronted with many untenable difficulties from the beginning and were irreparably damaged by the wartime factionalism, some ardent extremist nationalists with fascist or pro–German sympathies obstructively walked out and formed the Afrikaner Party. Hertzog on July 19 of 1940, after Nazi Germany's offensive from January to June 1940 and invasions of Low Countries and France, addressed a public letter to Smuts and accompanied it with a manifesto signed by himself and Malan protesting against South African continued participation in warfare and encouraged the Nationalist Afrikanerdom to organize public meetings and demonstrate in favor of peace. Dr. N.J. van der Merwe, a commander of the Nationalist Party in Free State, orchestrated a Republican Rally in Bloemfontein for 20th July, persuading loyalist Afrikaans "to take active and immediate measures, on constitutional lines, to bring about a republic."

Hertzog was incensed about inadequate consultation and the decision against informing him and condemned the demonstration, however his dissension failed in preventing an audience variously estimated at between 15,000 and 70,000 attending. The delegates resolved that the appropriate time had arrived for the inauguration of an independent South African republic, founded on principles of Christian-Nationalism and maintenance of white civilization. A committee of action was appointed to implement the resolutions. In his speech at the demonstration Dr. van der Merwe referred to "a certain British-Jewish influence which played an important part in the fashioning of fusion ... and is again at work," criticizing the National Party leadership and Hertzog.[5]

South African Domestic Pro-Axis Movements

Populist factions of pro–Nazi and extreme right wings groups appeared in South Africa during late 1930s, decentralized and uncoordinated but still representing serious national security dilemmas. With structural and financial assistance from both Nazi Germany and the Italian secret services the movement's priority combined opposition to the Allied military alliance and revolutionary goals. The domestic security and policing services, judging by an assessment of the contemporary intelligence reports, assessed the fascist organizations as a serious threat to political stability. The most prominent openly pro–Nazi organizations at this time were the Afrikaner Broederbond and Ossewa Brandwag. On mass the objectors re-diverted their sympathies into extra-parliamentary politics which included these diversified movements, well financed by secretly colluding establishment investors. Afrikaner Broederbond (Brotherhood) was the earliest conservative Afrikaner faction to deliberately align itself with Nazi Germany. The Broederbond began originally as a fraternity of male individuals devoted to promoting the Afrikaner community and redeveloping a cultural consciousness in 1918. In that year, a mob interrupted a Nationalist Party gathering in Johannesburg, this commitment impressed especially on three Afrikaner teenagers at the meeting, H.W. van der Merwe and Daniel du Plessis among them, who founded the movement.[6] Broederbond transitioned into a secret society in 1924 determined to strengthen their diffusion into other social spheres, the systems of underground cells were established according to independent sources in important institutions and organizations.

In this context the 1938 symbolic ox wagon trek, a traditional celebration of an incident in Afrikaner folklore, motivated a rejuvenated nationalist enthusiasm. Cultural organizations associated with the Broederbond popularized this ideology for mass consumption by staging demonstrations that glorified folk culture of this reimagined nationalism. Members of the Afrikaans community according to cultural mythology had become alienated and absorbed by the urban conglomerates, now it was possible to rediscover each other. Afrikaner nationalism consequently flourished and in the concerted efforts to perpetuate celebratory spirit the Ossewa Brandwag (OB) group was constituted in February 1939, ostensibly to promote Afrikaner heritage, but the organization developed into an underground military movement. The OB's members dressed in official uniforms, developed an armed militia and incorporated skietvereenigings (shooting associations) in a replication of military traditions. Aiming to accomplish the uniting of Afrikaners possessed with national ardor they organized festivals, the building of memorials, wreath laying at monuments and other traditional Afrikaner activities. There policy during this formative incarnation were devoted towards cultural appreciation and promoting reinvigorated cultural nationalism. Ossewa Brandwag would form a vanguard for this enthusiasm and ensure that it endured.

The OB was under leadership of a former Union Defense Force (UDF) commander, Colonel J.C.C. Laas, from February until development of the organization expanded beyond his managerial capabilities, prompting his resignation in October 1940. After Laas removed himself from leadership Ossewa Brandwag converted without reservation or disagreement into a significantly more militant in nature movement under the command of Hans Van Rensburg. He resigned as Administrator towards end 1940 and became Commandant-General on 15 January 1941. Rensburg directed great personal energy towards Afrikaner cultural revival and comprehended well propaganda influences, resurrecting trek names and traditional symbolism in the organization's mythology. This movement with the early Wehrmacht successes modified into a paramilitary culture in stated ambitions, clear parallels existed with the European fascist movements, an attraction to the Führer principle and other national socialist theories were discernible in the literature. Under Van Rensburg's leadership domestic political values were espoused, but outspoken attachment to fascism and Nazi Germany strengthened during 1941–42, the Ossewa Brandwag had openly welcomed Nazi military accomplishments. Hans Van Rensburg and other OB stalwarts enthusiastically admired Adolf Hitler, and proclaimed that natural symmetry was abundant in conjecture of Aryan superiority and doctrines of white supremacy. Afrikaner nationalism was inevitably empowered by the manifestation of fascism inside Continental Europe, while hostility to British imperialism naturally commended itself to Afrikaner ideologists.[7] OB was perceptibly the most radical organization and many obvious affinities with national socialist principles and primitive versions of German Nazi Party were transparent. Rensberg only marginally concealed his objectives to achieve political power within a national socialist framework through revolutionary methods. He commented in *Die Vaderland* on 8 August 1942 "The Ossewa Brandwag is of the opinion that a German victory is an obvious condition for and Afrikaner republic to come into existence. Liberation can happen only as a result of a German victory."[8]

An implicit conclusion was understood by the Ossewa Brandwag leadership who admitted realistically that securing objectives by traditional constitutional intervention was not practicable and paramilitary tactics were therefore justified. The transformed paramilitary organization modeled on Nazi SA engaged in actions of sabotage against the South African government to undermine British and Commonwealth war effort. The Orange Free State affiliate had galvanized a small fringe protest assemble into a substantive political force. By 1941, the OB was beginning to attract a diversified interest from Afrikaners splitting traditional political lines, its membership peaked at 130,000 in the Transvaal. Future Prime Minister John Vorster and radicalized establishment individuals joined the Ossewa Brandwag finding a convenient home. Vorster, the Assistant-hoof Kommandant in the Ossewa Brandwag, expressed his admiration of Adolf Hitler and quoted habitually Mein Kampf. After the war Hendrick van den Bergh another OB graduate ascended through divisional police ranks and achieved considerable notoriety as a prominent national security commanding officer, establishing in 1963 and directing the Bureau of State Security intelligence agency.[9]

Shortly into Van Rensburg governorship definite rumblings emanated from the National Party as he expanded the organization and adopted a more confrontational attitude. He openly declared a predestined obligation for overthrowing the South African government and abandoned the diplomatic approach of his predecessor.[10] Many Afrikaners permeating OB movements from the

Cape region were dissatisfied with indecisive mainstream attitudes, in the Transvaal OB had become an egregious dilemma for the National Party because the organization was comfortably surpassing their public and electoral popularity. A considerable number of Afrikaners in fact were no longer represented in the Parliament due to the direct election system, this reverberation drawing more dissatisfied converts. Inside industrial and railway communities the flourishing support for extra-parliamentary groups and in multiple districts an increased expression of malcontent and radicalism was discernible. In contrast, grassroots bases in the Southern regions tended to be aligned with their traditional party. Rank and file grassroots factions had required concessions and the National Party were compelled in performing the delicate balancing act of avoiding alienating their traditional strongholds, while maneuvering OB closer under its control. Broederbond and OB membership shared relatively comparable ideologies to Hertzog and undoubtedly large contingents of the Afrikaner populations, Forster and Rensburg found minimal transparent disagreements in practice with mainstream comrades. Nevertheless, Malan and Hertzog, despite their determination in spearheading the anti–British sentiment at national level and a standing commitment on withdrawing troops from the Allied armed forces, displayed reservations and distrust in their attitude towards the OB.

Documents captured after the war implicated Van Rensburg in actively supporting German espionage networks and proposing to orchestrate a coup on condition that Germany compensated his movement sufficiently and requisitioned the weaponry. In dialogue with the Nazi leaders in June 1940 Van Rensburg formally presented a strategy to provision the Third Reich with 100,000 soldiers in the instigation of a coup d'état and a replacement of the existing administration with an Axis friendly government. Cultivating an operational strategy, he had advocated to his Nazi alliances the concept of depositing the weapons and munitions inside South West Africa or on an airstrip in Zimbabwe (then Southern Rhodesia). After Axis powers accomplished their military objectives in Europe the Ossewa Brandwag was expected to govern South Africa completely. Canaris's assignments to Abwehr Section II personnel departing for South Africa accounted for infiltrating German heartland populations and contacting delicately the supporters of Ossewa Brandwag. Van Rensburg remained in dialogue with Nazi Germany, confirming targets for engagement in covert military action and sabotage to obstruct the pro–British elements. The Abwehr recognized that inciting mayhem and disorder within Southern Africa and Portuguese East Africa should inflict damage against the Allied military endeavors and conveniently force the re-positioning of troop divisions into other theaters. The first objective was to engender a power base among naturalized South Africans of German descent assimilated into the Afrikaner population and German nationals. The second major objective was to promote the national socialist cause not only among the German national communities but also non–Germans. A torrent of propaganda flooded South Africa dedicated towards influenced people in Afrikaner communities and remote rural areas into sympathy towards Nazi Germany.[11]

Pro-fascist propaganda was being distributed using radio broadcasts and other media. Nazi spymasters persevered with the employment of psychological manipulation techniques for promoting widespread civilian dissension in German populations with possible sympathies. Substantial German speaking communities were present in the Transvaal, Orange Free State and the Eastern Cape region. Sympathies for Nazi movement and pro–German nationalism were definitely noted from sections of the communities. Pro-German media programs and subversive newspapers attempted to motivate the adherents in these territories. Occupations were singled out for a bombardment with propaganda, for example operations to provoke agitation and unrest within the Rand miners.[12] Domestic friction was exploited, for Nazi propagandists the disaffected membership provided a fertile hunting ground for intelligence services in inciting dissent and recruiting informants.

Connections Between Nazi Germany and South Africa

After the Nazi Party consolidated state power in Germany the Afrikaner sections pronounced an inclination to defend Nazism, ideologically both national socialism and their Voortrekker heritage relied on concepts of community to promote the dialectic of racial supremacy. Nazis and Afrikaners construed their self-conceived identity as permitting a xenophobia that preserved a Western Christian tradition. Militant Afrikaner movements adapted Hitler's conceptualized master race and Nazism's nationalism to their situation shaping an insular ideology. A pre-war connection existed between the Third Reich and extreme-right South African political organizations, the philosophies of Afrikaner nationalism enabled sympathies to develop and a dedication to engineering alliances with pro-fascist movements in Europe. This linkage became critical to Broederbond with the appearance of Graf von Durckheim Montmartin in 1934, a representative of Nazi Germany and supposedly the Reich Ministry of Education, but secretly an espionage operative. Durckheim journeyed to South Africa under the subterfuge of attending a conference on education. According to secret documents confiscated from the German diplomacy headquarters for South African Union a divergent concealed purpose existed. Hitler charged Durckheim with the objective of determining what support

South Africa might confer on Germany in the world order that Hitler had envisioned and to assess the extent of pro–German sentiment. Durckheim held conferences secretly with the senior Broederbond leadership to commence negotiations on methodologies enabling the movement to service the Fatherland's interests.[13]

After this meeting with Durckheim the Afrikaner Broederbond reorganized itself structurally to resemble the Nazi Party. He expended six months in South Africa and discussed matters with the German descended or expatriate populations, he cautioned them on the importance of not abandoning Nazism's ideals. He encouraged both the Broederbond and interested civilian populations on investing productively in persuading possible converts about Nazism, the nationalism of Europe promoted by Durckheim and others energized the domestic culture in South Africa.[14] Daniel Malan, a leading politician and the Prime Minister between 1948 and 1954, was approached surreptitiously under the hidden pretext of a journalistic interview by a German spy in Cape Town. Documents captured by the Allied investigators postwar, from the decimated German Foreign Office headquarters, describe how a Mrs. Thyra Denk, acting on the instructions of Nazi military intelligence stationed at that time in Lourenço Marques, obtained permission for an interview with Malan in January 1940. As instructed by her superiors during mission briefing inside German consulate Mrs. Denk conveyed the message originating from the Nazi Foreign Minister, von Ribbentrop, that it was unequivocally in the self-interest of South Africa to cease hostilities against Nazi Germany and renounce Allied collaboration. The documents elaborated that the Nazi operative Mrs. Denk had transmitted to Dr. Daniel Malan an understanding on Germany's desire for comradeship and a mutually agreeable and profitable alliance with the Afrikaner movements. The Fatherland government insinuated in negotiations that formerly governed territories bordering South African Union would be returned to their jurisdiction, explicitly promising three British Protectorates of Swaziland, Bechuanaland, and Basutoland. The communiqué also expressed no impediments if South Africa decided on extending national territory northwards to encompass Southern Rhodesia. Ribbentrop's agent introduced into discussions a reserve contingency, harbored revealingly by German officials, insisting South-West Africa in exchange be relinquished to their control.

In reporting back to Nazi Foreign Ministry Mrs. Denk confirmed an unbounded admiration for Malan and his commitments to a diplomatic alliance. Malan had revealed before departing that he was sufficiently convinced to arrange a dialogue with J.B.M. Hertzog and other leading Nationalists in exploring parliamentary resolutions, purportedly issued assurances that he was influential enough to orchestrate maneuvering the other nationalist leaders into alignment. This incident had immediately preceded the commencing of 1940's parliamentary session. A successive week after Denk's meeting the National Party proposed a motion demanding a separate peace resolution and immediate cessation in hostilities, Nazi Germany had attempted to enlist interjections from the nationalist leadership in convincing South Africa to withdraw from conflict.

Malan's two hour speech at the Nationalists Congress of June 1941 opening proceedings was depicted as a consummate exposition of national socialist theories. Indeed, the political movement's composition and structure exemplified a similar pattern to Nazi conferences. An elitist mechanistic sequence of procedures mandated all resolutions were proposed from the governing platform based on a preconceived program and no debates ensued. Malan negotiated through backdoor channels with the OB's leadership in various complex permutations to achieve concessions from June to August 1941.[15] Van Rensburg and the other nationalists advocated collusion with Nazi Germany under a premeditated assumption that postwar an independently governed South Africa would therefore be accomplished in reimbursing their loyalty to Nazism. Support for Nazi Germany overtly detectable inside both the legitimate Afrikaner movement and OB senior command hierarchy did not proceed unnoticed by Allied or South African intelligence. Increasingly individuals and organizations suspected of collusion became a principle focal point of counterintelligence operations of British SOE and South African government.

Oswald Pirow declared his allegiance to Nazi Germany before most. The former Minister of Justice and Minister of Defense became an admiring proponent of national socialist cause during a 1933 European diplomatic expedition. He toured Germany as Justice Minister and organized meetings with high ranking Nazi politicians, Adolf Hitler and Herman Göring among the German leaders. In 1938, a second European overseas venture enabled Pirow to construct personal acquaintances with Italian and Spanish fascist politicians including Mussolini and Franco. In later recollections Pirow attempted to influence the national agenda in Germany by bargaining with Nazi officials about his government's non-interference on Eastern Europe, in exchange for Germany allowing the Jewish community to emigrate on mass from Europe.[16] Pirow was promoted to Minister of Defense, and consistently refused requests during 1938–39 for additional funding from South African Chief of the General Staff to combat pro-fascist subversive elements. He became convinced that European conflict an imminent Nazi victory was assured, in 1940 Pirow launched the radicalized New Order movement and obtained begrudging acceptance from Reunited National Party senior members.

Pirow transitioned in character and political agenda from parliamentarian and former adherent member of Hertzog's administration to a radicalized and more revolutionary figurehead. He endorsed Nazi Germany and organized the New Order movement alluding to the visions of a white racist state centered on fascist ideology, leadership by the "will of the Führer" and an authoritarian dictatorship. Democratic or parliamentary principles were rejected and further principles alluded to segregation. The extremist Afrikaner organizations and the momentum accumulated outflanked the National Party to a significant extent, the celebration of the Axis military triumphs emboldened the notion that Nazi political culture might be the future of humanity. This group took its name from his 1940 New Order in South Africa pamphlet in which Pirow embraced the ideology.[17] Extremely close relationships developed between Oswald Pirow and Hans Van Rensburg, the Ossewa Brandwag commander. He maintained communications with discerning outlets inside the Nazi infrastructure and accessed Van Rensberg as dependable conduit for transmitting messages to the Third Reich.[18] British intelligence reports analyzing the movement's interconnected structure identified a realistic conclusion that the central direction of Nazi mutual assistance pacts coveted Ossewa Brandwag rather than Malan.

Sabotage Operations Against Pro-British and South African Targets

The South African Police and Intelligence Records Bureau (IRB) jointly became conscious of sabotage incidents occurring predominantly in the Transvaal and Orange Free State regions from June to October 1940. Their surviving internal examination reports had attached the culpability squarely on Ossewa Brandwag's paramilitary division, the Stormjaers, the modus operandi was characterized as premeditated and coordinated, perpetuated at that time by an integrated nationwide movement. The majority of sabotage affected relatively small to medium scale targets, transport and communication networks, causing minimal degrees of damage. Ossewa Brandwag's cellular and compartmentalized structure represented a deviation from the normal local community-based networks. In railway worker and industrial communities of Orange Free State proclivities were documented towards the formation of cells affiliated to the OB, in this context interconnected systems of factory or workshop oriented cells were instituted. Elsewhere, similar underground divisions were founded, with the transportation and the railway communities targeted. In developing a national mass movement Rensburg's long-term objective was for the semi-independent paramilitary units to obstruct or control specific occupational and industrial zones. No longer a reactionary protest conference, Rensburg ensured that disaffected and decidedly pro–Nazi factions in his movement were influential across local government levels.[19]

Abwehr II in their capacity for masterminding covert operations were present in the dissident populations, encouraging sabotage and diverting requisite resources and finances to the Stormjaers or Ossewa Brandwag organizations. The Stormjaers with Van Heerien in command emerged as a militant splinter division of the OB, with originally the rather mundane intention of maintaining interest of younger members and disciplining their personnel for infractions, but evolved into a more radicalized culture. They engaged in hundreds of sabotage actions from March 1940 and Winter 1942 in Orange Free State and Transvaal, encompassing dismantling of telephone cabling and incendiary bombings of railways infrastructure, buildings and electricity pylons.[20] Punctually at 1:30 a.m. on the 29 January a sequence of violent explosions occurring at Vereeniging, Delmas and Potchefstroom had decimated power lines, ten substations conducting 80,000 to 132,000 volts were rendered inoperable. In January 1942, telegraph and telephone communication between Bloemfontein and the Union were dislocated in early hours of the morning. From January to March 1942 a heightened period developed with local governments and police registering widespread sabotage acts and disruptive incidents connected with the Stormjaers. They threatened to attacked high profile South African politicians including senior Nationalist Party leaders such as Dr. Hendrik Verwoerd.

Special Operations Executive (SOE) documents declassified in 2007 confirmed that a secret agreements existed between German military intelligence and OB leadership, equating to a strategic alliance. In exchange for mutual assistance the Nazi German government promised to guarantee that the Japanese refrained from entering South African territory under their control and similarly these geographic regions would be ignored by the Japanese Air Force and Navy stationed in Indian Ocean. Once Germany had defeated the Allied Nations theories were postulated envisioning the Stormjaers engineering general strikes to paralyze the Government facilitating the OB assembling a republican administration and replacing the present South African political structure. The Stormjaers collaborated with the Nazis during conflict's height utilizing other methods for instance harboring Axis POWs and escapees from South African Union usually in Portuguese East Africa. The POWs were transported to safer locations when necessary and distributed with supplies.[21]

A joint British Secret Information Service (MI5) and South African undercover investigation, covered in declassified files, disclosed reporting on sabotage actions allegedly perpetrated by Ossewa Brandwag and that organization's suspected connections with Nazi Germany. In February of 1942, a South African military intelligence (DDMI) operative penetrated an OB movement in Durban, his first report uncovered proposals by the underground faction to detonate explosives on trains and railway sections in Pretoria. He became associated with the Stormjaers organization in propitious course of investigations and recovered information that commanders in the Transvaal were receiving wireless transmissions directly from Berlin, imparting directives for sabotage missions and exchanging secret content matter. The Stormjaers had showed the undercover agent a recent communication from Nazi Germany to the effect that the Japanese planned on orchestrating an attack against Island View, and a substantive division of the German armed forces were now scheduled for deployment to South West Africa. Other nefarious incidents attributable to the OB sabotage actions were discovered. Another consignment of declassified Security Service (MI5) documents from 2002 determined how the South African Police's deliberative penetration of these subversive movements confirmed that the OB and affiliates garnished substantial disbursed financial and technical support from Nazi Germany and had equally uncovered the evidence concerning the organization director Van Rensburg, and his awareness and complicity in sabotage actions.[22] Van Rensburg was in communication with Dutch national H.J. Rooseboom, a Nazi intelligence asset, who was a former journalist and professor of literature. From 1939 to 1941 he was trained intensively and converted into a reliable conduit for communication with Nazi Germany via shortwave radio. He was protected by Rensburg and disseminated intelligence data to Berlin and apprised OB leadership of instructions. By mid–1940 he had become a prolific trafficker of sensitive content matter to Germany and public enemy number 1 to British intelligence, who while detecting his presence in radio intercepts struggled to ascertain his true identity.[23]

A tertiary splinter movement later gained some momentum within a power vacuum landscape, the X-group. Under the leadership of Pat Jerling this frustrated extremist faction declared loyalty to national socialism and dissatisfaction with Van Rensburg's authority and domination of the rebellious faction. This movement advocated more open collaboration with the Wehrmacht and Nazi Germany, military training for a damaging assailing of South African government and British armed forces and a definite break from the noncommittal pro-neutrality sections. However, these grand visions failed to materialize and the membership base dwindled. The military exercises and drilling had provocatively inciting government attention, motivating the initial campaigns of detention and internment targeting the OB leadership. This conversely at first prompted an acceleration in the rural expansion of support. Membership figures of Stormjaers fluctuated attaining a record of 12,500.[24]

The OB and other activist elements were declared a clear and present danger to state security by the Smuts governing administration, destruction of telephone and railway infrastructure and other violent actions were ubiquitous throughout the first six months of 1942. Other sabotage incidents from March to May 1942 comprised the destruction of railway telegraph and telephone cabling in various districts of Orange Free State. The detention of 350 police officers and 60 railway policemen on the suspicion of belonging to Stormjaers was followed by retaliatory campaigns of sabotage. Van Heerien intended to reconvene in Portuguese East Africa and remain in concealment at a German resident owned farm, a property screened previously as a secure and reliable rendezvous point after sabotage missions. Van Heerien identified as a ringleader was incarcerated in July 1942 and the other senior command personnel were rounded up. At Van Heerien's property the South African Police discovered boxes of dynamite, apparatus and glass tubing for the manufacturing of explosives and firearms. The contacts inside Nazi Germany were informed in July 1942 of the estimated statistics for the current membership numbers of the Stormjaers, decimated by the arrest and detention orders the answer was 3,500.[25]

South African police chief Colonel Kreft speculated in a memorandum to British intelligence in February 1941 that militant sabotage operations of the OB's inner circle were ordered by Leopold Werz, the German Consul in Lourenço Marques. In connection with an assessment of recent sabotage outrages in South Africa he delivered a verdict that Leopold Werz orchestrated these incidents and that ongoing collaboration was interdependent and regulated by transmitting encrypted messages. Kreft informed MI5 in June 1941 concerning other disclosures that permeating from their undercover agent working for South African military intelligence (DDMI) who infiltrated the Ossewa Brandwag's inner circle after months of groundwork. South African intelligence was now analyzing reproductions of the agent's reports detailing pro-fascist and Axis political movements including Pirow's New Order.[26] Pirow and Rensburg were discovered surreptitiously colluding in anti-government actions. In reality there appeared to be minimal functional difference between pro–Nazi Germany behavior of Pirow's New Orderites and the activists of Ossewa Brandwag. The interior police and wider security apparatus obviously did not regard on mass defending the Smuts administration as worthwhile, with security personal joining the rebellious groups. Chief of CID Colonel J.J. Coetzee, nominally responsible for investigation of subversive domestic elements, was a staunchly anti–British Afrikaner. Later, he was discovered to be duplicitously a member of Afrikaner Broederbond and had obstructed investigation wherever possible. Indeed, British and U.S. intelligence agencies acrimoniously reviled Coetzee and on occasion of Allied intelligence chiefs being informed of Coetzee's death in August 1944 little sympathy was expressed.[27]

While Oscar Pirow and Van Rensburg were undoubtedly prepared to accomplish objectives by unconstitutional and if necessary aggressive methods, at the other spectrum the Purified National Party and counterparts had rejected complete abolition of traditional parliamentary and constitutional systems. General Hertzog, Daniel Malan and many other senior Hereeigde Nasionale Partie members unquestionably developed underground contacts with Nazi representatives in their fervent antagonism and resistance to the Smuts government. Documented to the extent of back channel dialogue by Allied investigations.[28] But British MI5 analysis determined that full scale allegiance with Nazi Germany and collusion in military actions in their estimation had not occurred. In March 1943 a MI5 memo declassified in conjunction with batches of analysis reports on Rensburg in 2002 was unconvinced that a combined fusion of the opposition pro–Nazi factionalized groups inside South Africa could be accomplished. The surveillance and communication intercepts produced evidence of time consuming efforts at presenting a more united front, and previously in summer 1942 Hertzog was accepted as the Afrikaans leader by all but Malan's party.[29] Divisions protruded deep into foundations of the anti–Allied opposition movements and any confirmation dissipated with minimal accomplished. Hertzog died in 1943 and his replacement Havenga was not estimated to be harboring pro–German sentiments and merely advocated full neutrality.[30] The legitimate South African political opposition groups continued to navigate a tenuous game of clandestine support for Ossewa Brandwag and Dr. Hans Van Rensburg, without an irreversible confrontation being declared against Smuts's government or the British.

British and South African Security Force Response to Nazi Presence

The South African Union Defense Force had lobbied the national government for an intensive re-structuring and modernization of intelligence departments, countering the unfolding dissatisfaction with police response to internal dissent and foreign intervention in domestic politics. Reports of Nazi military intelligence considering Southern Africa to be an exigent region of interest and cultivating links with dissident groups outraged some sections of the military upper echelons. In May 1941, the South African government began to attach additional branches to their internal security network. Traditionally minor perfunctory intelligence agencies under the jurisdiction of the military and police were redeveloped into more prestigious national security departments. Within a matter of months the senior Intelligence Records Bureau (IRB) was established, reporting directly to Minister of Interior and the Prime Minister. The IRB functioned as the centralized coordination service for investigations and exchanging information between military intelligence and the other intelligence departments. In authorizing the standing priorities for the enactment of IRB the government had reinterpreted internal defense to be centered on preventing sabotage, surveillance of subversive communities and negating behavior which impaired security.

The British Special Operations Executive (SOE) commenced operations in European and pro-fascist populations in South Africa and the neighboring territory of then Portuguese East Africa. The Secret Information Service (MI6) and Security Service (MI5) also invested in elaborating on Southern African divisional teams, operatives specializing in counterespionage targeting the Nazi intelligence networks and representatives were appointed at the British embassies in the region. Across the wider Southern African region during intensification of World War II the possibility of increased Abwehr presence became a distinct priority.

Investigations into Stormjaers incidents and the suspected complicity of minimally sections of South African security infrastructure did not progress without provoking conflict, the factionalized culture and intensification of wartime emphasis exposed tensions. South African police and Criminal Investigation Department (CID) were perceived as encroaching on IRB's political operations and in particular the IRB's justification to behave with impunity as supreme institution in that domain, the monopoly on secret intelligence work was challenged and undermined in many quarters. A less than concrete compromise was finally achieved, the IRB now acknowledged as priority agency regarding political counterespionage activity but now subject to judicial procedure. Both sides expressed their dissatisfaction with agreements and no strict definitions were applied to general intelligence work or counterespionage. The IRB remained the dominant agency in military matters and a coherent focal point for Smuts's national defense policy and Ministry of Justice investigations. Surviving internal communication from the British delegations and South African security forces indicates that tensions gained irreparable footholds within British intelligence agencies and their South African counterparts. Competing national interests and varied differences surfaced to undermine ground level programs and posed unique challenges to SOE headquarters in London, conscious about avoiding destabilizing the relationships with South Africa and Portuguese territories.[31]

Smuts introduced new proclamations forbidding subversive materials in April of 1942 and instructed Criminal Investigation Department of South African Police to investigate individuals and organizations suspected of subversive or rebellious activities. The 1941 proclamations prohibited any civil servant from participating with or representing organizations classified as unlawful, deliberately in effect banning membership of Ossewa Brandwag and affiliates. The OB honorably discharged all the members who were prohibited from holding official membership under the new Act, subsequently retaining their support. Despite interruptions the reemphasized campaign against OB and Stormjaers in early 1942 exhibited the distinct symptoms associated with progress. Colonel Webster was a senior Security Service agent in Southern Africa, he had delineated assessment documents to his superiors explaining that Colonel Kreft of military intelligence (DDMI) had acquired possession after diligent police work from his personnel a directory of OB's prestigious and guarded inner circle. Webster had informed military intelligence about their interest in Ossewa Brandwag as it structurally encroached and overlapped an investigation they were enacting, Colonel Craft had responded with a surprised demeanor and inquired about the connections with Rensburg and other radicalized movements. Kreft was perhaps unconvinced about the British intelligence's genuine intentions and internal friction had developed previously in this unpredictable climate of multiple and sometimes competing foreign intelligence agencies.

Relationships however developed relatively smoothly and Colonel Kreft was a regular visitor to South Africa House in meeting with Colonel Webster, information and strategies were exchanged. Webster conveniently exploited the British Military Mission as believable cover camouflaging of his sensitive activities at MI5. The plethora of British intelligence agencies caused some confusion, with MI5, MI6, SOE and at times other organizations requesting information and contriving involvement in operations. Adhering to the security protocols reluctance was often practiced in revealing the exact nature of designations or mission specifics, despite their South African colleagues at times appearing unclear about which department they were dealing with.[32]

British intelligence working in conjunction with DDMI established X and Y signal stations to monitor communications and eavesdrop on Axis consulate traffic. Intercepting communiqués destined for Germany proved an essential technique in developing profiles of German undercover agents and from a counterintelligence perspective in derailing Axis missions. The X and Y stations decrypted Portuguese government codes among others, enabling a first-hand appreciation of that government's perspective interventions and colonial policies. British independently managed international listening stations also intercepted communications, but London headquarters was reluctant to employ the Ultra program and their awareness of Nazi encoding systems. Signals teams could expect minimal support in Southern Africa. In September 1941 United States

Radio Intelligence Division (RID) relay stations at Miami and Albuquerque intercepted unusual messages broadcasting from Lisbon, which apparently adopted language associated with coded information, over the course of two or three months tracking the location identified further messages with a similarly mysterious profile. Analysis by U.S. signals experts, primarily the FBI and Navy decryption teams, indicated the trafficking of covert intelligence information between Lisbon and two relay stations in Southern Africa. The codebreaking divisions after considerable time consuming labors translated considerable segments of the intercepted suspect transmissions, uncovering a clandestine communication network functioning as a channel for Nazi agents based in South Africa and surrounding territories. German agents were recorded reporting on the movements of ships, troops, and materiel and on political events.[33]

In the distant battlefields of Europe the Wehrmacht advancements of 1939–1940 had dispirited the opposing forces, from the occupation of France to other wartime deprivations. But early 1942 witnessed more ominous signs for the German military forces as their regiments were experiencing mounting difficult times. The Soviet Union invasion in Operation Barbarossa and other missions were not proceeding according to schedule and the causalities absorbed at an alarmingly faster rate than anticipated. U.S. forces were committed to unification with the Commonwealth against Germany's territorial ambitions. This uncertainty about the unpredictable expectations for Nazi Germany's future destiny appeared extremely counter-productive for a relationship building in Southern Africa. Allied commanders realized that a military intervention was necessary in Southern Africa, and the ensuing operations achieved some impressive results. The South African Prime Minister Jan Smuts professed concern to his supporters about Vichy French forces on Madagascar since the fall of France. With Japanese entrance into the conflict it appeared imperative to accomplish the securing of Madagascar, fundamental to controlling the Eastern border, before the Japanese launched their own incursion and possible invasion. Removing competition in the Western Indian Ocean and forming vantage points for mainland invasions of African territory was an irresistible prize. The planned invasion of Madagascar was code named Operation "Ironclad."

In May 1942 a joint British–South African taskforce headed for Madagascar and the first Allied amphibious assault of World War II was instigated by British forces at Diego Suarez on May 5. French Vichy armed contingents guarding the Diego Suarez base surrendered after a brief battle, Madagascar fell in November. Japanese naval threat to the Western Indian Ocean and Southern Africa terrain was realistically assessed as serious in the prelude to "Ironclad." By May 1942 the Japanese 8th Submarine Flotilla commanded by Rear Admiral Ishizaki was orchestrating assaults on shipping surrounding the coastal regions of Southern Africa. A combination of increasing South African antisubmarine air force and naval patrols traversing the coastal territories and Allied forces successful assault and capture of Madagascar motivated the Japanese 8th Submarine Flotilla in departing from the area.[34]

Portuguese East Africa Operations

Certain activities observed emanating from the legitimate diplomatic circles of Paul Trompke, German Consul stationed at Lourenço Marques (Maputo), Portuguese East Africa, were interesting to British intelligence. Lourenço Marques was an epicenter of intrigue and intelligence gathering, as the Portuguese East African (Mozambique) frontier was converted into a sanctuary for German, Italian and South African dissidents either evading or escaping from internment in the Union. Trompke was assisted in Consulate business by Consul Dr. Werz, Vice-Consul Schwartz and delegating under him four Consuls stationed in Beira, Port Amelia, Mozambique and Quelimane districts. Contemporary intelligence assessments verify that Paul Trompke the Consul General was unmasked prematurely as the senior commander of the German Abwehr intelligence system in that area, however speculation circled that Trompke represented a figurehead distorting the presence of other assets. This network extending throughout Southern Africa was hampered temporarily by the enforced shutdown of the German Embassy in South Africa and several sub-agents were instead installed inside Mozambique and Madagascar.

Minimal information was understood about Trompke, but MI5 analysis documents postulated that the diplomatic official was a convenient channel for more energetic subordinates. Other principal characters in this underground organization were code named Felix, Leo, O and Tino, the interactions of operatives was originally determined by the analyzing of shortwave radio intercepts, but genuine identities of agents remained a mystery in some instances for considerable time. Instructed by Abwehr II headquarters in Berlin, Trompke's network had instigated contact and controlled relationships with sympathetic South African politicians, collected any operational intelligence and assumed obligations in handling Portuguese agents collaborating with military intelligence in Lisbon. The transmission of shipping intelligence was referred to as clear primary objective.[35]

Rumors in Mozambique circulated that German Consul Dr. Werz was an alleged member of the Gestapo. Correspondents returning from Southern Africa to Britain reported on the accumulating evidence pertaining to suspicious activities of certain German consulate officials and citizens in the territory of Portuguese East Africa. The declassified 2002 Security Service (MI5) documents reveal that Leopold Wertz was in reality commanding the Abwehr intelligence services. The German consul inhabiting Lourenço Marques since January 1940 was a former senior leader at German Consulate in Pretoria who escaped internment to the still neutral Portuguese East Africa.[36] When the remaining diplomatic consular representatives proceeded to Germany on outbreak of conflict Werz had remained behind presumably with the objective of organizing the German populations within Mozambique and establishing information gathering and espionage services.

Born in Munich, the thirty-seven-year-old was architect and controller of German espionage actions inside Southern Africa, which possibly numbered approximately 100 agents. Characterized as educated and charming he maneuvered effortlessly inside diplomatic circles and social environments. Leopold Werz had discreetly engendered a substantial reputation for espionage against Allied interests in Portuguese East Africa and the neighboring Union. The Security Service report speculated that Leopold Werz controlled agents across Cape Town and Johannesburg, but it was later assessed that predominantly this information was obtained from seamen and travelers. By February 1941, it was a contention that German intelligence had assembled underground networks in Southern Africa and were organizing on a military basis German settlers inhabiting and working on agricultural plantations in both Portuguese East Africa and Bloemfontein with the exact magnitude of populations engaged widely debated. Leopold Werz resided in the Polana Hotel and under twenty-four hour surveillance he was monitored in conference daily with other local German nationals. His attachment to the German Consulate had conferred diplomatic immunity and investigations were required to maneuver carefully in avoiding ruptures with the Portuguese government.

Werz's confidant and personal secretary was an individual named Ernst Paasche, another former employee from Pretoria. This deployment shifted communications fundamentally as Paasche couriered advanced ciphers to the German Consulate in Lourenço Marques in August 1942, from that specific date Consular communications were transmitted in cipher rather than code. Trafficking of the secretive intelligence without enemy detection from this distant location back to Germany presented obstructions, the standard model involved field agents transferring data to Mozambique Consulate. Werz collated this content material and transmitted the communiqués to Germany. MI5 managed to retrieve resource files from the Consulate suggesting that Werz daily expenditure on cable charges fluctuated between £100 and £200.[37]

The Abwehr networks obtained its most prolific maritime and Naval information from a distinct principle source, "Leo," who collected intelligence about shipping in East Africa and Union ports. The nature of these updates implied strongly that Leo was coastal based. British intelligence field analysis reports described how on 20th February Leo confirmed SS Pennsylvania as docking "here yesterday," the identical maritime vessel that disembarked from Lourenço Marques on 19 of February. Therefore, evidence inferred that Leo resided somewhere in Portuguese East Africa. Nine reports from this source "Leo" intercepted commencing from the 13th of January covered primarily the Allied and merchant navy shipping movements with locations spanning from Cape Town, Port Elizabeth, Durban, East London, Mombasa and Dar-es-Salaam. Communiqués comprised statistics on the political and economic information from the Union, e.g., recruiting of women, war production and labor troubles. In general, MI5 analysis proposed that significant quantities of this content matter were classified as a type that could feasibly be obtained from travelers, sailors and local newspapers. This ubiquitous character was unmasked as Basil Batos a Greek national. MI5 noted with interest that on 20th February Trompke asked Berlin for an estimate of the value of Leo's reports.[38]

The German and Italian intelligence groups targeting shipping worked in close collaboration and in fact formed a joint organization commanded by Nils Olaf Paasche and later his replacement another German named Kolb. Campini, the Italian Embassy official, was unmasked by Allied counterintelligence as telegraphing messages with deliberate time delays containing articles identically found appearing inside Leo's reports, but without referencing original sources. From ten articles comprising Campini communiqués on March 1, eight were extracted verbatim from Leo's documents forwarded by Trompke on the 20th, 20th and 27th of February. Both Consulates reported with a comprehensive exactitude the arrivals and departures from Lourenço Marques. The messages intercepted originating at Lourenço Marques consulate in early 1943 contained information discussing the arrival of 1,000 Canadian forces in Cape Town and explained the reasons for reductions in traffic surrounding South Africa as extenuating from the deployment of naval vessels in the invasion of Europe. Leo appeared to be in communication with the American Consulate, collaborating with either logically an informant or at minimum had cultivating access to the circulars.[39] He alluded to "receiving daily information telegrams" conveniently procured by individuals stationed inside the Consulate, ascertaining from the documents that Russia was unenthusiastic about the recent Casablanca accords.

The South African admiralty confirmed generally that Leo correctly portrayed the itinerary of maritime vessels he reported on. MI5's evaluations indicated that after stringent analysis the reports originating from the source appeared to contain minimal content materials of "hot news," for example intelligence strategically focusing on submarines was absent, and obvious inaccuracies appeared. A notable example pertained to advanced and mistaken reportage featuring two convoy movements. Leo's reports definitely at times resorted unprofessionally to simply reproducing intel derived partially from gossip or scuttlebutt, proclaiming falsely that Soviet Marshall "Timoshenko was in the USA" and a discussion intercepted on "Turkey occupying the Dodecanese."[40]

A Nazi agent "Felix" was identified as the acting liaison component with pro–Axis subversive elements in the Union. His headquarters were in Pretoria and he controlled a wireless transmitter a distance away in the country. Felix was conversant with and implicated in the inner politics of Ossewa Brandwag. He was first detected by British intelligence after a radio message was intercepted on 16 December 1942, in which Paul Trompke stated that Felix "did not reply yesterday" and recommended suspiciously that at the next attempt the "call sign should be transmitted for fifteen minutes" before the telegram was then repeated. On the 11th of January 1943 Trompke broadcast to Berlin the "long Felix transmission," contents enclosed as recorded in British-South African X and Y intercepts, concerned the program for South African Parliament meetings on 16 January and a statement by the Minister of Labor. As dialogues progressed Felix confirmed that he had received the encoded transmissions and instructions demanding production of political and economic intelligence from Berlin on December 20th, 22, and 24. British intelligence opportunely gained an invaluable awareness of entangled inner workings of Trompke-Felix communication system. Trompke reassured Felix that secret ink and the German Press Code system, the standard methods of encryption in that theater, were not known by South African or Allied authorities.[41]

Technical limitations were exposed as Felix intimated to the Berlin reception stations that subsequent messages should be transmitted progressively as his operators were unskilled, by accounts the reason behind his unscheduled radio silence. The complex verification procedure was recounted in considerable detail, Felix would start transmitting on 41.6 meters with the call sign GQR. When the message was received in Germany the return acknowledgment should be confirmed in German Press Code or else English, and then Germany following procedures would begin launching transmission. Felix was instructed in another contingency measure to share his transmissions and returns involving Berlin with personnel on Lourenço Marques. He advocated against repetition of their transmissions every weekend as too dangerous in risking detection, but acquiesced on inducting security protocols. He transmitted military information and data on munitions and production, informing superiors on the future perceived capabilities of expropriating or trading Naval and shipping intelligence of interest to U-boats.

Abwehr Section II persistently instructed their African division to cultivate any contacts with movements sympathetic to national socialism and extreme right or white supremacist movements in the dominion. Felix as a seasoned and senior Nazi operative in South Africa cooperated extensively and was on confidential terms with the OB leader Van Rensburg. The dominant themes contained in the intelligence reports stemming from this secret collusion, clarified by the signals interceptions and decryptions, were the internal political information, military targets, advice on the German broadcasts from Zeisel and the Ossewa Brandwag affairs. His information production was assessed by MI5 to be much more detailed than Leo's and at minimum a moderate quantity of his military information was obtained from Van Rensburg. This sustained relationship with the various dissenting anti-government factions proved profitable. Felix as documented in intercepts provided information amounting to a warning to Berlin about Dutch agent Rooseboom who had incurred displeasure of Ossewa Brandwag. The British obtained improved awareness about the Stormjaers, depicted as comparable to Rensburg's personal paramilitary force. Information on the membership and the extent of individual control by loyalty to Hans Van Rensburg was compiled from this intrusion into communications.[42]

Van Rensburg was apparently in sufficiently close proximity with Felix to the extent of being regarded as a permanent asset by the Abwehr Section II, a formalized exchange system for relaying the communications was established. On January 1943 Felix reported that Van Rensburg had returned from a successful tour and extrapolated on the assertion that reactions to German propaganda were splendid. He advised to expect further military information on the South African and Allied forces in the region, and proceeded to disseminate statistics on machine factories in Pretoria, believed to be trafficked from sources by Van Rensburg. On 16 January Felix referred messages to Berlin with substance pertaining to the Stormjaers calculated as being in a suitable position to manufacture for the Ossewa Brandwag electoral turnout to assist in forming a coalition front against Smuts. By mid–1943 the identity of Felix continued to elude British intelligence. The adoption of the Press Code system by Felix implied that an individual with a journalist background was distributing plain language code telegrams to Lourenço Marques, embodied in this intelligence as corroboration appeared some themes contained in published local press reports. Fostering negative sentiments towards the South African government and destabilizing Allied military ventures increased in possibility with this collaboration. German operatives debating installing a secondary radio transmitter with Rensburg's assistance, Felix dispatched communiqués on the 10th of January 1943 attempting to persuade Berlin concerning his perception of events.

Your proposal to relay to the wireless station was understood. The chief difficulty is that there is no condenser. Spare parts must all be stolen, a dangerous business. The weak point is still the link between the source of the intelligence and the wireless station. Hence our proposal to send shipping intelligence direct to the U-boat. In spite of difficulty this will under all circumstances be done ... in agreement with Rensburg I make the following suggestion: A U-boat should also embark a (first-class) technician with several wireless sets, spare parts, money and weapons for sabotage, and should return with representative, and diamonds; details to be arranged.

Felix continued throughout first six months of 1943 to communicate using the shortwave radio transmitter to Berlin and Lourenço Marques, the latter insurance method it transpired involved Trompke forwarding messages to Berlin. Hypothetically if contingencies were obediently complied with as minimal direct contact as feasibly possible was practiced.[43] MI5 investigations realized that the security procedures of the Nazi coconspirators had resulted in "blind" transmissions. A level of compartmentalization was preferred and conformed to relatively consistently by most of the operators. Serious lapses in judgment and protocol definitely occurred, in some instances agent identities were accidentally revealed. Felix continued transmitting information at fixed times as instructed by his superiors, generally twice weekly post mid–1943. MI5 dossiers commenting on interceptions analysis identified limitations in the Felix operation, for instance the assessments implied that critical shipping information was inadequately collected. The Nazi agent's specialist skills did not MI5 had speculated penetrate dockyard or harbor installations. Two references to Saldanha Bay in Cape Province on the West coast, approximately 100 miles north of Cape Town, originating from Felix displayed conjecture with relevancy to convoy arrangements, but naval or military base information was not mentioned as standard. Presumably, this maritime content was therefore problematic to ascertain. In discussions the inventive proposal was circulated of developing South African Navy contacts in coordination with Nazi Germany, Felix had tailored a scenario for collecting shipping intelligence and for trafficking data to reach the nominated U-boat. A program to detect and evaluate Naval movements in the Cape of Good Hope region was a tempting interference in Allied defensive systems. Potential impediments were declared stemming from the communications unreliability and this planning deviation was later abandoned.

It was later determined by British investigators that Felix was a code name used to describe the mission and involved two agents—Lothar Sittig and Nils Olaf Paasche. The second individual was the brother of Leopold Werz's assistant who had escaped from Pretoria avoiding internment in the Union. He was inconspicuously smuggled into South Africa to improve communication, stationed after arrival at a country house serving as location of "Felix" radio transmitter.[44]

H.J. Rooseboom, the Nazi intelligence asset, previously corresponded with Berlin under this code name.

Uncovering Other Nazi Agents in Southern Africa

MI5 tentatively identified prominent Abwehr agent "Tino" as Eduardo Quintinho, a renowned Portuguese Marconi radio communications expert. In early 1942 Tino had pursued his supplementary assignment in identifying a residential setting for the installing of a radio system, he discussed with Trompke the necessity for new technology and requested further instructions from his couriering route in Lisbon about timescale and rapidness he should devote to fulfilling his objectives. "Tino" informed his handlers about operational constraints of both obtaining a residence and the specialist apparatus, purchases of these specific items would encourage attention from the authorities. Intercepts indicate he transmitted data continuously through his Iberian contacts until he was uncovered as a Portuguese radio operator. In an unfortunate miscalculation he was mistakenly addressed as "Tino" in a letter in July 1942.[45] Nils Olaf Paasche or possibly his brother was floated inaccurately in speculation on the genuine identity of an Abwehr agent connected to Felix, however gradually all German agents were unmasked and true identities discovered.

As ascertained from resume of intercepted messages the interconnected structures definitively encouraged mutual cooperation in the espionage field between the Italian Consul Umberto Campini and Werz. The Felix messages from early 1943 dealing with American journalists in South Africa and a statement that Saldamha Bay had been mandatorily restricted to convoy traffic was passed on to Campini. Two further encrypted messages regarding the production of shells for artillery weapons and Howitzers were also shared with Campini. The Italian Consul was accomplished enough to cultivate a source who produced accurate information on several occasions from steel works inside Pretoria. Intelligence in September 1943 was trafficked from Italian agents, functioning under the protection of the Consulate, to Leopold Werz, on surveillance missions recording movements of British military officer Brigadier Treatt and Captain Cruz in Lourenço Marques. The Germans were displaying some considerable interest in the Brigadier's expedition. Campini dispensed updates on meeting points and destinations of the two individuals and reproductions of the conversation fragments recovered by the surveillance teams. The intelligence analysis indicated that conversations were discussing a potential alliance and the drawing up of joint working documents.[46]

An important center of German subversive activity located in Portuguese East Africa was the Radio Club Mozambique in Matola district of Lourenço Marques. A major proportion of employees were pro–Axis powers, obliging confederates included the Publicity Manager Campo, apparently an ardent national socialist propagandist, a Miss Sadie Merber and a French citizen called Darnat who was a paid German informant. Sadie Merber formerly an employee of the South African Broadcasting Corporation was dismissed after conspicuously provoking the authorities suspicion and a consequent "blacklisting." This Radio Club constructed its own 10kw shortwave radio transmitter on the surface managed legitimately to transmit messages from Portuguese soldiers to relatives in Portugal. But agents expeditiously exploited this transfer stream for transmitting encrypted messages to colluding Nazi respondents in Lisbon. A scheme was proposed but later rejected to hijack the facility to transmit private German communiqués directly to Germany.

Erich Kellerman was believed accountable for operation of a portable shortwave radio system in an isolated neighborhood of Lourenço Marques. The transmitter technology was constructed by Kellerman, a representative of Germany private company Telefunken Berlin, possessing the ability to cover his sedulous obligations behind the respectable persona of a radio technician. He was closely connected with Leopold Werz who relayed instructions. It was observed with interest by the South African military intelligence (DDMI) and their counterparts at MI5 that recurrent incidents between periods of July–November 1943 implicated Erich Kellerman in receiving and transmitting information referencing Eduardo Quintinho (Tino). Further relationships embedded within the Abwehr's network were gradually being unraveled. The underground activities of the Radio Club Mozambique had been the subject of investigations by the DDMI. Departmental personnel in Pretoria informed headquarters that the transmissions intercepted from the radio station included messages in code which referred to troop movements and other military information in Southern Africa. Another proficuous information channel relied on by Leopold Werz was discovered in his secretive association with a German aviation engineer named Maas, conveniently employed by Delta Air service. Maas had inhabited Lourenço Marques and Portuguese East Africa since delivering the first junkers for Delta airways approximately two years before the outbreak of warfare. He resided at Polana Hotel, a hunting ground for German government assets and was observed by the surveillance teams almost daily in intimate and guarded conversation with Dr. Werz. At times he appeared to be conveying information from paperwork in his possession. As the Delta airways service operated between Germiston and Lourenço Marques it was possible for Maas to personally transport covert information from the South African territories to Dr. Werz.[47]

On the surface the command structure designated that the senior Nazi intelligence leader in Lourenço Marques, who theoretically outranked Werz, was Leidenberg. But since the conflict began he appeared to be demoted in a departmental reshuffling and was then replaced by Dr. Werz. He still inhabited Portuguese East Africa and certainly implicated himself in intelligence work, Leidenberg nominally handled an import and export channel in partnership with another German national named Schroeder. The latter departed for Europe shortly before the conflict in the company of several other German citizens before returning by Abwehr mandate.

Schroeder and Leidenberg resided on the East Coast of Africa for many years and developed intriguing connections inside resident Portuguese community. Recurrently they demanded financial reserves in their ventures for recruiting informants and sympathizers, who were generally high level government officials or business community leaders who could prove immensely useful. Leidenberg married a local Portuguese woman who was the daughter of a prominent local lawyer named Costa, on several occasions he displayed anti-British sentiments. But penetrating the Portuguese expatriate community demonstrated minimal value long-term and with only uneventful scuttlebutt uncovered and minor open source intelligence Berlin headquarters were reluctant on investing any additional resources. The Portuguese community in Lourenço Marques and Mozambique was evaluated by MI5 analysts as predominantly anti–German in sentiment. This applied particularly to the local and national government officials who on occasions publicly snubbed Colonel Werz and his associates. There were estimated to be approximately 250 to 300 German nationals inhabiting Portuguese East Africa and 80 of whom populated Lourenço Marques, but little sympathy was developed for national socialism or the Axis powers.

Portuguese military authorities and Vacuum and Shell oil companies organized special guards to prevent sabotage affecting their storage plants at Mazola as a consequent result of rumors that the fascist crews of German ships in Mozambique planned the destruction of petrol supplies and other facilities. But no single incident of sabotage or military assault were recorded against Allied industry or personnel stationed in Mozambique. The Portuguese military and diplomatic establishment were generally perceived as satisfactorily well disposed towards the Allied cause and obliged assistance in any respect that did not palpably conflict with the neutrality. As a result of the war business commerce was modest in both Lourenço Marques and Mozambique, but the conditions detached from conflict attained classification as relaxed and passive. Minimal transparent fear was detected about serious German intrigue in the colony.[48]

British and South African Security Response

By mid–1943 the momentum of World War II had contrived to surmount considerable military disadvantages against Nazi Germany and its declared interests, the OB was steadily depleted in both its members and ideological impetuous. Colonel Webster and the Special Operations Executive were instrumental in compiling concrete evidence for South African and indeed the Portuguese authorities that culminated in the expulsion in October 1944 of leading Nazi and spy master Dr. Leopold Werz from the Portuguese East African territory. The Portuguese government expelled other implicated and exposed Nazi diplomats, the South African authorities were anxious to avoid offending the Afrikaner communities on mass and generally adhered to a conservative strategy of interning suspected foreign intelligence assets. Requesting the presentation of evidence of individual connections to subversive or pro–Nazi movements before issuing a detention order. The Director of Military Intelligence noted in his biography that 6,636 people were interned during the war. Establishment of multiple British-South African liaison and intelligence gathering agencies that patrolled Southern Africa, while displaying fractured pressures and arguably threatened coordinated interactions, produced Allied successes that were impressive.

The Special Operation Executive (SOE) activities ranging from monitoring Axis wireless to identifying German agents were an influential intercession in preventing the pro–Nazi ambitions from becoming realized and defending Allied Navy and merchant convoys. The Cape was transformed into a route of vital performance in spring 1941, British intelligence services inside Central and Southern Africa had not developed substantially from the peace time standing before this period and minimal prominent enemy activity had in fact been observed. In July 1941, both SIS and DFO stations were established in multiple African cities continent-wide from North to South. South Africa presented a complex territory to secure, the borders with Mozambique and Lourenço Marques were classified as security risks pertaining to both intrusion and insurrection. Persistent vigilance against any domestic subversion and espionage then became mandatory. The British government invited the South African authorities to accept appointment of British Security Liaison Officers.[49]

The reputed penetrations by the Broederbond deeply into the local police and civil service provoked anxiety on the reliability of their South African counterparts. Agent Leo otherwise known as Basil Batos was captured in a joint British and South African operation, precipitating the detention of principal Nazi agents in underground networks connected insidiously to him. The operative confirmed a bargain agreement to reveal all to British intelligence.

He informed interrogators about the internal structure and operations of the Abwehr and a complete general picture was ascertained of insular field operations, missions and the senior command leadership. This information was passed on to the U.S. authorities and influenced their counterintelligence operations.

Documents declassified in 2003 portray the events surrounding a British intelligence mission to abduct an opposite number in Mozambique. In May 1943 a high ranking Axis agent was captured after an Allied task force apprehended Alfred Manna, an Italian operative associated with Campini and the Abwehr officials. The SOE in a meticulously well-orchestrated and executed mission, acting on intel from the Portuguese officials, decided on exploiting Alfred Manna's penchant for women. Adopting a honeytrap scheme the SOE managed on enticing the Italian foreign intelligence agent to a suitably discreet location, he was then kidnapped and transferred safely into British custody. Alfred Manna had a reputation for stubbornness and originally refused any inducements to cooperate, but in the course of confinement and assessing the various options he was converted into a cogent source of information in identifying other the Axis agents and confirming the analysis of radio intercepts.[50] Special Operations Executive records released in 2002 on Operation "Malpas" revealed a second more adventurous plot, undoubtedly inspired by the Manna kidnapping. SOE in South Africa had circulated scenarios for assassinating Leopold Werz their primary adversary at German intelligence. Initially, the SOE planned to eliminate him using a car bomb. London headquarters had intervened to ensure the mission's cancellation and proposals were not advanced forwards.[51]

Robey Leibbrandt and an Abwehr Inspired Revolution

Abwehr Section II at the Tirpitzufer headquarters was cognizant of the pro-fascist domestic environment, acknowledged as abundantly fertile for ideological development, and launched a daring scheme to orchestrate a revolution and permanently eradicate the pro–British Smuts government in the South African union. Robey Leibbrandt a South African Springbok boxer transformed into a fervent Nazi was instrumental to the Abwehr objectives. According to this proposition code named Operation "Weissdorm" Hans Van Rensburg, the Stormjaers and pro-fascist elements received direction from Germany to present all necessary operational support to the mission in June of 1941. The Abwehr's expectations rested almost entirely on Robey Leibbrandt, inducted as a Nazi government and military intelligence agent to command the mission.

Preparations were underway in April 1941 for dropping Leibbrandt on the Western coast of South Africa, and awaited final authorization, with a fundamental objective of assassinating Jan Smuts.

He was trained with comrades of the Brandenburgers at a sabotage training course of Abwehr II near Brandenburg an der Havel, in close proximity to the Quenz Lake facility staging Operation Pastorius training. Leibbrandt had gained some celebrity status in his native South Africa for exploits as a heavyweight boxer, he had competed commendably in the 1932 Olympics and was selected for the 1936 national team. A whistle-blower on November 13th, a German prisoner incarcerated in Cairo, Egypt, commented that Leibbrandt to his awareness participated at the Buckhart Parachutist Group in January–February 1941. The Cairo informant had referenced the objectives of Operation" Weissdorm" but was ambiguous on the exact pathway Leibbrandt would employ to infiltrate the border, theorizing either French Vichy vessel or a German submarine. Documents later confirmed that the French yacht Kyloe was the culprit vehicle under command of Lieutenant Cristian Nillsen.

Leibbrandt disembarked on the West African territory of Namaqualand in June of 1941.[52] According to his circular pamphlets and verbal statements by witnesses he returned to South Africa on the date of 15 June. Intelligence channels had in fact discovered and enacted the proceedings for tracking a small sailing ship which departed from Lisbon or possibly a port on the French coast to South Africa in the spring of 1941. Involvement of Abwehr II had been theorized, but the details were not checked upon further until after the landing.

Robey Leibbrandt had completed this Southern bound journey and recalled his appreciation at setting foot on South African territory again. He contacted a farmer loyal to Germany named Smit in the Springbok district as he was instructed to proceed in mission training and briefings in Berlin. The distant agrarian property was converted into a convenient temporary stopover location and hide-out for Abwehr field agents and escaped POWs with the owner's permission. Smit discreetly dispatched a messenger to inform the organizing secretary of the Ossewa Brandwag about their prestigious new arrival. After about three days Leibbrandt traveled to Cape Town by automobile and was introduced to the local branch organizing secretary. The South African apprised him of the mission's purpose and announcing Abwehr II's instructions on preparing the underlying foundations for a second phase. He remained in Cape Town for approximately a week and then journeyed to Bloemfontein brokering an interchange with an individual called De Jager, an Assistant Commandant General of the OB, with directives from Berlin for relaying to Van Rensburg. Discussions were consequently surreptitiously activated with figures in the Ossewa Brandwag leadership exactly as military intelligence in Berlin had preconceived. Leibbrandt investigated the possibility of joint action in assassinating Smuts and bringing about the coup d'état. Lacking adequate arms supplies in South Africa, he initiated contact with Stormjaers commanders and was smuggled to Pretoria for a meeting with Rensburg personally.

Leibbrandt in dialogue with Rensburg elaborated on Abwehr expectation that the OB General form an integral link in the months ahead, and submitted proposals concerning re-organization of the existing movement. It appears that Rensburg and De Jager had both expressed doubts and ominously did not conform to the recommendations forwarded by Leibbrandt. Unconvinced about the prevailing wisdom of counting on Van Rensburg and under present conditions focused on ensuring continuity of operations Leibbrandt next announced a decision to establish an independent organization, entitled "Nasionaal Sosialistiese Rehelle." He contacted prominent and well connected nationalist individuals and at secretive meetings with the nominated persons recollected his story of being dispatched to South Africa with mandate by the Nazi Government. He unreservedly divulged to his audiences that Germany had supplied him with a radio transmitter, a secret code and approximately ten thousand U.S. dollars. The resources represented a calculated investment to enable the pro-fascist underground segments to re-engineer insular scattered movements and ferment rebellion.[53]

Reaching the conclusion that a trustworthy and distinct movement was necessary to maintain the duration of activity that was essential to accomplishing the mission Leibbrandt rejected the OB as a feasible vehicle. His passion and fanaticism was appealing to some grassroots sentiments and he managed to encourage defections from the Ossewa Brandwag membership base. Leibbrandt and his supporters traveled extensively through the Transvaal and Orange Free State areas, and obtained he further advocates and dejected followers to his organization. When the activities of the movement had sufficiently covered both regions an attempt was implemented to contact the headquarters in Germany by radio utilizing a telegraphist employed in a compromised post office at Potchefstroom seconded to the mission. But reception by Berlin was not confirmed.

At about this time incidents of sabotage occurred at various places in the Transvaal, and it is clear from direct and circumstantial evidence that these crimes were being perpetrated by members of Leibbrandt organization. He managed to commandeer a personal paramilitary force of 60 resistance fighters he was instructing from inside Transvaal. In September 1942 after a violent confrontation and intense gun battle with South African soldiers confusion had descended on the movement as members scattered. Leibbrandt was uncontactable and presumed missing in the ensuing aftermath, it transpired the revolutionary leader had departed in time fortuitously to forestall capture, the South African police were searching all suspected residence for the wanted man.

Nothing however ultimately came of Leibbrandt's attempted infiltration of South Africa. His megalomania and decision to exert authority over the existing movements had counterproductively generated tangible acrimony and sufficient deterrence for domestic movements to reject cooperation with him. The individual earmarked in planning stages as an indispensable contact Van Rensburg had disavowed personal involvement with Leibbrandt.[54] Documents first drafted by MI5 in 1942 and released in 2002 delved intriguingly into the background of the mission and its failure. It appears that Rensburg, almost precisely at the halfway mark in the operation, informed on Robey Leibbrandt to the South African government himself.

SOE reports indicated that Van Rensburg had severe reservations and questioned Leibbrandt's function in South Africa within the movement, in particular his assuming of hands-on control. South African DDMI official Major Luke covered the circumstances in an official assessment and concurred that information leading to the arrest was supplied by Van Rensburg. A definite split occurred between the Ossewa Brandwag and Leibbrandt, disastrously for the operation.[55] The arrests took place on 24 December of 1941 without the fundamental stages being implemented by the cohorts. Leibbrandt was arrested during an automobile journey from Pretoria destined for Johannesburg, in company with various supporters. Following detentions other individuals implicated in the conspiracy were rounded up. Leibbrandt was subsequently prosecuted on charges of high treason and sentenced to death, with several others receiving convictions and prison sentences. In the event, Leibbrandt's death sentence was commuted and he was released with a majority of wartime internees and prisoners in 1948.

Conclusion to the Southern African Question

In Europe, the Allied Nations from 1944 decisively reversed Germany's earlier succession of victories and the Nazi's vision of the continent and a post-war fascist utopia was crumbling. On the Russian front the material deprivations and incessant advancement of Soviet Red Army forces were causing traumatic damage to morale, many of Hitler's finest generals were exhibiting inclinations of deserting the sinking ship. The Axis coalition was hampered with Italy's withdrawal and switching of allegiances to the Allies, now Germany and Japan alone would continue hostilities. It was distinctly observable that the once indomitable Wehrmacht that achieved significant military accomplishment on battlefields from East to West was in retreat on all frontiers. Industrially, the Allied nations and Soviet Union were out competing their enemies, with Russian and American factories producing munitions and war materials at accelerated rates, not feasibly attainable to the Fatherland.

Conspiracies for a South African revolution failed to develop into fruition and the sabotage campaigns were exhibiting a deficiency in coherent methods and the necessary financial capabilities. In 1944, the prospects for a Nazi inspired changeover in government appeared more distant than ever previously. The OB had placed its visionary ideology on a German and Axis power victory in World War II, since this would logically achieve the collapse of the British Empire. The reversal of Axis advancement and impending demise produced sobering repercussions with the Ossewa Brandwag's membership plummeting. Elements of domestic communities previously aligned with Nazi and Axis objectives became disillusioned with some of the non-mainstream extreme right in South Africa.

Union citizens contravening the emergency regulations proclaimed by the Smuts government and especially those suspected of subversive activities were held under the War Measures Act without trial and faced internment, in company with the alleged enemy spies and foreign nationals implicated in subversive acts. In 1944, Jan Smuts had demanded that all Broederbond members still attaining public service occupations resign either from that movement or their government positions. After this order, 1,094 Broederbond members decided on resigning from the organization but an even higher proportion abandoned their civil service posts. Investigations of pro–Nazi influences were directed by IRB and South African police authorities inevitably at their department's internal rank and file. This unraveling of coconspirators and sympathizers in the police forces by May 1942 accounted for over 400 arrests.

Successively protracted groups of political prisoners were interned continuing up until August 1945, severely disrupting organization tactics and Abwehr capability in penetrating sensitive factions. Ossewa Brandwag's rapid evolution from cultural organization to a movement practicing transparent commitment to the disruption of the South Africa interior represented a legitimate security risk, but the internment campaigns as popular support fragmented in the culminating months of 1944 proved insurmountable blows. High profile individuals in Dr. J.D. Vorster and van der Bergh both outspoken Nazis committed to Hitler's revolution were arrested and interned, incarcerated by the government under wartime emergency laws for their subversive activities. The former was later convicted of spying and sentenced to three years imprisonment.

By 1944, Van Rensburg was interned and removed from the organization he conspired with in relentlessly promoting his interpretation of the Afrikaner future. The consequence was a reduction of political and social relevance. Bruising conflicts with traditional heartland communities had occurred, but Malan managed on retaining control of the National Party now absorbing sections deserting from other disparate factions. With the OB's virtual obsolescence the allegiance of Broederbond and other Afrikaner cultural and economic organizations was directed to Malan's camp.[56] As the prospects of a German victory irreversibly dwindled the legitimate concerns about secret agreements or espionage operations stemming from collaborations with parliamentarians and political class diminished.

Chapter Notes

Introduction

1. Jefferson Adams, *Historical Dictionary of German Intelligence* (Lanham, MD: Scarecrow, 2009), 446.
2. Michael Herman, *Intelligence Power in Peace and War* (UK: Cambridge University Press, 1996), 16.
3. Richard Basset, *Hitler's Spy Chief: The Wilhelm Canaris Betrayal; The Intelligence Campaign Against Adolf Hitler* (New York: Bantam Doubleday, 2013), 114.
4. Norman Tobias, *The International Military Encyclopedia* (Gulf Breeze, FL: Academic International, 1992), 175.
5. Helmut Krausnick et al., *Anatomy of the SS State* (New York: Walker, 1968), 261.

Chapter 1

1. Henry L. Stimson, Diary, September 26, 1942, Roll 7 at 128–29, Manuscript Room, Library of Congress.
2. Curtis Munson, Summary of Report on Program for Loyal West Coast Japanese, December 19, 1941, A7378, Reel 10, Box 11, University of Washington Libraries.
3. Naval Historical Center (U.S), Office of Naval Intelligence, *United States Naval Administration in World War II* (Dept. of the Navy, Naval Historical Center, Washington, D.C.).
4. Barry M. Katz, *Foreign Intelligence: Research and Analysis in the Office of Strategic Services, 1942–1945* (Cambridge, MA: Harvard University Press, 1989), 131.
5. Richard Gid Powers, *Broken: The Troubled Past and Uncertain Future of the FBI* (New York: Simon & Schuster, 2004), 188.
6. Presidential Military Order, June 13, 1942, Administrative History, Office of Strategic Services Records, RG226.1, NARA.
7. D.M. Ladd to the Director, October 26, 1942, SIS Administrative Records, FBI Files, RG65 Folder 6, File 64-4104, NARA.
8. Jens-Uwe Guettel, *German Expansionism, Imperial Liberalism and the United States, 1776–1945* (UK: Cambridge University Press, 2012), 206.
9. Leland V. Bell, "The Failure of Nazism in America: The German American Bund, 1936–1941," *Political Science Quarterly* 85 (December, 1970), 598.
10. Jens-Uwe Guettel, *German Expansionism*, 204.
11. Hans Luther, Report to German Foreign Office, "Cultural Policy Questions in the United States," June 28, 1935, series C, vol.4, ADAP.
12. "A Report on the Un-American Activities of Various Nazi Organizations and Individuals in the United States," 76th Congress, 3rd session, Appendix Part 2, House Report 153(A).
13. Special House Committee, Investigations of Nazi and Propaganda, 74th Congress, 1st session, House Report 153(A).
14. German American Federation Bund, FBI Files, Seized Records, RG131.2, NARA.
15. J. Edgar Hoover, Memorandum to assistant attorney general McMahon, March 15, 1939, German American Federation Bund, FBI Files, Seized Records, RG131.2, NARA.
16. Ernest Lundeen, Letter to George Viereck, 1937–1940, Papers of George Sylvester Viereck, Special Collections Department, University of Iowa Libraries, Iowa City.
17. Francis MacDonnell, *Insidious Foes: The*

Axis Fifth Column and the American Home Front (UK: Oxford University Press, 1995), 126.

18. George Viereck, Letter to Franz von Papen in Berlin, August 20, 1938, Papers of George Sylvester Viereck, Special Collections Department, University of Iowa Libraries.

19. American Fellowship Forum, FBI Files, RG65 HQ 0010003415, NARA.

20. E.A. Tamm, Memorandum for the Director, German American Federation Bund, Seized Records, RG131.2, NARA.

21. Sumner Welles, Memorandum to Franklin D. Roosevelt, July 27, 1942, FDR Library.

22. MacDonnell, *Insidious Foes*, 32.

23. Ignatz Griebl, Statement, State Department Records, RG59 862.20211, Box 6773, NARA.

24. William Breuer, *Hitler's Undercover War: Nazi Espionage Invasion of the USA* (New York: St. Martin's, 1989), 16.

25. Ignatz Griebl, Statement, State Department Records, RG59 862.20211, Box 6773, NARA.

26. Ibid.

27. Cordell Hull, *Memoirs of Cordell Hull*, vol.1 (New York: Macmillan, 1948), 1102.

28. Leon Turrow, *The Nazi Spy Conspiracy in America* (Freeport, NY: Books for Libraries, 1969), 17.

29. "Espionage Report on Rumrich," FBI Files, RG65 37193, Serial 332, v. 1, NARA, 40.

30. Ron Grossman, "Hero, Traitor," *Chicago Tribune*, 1989.

31. Charles Whiting, *Hitler's Secret War: The Nazi Espionage Campaign Against the Allies* (UK: Pen & Sword Books, 2000), 33.

32. Guenther Rumrich, Correspondence alias "Crown," January 1938–April 1938, Security Service, KV 2/3421, National Archives.

33. Guenther Rumrich, Statement, FBI Files, RG59 6773, NARA.

34. "Espionage Report on Rumrich," FBI Files, RG65 37193, serial 332, v. 1, NARA, 40.

35. J.D. Swenson, Special Agent Report Re German Activities in the United States, October 10, 1939, FBI Files, RG65 7560-3022, NARA.

36. Francis MacDonnell, *Insidious Foes: The Axis Fifth Column and the American Home Front* (UK: Oxford University Press, 1995), 56.

37. Judge John Knox, Comments, December 2, 1938, *United States of America vs. Otto Voss et al.*, Southern District of New York, United States District Court.

38. Walter Kappe, Personal File, FBI Files, RG65 9811449, NARA.

39. Erwin Lahousen, Affidavit A, January 21, 1946, Nuremberg War Crime Tribunal, Vol. 8.

40. Ibid.

41. German Saboteurs Landed in the USA from U-boats, 1942, Secret Service, KV3/413, 1942, 10.

42. Bodo Herzog, *60 Jahre Deutsche Uboote* (München: J. F. Lehmann, 1968), 239.

43. Nigel West, *Historical Dictionary of International Intelligence* (Lanham, MD: Scarecrow, 2006), 46.

44. "Decree on the Command of the Armed Forces by Adolf Hitler," *Reichsgesetzblatt*, RGBI, 5 Part 1, February 4, 1938, p. 111.

45. Wilhelm Canaris, Letter to Reinhard Heydrich, February 7, 1941, RW 5 v.690, BA-MA.

46. John H. Waller, "The Double Life of Admiral Canaris," *International Journal of Intelligence and Counter Intelligence* 9, no. 3 (1996), 287.

47. Walter Schellenberg, *Walter Schellenberg: The Memoirs of Hitler's Spymaster* (London: Andre Deutsch, 2006), 400.

48. Richard Basset, *Hitler's Spy Chief: The Wilhelm Canaris Betrayal; The Intelligence Campaign Against Adolf Hitler* (New York: Bantam Doubleday, 2013), 231.

49. Major General Lahousen, Diary, April 16, 1942, War Crimes Records, RG 238 Entry 2, Box 18, NARA.

50. Ibid.

51. George Dasch, FBI Statement, FBI Files, RG65 98-10288-1163, NARA.

52. German Saboteurs Landed in the USA from U-boats, 1942, Security Service, KV3/413, National Archives, p. 10.

53. George Dasch, Statement to FBI Special Agent Traynor, Defendant's C-1 original, June 25, 1942, Office of the Judge Advocate General Records (Army), RG 153, NARA.

54. Walter Kappe, Personal File, FBI Files, RG65 9811449, NARA.

55. Ernst Burger, FBI Statement, FBI Files, RG65 98-10288-1172, NARA.

56. German Saboteurs Landed in the USA from U-boats, 1942, Security Service, KV3/413, National Archives, p. 12.

57. Kerling letters, Letter to Marie Kerling, FBI Files, RG65 98-10288-2088, NARA.

58. Richard Quirin, Statement, July 3, 1942, Office of the Judge Advocate General Records (Army), RG 153, NARA.

59. Saboteur School of Axis Powers, Sabotage Documents, FBI Files, RG65 98-18606, NARA.

60. Richard Quirin, Statement, July 3, 1942.

61. Ibid.

62. German Saboteurs Landed in the USA from U-boats, 10.
63. D.M. Ladd, Memorandum for Mr. Tamm, June 22, 1942, FBI Files, RG65 98-15929, NARA.
64. George Dasch, FBI Statement, FBI Files, RG65 98-10288-1163, NARA.
65. Ibid.
66. George John Dasch, *Eight Spies Against America* (New York: R.M. McBride, 1959), 98.
67. Dennis L. Noble, *The Beach Patrol and Corsair Fleet* (Washington, D.C.: Coast Guard Historian's Office, 1992), 11.
68. George Dasch, FBI Statement, FBI Files, RG65 98-10288-1163, NARA.
69. George, Dasch Statement to FBI Special Agent Traynor.
70. German Saboteurs Landed in the USA from U-boats in 1942, Secret Service, KV3/413, National Archives, p. 2.
71. "Spy Crew Escaped from a Coastguard," *New York Times*, June 28, 1942.
72. Michael Dobbs, *Saboteurs: The Nazi Raid on America* (New York: Knopf, 2004), 37.
73. Francis Biddle, Memo to FDR, June 19, 1942, FBI File 146-7-4219, Justice Folder, FDR Library.
74. Ibid.
75. German-Americans of Chicago, August 24, 1942, Office of Strategic Services Records, RG226 Int 13 GE345, NARA.
76. FBI Memorandum, June 25, 1942, FBI Files, RG65 98-10288, NARA.
77. George Dasch, Statement to FBI Special Agent Traynor.
78. Ibid.
79. Dobbs, *Saboteurs*, 116.
80. P.E. Foxworth, Assistant Director, Memorandum to New York Director, August 23, 1942, FBI Files, RG65 9815929, NARA.
81. Francis Biddle, *In Brief Authority* (Garden City NJ: Doubleday), 1962, 337.
82. Major General, Lahousen, Diary, June 27, 1942, 1933-1946, War Crimes Records, RG 238 Entry 2, Box 18, NARA.
83. German Saboteurs Landed in the USA from U-boats in 1942, 75.
84. Edgar J. Hoover, Memorandum to Marvin McIntyre, June 22, 1942, Report 2192, Box 16, FDR Library.
85. Henry L. Stimson, Diary, June 28, 1942, Roll 7, 128-29, Manuscript Room, Library of Congress.
86. Major General Cramer, Letter to Secretary Stimson, June 28, 1942, Myron Cramer, Official Military Personnel File, National Personnel Records Center, St. Louis, Missouri.

87. Francis Biddle, Memorandum to FDR, June 30, 1942, FDR Library.
88. Franklin Roosevelt to Attorney General Francis Biddle, June 30, 1942, Justice Department 1938-44, PSF 76, FDR Library.
89. Franklin Roosevelt to Attorney General Francis Biddle, June 19, 1942, Justice Department 1938-44, PSF 76, FDR Library.
90. Denying Certain Enemies Access to the Courts, July 2, 1942, p. 75, Proclamation 2561, President Franklin Roosevelt.
91. Dobbs, *Saboteurs*, 210.
92. Trial transcript, Court-Martial Case Files, CM 334178, "German Saboteur Case," Volume 10 of 18, Office of the Judge Advocate General Records (Army), RG 153, NARA.
93. Ex Parte Quirin, U.S. Supreme Court, July 31, 1942, 17 AILC, 4-85.
94. *United States v. Hebert Haupt*, June 29, 1943, 136 F.2d 661, U.S. Court of Appeals, Seventh Circuit.
95. George Lardner, Jr., "Nazi Saboteurs Captured," *Washington Post Magazine*, January 13, 2002, p. 16.

Chapter 2

1. Richard Basset, *Hitler's Spy Chief: The Wilhelm Canaris Betrayal: The Intelligence Campaign Against Adolf Hitler* (New York: Bantam Doubleday, 2013), 117.
2. Reinhard R. Doerries, *Hitler's Intelligence Chief: Walter Schellenberg* (New York: Enigma Books, 2008), 18.
3. Helmut Krausnick et al., *Anatomy of the SS State* (New York: Walker, 1968), 260.
4. Earl Morrell, New York SOI Organization, July 10, 1941, Political Warfare Executive, PRO F0898, File 103, National Archives.
5. Memorandum to Secretary of State, September 5, 1941, Adolf Berle Diary, Berle Papers, 0308.
6. "Espionage Report on William Sebold," FBI Files, RG65 Serial 332, v. 1, 3713, NARA, 236.
7. Ibid.
8. Michael J. Sulick, *Spying in America: Espionage from the Revolutionary War to the Dawn of the Cold War* (Washington, D.C.: Georgetown University Press; Reprint edition, 2014), 139.
9. "Sebold's Testimony," *U.S. vs. Herman Lang*, US District Court for East District New York, RG21, NARA
10. Raymond J. Batvinis, *Hoover's Secret War Against Axis Spies: FBI Counterespionage*

During World War II (Lawrence: University Press of Kansas, 2007), 227.

11. Frederick Duquesne Case File, FBI Files, RG65 1819, NARA, 4.

12. "Fritz Joubert Duquesne," Obituary, *Time*, June 4, 1956.

13. Fritz Joubert Duquesne, Secret Service, KV2/1955, National Archives.

14. FBI Surveillance of William Sebold, March 28, 1940, Duquesne Spyring, FBI Files, RG65 1819, NARA.

15. *Frederick Duquesne Case File*, FBI Files, RG65 1819, NARA, 31.

16. FBI transcript of electronic surveillance of William Sebold's office, April to May 1940, *U.S. vs. Herman Lang*, U.S. District Court for East District New York, RG21, NARA.

17. William Sebold, Personal File, FBI Files, Sections 1 & 2, RG65 100 HQ3738, NARA.

18. Rudolf Ebeling, Statement, Duquesne Spyring, FBI Files, RG65 1819, NARA, 132.

19. FBI Surveillance of William Sebold and Eichenlaub, May 16, 1940, Duquesne Spyring, FBI Files, RG65 1819, NARA.

20. FBI transcript of electronic surveillance of William Sebold's office, May 16 to June 24, 1940.

21. Sulick, *Spying in America*, 140.

22. William Sebold, Personal File, FBI Files, Sections 1 & 2, RG65 100 HQ3738, NARA.

23. Bayard Stockton, *Flawed Patriot: The Rise and Fall of CIA Legend Bill Harvey* (Washington, D.C.: Potomac, 2007), 2.

24. Frederick Duquesne Case File, FBI Files, RG65 1819, NARA, 35.

25. Mail intercepts of William Sebold, June 2 to July 16, 1940, FBI File, RG65 1819, NARA.

26. Edmund Carl Heine, Subject File, Duquesne Spyring, FBI Files, RG65 1819, NARA.

27. F.J. Duquesne, Letter to Chief of Chemical Warfare Service, December 26, 1940, Duquesne Spyring, FBI Files, RG65 1819, NARA.

28. Frederick Duquesne Case File, FBI Files, RG65 1819, NARA, 7.

29. Mail intercepts of William Sebold, June 2 to July 16, 1940.

30. Edmund Carl Heine, Subject File, Duquesne Spyring, FBI Files, RG651819, NARA.

31. FBI transcript of electronic surveillance of William Sebold's office, April to May 26, 1940.

32. FBI Surveillance of William Sebold and Waalen, January 12, 1941, Duquesne Spyring, RG65 1819, NARA.

33. Heinrich Clausing, Statement, Duquesne Spyring, FBI Files, RG65 1819, NARA, 134.

34. FBI transcripts of William Sebold and Roeder meeting at Japanese restaurant, May 22, 1941, Duquesne Spyring, FBI File, RG65 1819, NARA.

35. Edgar J. Hoover, Letter to Watson, June 3, 1940, OFI0b, Box 3, FDR Library.

36. "Espionage Report on Ludwig," FBI Files, RG65 Serial 332, v. 1, 3713, NARA, 236.

37. Ibid.

38. Batvinis, *Hoover's Secret War*, 168.

39. *U.S. vs. Herman Lang*, U.S. District Court for East District New York, RG21, NARA.

40. *U.S. vs. Ebeling*, 146 F 2d 254, U.S. Court of Appeals, Second Circuit.

41. *United States vs. Heine*, 149 F.2d 485, U.S. Court of Appeals, Second Circuit.

42. Krausnick et al., *Anatomy of the SS State*, 260.

43. Marie Vassiltchikov, *Berlin Diaries, 1940–45* (New York: Vintage, 1998), 211.

44. Basset, *Hitler's Spy Chief*, 180.

45. Oster, Hans, Personal Service Record, Folio 87, IfZ.

46. Himmler to Schellenberg, Feb 25, 1943, Berlin Documentation Centre Microfilm, A3343, SSO-074B.590, NARA.

47. Erich Gimpel, *Spy for Germany*, with Will Berthold (London: Robert Hall, 1957), vii.

48. Edgar J. Hoover, Letter to Harry Hopkins, February 9, 1945, Manhattan Project, RG77 6248, NARA.

49. Report on the Interrogation of German Agents Gimpel and Colepaugh, January 13, 1945, Chief of Naval Operations, RG38 21, NARA.

50. Ibid., 8.

51. Gimpel and Berthold, *Spy for Germany*, 14.

52. Ibid.

53. Report on the Interrogation of German Agents Gimpel and Colepaugh, January 13, 1945, Chief of Naval Operations, RG38 21, NARA.

54. Gimpel and Berthold, *Spy for Germany*, 57.

55. Ibid., 111.

56. Report on the Interrogation of German Agents Gimpel and Colepaugh, January 13, 1945.

57. David Kahn. *Hitler's Spies: German Military Intelligence in World War II* (New York: Macmillan, 1978), 24.

58. Richard Willing, "The Nazi Spy Next Door," *USA Today*, February 27, 2002.

59. Gimpel and Berthold, *Spy for Germany*, 74.

60. "Governor Island Spy Trail Resumed," *Daily Chronicle*, February 14, 1945.

Chapter 3

1. James J. Barnes and Patience Barnes, *Nazis in Pre-War London, 1930–1939: The Fate and Role of German Party Members and British Sympathizers* (Sussex, 2005), 46.
2. Memorandum of conversation between the Fuhrer and Horace Wilson, September 27, 1938, D/11, No 634, DGFP, 965.
3. Erich Kordt, *Nicht aus den Akten* (Stuttgart: Union Deutsche Verlagsgesellschaft, 1950), 235.
4. Richard Basset, *Hitler's Spy Chief*, 174.
5. David T. Zabecki, *World War II in Europe: An Encyclopedia*, vol. 1 (New York: Routledge, 1999), 1217.
6. Walter Görlitz, *The Memoirs of Field-Marshal Wilhelm Keitel* (Lanham, MD: Rowman & Littlefield, 2000), 117.
7. Kurt Assmen, *Operation Sea Lion*, Official History, 1946, Cabinet Office Records, CAB 101/347, National Archives.
8. Sir David Petrie, Report on the Security Service, Cabinet Office Records, CAB 301/25, National Archives.
9. James J. Barnes and Patience Barnes, *Nazis in Pre-War London, 1930–1939: The Fate and Role of German Party Members and British Sympathizers* (Sussex Academic, 2005), 252.
10. Oliver D. Hoare, *Camp 020: MI5 and the Nazi Spies* (London: National Archives, 2000), 114.
11. Ben Macintyre, *Agent Zigzag: The True Wartime Story of Eddie Chapman; The Most Notorious Double Agent of World War II* (London: Bloomsbury, 2010), 46.
12. Hans-Adolf Jacobson and Charles Burdick, *The Halder War Diary*, February 18, 1940 (New York: Presidio, 1988).
13. Tyler Kent, Personal File, Dec 1944–Oct 1949, Security Service, KV2/54, National Archives.
14. Joseph E. Persico, *Roosevelt's Secret War: FDR and World War II Espionage* (New York: Random House, 2001), 24.
15. General Interrogation of Tyler Kent by Ambassador Kennedy, May 20, 1940, FDR Library.
16. Hamburg-Berlin Reports, September 18, 1940, German Military Records, RG242 T77 1540, NARA.
17. Major Ritter, Interrogation report, January 16, 1946, Agent Snow—Selected Historical Papers, Security Service, KV2 451, National Archives.
18. Walther Brauchistch, Directive on September 9, 1940, RW35 241, German Military Archives.
19. Major Ritter, Interrogation report, January 16, 1946.
20. Ibid.
21. Jose Waldberg, Interrogation by Colonel Hinchley Cooke, Carl Meier Personal File, Security Services, KV 2/1700, National Archives.
22. "Landing of Enemy Agents," Home Office Memorandum, September 6, 1940, Kieboom, Charles Albert Van Den, Home Office Records, HO 144/21472, National Archives.
23. Immigration Officer Report on Charles Albert Van Den Kieboom, September 5, 1940, Charles Albert Van Den Kieboom, Home Office Records, HO 144/21472, National Archives.
24. Ibid.
25. Dr. Friedrich Praetorius, Interrogation Report, Oct 1945, FBI Files, RG65 IWG 169, NARA.
26. Gosta Caroli, Statement to Captain Stephens, September 7, 1940, Gosta Caroli—Personal File, Security Service, KV 2/60, National Archives.
27. Ibid.
28. Gosta Caroli, Statement to Captain Stephens, September 9, 1940.
29. James Hayward, *Hitler's Spy* (Simon & Schuster UK, 2014), 160.
30. Oslo's "Norgenbladst," September 5, 1945, Tor Glad Personal File, Security Service, KV 2/1068 National Archives.
31. TAR Robertson, "Interrogation of Jeff," October 21, 1941, Tor Glad Personal File, Security Service, KV 2/1068 National Archives.
32. Transcripts from May 5, 1943, Eric Arthur Roberts, alias Jack King: British—The Fifth Column Case, Security Service, KV 2/3874, National Archives.
33. Ibid., July 1, 1943.
34. Mary Katherine Barbier, "*Clash of the Titans*" in *Arms and the Man: Military History Essays in Honor of Dennis Showalter*, edited by Michael S. Neiberg (The Netherlands: Brill, 2011), 61.
35. Ibid.
36. Ben Macintyre, *Double Cross: The True Story of the D-Day Spies* (London: Bloomsbury, 2012), 4.
37. J.C. Masterman, *The Double-Cross System* (Guilford, CT: Lyons, 2000), 37.
38. Oliver D. Hoare, *Camp 020: MI5 and the Nazi Spies* (UK: National Archives, 2000), 101.

39. Deception Policy for the War Against Germany, September 22, 1943, Cabinet Office Records, PRO CAB 119/66, National Archives.
40. Karl Heinz Kramer, Personal File, War Office, WO 208/5212, National Archives.
41. Eddie Chapman Statement, December 16, 1942, Agent Zigzag, Security Service, KV 2/455, National Archive.
42. Ben Macintyre, *Agent Zigzag: The True Wartime Story of Eddie Chapman, the Most Notorious Double Agent of World War II* (London: Bloomsbury, 2010), 81.
43. Eddie Chapman Statement, December 16, 1942, Agent Zigzag, Security Service, KV 2/455, National Archive.
44. Ibid.
45. Report of Eddie Chapman and MI5 Officers' Visit to the De Havilland Factory, December 30, 1942, Agent Zigzag, Security Service, KV 2/455, National Archive.
46. Ibid.
47. Discussions with Robertson, White and Rothschild about Sabotage on City of Lancaster, March 29, 1943, Zigzag; Guy Maynard Liddell, *The Guy Liddell Diaries, MI5's Director of Counterespionage in World War II*, Vol. 2, 1942–1945, ed. Nigel West (London: Routledge, 2006).
48. Eddie Chapman, Interview with Lord Rothschild, January 1943, Agent Zigzag, Security Service KV 24/58, National Archives.
49. Plot to assassinate Hitler, December 16, 1942, Agent Zigzag, Security Service, KV 2.457, National Archives.
50. A Summary of the Garbo Case, January 1–December 30, 1945, Juan Pujol-Garcia, Security Service, KV 2/41, National Archives, 6.
51. Ben Macintyre, Double Cross, 161.
52. Letter to Kuhenthal, July 25, 1943, Juan, Pujol-Garcia, Security Service, KV 2/41, National Archives.
53. A Summary of the Garbo Case, Jan 1–Dec 30, 194.5
54. Memo to Hinchley Cooke, March 24, 1939, Agent Snow, Security Service, KV2/466, National Archives.
55. Hayward, *Hitler's Spy*, 8.
56. Interview with Snow, September 6, 1939, Agent Snow, Security Service, KV2/466, National Archives.
57. Report, 19, May 1940, Agent Snow, Security Service, VK2/466, National Archives.
58. Interview with Snow, April 3, 1941.
59. Ibid.
60. John Alanis, *Double Cross: The True Story of "Tricycle," the Original Master Spy* (Austin, TX: Arts of Steel, 2013).

61. Case Summary, Dusko Popov, Security Service, KV 2/845, National Archives.
62. German Questionnaires, February 1941, Dukso Popov Security Service, KV 2/845, National Archives.
63. Abwehr report on Tricycle, Dusko Popov Dec 1943–Feb 1944, Security Service KV 2/856, National Archives.
64. Little Memorandum to Ladd, July 6, 1943, Dusko Popov FBI File, RG65 36994, FBI Reading Room, Washington, D.C.
65. Nigel West, *The A to Z of British Intelligence* (Lanham, MD: Scarecrow, 2009), 428.
66. Alanis, *Double Cross*.
67. Dusko Popov, Security Service, KV 2/845, National Archives.
68. J.C. Masterman, Report, September 1941, Gelatine, Security Service, KV 2/1276, National Archives.
69. Ewen Montagu, Twenty Committee, September 8, 1944, Ministry of Defense, PRO ADM 223, National Archives.
70. Deputy Head of the Government Code and Cypher School, Letter to John Masterman, May 26, 1944, Security Service KV 2/466, National Archives.
71. Barbier, *"Clash of the Titans,"* 94.
72. Donal O'Sullivan, *Dealing with the Devil: Anglo-Soviet Intelligence Cooperation in the Second World War* (New York: Peter Lang, 2010), 205.
73. Kiss, Security Service, KV2 1282, National Archives.
74. Torch Cover and Deception Plans, Lessons Learnt, December 7, 1942, Cabinet Office Records, PRO CAB 81/76/12, National Archives.
75. ZIGZAG, Memorandum on Berlin GIS Personnel, October 31, 1945, Office of the Strategic Services Records RG226 Entry 213, Box 2, NARA.
76. Koutrik, Personal File, Secret Information Service, KV 2/3643, National Archives.
77. Ministrie Van Justite letter to Captain Corin, August 7, 1946, Koutrik Personal File, Secret Information Service, KV 2/3643, National Archives.
78. Report on Spanish Falange, Files of RSHA Amt IV D, Foreign Records, RG242 Box 28 173b-24, NARA.
79. Lauran Paine, *German Military Intelligence in World War II: The Abwehr* (New York: Stein and Day, 1984), 72.
80. John H. Waller, *The Unseen War in Europe: Espionage and Conspiracy in the Second World War* (London: B. Taurus, 1996), 274.
81. Ibid.

82. Axis Governments and Switzerland, Intelligence Report, Office of Strategic Service Records, RG226 60459, NARA.
83. U.S. Military Intelligence, Office of Assistant Chief of Staff, G-2, RG319, NARA.
84. Report on employment of German aviation engineers, December 16, 1942, *Operation Safehaven*, Office of Strategic Services Records, RG226 Box 6 0499, NARA.
85. "Foreign funds control activities," Annual Report of the Secretary of the Treasury on the State of the Finances, June 30, 1942, FBI File, RG65 112 567747, NARA.
86. Michael Arthur Jones, *Swiss Bank Accounts* (New York: Liberty House, 1990), 37.
87. OSS Dossier on Jacob Fuerst, April 1946, Office of Strategic Services Records, RG226 Entry 211 Box 35, NARA.
88. *Ibid.*
89. Mark Aarons and John Loftus, *The Secret War Against the Jews* (New York: St Martin's), 86.
90. Greg Bradsher, "A Time to Act: The Beginning of the Fritz Kolbe Story, 1900–1943," *Prologue: Quarterly of NARA* 34, no. 1 (2002), 32.
91. Frederick J. Stalder, Activity Reports, August 5, 1942, to April 13, 1945, *Operation Safehaven*, Office of Strategic Services Records, RG226 Box 6 0499, NARA.
92. *Operation Sunrise*, OSS Report, Office of Strategic Service Records, RG226 Box 8 E190C, NARA.
93. *Operation Gehlen*, Document 41, National Security Archive, George Washington University, Washington, D.C.
94. Guido Zimmer, Name File, Central Intelligence Agency Records, RG263, NARA.
95. Dr. Klaus Huegel, Interrogation Report, June 21, 1945, Office of Strategic Services Records, RG226 Box 71E119A.
96. Jupp Hoven, Personal File, Security Service, KV7 79, National Archives, 86.
97. Wilhelm Hollmann, Interrogation Report, February 27, 1945–April 5, 1945, Security Service, KV2 2/300, National Archives.
98. "The Irish Interlude: German Intelligence in Ireland, 1939–43," *Journal of Military History* 66 (July 3, 2002), 699.
99. "New Evidence on IRA/Nazi Links: The Emergency," *20th Century Contemporary History* 19, no. 2 (March/April 2011).
100. Frank Ryan to Leopold Kerney, December 11, 1940, DFA Secretary's files, A20/4, National Archives of Ireland.
101. Policy Re Control of the IRA, Policy (P) Files, Security Services, KV4 232, National Archives.
102. Weber-Drohl, Summary, G-2 1928, Irish Military Archives.
103. Photostats of Operation Kathleen Documents, Stephen Held, Security Service, KV 2/1449, National Archives.
104. "The Irish Interlude: German Intelligence in Ireland, 1939–43," 702.
105. Summary of Encrypted German Legation Messages, September 19, 1939 to October 2, 1943, TNA, DO 121/87.
106. Chief Constable Letter, Special Branch, May 31, 1940, Stephen Held, Security Service KV 2/1449, National Archives.
107. Photostats of Operation Kathleen Documents, Stephen Held, Security Service, KV 2/1449, National Archives.
108. Summary of encrypted German legation messages, September 19, 1939 to October 2, 1943, TNA, DO 121/87.

Chapter 4

1. Ernst Wilhelm Bohle, G-2 Interview, Army Intelligence, September 8, 1945, RG165 946, Drawer 1, NARA.
2. *Ibid.*
3. Hans Adolf Jacobsen and Arthur Lee Smith, *The Nazi Party and the German Foreign Office* (London: Routledge, 2007), 113.
4. Leslie B. Rout Jr. and John F. Bratzel, "Origins: U.S. Intelligence In Latin America," *Studies in Intelligence* (1985), 5.
5. *Ibid.*
6. "German Espionage and Sabotage Against the United States," January 1946, Office of Naval Intelligence, R4551, 1, no.3, NARA, 31.
7. *Operation Bluebook*, U.S. State Department, RG59 862.20235, NARA, 7.
8. Randolph Paul, Memorandum to Henry Morgenthau Jr., February 3, 1944, Diaries of Henry Morgenthau Jr., Volume 700: February 3–9, 1944, FDR Library.
9. James Boxwell, "MI5 Claimed Siemens a Cover for Nazi Spies," *Financial Times*, August 26, 2011.
10. George S. Messersmith, Letter to Cordell Hull, July 2, 1944, U.S. State Department, RG59, DS862.20212, NARA.
11. Pierre De Lagarde Boal, Letter to George S. Messersmith, December 22, 1939, U.S. State Department, RG59 DS862.20212, NARA.
12. Thomas D. Schoonover, *Hitler's Man in Havana: Heinz Luning and Nazi Espionage in Latin America* (Lexington: University Press of Kentucky, 2008), 35.

13. María Emilia Paz Salinas, *Strategy, Security, and Spies: Mexico and the U.S. as Allies in World War II* (University Park: Pennsylvania State University Press, 2012), 5.
14. Joseph E. Persico, *Roosevelt's Secret War: FDR and World War II Espionage* (New York: Random House, 2001), 84.
15. "Nazi Groups in America," Memorandum, Assistant Secretary of State Adolf Berle, July 7, 1941, RG59 82400 NARA.
16. *Ibid.*
17. Cordell Hull, *The Memoirs of Cordell Hull* (New York: Macmillan, 1948), 601.
18. Study of the Joint Action, RG165 JB325, serial 634, 4.5, NARA.
19. "Radio Intelligence," April 3, 1942, Office of Naval Communication, Military Agency Records, RG38 21, NARA.
20. German Activities in South America in World War II, National Security Agency, Office of National Archives, George G. Meade, MD, 40.
21. Edward A. Tamm, Memorandum to the Director, May 13, 1941, SIS Records, FBI Files, RG65 1644104, NARA.
22. D.M. Ladd, Memorandum to the Director, Oct 26, 1942, SIS Records, FBI Files, RG65 1644104, NARA.
23. Darlene J. Sadlier, *Americans All: Good Neighbor Cultural Diplomacy in World War II* (Austin: University of Texas Press, 2012).
24. *Ibid.*
25. Max Paul Friedman, *Nazis and Good Neighbors: The United States Campaign Against the Germans of Latin America in World War II* (UK: Cambridge University Press, 2003), 21.
26. Leslie Bethell, *Latin America Between the Second World War and the Cold War, 1944–1948; Crisis and Containment, 1944–1948*, 33.
27. Sumner Welles to Cordell Hull, January 18, 1942, FRUS.
28. "Interrogation of Ernst Bohle," September 8, 1945, State Department Special Interrogation Mission, RG59 M679/1/12, NARA.
29. FBI Report to Donovan Concerning Brazil and Axis Nationals, January 1942, Office of Strategic Services, RG226 158339, NARA.
30. Hans Adolf Jacobsen and Arthur Lee Smith, *The Nazi Party and the German Foreign Office* (London: Routledge, 2007), 115.
31. Flight of Axis Capital, Brazil, FBI File, Foreign Funds, RG65, 112 567747, NARA.
32. Stanley E. Hilton, *Hitler's Secret War in South America, 1939–1945: German Military Espionage and Allied Counterespionage in Brazil* (Baton Rouge: Louisiana State University Press, 1981), 208.
33. Earl Morrell, New York SOI Organization, July 10, 1941, Political Warfare, KV PRO/103, National Archives.
34. "Nazi Groups in America," Memorandum, Assistant Secretary of State Adolf Berle, July 7, 1941.
35. *Ibid.*
36. Jefferson Adams, *Historical Dictionary of German Intelligence* (Lanham, MD: Scarecrow, 2009), 98.
37. Reinhard R. Doerries, *Hitler's Intelligence Chief: Walter Schellenberg*, 141.
38. Johannes Becker, Security Service, KV 2/89, National Archives, p. 6.
39. German Activities in South America in World War II, National Security Agency, Office of National Archives, George G. Meade, MD, 26.
40. German Activities in Brazil, U.S. Embassy in Rio, February–November 1941, PRO FO371/25800.
41. *Ibid.*
42. "Nazi Groups in America" Memorandum, Adolf Berle, July 7, 1941.
43. "German Espionage and Sabotage Against the United States," January 1946.
44. Hilton, *Hitler's Secret War*, 45.
45. Jefferson Caffery, Letter to Secretary of State, September 7, 1942, War Department Records, Military Intelligence Division, RG165 261, NARA.
46. FBI Memorandum on the SIS, February 12, 1946, SIS Records, FBI Files, RG65 11/64-4104, NARA.
47. A. Berle, Memorandum to J. Edgar Hoover, June 27, 1940, Special Activities Branch, ONI, RG38, NARA.
48. Johannes Becker, Security Service, Personal File, KV 2/89, National Archives.
49. Aranha to Vargas, Rio, January 25, 1943, AOA, CPDOC.
50. Little, Memorandum to Ladd, July 6, 1942, Dusko Popov, FBI File, 65-36994, FBI Reading Room, Washington, D.C.
51. Ernst Wilhelm Bohle, G-2 Interview, September 8, 1945, RG165 946, Drawer 1, NARA.
52. Max Paul Friedman, *Nazis and Good Neighbors*, 23.
53. Rout and Bratzel, "Origins, 166.
54. Ludwig von Bohlen, KV 2/1975, National Archives.
55. Chile, Justice Department, Records of the Economic Warfare Section, RG60 285B Boxes 5–226, NARA.
56. FBI Summary Report, SIS, October 1942, RG65 44610-164, Sec 5, NARA, 6.

57. Ibid.
58. "German Espionage and Sabotage Against the United States," January 1946, Office of Naval Intelligence, 1, no.3, R4551, NARA, 15.
59. Montt to Foreign Minister, October 6, 1941, File E 11-6-0, Chilean National Archives.
60. Special Intelligence Service, Annual Report 1944–1945, U.S. State Department, RG59 1159457, NARA, 33.
61. Ibid 35.
62. "Radio Messages in Valparaíso," March 10, 1942, FBI Files, SIS Records, FBI Files RG65 6/64, NARA.
63. Rout and Bratzel, "Origins," 46.
64. Cordell Hull, *The Memoirs of Cordell Hull*, vol. 2 (New York: Macmillan, 1948), 1411.
65. Factors Affecting Chile's Decision on Severance of Relations with the Axis, June 1943, RG226 15 13515, NARA.
66. German Assets, Argentina, Foreign Affairs Records, US State Department, RG84 Box 24, File 711.3, NARA.
67. "The Pinedo Plan to Stimulate the Export of New Articles from Argentina," November 29, 1940, Trading with American Republics, U.S. State Department, RG 59 611, NARA.
68. "Concern of the United States Over Enemy Attempts to Secrete Funds or Other Assets in Neutral Countries, Implementation of the Safehaven Program," vol. 2, 1945, FRUS, 929.
69. Ronald C. Newton, *The "Nazi Menace" in Argentina, 1931–1947* (Stanford, CA: Stanford University Press, 1992), 52.
70. "Summary of Opinion in Latin America," October 1941, Office of Strategic Services, RG226 15 1139, NARA, 70.
71. History of the SIS, Operations in Argentina, vol. 2, FBI Files, RG59 11594, NARA, p. 6.
72. Captain Dietrich Niebuhr, Interrogation, October to November 1943, RG59 862.20232, NARA.
73. Ibid.
74. Director of the Political Department, Memorandum, August 25, 1941, Büro des Staatssekretärs: Argentinian Band 2, RG242 T120/207, NARA.
75. German Embassy Buenos Aires to Reich Foreign Office, June 14, 1940, German Foreign Ministry Records, RG242, NARA.
76. Johannes Becker, Security Service, Personal File, KV 2/89, National Archives, 6.
77. "The Foreign Minister to the Embassy in Argentina," July 16, 1941, Doc. 112, DGFP, 142.
78. "Affidavit of Walter Schellenberg," February 6, 1946, RG59 ABB, Box 6740, NARA, 4.

79. "Hellmuth Interrogation," FBI Files, RG 65 64-27116, Box 19, NARA, 2.
80. Captain Dietrich Niebuhr, Interrogation.
81. German Agent Enciphered Messages from Argentina to Spain, National Security Agency Records, RG445 604, NARA.
82. Otto Reinebeck, Interrogation, February 4, 1946, Operation Bluebook Report, US State Department, RG59 862.20235, NARA.
83. Operation Bluebook, *Argentinian Blue Book*, U.S. State Department, RG59 862.20235, NARA, 7.
84. History of the SIS, Operations in Argentina, Vol. 2, FBI Files, RG59 11594, NARA, 2.
85. German-Latin America Communications, Jan–May 1942, Magic Diplomatic Summaries, National Security Agency, RG457 1439, NARA.
86. Ibid.
87. Hugo Fernandez Artucio, *The Nazi Underground in South America* (New York: Farrar & Rinehart, 1942), 116.
88. Newton, *The "Nazi Menace,"* 257.
89. Hellmuth Interrogation, FBI Files, 4.
90. "Hellmuth Mission," October 28, 1943, "Magic" Diplomatic Summaries, 1942–1945, National Security Agency, RG 457 Box 7, NARA.
91. "Berlin to Argentina," January 2, 1944, OSS Communication Office Records, Ultra Decrypts, RG 226 188, NARA.
92. Operation Bluebook, *Argentinian Blue Book*, U.S. State Department, RG59 862.20235, NARA, 9.
93. George S. Messersmith, Letter to Cordell Hull, July 21, 1944, U.S. State Department, RG59, DS862.20212, NARA.
94. "German Capital in Argentina," *Economist*, September 22, 1945.
95. Memorandum re Argentine Safehaven programme, Foreign Funds Control, Subject File, RG131 Box 20, NARA.
96. Report on German Commercial Activities in Mexico 1943, OSS Central Files, 1942–1946, RG226 92, Box 446, Folder 40, NARA.
97. "Affidavit of Walter Schellenberg," February 6, 1946, RG59 ABB, Box 6740, NARA, 4.
98. Operation Bluebook Report, *Mexican Blue Book*, U.S. State Department, RG59 862.20235, NARA, 7.
99. María Emilia Paz Salinas, *Strategy, Security, and Spies*, 25.
100. Attorney General of Mexico report on Persons Engaged in Espionage Activities, April 17, 1942, RG226, NARA.
101. Aaron W. Navarro, *Political Intelligence*

and the Creation of Modern Mexico, 1938–1954 (University Park: Pennsylvania State University Press), 128.

102. Confidential Report on Nazi Activities in Mexico, ONI, RG38 C-10K/22512-1, NARA.

103. George Messersmith, Letter to Roosevelt, October 2, 1943, George S. Messersmith Papers, University of Delaware, Newark.

104. María Emilia Paz Salinas, *Strategy, Security, and Spies: Mexico and the U.S.*, 5.

105. Presidente De La Republica DF, January 17, 1942, Manuel Avila Camacho, Box 824 bis, Folder 550-991, AGN.

106. Engaging Latin American Republics in Defending the Hemisphere Against Nazi Aggression, Propaganda Materials, 1941–45, U.S. Office of War Information, RG229 PG71, NARA.

107. Maria Teresa, Statement to the FBI, FBI Files, RG65, NARA.

108. Georg Nicolaus, Security Information Service, KV 2/2663, National Archives.

109. Georg Nikolaus, Letter to Abwehr, August 20, 1941, RG59 800.727, NARA.

110. Georg Nicolaus, Letter to Vogel, October 2, 1940, Nicolaus, Georg, KV 2/2663, National Archives.

111. Military Attaché Report 2761, November 27, 1943, Mexico City, RG165 656, NARA.

112. Georg Nicolaus, Security Information Service, KV 2/2663, National Archives.

113. Aaron W. Navarro, *Political Intelligence and the Creation of Modern Mexico*, 128.

114. Ibid., 176.

115. Harold D. Finley, Memo to Secretary of State, "The Mexican Political Situation," September 1943, RG59 812.00/32916, NARA.

116. Military Attaché Report 2761, November 27, 1943, Mexico City, RG165 656, NARA.

117. Edgar J. Hoover, Letter to Adolf Berle, "Mexican Matters," May 27, 1940, RG59 812.00, NARA.

118. Letter from Messersmith to de Boal, January 24, 1940, George S. Messersmith Papers, University of Delaware, Newark.

119. Mexico, SIS History, RG65, NARA, 319.

120. William Dirk Raat and Michael M. Brescia, *Mexico and the United States: Ambivalent Vistas* (Athens: University of Georgia Press, 1992), 163.

121. Attorney General of Mexico, Report on Persons Engaged in Espionage, April 17, 1942, RG226, NARA.

122. Ibid.

123. Raat and Brescia, *Mexico and the United States*, 163.

124. History of the SIS, Operations in Cuba, vol. 1, FBI Files, RG59 11594, NARA, 5.

125. Adolf Berle, "Patterns of Nazi Organisations and Their Activities in the American Republics," February 6, 1945, RG59 862, NARA.

126. Schoonover, *Hitler's Man in Havana*, 81.

127. J. Edgar Hoover, Memorandum to Berle, November 24, 1942, Luning File, Army Intelligence, RG319 X8536413, Box 131E, NARA.

128. Clifford L. Staten, *The History of Cuba* (New York: Palgrave Macmillan, 2005), 66.

129. Ibid.

130. Schoonover, *Hitler's Man in Havana*, 40.

131. German Activities in South America in World War II, Center for Cryptologic History, National Security Agency, George G. Meade, MD, 7.

132. "The Jolle Operation," August 25, 1944, Chief of Naval Operations, RG35 3200/5 Box 11, NARA.

133. Memorandum to the FCC, January 5, 1942, Chief of Naval Operations, RG35 3200/5 Box 11, NARA.

134. SIS Statistics, SIS Administrative Records, FBI Files, RG65 10, File 64-4104, NARA.

135. FBI Report to Donovan Concerning Brazil and Axis Nationals, January 1942, Office of Strategic Services, RG226 15 8339, NARA.

136. J. Edgar Hoover, Memorandum to Attorney General Clark, August 29, 1945, Troy Papers, Central Intelligence Agency, FBI Documents, RG263, NARA.

Chapter 5

1. Leonard Thompson, *A History of South Africa* (New Haven, CT: Yale University Press, 2001), 177.

2. William Beinart, *Twentieth-Century South Africa* (UK: Oxford University Press, 2001), 125.

3. Jack Harris, U.S. observer interview with Van Rensburg, August 15, 1944, General Commandant Van Rensburg, Security Service, KV 2/907, National Archives.

4. War Measures: Validated By, and Issued Under, the War Measures Act, 1940 (Act No. 13 of 1940), as Amended by the War Measures (Amendment) Act, 1940 (Act No. 32 of 1940), Union of South Africa.

5. K. Fedorowich, "German Espionage and British Counter-Intelligence in South Africa and Mozambique, 1939–1944," *Historical Journal* 48, no. 1 (March 2005), 210.

6. Ibid.

7. Auswärtiges Amt (Foreign Office)

Bonn, 1939-1943, f. 24, 1102-S9, Archives StSAfrika, ADAP.
8. Christoph Marx, *Oxwagon Sentinel: Radical Afrikaner Nationalism and the History of the "Ossewabrandwag"* (Münster: LIT Verlag, 2009), 322.
9. R.W. Johnson, *South Africa: The First Man, the Last Nation* (London: London: Orion), 134.
10. Ontstaan van Ossewabrandwag, May 1962, R. Meyer Collection, PV 104, Archive of the Institute for Contemporary History, University of the Orange Free State.
11. Christopher Marx, "'Dear Listeners in South Africa,' German Propaganda Broadcasts to South Africa, 1940-1941," *South African Historical Journal* 27 (1992), 170.
12. Christoph Marx, *Oxwagon Sentinel: Radical Afrikaner Nationalism and the History of the "Ossewabrandwag"* (Münster: LIT Verlag, 2009), 322.
13. Ibid.
14. Jack Harris, U.S. observer interview with Van Rensburg, August 15, 1944, General Commandant Van Rensburg, Security Service, KV 2/907, National Archives.
15. Pirow's visit to Hitler, 1938, Code 18 File 1356, Foreign Office Files, FO 371, National Archives.
16. R.W. Johnson, *South Africa: The First Man, the Last Nation* (London: Orion Books), 134.
17. Oswald Pirow, May 1935-December 1951, Security Service, KV 2/908.
18. Hans Van Rensburg, *Die Vaderland*, August 1942.
19. Lt. Col. A. Stanford, Report on the OB to the Cabinet Subcommittee Internal Security, June 28, 1940, BC 640, E3.203, University of Cape Town.
20. Intelligence Summaries, September 20, 1940, Civil Section Documents, Box 265 F B120, Vol. 1, South African Defense Force Archives, Pretoria.
21. Report on Webster's undercover operation, South Africa Mission: SOE directive; Joint Intelligence Committee at Capetown, SOE Records, HS 3/8, National Archives.
22. The Durban Saboteurs, Undercover Reports, February-July 1942, Trompke Organisation for German Espionage in South Africa, Security Service KV2 275, National Archives.
23. Rooseboom, Accusations about Van Rensburg, General Commandant Van Rensburg, Security Service, KV 2/907, National Archives.
24. Intelligence Summaries, February 18, 1942, Chief of General Staff, Box 93 F 169/7, Vol. 1, South African Defense Force Archives, Pretoria.
25. The Durban Saboteurs, Undercover Reports, February-July 1942.
26. Colonel Kreft, Report on Ossewa Brandwag, March 19, 1943, Trompke Organisation for German Espionage in South Africa, Security Service KV2 275, National Archives.
27. K. Fedorowich, "German Espionage and British Counter-Intelligence in South Africa and Mozambique, 1939-1944," *Historical Journal* 48, no. 1 (March 2005), 219.
28. Van Rensburg, Letter to D.F. Malan, November 29, 1941, 111915, DF Malan Collection, University of Stellenbosch.
29. German Sabotage in the Union and PEA, March 16, 1943, General Commandant Van Rensburg, Security Service, KV 2/907, National Archives.
30. D.F. Malan, Letter to Van Rensburg, January 7, 1942, 111936, DF Malan Collection, University of Stellenbosch.
31. K. Fedorowich, "German Espionage and British Counter-Intelligence," 215.
32. Report on Webster's undercover operations, South Africa Mission: SOE directive; Joint Intelligence Committee at Capetown, SOE Records, HS 3/8, National Archives.
33. Trompke Radio Transmissions, January 16-February 27, 1943, Trompke Organisation for German Espionage in South Africa, Security Service, KV2 275, National Archives.
34. Plans for the Capture of Madagascar, November 19, 1940 to April 4, 1942, Cabinet Office Records, CAB 121/622, National Archives.
35. Intelligence Summary, German Activities in Portuguese East Africa, January 12, 1940, Trompke Organisation for German Espionage in South Africa, Security Service, KV2 275.
36. Interim Report on the Case of Colonel Werz, September 9, 1945, Camp 020, General Commandant Van Rensburg, Security Service, KV 2/907, National Archive.
37. Telegraph from Cape Town, Police Records, Paasche, Lothar Sittig/Nils Paasche, Alias Felix, Security Service, KV2 939, National Archives.
38. Trompke Radio Transmissions, March 12, 1942-February 27, 1943.
39. German Consulate in Lourenço Marques, Trompke Organisation for German Espionage in South Africa, Security Service, KV2 275, National Archives.
40. Leo Radio Transmissions, January 1942-

December 1943, Trompke Organisation for German Espionage in South Africa, Security Service KV2 275, National Archives.

41. Felix Radio transmissions, February 1943–October 1943.

42. Letter from SIS to B1B regarding Van Rensburg, September 1, 1944, General Commandant Van Rensburg, Security Service, KV 2/907, National Archive.

43. Felix Radio Transmissions, Trompke Organisation for German Espionage in South Africa, Security Service, KV2 275, National Archives.

44. Felix Identity, April 3, 1943, *Guy Liddell Diaries*, vol. 2: 1942–1945: *MI5's Director of Counter-espionage in World War II*, ed. Nigel West (London: Routledge), 2006.

45. "Quintinho Letter," July 30, 1942, Trompke Organisation for German Espionage in South Africa, Security Service KV2 275, National Archives.

46. Report on the Leopold Werz case, May 12, 1944, Office of Strategic Services Records, RG226 Box 6 244, NARA.

47. *Ibid.*

48. Interim Report on the Case of Colonel Werz, September 9, 1945, Camp 020.

49. South Africa Mission: SOE directive; Joint Intelligence Committee at Capetown, SOE Records, HS 3/8, National Archives.

50. Report on the Leopold Werz case, May 12, 1944, Office of Strategic Services Records, RG226 Box 6 244, NARA.

51. *Operation Malpas*, Special Operation Executive, HS 8/891, National Archives.

52. Robey Leibbrandt, October 18, 1941–January 23, 1942, KV 2/924, Security Service, National Archives.

53. *Ibid.*

54. Rooseboom, Accusations about Van Rensburg, General Commandant Van Rensburg, Security Service, KV 2/907.

55. Robey Leibbrandt, October 18, 1941–January 23, 1942, KV 2/924, Security Service, National Archives.

56. Leonard Thompson, *A History of South Africa*, 3rd ed. (New Haven, CT: Yale University Press, 2001), 184.

Bibliography

Books

Aarons, Mark, and John Loftus. *The Secret War Against the Jews*. New York: St. Martin's, 1997.
Adams, Jefferson. *Historical Dictionary of German Intelligence*. Lanham, MD: Scarecrow, 2009.
Alanis, John. *Double Cross: The True Story of "Tricycle," the Original Master Spy*. Austin, TX: Arts of Steel, 2013.
Artucio, Hugo Fernandez. *The Nazi Underground in South America*. New York: Farrar & Rinehart, 1942.
Barbier, Mary Katherine. *"Clash of the Titans" in Arms and the Man: Military History Essays in Honor of Dennis Showalter*. Edited by Michael S. Neiberg. The Netherlands: Brill, 2011.
Barnes, James J., and Patience P. Barnes. *Nazis in Pre-War London, 1930–1939: The Fate and Role of German Party Members and British Sympathizers*. Brighton: Sussex Academic, 2005.
Bassett, Richard. *Hitler's Spy Chief: The Wilhelm Canaris Betrayal; The Intelligence Campaign Against Adolf Hitler*. New York: Bantam Doubleday, 2013.
Batvinis, Raymond J. *Hoover's Secret War Against Axis Spies: FBI Counterespionage During World War II*. Lawrence: University Press of Kansas, 2007.
Beinart, William. *Twentieth-Century South Africa*. Oxford: Oxford University Press, 2001.
Biddle, Francis. *In Brief Authority*. Garden City, NJ: Doubleday, 1962.
Dasch, George John. *Eight Spies Against America*. New York: R.M. McBride, 1959.
Dobbs, Michael. *Saboteurs: The Nazi Raid on America*. New York: Knopf, 2004.
Doerries, Reinhard R. *Hitler's Intelligence Chief: Walter Schellenberg*. New York: Enigma, 2008.
Friedman, Max Paul. *Nazis and Good Neighbors: The United States Campaign Against the Germans of Latin America in World War II*. Cambridge: Cambridge University Press, 2003.
Gimpel, Erich, and Will Berthold. *Spy for Germany*. London: Robert Hall, 1957.
Görlitz, Walter. *The Memoirs of Field-Marshal Wilhelm Keitel*. Lanham, MD: Rowman & Littlefield, 2000.
Guettel, Jens-Uwe. *German Expansionism, Imperial Liberalism and the United States, 1776–1945*. Cambridge: Cambridge University Press, 2012.
Hayward, James. *Hitler's Spy*. London: Simon & Schuster, 2014.
Herman, Michael. *Intelligence Power in Peace and War*. Cambridge: Cambridge University Press, 1996.
Herzog, Bodo. *60 Jahre Deutsche Uboote*. München: J.F. Lehmann, 1968.
Hoare, Oliver D. *Camp 020: MI5 and the Nazi Spies*. London: National Archives, 2000.
Hull, Cordell. *Memoirs of Cordell Hull*. Vol. 1. New York: Macmillan, 1948.
Jacobsen, Hans-Adolf, and Arthur Lee Smith. *The Nazi Party and the German Foreign Office*. London: Routledge, 2007.

Jacobson, Hans-Adolf, and Charles Burdick. *The Halder War Diary*. New York: Presidio, 1988.
Johnson, R.W. *South Africa: The First Man, the Last Nation*. London: Orion, 2006.
Jones, Michael Arthur. *Swiss Bank Accounts*. New York: Liberty House, 1990.
Katz, Barry M. *Foreign Intelligence: Research and Analysis in the Office of Strategic Services, 1942–1945*. Cambridge, MA: Harvard University Press, 1989.
Khan, David. *Hitler's Spies: German Military Intelligence in World War II*. New York: Macmillan, 1978.
Kordt, Erich. *Nicht aus den Akten*. Stuttgart: Union Deutsche Verlagsgesellschaft, 1950.
Krausnick, Helmut, et al. *Anatomy of the SS State*. New York: Walker, 1968.
Liddell, Guy. *Guy Liddell Diaries*. Vol. 2, 1942–1945. *MI5's Director of Counter-espionage in World War II*. Edited by Nigel West. London: Routledge, 2006.
MacDonnell, Francis. *Insidious Foes: The Axis Fifth Column and the American Home Front*. Oxford: Oxford University Press, 1995.
Macintyre, Ben. *Agent Zigzag: The True Wartime Story of Eddie Chapman, the Most Notorious Double Agent of World War II*. London: Bloomsbury, 2010.
Macintyre, Ben. *Double Cross: The True Story of the D-Day Spies*. London: Bloomsbury, 2012.
Marx, Christoph. *Oxwagon Sentinel: Radical Afrikaner Nationalism and the History of the "Ossewabrandwag."* LIT Verlag Münster, 2009.
Masterman, J.C. *The Double-Cross System*. New York: Lyons, 2000.
Navarro, Aaron W. *Political Intelligence and the Creation of Modern Mexico, 1938–1954*. University Park: Pennsylvania State University Press.
Newton, Ronald C. *The "Nazi Menace" in Argentina, 1931–1947*. Stanford, CA: Stanford University Press, 1992.
Noble, Dennis L. *The Beach Patrol and Corsair Flee*. Washington, D.C.: Coast Guard Historian's Office, 1992.
O'Sullivan, Donal. *Dealing with the Devil: Anglo-Soviet Intelligence Cooperation in the Second World War*. New York: Peter Lang, 2010.
Paine, Lauran, *German Military Intelligence in World War II: The Abwehr*. New York: Stein and Day, 1984.
Persico, Joseph E. *Roosevelt's Secret War: FDR and World War II Espionage*. New York: Random House, 2001.
Powers, Richard Gid. *Broken: The Troubled Past and Uncertain Future of the FBI*. New York: Simon & Schuster, 2004.
Raat, William Dirk, and Michael M. Brescia. *Mexico and the United States: Ambivalent Vistas*. Athens: University of Georgia Press, 1992.
Sadlier, Darlene J. *Americans All: Good Neighbor Cultural Diplomacy in World War II*. Austin: University of Texas Press, 2012.
Salinas, María Emilia Paz. *Strategy, Security, and Spies: Mexico and the U.S. as Allies in World War II*. University Park: Pennsylvania State University Press, 2012.
Schellenberg, Walter. *Walter Schellenberg: The Memoirs of Hitler's Spymaster*. London: Andre Deutsch, 2006.
Schoonover, Thomas D. *Hitler's Man in Havana: Heinz Luning and Nazi Espionage in Latin America*. Lexington: University Press of Kentucky, 2008.
Staten, Clifford L. *The History of Cuba*. New York: Palgrave Macmillan, 2005.
Stockton, Bayard. *Flawed Patriot: The Rise and Fall of CIA Legend Bill Harvey*. Washington, D.C.: Potomac, 2007.
Sulick, Michael J. *Spying in America: Espionage from the Revolutionary War to the Dawn of the Cold War*. Washington, D.C.: Georgetown University Press; reprint edition, 2014.
Thompson, Leonard. *A History of South Africa*. New Haven, CT: Yale University Press, 2001.
Tobias, Norman. *The International Military Encyclopedia*. Gulf Breeze, FL: Academic International Press, 1992.
Turrow, Leon. *The Nazi Spy Conspiracy in America*. Freeport, NY: Books for Libraries, 1969.

Vassiltchikov, Marie. *Berlin Diaries, 1940–45.* New York: Vintage, 1998.
Waller, John H. *The Unseen War in Europe: Espionage and Conspiracy in the Second World War.* London: I.B. Taurus, 1996.
West, Nigel. *Historical Dictionary of International Intelligence.* Lanham, MD: Scarecrow, 2006.
Whiting, Charles. *Hitler's Secret War: The Nazi Espionage Campaign Against the Allies.* UK: Pen & Sword, 2000.
Zabecki, David T. *World War II in Europe: An Encyclopaedia.* Vol. 1. New York: Routledge, 1999.

Articles

Bell, Leland V. "The Failure of Nazism in America: The German American Bund, 1936–1941." *Political Science Quarterly* 85 (1970): 598.
Bradsher, Greg. "A Time to Act: The Beginning of the Fritz Kolbe Story, 1900–1943." *Prologue: Quarterly of NARA* 34, no. 1 (2002), 32.
Decree on the Command of the Armed Forces by Adolf Hitler. *Reichsgesetzblatt* [Reich Legal Gazette], 5, Part 1 (February 4 1938): 111.
Fedorowich, K. "German Espionage and British Counter-Intelligence in South Africa and Mozambique, 1939–1944." *Historical Journal* 48, no. 1 (2005): 219.
"The Irish Interlude: German Intelligence in Ireland, 1939–43." *Journal of Military History* 66 (2002): 699.
Marx, Christopher. "Dear Listeners in South Africa, German Propaganda Broadcasts to South Africa, 1940–1941." *South African Historical Journal* 27 (1992): 170.
"New Evidence on IRA/Nazi Links" *20th Century Contemporary History* 19, no. 2 (2011).
Rout Jr., Leslie B., and John F. Bratzel. "Origins: U.S. Intelligence in Latin America." *Studies in Intelligence* (1985): 5.
Waller, John H. "The Double Life of Admiral Canaris." *International Journal of Intelligence and Counter Intelligence* 9, no. 3 (1996): 287.

Newspapers

Boxwell, James. "MI5 Claimed Siemens a Cover for Nazi Spies." *Financial Times*, August 26, 2010.
"German Capital in Argentina." *Economist*, September 22, 1945.
"Governor Island Spy Trail Resumed." *Daily Chronicle*, February 14, 1945.
Grossman, Ron. "Hero, Traitor." *Chicago Tribune*, 1989.
Lardner, George, Jr. "Nazi Saboteurs Captured." *Washington Post Magazine*, January 13, 2002.
Lissner, Will. "Spy Crew Escaped from a Coastguard." *New York Times*, June 28, 1942.
Obituary. Fritz Joubert Duquesne. *Time*, June 4, 1956.
Rensburg, *Die Vaderland*, August 1942.
Willing, Richard. "The Nazi Spy Next Door." *USA Today*, February 27, 2002.

Archival Materials

Administrative History, Office of Strategic Services Records. RG226. NARA.
Adolf Berle Diary. Reel 3, Berle Papers. FDR Library.
Argentina, Foreign Affairs Records. Foreign Service Posts. RG84 Box 24 711.3. NARA.
Argentine Bluebook Report, Special Subjects 1794–1976. State Department, RG59.52. NARA.
Army Intelligence Files. Office of Chief of Staff. RG319/RG165. NARA.
Auswärtiges Amt. 1939–1943, f. 24, Archives StS Afrika. ADAP (German Foreign Office Archives).

Berlin Documentation Centre Microfilm. Captured German Records, A3343. SSO-074B.590. NARA.
Brazil, General Correspondence, 1906-66. Foreign Office, FO371/25800. National Archives.
Büro des Staatssekretärs: Argentinean Band 2. Seized Foreign Records. RG242. NARA.
Cabinet Secretary's Files, Cabinet Office Records. CAB 301/25. National Archives.
Cabinet Subcommittee Internal Security, 1940. BC 640. South Africa: University of Cape Town.
Center for Cryptologic History, National Security Agency. George G. Meade, MD.
Charles Albert Van Den Kieboom, Home Office Records. HO 144/21472. National Archives.
Chief of Naval Operations, Military Agency Records. RG38 21. NARA.
Commission on Wartime Relocation and Internment of Civilians, A7378, University of Washington Libraries, Seattle.
D.F. Malan Collection, J.S. Gericke Library. University of Stellenbosch, South Africa.
Diaries of Henry Morgenthau, Jr., 1933-1945. Volume 700: February 3-9, 1944. FDR Library.
Directorate of Operations, Central Intelligence Agency Records, RG263, Boxes 1-2. NARA.
Dusko Popov, RG65 36994. FBI Reading Room, Washington, D.C.
Economic Warfare Section Records, Justice Department. RG60 285B Box 50. NARA.
Espionage Collection, FBI Files. RG65 37193, Serial 332, v. 1. NARA.
FBI Documents, 146-7-4219, Justice Folder. FDR Library.
Frederick Duquesne Case File, FBI Files. RG65 37193. NARA.
George S. Messersmith Papers. Special Collections, University of Delaware, Newark.
George Sylvester Viereck Papers. Special Collections Department, University of Iowa Libraries, Iowa City.
German Foreign Policy records 1918-1945. Series C, Vol. 4, 1933-1937. ADAP (German Foreign Office Archives).
German Legation in Dublin Reports. Commonwealth Offices Relations, TNA, DO 121/87. National Archives.
German Military High Command (OKW) files, German Military Records. RG242 T77. NARA.
Hans Oster Files, Folio 87. Institute of Contemporary History (IfZ), Munich.
Henry L. Stimson. Diary. Roll 7, at 128-29. Manuscript Room, Library of Congress.
Intelligence Summaries, Civil Section, Box 265. South African Defense Force Archives, Pretoria.
Internal Affairs of States, Central Files, U.S. State Department, RG59 DS 600-865.2000. NARA.
Joint Intelligence Committee at Capetown, SOE Records, HS 3/8. National Archives.
Joint Planning Staff Files, Cabinet Office Records, PRO CAB 119/66. National Archives.
Latin America, Foreign Funds. FBI File. RG65 112 567747/RG131. NARA.
Major General Cramer, Official Military Personnel File. National Personnel Records Center, St. Louis, Missouri.
Manhattan Project, Records of the Office of Chief of Engineers, RG77 6248, NARA.
Manuel Avila Camacho. Box 824, folder 550-991. National General Archive (AGN), Mexico.
Mexico, Military Attaché Reports.War Department Records. RG165 656, NARA.
Military Commander in France, RW35 241. Bundesarchiv-Militärarchiv. BA-MA (German Military Archives), Freiburg.
Ministry of External Relations 1940-1945. File E 11-6. Chilean National Archives.
Naval Historical Center. *United States Naval Administration in World War II*. Naval Historical Center, Washington, D.C.
Naval Intelligence Papers, Ministry of Defense, PRO ADM 223. National Archives.
Office of Naval Intelligence, Naval Records Collection. R4551, 1, no.3. NARA.
Office of Strategic Services Records. RG226 Box 2-6. NARA.
Office of the Judge Advocate General Records (Army), RG153. NARA.

Operation Gehlen, CIA History. National Security Archive, George Washington University, Washington, D.C.
Operation Malpas, Special Operation Executive, HS 8/891. National Archives.
Oswaldo Aranha Archives, 1941–1944. Center for Research and Documentation of Contemporary History (CPDOC), Brazil.
Personal Files, Security Service, KV2 1–7. National Archives.
Political Warfare Executive, Foreign Office Files, PRO F0898, File 103. National Archives.
President's Official File (OFI) 10-B: Justice Department; FBI Reports, 1940. FDR Library.
President's Staff Files, Box 56, FDR Papers. FDR Library.
Radio Intelligence Division Record, Federal Communication Commission, RG 173.111. NARA.
R. Meyer Collection, PV 104. Archive of the Institute for Contemporary History, University of the Orange Free State.
RSHA Amt IV, Seized Foreign Records, RG242 Box 28. NARA.
Secretary's Files, A20/4 Department of Foreign Affairs (DFA). National Archives of Ireland.
Seized records of enemy-controlled organizations, Records of the Office of Alien Property. RG131.3.2 NARA.
SIS Administrative Records, FBI Files. RG65 Folder 6, File 64-4104. NARA.
State Department Report, Foreign Relations of the U.S. (FRUS), 1942–1945.
Subject Files, Security Service Records, KV3/413. National Archives.
Sumner Welles Papers. FDR Library.
Trading with American Republics, Central Files. U.S. State Department. RG59 611. NARA.
Troy Papers, Central Intelligence Agency. RG263. NARA.
Tyler Kent Papers, 1926–1989. FDR Library.
U.S. District Court for East District New York. Criminal Cases, District Courts of the United States. RG21.34.4. NARA.
War Crimes Records. RG 238 Entry 2, Box 18. NARA.
Wartime Files. Director of Intelligence, G2 1928. Irish Military Archives.
Wehrmacht General Office, RW 5 v.690. Bundesarchiv-Militärarchiv BA-MA (German Military Archives), Freiburg.
William Sebold Files. Domestic Security, FBI Files. RG65 100 HQ3738. NARA.
World War II Case Files. Investigative records, FBI Files. RG65 7560-985000. NARA.

Index

Abwehr 31, 46, 50, 83, 118, 229, 259, 275, 295, 304; history 3, 6, 84; structure 8, 85–6, 120, 137
Agero, Colonel Sanz 256
Almazan, Juan 257
American Fellowship Forum 27, 133
Anti-Nazi Resistance 119–20, 181
Army Intelligence Service (SIM) 208, 256–7
Auhagen, Dr. Friedrich A. 27, 133
Ausland Organization (Foreign Office of the Nazi Party) 45, 199, 215, 230, 255, 274

Barbarossa, Operation 292
Batista, Fulgencio 267, 270
Beck, General Ludwig 14, 118
Becker, Johannes Siegfried 202, 220, 228, 242, 272
Benecke, Berthhold 150
Bentivegni, Colonel Egbert 8
Berle, Adolf 20, 88, 227
Berlin 8, 30, 50, 135
Biddle, Francis 19, 66, 78–9, 82
Bletchley Park 135, 155; see also Ultra
Blue Book Report 246, 251
Boal, Pierre de Lagarde 206, 264
Bohle, Ernst 217, 230
Bolivar, Operation 198, 202, 221 232, 270
Broederbond 279, 283, 302
Bruggman, Dr. Charles 188
Buenos Aires 202, 228, 239, 245
Buerkner, Vice-Admiral Leopold 9
Burger, Ernst 46, 70

Caffery, Jefferson 218, 226
Camacho, Manuel Avila 258, 266
Campini, Umberto 295, 299, 303
Campos, Francisco 215

Canaris, Adm. Wilhelm 34, 41, 112, 133, 181, 274; death 121; history 5, 7, 201; leadership 30, 48, 74, 85, 117
Cárdenas, Lazaro 257–8, 264
Castillo, Ramón 243, 246
Chapman, Eddie 157, 163
Chicago Tribune 61
Cicero 184
Colepaugh, William 123, 128
Confessions of a Nazi Spy 25
Connelley, Earl J. 67, 114
Coordinator Inter-American Affairs (CIAA) 211

Daldorf, Julius 249
Dasch, George 45, 51, 70
Dickstein, Samuel 24
Dönitz, Karl 18, 45, 121
Donovan, William 20, 212
Double Cross 154, 163, 193
Dulles, Allen 188
Duquesne, Fritz 93, 104
Duquesne Spy Ring 89, 117
Dusty, Operation 189

Elster, Operation 127
Engels, Albrecht 202, 219

Falange 207, 255–7
Farrell, Edelmiro 270, 272
Faupel, Wihelm 256
Federal Bureau of Investigation (FBI) 20, 25, 30, 40, 66, 95, 102, 210, 272
Federal Communications Commission (FCC) 111, 210, 237
First U.S. Army Group (FUSAG) 180
Flores, Alberto 208
Flossenberg Concentration Camp 121

Fortitude, Operation 176, 179
Franco, Gen. Francisco 164, 207, 214, 256
Friends of New Germany 21, 24
Fuerst, Jacob 188

Garby-Czerniawski, Roman 177
García, Juan Pujol 164
Geneva 85, 185
German-American Bund 21, 25, 41, 99
German Foreign Office 14, 19, 85, 116, 189, 203
German Propaganda Office 21, 26, 203
German War Ministry 132
Gestapo 8, 10, 45, 99, 187, 256
Gimpel, Erich 123, 128
Goebbels, Joseph 26, 42, 254
Gortz, Hermann 194–197
Griebl, Ignatz T. 29, 32, 99
Grohl, Karl Otto 241

Halder, General Franz 14
Hamburg 27, 33, 90, 95, 147
Hamburg Ast Station 84, 89, 94, 113, 137, 178
Hamburg-Wohldorf radio station 204
Hansen, Col. Georg Alexander 121
Harnisch, Hans 243, 246, 272
Haupt, Herbert 35, 55, 68, 73
Hellmuth, Osmar 243, 250
Hertzog, J.B.M. 275, 283, 289
Heydrich, Reinhard 7, 10 48, 50, 86
Himmler, Heinrich 7, 48, 118, 188, 190
Hitler, Adolf 18, 26, 133
Hoettl, Wilhelm 190
Hoover, J. Edgar 19, 66, 78, 227
Hull, Cordell 19, 88, 238, 247, 268
Husky, Operation 181

Integralists 214, 228, 231
Intelligence Records Bureau (IRB) 285, 289
Inter-American Emergency Advisory Committee 234, 251

Jodl, Alfred 47, 189
Justice Department (United States) 20, 80, 101

Kaltenbrunner, Ernst 12, 48, 87, 118
Kappe, Walter 41, 50, 54, 74
Keitel, Wilhelm 47, 133, 136, 143, 189
Kent, Tyler 140–1
Kerling, Edward John 46, 56, 67, 73
King, Jack 152–3
Kiss 179
Knappe-Ratey, Friedrich 164

Kolbe, Fritz 188
Kriegsmarine 6, 28, 85, 117
Kriminalpolizei (Criminal Police) 10
Kuhlenthal, Karl-Erich 165
Kuhn, Fritz 25, 30, 97

Ladd, D.M. 72
Lahousen, Erwin von 8, 41, 63, 74, 241
Leibbrandt, Robey 303–4, 306
Leissner, Wilhelm 183
Lena, Operation 142, 144, 147, 168
Liddell, Guy 149, 154
Lisbon 85, 124, 163, 176, 183
Lobster, Operation 143
Lonkowski, William 29
Lourenço Marques 283, 293, 298
Ludwig, Kurt 115
Luftwaffe 34, 86, 126
Lüning, Heinz 267–68, 270

Madrid 85, 164, 183
Malan, Daniel 276, 283, 289
Malpas, Operation 303
SS *Manhattan* 104, 108
Manhattan Project 122, 229
Masterman, John Cecil 154, 166, 177, 194
McCombs, Holland 265
McIntyre, Marvin 76
Menninger, Ernst 173
Meynen, Erich Otto 247
Military Intelligence Division 186, 211, 269
Moebius, Otto 254
Movimiento Nacional Socialista de Chile 231
Mowrer, Edgar 88
Moyzisch, L.C. 184
Mozambique 275, 293, 301
Muller, Heinrich 118

National Geographic 265
National Socialist German Workers' Party (NSDAP) 5, 52, 199
Nebe, Arthur 49
Nicolaus, Georg 202, 220, 259
Niebuhr, Dietrich 202, 241, 244

Oberkommando der Wehrmacht (OKW) 4, 41, 48, 136, 215
Office of Naval Intelligence (ONI) 147, 211
Office of Strategic Services (OSS) 16, 20, 188, 212
Order 76 23
Ossewa Brandwag 276, 279, 286, 297, 307
Oster, General Hans 119–20
Owens, Arthur 135, 144, 167

Index

Padilha, Raimundo 228
Paeffgen, Theodor 122, 126
Panama Canal Zone 126, 208, 234
Paperclip, Operation 189
Pastorius, Operation 41, 54, 68
Patzig, Walthar 5, 10
Paukenschlag, Operation 266
Perón, Juan 228, 236, 251, 253
Petrie, David 43
Pheiffer, Erich 28, 32, 40
Piekenbrock, Colonel Hans 8, 11, 94, 120, 134, 199
Pirow, Oswald 276, 285, 288
Popov, Dusko 172, 229
Príncipe Fortress 270
Prufer, Curt 217

Raeder, Admiral Erich 14, 18, 137
Ramírez, Pedro 247, 250, 270
Reichsbank 186, 188
Research Office of the Reich Air Ministry 135
Rio Conference (1942) 235, 269, 272
Rio de Janeiro 199, 210, 219, 221
Ríos, Juan Antonio 231
Ritter, Nikolaus 18, 35–6, 89, 92, 142, 170, 181
Rivera, Diego 265
Rockefeller, Nelson 211
Rohleder, Joachim 178
Roosevelt, Franklin 17, 79, 88, 2012
Rothschild, Lord 43, 164; report 44, 65, 75
RSHA 9, 11, 48, 87, 120, 188, 199, 242
Rumrich, Guenther 38, 99

Schellenberg, Walter 10, 48, 87, 118, 191, 199, 224, 242, 250
Sea Lion, Operation 136, 139, 142
Sebold, William 90, 99, 105, 226
Secret Intelligence Service (MI6) 134
Security Service MI5 16, 36, 43, 134, 160, 286
Sicherheitsdienst (SD) 5, 9, 86, 220; SD VI Foreign Intelligence 29, 48, 87, 182, 198, 214, 230, 244
Silvershirts 26, 95
Sinarquista 255–6

Smuts, Jan Christian 275, 277, 290, 307
Soviet Union 6, 52, 85, 180
Special Intelligence Service (SIS) 20, 210, 236, 248, 265, 272
Special Operations Executive (SOE) 16, 88, 286, 290, 302; SOI Department 88
SS 26, 48, 86, 118
State Department (United States) 19, 38, 88, 217, 234, 251
Stephenson, William 88
Stimson, Henry L. 18, 78, 82
Stormjaers 276, 285–7, 290
Sulzburger, Arthur Hayes 88

Thompson, Dorothy 88
Tirpitzufer 30, 118, 126
Today's Challenge 26–7
Torch, Operation 181
Trompe, Paul 294, 296
Truman, Harry S. 83, 131

Ultra 62, 160, 186; *see also* Bletchley Park

Van Heerien, F.J. 286, 288
Van Rensburg, Jan 276, 287, 297, 305
Vargas, Getúlio Dornelles 212, 216, 223, 271
Viereck, George Sylvester 26
Villarroel, Gualberto 247
Vogel, Ernst Max 261
von Brauchitsch, Gen. Walther 14
von Dohnanyi, Hans 119
von Gröning, Stephan 158
von Karstoff, Major 176
Vorster, John 280, 307
Vos, Otto Hermann 33, 41

Walbach 183
Wannsee Conference 48
Weber-Drohl, Ernst 194
Wehrmacht 5, 28, 132, 199
Weissdorn, Operation 303
Welles, Sumner 258, 265, 269
Wertz, Leopold 294, 298
Whiteshirts 22
Williams, Owen 265
Wolf, Gen. Friedrich 245
Wolfsschanze Conference 137

www.ingramcontent.com/pod-product-compliance
Ingram Content Group UK Ltd.
Pitfield, Milton Keynes, MK11 3LW, UK
UKHW041923140426
5217IPUK00014B/286